The Study of

THE UNIVERSIT
WINCHES

TITLES ALSO PUBLISHED BY BLOOMSBURY

The Daoist Tradition: An Introduction, Louis Komjathy
PB: 9781441168733
HB: 9781441116697

Secular Steeples 2nd edition: Popular Culture and the Religious Imagination,
Conrad Ostwalt
HB: 9781441156174
PB: 9781441172860

Religions and Environments: A Reader in Religion, Nature and Ecology,
Richard Bohannon
HB: 9781780937625
PB: 9781780938028

The Study of Religion

An Introduction to Key Ideas
and Methods

SECOND EDITION

**GEORGE D. CHRYSSIDES
AND
RON GEAVES**

BLOOMSBURY
LONDON · NEW DELHI · NEW YORK · SYDNEY

Bloomsbury Academic

An imprint of Bloomsbury Publishing Plc

50 Bedford Square	1385 Broadway
London	New York
WC1B 3DP	NY 10018
UK	USA

www.bloomsbury.com

Bloomsbury is a registered trade mark of Bloomsbury Publishing Plc

First edition published in 2007
This second edition published in 2014

© George D. Chryssides and Ron Geaves, 2007, 2014

George D. Chryssides and Ron Geaves have asserted their rights under the Copyright, Designs and
Patents Act, 1988, to be identified as Authors of this work.

British Library Cataloguing-in-Publication Data
A catalogue record for this book is available from the British Library.

ISBN: HB: 978-1-78093-700-7
PB: 978-1-78093-840-0
ePub: 978-1-78093-670-3
ePDF: 978-1-47256-732-1

Library of Congress Cataloging-in-Publication Data
A catalog record for this book is available from the Library of Congress.

Typeset by Newgen Knowledge Works (P) Ltd., Chennai, India
Printed and bound in Great Britain

Contents

Illustrations   vi

Acknowledgements   vii

Website   viii

Introduction   1

1   The tools of the trade *George Chryssides*   7

2   Methodology in religious studies *George Chryssides and Ron Geaves*   39

3   Insiders and outsiders *George Chryssides*   67

4   Does size matter? *George Chryssides*   89

5   Key figures in the study of religion *George Chryssides*   127

6   Phenomenology and its critics *George Chryssides*   157

7   Colonialism and postcolonialism in the study of religion *Ron Geaves*   183

8   Authenticity and diversity *Ron Geaves*   211

9   Fieldwork in the study of religion *Ron Geaves*   241

10   Religion and gender *Ron Geaves*   275

11   The question of truth *Ron Geaves*   303

12   The internet as a resource in the study of religion *George Chryssides*   339

Bibliography   361

Index   377

Illustrations

1.1 Wat Ong Teu, fortune-telling at a Buddhist temple   31

2.1 The Dome of the Rock, Jerusalem   48

3.1 Ma-tsu (Chinese) Temple, San Francisco   73

4.1 Adult Church attendance, Britain, 1851–1989   103

4.2 St Michael the Archangel, exterior (Church of England)   108

4.3 Hassan II Mosque, Casablanca   114

5.1 Hindu shrine, Pushkar, India   135

5.2 Synagogue interior, Vilnius, Lithuania   150

5.3 Wolverhampton Buddha Vihara   155

6.1 St Michael the Archangel, interior (Church of England)   167

6.2 *Arati* at the Hare Krishna Temple, Birmingham   177

7.1 Sufi leaders and Muslim dignitaries process in the streets of Manchester   194

7.2 The Jade Emperor Pagoda, Ho Chi Minh City, Vietnam   196

7.3 Village Temple, Pushkar   199

8.1 Guru Nanak Sikh Temple, Wolverhampton   214

8.2 Wudu tank   222

8.3 Tomb and shrine of Pir Wahhab Siddiqi, England   234

9.1 Murugan devotees, Ealing   242

9.2 An image of Baba Balaknath   249

9.3 Ek Niwas, Wolverhampton   254

9.4 Narasimha Temple, Pushkar   261

10.1 Marian Shrine, Portugal   280

10.2 Women's ordination as deacons   284

12.1 Fo Guan Shau Monastery, Taiwan   355

Acknowledgements

It is always the authors who take the credit for their work, and sometimes the blame! However, books can seldom, if ever, be written without the help and support of others. The authors would like to express their thanks to their spouses Margaret Wilkins and Catherine Barnes respectively, for their encouragement and patience as we spent long hours in our studies. We would both like to thank the staff at Bloomsbury for their constant support, especially Lalle Pursglove and Dhara Patel, who have been closely involved with this project. We are grateful to Margaret Wilkins for indexing the work.

The book would not have been conceived if it had not been for our students, who have struggled with these methodological issues over the years. Their seminar discussions, assignments and queries have all provided invaluable stimulation, for which we are grateful. We hope that this volume will prove to be helpful to their successors.

Website

www.bloomsbury.com/the-study-of-religion-2nd-edition-9781780938400

Levels of Religion by Ron Geaves (Chapter 5 in the 1st edition of *The Study of Religion,* which has been removed from this 2nd edition) can be found on the website above, along with the following case studies:

1   Case Study: The death and resurrection of Jesus Christ

2   Case Study: Where is Britain's 'Christian' population?

3   Case Study: Sikhism and religious diversity

Introduction

The first edition of *The Study of Religion* appeared in 2007, and aimed at introducing students – particularly those embarking on undergraduate courses – to fundamental methods and issues in this field. The material was well received by students and tutors, but some updating has proved desirable some five years on. In particular, there have been many developments in online religion, and the authors felt that discussion of the so-called insider/outsider problem and the legacy of colonialism were desirable.

There are many good books that introduce the world's religions as well as specific religious traditions. Yet students who are embarking on the study of religion are typically introduced to more abstract methodological issues, rather than the religions themselves. And rightly so: if we do not approach the religions of the world with some definite purpose and method of dealing with them, we are likely to end up with either trivia, stereotypes or sensationalized pieces of misinformation supplied by certain sectors of the media.

There are not so many books on methodology, however. Ninian Smart's writings have served generations well and made the subject accessible. However, the study of religion has now advanced beyond phenomenological study, and studying a religion entails more than a 'seven-dimensional' approach, although his work remains valuable. Other more recent approaches are somewhat daunting, and rather indigestible, at least to first-year undergraduates. Several of these are anthologies, in which individual authors pursue their area of specialism competently, but at the risk of leaving the beginner behind.

Historically, the study of religions has derived from a number of parallel lines of development of varying age with little horizontal contact between them. The oldest and most venerable is the study of Christianity which, of course, has its roots in the Western world's historical heritage. This study of Christianity remains linked to the Christian Church, in a quest to understand Christianity's key doctrines and to instruct the faithful. In this context it has been joined by Biblical Studies and Church history. Biblical Studies, as it borrows from the disciplines of literary criticism, historiography and discoveries in archaeology, has been the most challenging in regard to theology's main thrust of more fully understanding God's presence in history. Such attempts to enhance one's understanding of the Christian faith have not always been welcomed: many Christians continue to contend that the scholarship of the last two centuries has tended to undermine rather than strengthen faith. However, the three disciplines have essentially remained the preserve of Christian scholars rather than scholars of

Christianity although there are signs that this is changing. The direction of knowledge has been essentially top downwards rather than from the bottom up, with a consequent emphasis on textual study and knowledge derived from a small group of elite scholars and eminent churchmen.

The development of the study of religion as an academic subject originally borrowed heavily from this methodological framework for the study of Christianity. The original study of other traditions or even comparative religion was often undertaken by Christian scholars anxious to demonstrate that their own tradition's truth-claims were paramount. They often adopted the methodologies used for the study of Christianity to explore other faith traditions, and a division was made between the study of correct doctrine (theology), textual criticism (Biblical Studies) and history. This methodological compartmentalization appropriates a tradition into the hands of scholars whose systematization and categorization do not reveal the fact that religious conviction is messy and idiosyncratic. In addition, this kind of study tends to focus on the *diachronic*, that is, the historical development of a faith tradition, from its origins to the present, rather than the *synchronic*, looking across the various forms of the tradition as it manifests in its contemporary forms. Thus the beliefs and practices of everyday believers are generally ignored.

In the eighteenth and nineteenth centuries, an interest in Islam, Hinduism and Buddhism began to develop through contact with the Orient through empire and trade. The plus side of this interest was that these religions began to appear in British universities and their doctrines began to be taken seriously as competitors by Christians, rather than being perceived as superstition, idolatry or falsehoods. However, the downside was the study of these traditions followed closely the methods of study utilized in Christianity. However, in the nineteenth and twentieth centuries, the study of religion was transformed by the new attempts to develop a scientific paradigm for the study of human behaviour; and increasingly, the social sciences of psychology, anthropology and sociology muscled in on the act of explaining religious phenomena. Today, this trend is continued within cultural studies. Increasingly in the second half of the twentieth century, the study of religions has drawn upon the research of social scientists working in the disciplines of sociology and anthropology. Both of these disciplines have long traditions of field and ethnographic studies with well-established methodologies, however these scholars are often criticized for taking 'the religion out of religion', or to put it in a more scholarly context, they lean towards reductionism.

The fourth strand to be considered in the British context, developed in the new universities and teacher training colleges, involved creating departments to train teachers. This has developed since the 1944 Education Act insisted upon religious education being an essential part of both primary and secondary curricula. The increasing multiculturalism of Britain in the second half of the twentieth century has introduced new Acts that insist that British children are introduced to the main faiths present in the nation. Thus in the British context, since the 1945 and 1988 Education Acts, the teaching of religions has been compulsory in schools. However, this approach to the study of religion in schools is markedly different to that adopted in the United

States and India, where both nations have attempted to protect their secular status by refusing to teach any religious tradition in state schools. This policy has been challenged by evangelical Christians in the United States and recently the last BJP government in India decided to change the law there. However, there is justifiable suspicion that in both cases, those that pursue the requirement to teach religion to children, do so to promote a dominant faith and envisage confessional approaches rather than the neutral academic approach to the study of religions.

In Britain, the increasing plurality and focus on promoting multicultural values has led to many Religious Education teachers taking their pupils to visit places of worship. Consequently, most teacher-training programmes in higher education, and Religious Studies departments that have developed in colleges whose historical focus has been teacher training, have provided fieldwork activities on their degrees. In addition, the teachers of religious education in British schools are required to introduce their students to more than one faith tradition. The impact of multiculturalism and its demands on the education system have helped develop Religious Studies departments that focus on several religions utilizing a broadly phenomenological approach heavily influenced by the late Ninian Smart.

Most departments of Theology and Religious Studies in Britain will probably have originated from the study of Christianity, introducing other discrete religions such as Islam, Hinduism, or Buddhism and the social science contributions to the study of religions as they developed historically. Their curriculum may well be influenced by the research interests of their respective staff and it is only since the 1960s that the fledgling subject of Religious Studies began to be fitted into these existing frameworks, introducing methodology modules and a broadly phenomenological framework. To the present time Religious Studies remains as Ninian Smart described it – a polymethodic approach. This poses its own problems and Peter Connolly referring to Smart's description of the subject as polymethodic makes the observation that the student of religions faces the challenge of being a specialist and a generalist simultaneously. One one hand, it is necessary to be familiar with the methods of a number of subjects, on the other hand, it may become necessary to master one in more detail with contributions to its knowledge base borrowed from scholarship that arose from specialist contributions focusing on one methodology utilized by a discrete discipline. Broadly speaking the approach is 'methodological agnosticism' where the existence of a divine being is neither affirmed or negated but recognizing that a particular belief will lead to certain kinds of actions which, in turn, create their own unique social and cultural forms.

Within this increasing complexity this volume seeks to be a 'user-friendly' approach for the undergraduate, introducing a number of key methodological issues surrounding the study of religion, and explaining why they are needed. A jointly authored book enables the writers to draw on their respective areas of expertise, while affording continuity. In Chapter 1 we begin with key questions such as definitions of religion, we explore how the study of religion differs from cognate subjects, and how it has come to define its subject-matter. In Chapter 2 we look at methodology and the various disciplines that have or are still contributing to the ways of studying religion. In particular, this chapter introduces new developments along with an overview of historic contributions to the study. Those who study religion may or may not belong to the traditions they are studying, and Chapter 3 explores the relationship between 'insiders' and 'outsiders' – how (or indeed whether) one can comprehend unfamiliar forms of spirituality, and how one can maintain a critical distance from religious communities with which one may be overfamiliar.

One may not readily associate numerical skills with the study of religion, but a sizeable amount of statistical information has now been amassed on religions and religious organizations – both by the religions themselves, as well as by scholars. While it is not our aim to make students into statisticians, a certain amount of guidance is needed on how (or whether) to collect statistical data, how to interpret statistics and how to avoid some of the pitfalls in handling numbers. Chapter 4 is devoted to this.

Methodology was not built in a day, and consideration is given in Chapter 5 to how the West's interest in religion developed through time, from around the late eighteenth century to the present day. It is all very well to say that one is studying religion, but religions are understood in different ways, at different levels, for different people, and for different purposes. It is therefore important to discuss how practitioners use their religion in different ways, and how one reflects this in how we write about their beliefs and practices.

Scholars have often agreed that the study of religion should be as objective as possible. The phenomenologists' agenda was to see religion in its true form, unimpeded by our own assumptions. In Chapter 6, our discussion considers whether this is possible, and what alternatives there might be. Chapter 7, on Colonialism and Postcolonialism, develops the theme of neutrality by examining the ways in which the study of religions – especially eastern religions – has been influenced by the traditional ways in which Christianity has been studied, and explores various levels which exist over and above their doctrines and sacred texts. The ensuing Chapter 8 (Authenticity and Diversity) explores how religious traditions can assume different forms with the passage of time, and questions whether any one such expression can claim authenticity.

Because religions do not exist simply in books, many Study of Religion departments now like to encourage students to undertake field work and hear the accounts of rank-and-file practitioners, rather than scholars who are writing at second remove. In Chapter 9 field work is a major topic, with a focus on practical tips for undertaking fieldwork, especially the short site visit which may be many students' only experience.

Much debate, both in religions themselves, as well as in the study of religion, has been focused on gender issues. (Gender issues should not be confused with feminist issues, although the two areas are related.) As a reader of such an introduction might expect, we have attempted to survey this area here in Chapter 10. The last two chapters introduce two further topical themes. In the present climate of interfaith dialogue, questions of truth inevitably arise. Does one religion offer a unique claim to truth, or are the various religions of the world equally pointing towards the same transcendent reality? Finally Chapter 12 describes the advent of the World Wide Web and its considerable impact on how religions promote their message, as well as providing a powerful new research tool. The rapid strides that the cyber-revolution has made in the last ten years make it difficult to write material that has enduring relevance, but it would be a serious omission if we did not attempt it.

In addition to these various broad themes, we have included some case studies relating to each chapter. These serve to illustrate or amplify some of the salient issues that we have raised. We have also added some discussion questions, which can be used either for further personal reflection, or by tutors for class discussion. We have tried to make the book a genuine attempt to write for students rather than a book which focuses on the research interests of scholars and to include wherever possible 'how to do it' as well as identifying the study of religion.

George Chryssides
Ron Geaves

1

The tools of the trade

George Chryssides

Chapter Outline

Why be religious, and why study religion?	7
Studying religion and studying religions	8
RK, RE, RI and RS	11
Theology, divinity and Religious Studies	14
Comparative religion	16
Defining religion	17
Some definitions of religion: Substantive and functional	19
'Functionalist' definitions of religion	24
Religion and 'ultimate concern'	27
The 'salient features' approach	30
Discussion points	37

Why be religious, and why study religion?

Religious behaviour can often seem strange to the outsider. Why should people meet together for an hour or so on a Sunday morning, and stand, sit or kneel at predetermined intervals, sing hymns, perhaps burn incense and light candles, and do many more things that would be regarded as downright bizarre if an individual performed them outside the context of organized worship? If the reader doubts their apparent strangeness, he or she might try singing a hymn on the bus to work, or even be seen reading a Bible in public. What do such actions achieve, and why do some people engage in them? The aim of studying religion is to make sense of religious behaviour: neither to endorse it, nor to criticize it, but to endeavour to understand it.

As we shall see, different people are religious for different reasons. Some believers may feel that their everyday lives are enhanced by worship; a practising Christian once told one of the authors that he went to church each Sunday 'to psych myself up for the week'. Other believers may hope for more definite benefits, like healing, or coping with a disappointment or bereavement. Some may feel that religion offers guidance for life in the form of a moral code, and hence improves their way of living. Others may have concerns such as what happens after they die, and how they can achieve salvation or liberation, attaining whatever hope their religion offers.

Some students of religion are themselves followers of religions; others are heavily critical of religion, perhaps believing that it is simply illusion, or that it encourages strife and human divisions; while others may classify themselves as 'interested enquirers', feeling that there may be 'something in religion' but not having found any particular religious niche that suits them. These different types of enquirers all have a place in the study of religion. Whether or not any one category makes for a better student of the subject is a matter for discussion, but past and present scholars of Religious Studies have variously fitted into all three of these categories.

Just as religious believers have different reasons for being religious, students of religion have different reasons for studying the subject. There are those who have been troubled with questions like whether there is a god, and whether God can miraculously intervene in the world's affairs, whether there is a life after death and indeed why we are here in the first place. Other students may have more worldly interests in studying religion. Religion is part of human behaviour, so understanding religion is important for understanding individuals and the societies in which they live.

Studying religion and studying religions

Students who are new to the study of religion often expect to receive sets of information on the various living faiths of the world, usually the 'big six': Buddhism, Christianity, Hinduism, Islam, Judaism and Sikhism. Instead of an introductory course on the world's religions, they often find themselves involved in an enquiry which is one step removed from the religions themselves. Instead of asking how specific religions began, an introduction to the study of religion focuses on how the study of religion began, beginning with scholars such as Sir J. G. Frazer, E. B. Tylor, R. R. Marett, Rudolf Otto and William James. The study often consists of seemingly abstruse theories such as evolutionism, phenomenology, postmodernism, debates about whether 'insider' or 'outsider' approaches to religion are preferable, and even what the word 'religion' itself truly means. The study of religion involves a variety of academic disciplines including anthropology, sociology, philosophy, theology and psychology, and asks how they contribute to understanding religion.

Most students find theoretical issues more demanding and more difficult than accounts of a religion's practices. We can see in our mind's eye (or in reality) a Muslim facing Mecca, a Buddhist monk sitting cross-legged in meditation or a Christian kneeling before the altar to receive the sacrament. Getting to grips with abstract theories, whose very names are frightening, is much harder. Why engage in academic study, rather than simply obtain a reasonable amount of general knowledge from quality newspapers, television documentaries and the internet?

Questions about the value of formal academic study can be asked of any subject area. A self-taught piano player may be able to play tunes 'by ear' at the audience's request, impressing the listeners. The pianist may not wish to undertake formal study of the discipline, but if she wants a professional career in music, being able to play Beethoven and Schubert with accuracy and panache, then self-effort is not enough. Hours of practice are needed, often involving tedious scales and finger exercises. Moreover, good musicianship is not simply a matter of playing notes proficiently: technical expertise needs to be combined with a knowledge of the history and theory of music, and, most especially, of musicology – the study of the principles of interpreting musical writings.

Similarly, some people can learn enough about religion to meet their non-academic needs. Those who practise a religion will certainly know the fundamental practices required of its adherents, how the festival year is celebrated and how rites of passage are marked. They will know something about their religion's founder-leaders and the stories associated with them, and probably something of their faith's history. This is no doubt sufficient for religious practice, and they may not need academic study. Equally, there is nothing inherently wrong in having a mild interest in religion – perhaps enough to prompt oneself to read the odd coffee-table book, watch the occasional television documentary, keep up with religious affairs in the news, and perhaps attend an occasional religious gathering, extra-mural lecture or evening class. To maintain such a level of interest is certainly better than being ignorant about religion, or dismissing it as trivial or unimportant. Such activities, however, commendable as they are, cannot yield the level of understanding and expertise that are needed to study religion professionally or undertake a career associated with it, any more than bashing out a few tunes on a piano and attending the occasional concert makes someone a competent musician.

To understand religion, there are obvious problems in simply relying on media reports and popular pieces of writing. The most obvious drawback is that the media are frequently unreliable, biased or sensationalist. While this chapter was being written, one internet provider used the headline 'Indian woman marries statue' (AOL News, 29 June 2002), claiming that in a Hindu ceremony a woman was literally married to a stone image of a deity; and a television documentary alleged that the Jehovah's Witnesses' headquarters in Brooklyn, New York, kept tens of thousands of secret files on known paedophiles in their ranks, about whom the organization refused to act. Meanwhile, in the wake of 11 September 2001, various news agencies continue to propagate misleading information about 'Islamic fundamentalism' and *jihad*.

No serious student of religion can accept such accounts uncritically, and it is important to learn how to evaluate one's sources and to raise critical questions about such stories. What kind of Hindu ceremony was being enacted? For what purpose, and with what consequences? How typical is it of Hindu practice as a whole, and how would it be understood and explained by those taking part? What do the Jehovah's Witnesses teach about family life and protecting children? What kind of evidence is needed before their ministerial elders will take sanctions against an erring member? How do they see their relationship with civil authorities, and does this affect their decisions as to whether to report crimes or to deal with malpractices internally? With regard to the alleged phenomenon of Islamic fundamentalism, a student of religion needs to explore what the word 'fundamentalism' actually means. Is it a term Muslim extremists use of themselves and if not, why not? Is Islam as a religion really bound up with acts of terrorism? After all, the word 'Islam' comes from the same etymological root as the Hebrew shalom, meaning 'peace'. How does this relate to the concept of *jihad*, and does the concept really mean 'holy war'?

These are all examples of questions that would be raised within the academic study of religion. It is worth mentioning, too, that whereas the media typically disseminate 'stories' that are intended to gain immediate impact, academic study involves systematic study. Academic study involves more than 'sound bytes' of information, whether these are items of news or hagiographical tales. As we shall see, the 'narrative dimension' is an important aspect of most religions, but it is not the only one. Understanding a religion means knowing the fundamental doctrines that underpin it, and how they influence its scriptures and other sacred writings, its rituals and festivals, and its forms of devotion.

'Systematic' study has two crucial aspects. First, it views religions as 'systems': that is to say, it seeks to explore how the various components of religions hang together and interrelate, rather than simply reporting individual or un-connected pieces of information. Second, it critically examines its sources. Unlike certain sectors of the media, who may keep their sources confidential and publish on the basis of slender evidence, the academic study of religion identifies the sources of information. Unless such sources are declared, we have no means of knowing whether they are reliable or biased, whether they come from adherents of a religion, from outsiders or from critics, and whether they are 'official' statements or individual opinions. To say this is not to imply that unreliable, biased or idiosyncratic sources are to be disregarded, but rather that all sources should be known, and assessed accordingly.

It is unfortunate that the term 'academic' is so often used in a dismissive or even pejorative way. In popular parlance, to say that a matter is 'merely academic' is to dismiss it as unimportant, abstruse, irrelevant or pedantic. The medieval Christian scholar-saint Anselm of Canterbury (1033–1109) is often credited with speculating how many angels could dance on the head of a pin – although there is no evidence that he ever discussed this topic – and such speculation is assumed to epitomize academic study. While academics have spent years studying topics of little general interest, the study of contemporary World Religions is a much-needed corrective to media stereotyping, which fosters misunderstanding and prejudice. Common to popular assumption, studying religion academically does not entail journeying through long dark alleys of abstruse erudition. It is simply a quest for reliable, accurate understanding of the world's religious traditions, carried out in a manner as free from prejudice as is humanly attainable. As with all other academic disciplines, there are methods and techniques the student needs to learn.

RK, RE, RI and RS

There are a number of fields of study related to religion. Students who are unfamiliar with the study of religion, not to mention some colleagues in other subject areas, often wrongly equate RS (Religious Studies) with RE (Religious Education), RI (Religious Instruction) and RK (Religious Knowledge). The nature and purpose of Religious Studies has been clouded, first by the history of its role in schools and second by successive British governments, who have viewed Religious Education as likely to foster and develop morality, or by teachers who believe that the study of religion has the effect of creating and developing one's 'spirituality'. Some unpacking of these different labels and different rationales for Religious Studies is therefore necessary.

In the first half of the twentieth century Britain could be described as a 'Christian country'. There were few rivals to mainstream Christianity: apart from church buildings, virtually the only other signs of religion were Jewish synagogues, gospel halls, Christadelphian ecclesia, and Unitarian and Quaker meeting houses. Even the Church of Jesus Christ of Latter-day Saints (better known as the Mormons) and the Jehovah's Witnesses had not yet attracted the thousands that they now do. A very small number of Muslim communities existed, but only one purpose-built mosque, in Woking, Surrey, erected in 1894.

It is therefore understandable that school education should have been placed in the context of mainstream Christianity. It was customary for a morning assembly to begin with the singing of a Christian hymn, the reading of a Bible passage and Christian prayers. Schools typically had chaplains, whose function was to conduct services to mark the beginning and end of each school term. A weekly lesson, variously called 'RK' or 'Scripture', was generally taught by a non-specialist teacher, who would select a passage from a 'school Bible' – a children's anthology of Bible stories. In a culture where the Christian faith remained virtually unchallenged, the assumption was that the school could safely replicate the function of the Church, teaching the Christian Bible as if its stories were indisputably historical, and instilling virtuous habits such as prayer and devotion.

All this changed in the 1960s, for two reasons. First, secularization took a toll on mainstream churches, whose membership declined substantially from 1960 onwards. Secularization, however, meant more than simply dwindling congregations on Sundays: the Church had lost its hold on people's lives and minds. (We shall have more to say about secularization in Chapter 4.) The second factor was the substantial immigration that began in the late 1950s, when the British government invited people from India,

Pakistan and the West Indies to enter Britain to solve a labour shortage problem. With the people came their religions, whose presence is visibly part of Britain's religious landscape today.

Studying religion – at least within an educational establishment – can therefore no longer be equated with the transmission of any specific faith, such as Christianity. In the face of a multiplicity of faith traditions, the study of religion is not about passing on an agreed body of knowledge, increasing one's faith or training students to become officials within religious organizations. Our students have sometimes reported that, having mentioned to someone that they are studying religion, they have received the response, 'You're training to be a vicar, then?' Such a response, of course, conflates studying a subject with practising it. There is no more reason to assume that a student of religion is religious than there is to assume that a student of criminology is a criminal, or that a student of French Studies is French! Whether a follower of a religion has a better understanding of religion than the outsider has been much debated, but both insiders and outsiders have contributed to the study of religion. We shall not enter the debate here, but instead clarify the respective roles of RS, RK, RI and RE.

RI (Religious Instruction) is a term that derives from the practice, mainly within churches, of transmitting one's faith. The term 'instruction' means an attempt to pass on an agreed body of knowledge and set of practices, which simply have to be learned without question. The use of the term 'instruction', for example, prevails in schools of motoring, where the pupil's task is unquestioningly to learn and apply the rules of the road, and to operate the vehicle in the way the instructor dictates, without criticism, deviation or innovation. In a similar way instruction of converts, and of new generations of believers, has often taken place within religious institutions. It used to be common practice in mainstream churches for children to have to learn the Catechism, a short book set out in question-and-answer form, whose answers the catechumen learned to recite verbatim. Anyone seeking admission to a religious community will of course be expected to know the protocol associated with participation in its practices, as well as the underlying rationale for them. Religious instruction is therefore 'confessional': its teachers were unashamedly committed to the religion that they taught, and the aims of teacher and pupil alike were to build and strengthen understanding of and commitment to the religion for which instruction was given.

RK (Religious Knowledge) is an expression that has almost become obsolete. About half a century ago it was used in some British schools to name lessons in (almost exclusively Christian) religion. The word 'knowledge', of course, is somewhat problematic. To claim to know something is to claim that it is true, and, even if some students of religion may claim to 'know the truth', any such claim can be contested by others. One cannot assume a body of agreed knowledge within a field that is fraught with controversy. Certainly, there exist some basic facts that might be acknowledged by all who study religion: for example, it is very rare to find scholars and teachers who deny the existence of founder-leaders such as Abraham, Moses, Gautama the Buddha, Jesus of Nazareth, Muhammad or Guru Nanak. However, once one goes much beyond their names, approximate dates and places, there is relatively little within religions that commands universal agreement. Even incidents in the lives of these leaders tend to be disputed by historians, and Western scholars of religion tend to view them as 'myth' (inspiring narratives) rather than solid fact about the past. To claim that Moses received the Torah in its totality on Mount Sinai, that Christ died for the sins of the world, that Muhammad is God's final messenger, are all claims that are firmly believed by practitioners of the respective religions themselves, but are of course largely rejected by those outside these faith traditions. In a bygone era where there was virtually only one main religion, and where commitment was regarded as desirable, it was understandable that the teaching profession conflated the study of religion with religious instruction and sometimes employed the term 'religious knowledge'. However, in a multifaith culture and a secularized society, there can be little justification for assuming that the teacher of religion is imparting an agreed body of knowledge that can be uncritically imbibed by pupils and students.

RE (Religious Education) is a somewhat ambiguous term. It is sometimes used in British schools as a synonym for RS (Religious Studies), but is also used in US churches to refer to their programmes of religious instruction for children and youth. More commonly in Britain, the term 'Religious Education' is part of Education Studies, which addresses questions about the nature and role of Religious Studies within the school curriculum. Thus, RE includes issues such as the legal requirements relating to the teaching of religion, the rationale that underlies it, the curricula that education authorities have set down, and the resources and methods of teaching religion in the classroom.

RS (Religious Studies) is the academic study of religion. Some university departments have expressed disquiet about the adjective 'religious', claiming that it might be taken erroneously to mean that the activity of studying religions is itself religious, or that staff and students are expected to have religious commitments as a prerequisite for study. Such departments have commonly opted for the alternative label, 'The Study of Religion'. Religion is thus the subject-matter of enquiry, rather than something that teachers and students bring to bear upon their studies. It is not unduly pedantic to distinguish between the study of religion and the study of religions. The latter examines the origins, beliefs and practices of various religions of the world, while the former is about the methods of studying religion – the tools of the trade, so to speak. This book focuses on religion rather than religions: it is about methodology, and raises the types of question that are indicated by the various chapter headings. What are the defining characteristics of religion? How does religion differ from philosophy or ideology? What are the differences between a religion, a cult, a sect and a denomination? Who defines the authentic form a religion takes? Is it the saint, the scholar, the religious officials, or should the student of religion be equally authoritative in defining religion as it is practised by its followers? Should we define Roman Catholicism in terms of papal pronouncements, the Catholic Church's councils, the solemn sacraments over which its priesthood presides? Or is Catholicism about wearing St Christopher medallions to fend off danger, visiting Lourdes for miraculous healings, or venerating weeping statues? And should one's study of Roman Catholicism also include those who do not accept or live up to the norms of that religion: campaigners for women's ordination, pregnant women who seek abortions, paedophile priests? Students of religion need to bear in mind that what starts off as deviant practice often becomes an important reform movement within a religion, or even the cause of a significant schism. Even in indefensible matters such as paedophilia, bad practice can lead to important changes.

It is tempting to think of religions in terms of their high ideals, but no one is a perfect practitioner of his or her religion. Following a religion is more like making a journey than arriving at a destination. One might respect legal codes such as the Ten Commandments of Judaism and Christianity, and conclude that the ancient Hebrews invariably refrained from theft, murder and adultery: on the contrary, however, such commandments would have been unnecessary if these offences were not already occurring. While one should not totally rule out the possibility that some legislation can be proactive, most societal rules are designed retrospectively to deal with malpractices that are already prevalent.

Religions are notoriously disparaging of the world's condition and of human behaviour. According to Judaism and Christianity, we are all 'born in sin'; Buddhism teaches that everything is *dukkha* (unsatisfactoriness) and that we are fundamentally ignorant; Hinduism avers that, in the world that we inhabit, all is maya (illusion). Attaining a religion's goal is no easy matter: it is not simply a matter of making a few improvements in one's lifestyle, such as praying more often, giving more to the poor, or kicking the odd bad habit: according to the vast majority of religions there is something much more radically wrong with the human condition, and it is very rare to find anyone who plausibly claims to have become enlightened, achieved perfection or attained complete oneness with God. Religions typically use metaphors that connote journeys: Judaism teaches that the Torah is a lamp to guide one's path (Ps. 119.105); the early Christians were originally known as followers of 'the Way' (Acts 9.2); the three principal Buddhist traditions are known as the three 'vehicles', or yanas. Academic study would therefore leave out some very important aspects of religion if it focused on the ideal, at the expense of the real.

Theology, divinity and Religious Studies

Thus far we have examined related subject areas with an initial 'R', but there are two others that need some comment: theology and divinity. It is important to distinguish between theology and Religious Studies. The word 'theology' literally means 'discourse about God' and the making of theology is generally an activity that is done from inside a religion, and hence presupposes religious commitment. Take, for example, the question, 'How is it possible for Jesus Christ to be both fully human and fully divine?' This is a theological question – one about which much has been written, and which has caused considerable controversy throughout the history of Christianity.

The question presupposes at the outset that there is a God – an assumption, of course, which would not be accepted by atheists and agnostics. Even religions such as Buddhism and Jainism would be uncomfortable with this starting point. The question assumes that God is either a person or is in some way 'personal' (Christianity often makes this distinction) – again, an assumption that would be inimical to Hindu thinkers in the *advaita* (non-dualist) schools, who would hold that the divine is fundamentally some kind of impersonal substance (typically called *brahman*), and that personal manifestations of divinity form part of the illusion to which unenlightened beings are still subject. The question uses the word 'Christ': a word that derives from the Greek *Christos*, which literally means 'anointed', and is the Greek translation of the Hebrew *mashiach*, which comes into Judaism and Christianity as 'messiah'. To refer to Jesus as 'Christ' is thus to endow him with a status which can really be endorsed only by Christianity; certainly the vast majority of Jews dissociate themselves from the Christian claim that Jesus is God's chosen messiah. The question further assumes that, in some sense, there is an identity between Jesus and God: such a claim is inimical to followers of Islam, which teaches that any association of the physical with the divine, which is defined as *shirk*, is a serious sin. The Qur'an teaches, referring to the Christian doctrine of the Trinity: 'Unbelievers are those that say: "Allah is one of three." There is but one God' (Qur'an, sura 5.70), and 'Allah . . . has never begotten a son' (Qur'an, sura 17.111).

The question, 'How can Christ be human and divine?' is thus a question that arises from within mainstream Christianity, and is really only a live issue for the Christian. A theologian who undertakes to address the question is therefore tacitly declaring his or her allegiance to the Christian faith, and effectively undertaking to be a spokesperson on behalf of Christianity – or, more likely, for a particular tradition within Christianity (such as Eastern Orthodoxy, Roman Catholicism or Protestantism). One cannot simply be a theologian: one is a Christian theologian, an Islamic theologian, a Jewish theologian and so on. Belonging, as the theologian does, to a specific faith tradition, he or she is not at liberty to devise any solution whatsoever to a problem such as Christ's incarnation. The tradition itself has laid down ground rules about what is and is not acceptable. Some thinkers in Christianity's early centuries suggested that Christ could be simultaneously divine and human by virtue of being the first of God's creation, or that Jesus had a divine mind and a human body, or that he was born human but subsequently promoted to divine status. These – and other – proposed explanations of the incarnation did not gain acceptance into what became Christianity's orthodox position, and any theologian who desires to remain within the Christian fold is bound by the creeds of the faith and the decisions of its councils.

Writing theology, then, is essentially an 'insider' activity: for those who do not share the belief in the deity and humanity of Jesus Christ, questions about reconciling divine and human attributes simply do not arise. This does not mean that the 'outsider' is totally excluded from considering such questions. Most students are not themselves theologians, any more than music students are composers; they are not writing theology but studying it, and that can be done by insider and outsider alike. Both can trace the history of the Christological debates for example, examining how doctrines developed, and identifying key events in the formulation of doctrine. Outsiders as well as insiders can also explore the variety of forms that Christian theology takes, showing how they make up the complex phenomenon of Christianity. Studying history and phenomenology can both be done without entering into the debates themselves, and without endorsing or criticizing the religion's proposed solutions, and both history and phenomenology come under the umbrella of the study of religion.

A brief word about 'divinity' may be helpful at this point. 'Divinity' is a somewhat quaint, slightly old-fashioned word, although it is still used in a handful of British universities. 'Divinity' is wider than theology, and is an umbrella term for the range of studies that are associated principally with the Christian faith. These include Biblical Studies (usually divided into two, reflecting the two 'testaments' – the Old Testament and the New Testament – that comprise the Christian Bible), Church History, and various practical studies such as pastoral care and counselling, liturgics and homiletics, as well as theology itself. (Liturgics is the study of the liturgy – Christian worship – and homiletics is the study and practice of how to preach.) These are all subjects that are relevant to training for the Christian Church's priesthood or ministry (different denominations use different terms here) and, in contrast with the study of religion, are the academic disciplines pursued by those who truly want to be vicars.

Comparative religion

One sometimes comes across the term 'comparative religion' (occasionally 'comparative religions') as a phrase that is seemingly coextensive with 'Religious Studies'. The expression has now fallen into disfavour in Britain, since it suggests that academic study of religion involves the comparison of one religion with another. Very occasionally, comparison with another religion can illuminate a religion that is being studied, but in general one's aim in studying religion is not to draw out points of comparison or contrast, or to establish a 'league table' of religions – with the inevitable consequence of placing one's own religion on top! Religions tend to generate their own distinctive concepts and vocabulary, and the use of expressions that are borrowed from other traditions can easily result in distortion or confusion. It used to be common for early writings on World Religions to talk about the 'Buddhist Church' instead of the Buddhist *sangha* (monastic order), to describe the Dalai Lama as 'Tibet's priest-king' (Waddell, 1895, p. 227), and *bodhisattvas* (a type of celestial being in the Buddhist tradition) as 'incarnations of divinity'. Each of the world's religions has developed its own distinctive vocabulary, and to do justice to its ideas requires learning and using its own key terms. Looking to another faith to help explain should not be necessary.

The term 'comparative religion' will be considered more fully when we discuss the history of the study of religion (Chapter 7). In the meantime we need to turn to another key question relating to the study of religion. Up to this point we have focused on the study of religion, and how it differs from other related disciplines. We now turn to the concept of religion itself. What is the nature of our subject-matter? What is the object of enquiry in the study of religion?

Defining religion

What is religion? It is commonplace for introductions to any subject to begin by attempting a good definition. To the student who is embarking on the subject, this question may seem unnecessary. Doesn't everyone know what religion is? We all know it when we see it: the Muslim who faces Mecca to pray, the Christian receiving the bread and wine at the altar, the Buddhist monk sitting in meditative posture, and the Hindu brahmin studying scriptures, are all examples of people practising their religion. Anyone who picks up a book of this kind must already have some idea of what religion is, and be able to recognize it. If we genuinely did not understand the word, or if our problem was simply providing a snappy definition of the term, could we not simply reach for our dictionary?

Starting off with a dictionary definition of 'religion' is hardly likely to grab the reader's attention, and students who have been advised always to begin essays by 'defining their terms' might well consider whether starting with a dictionary is really the best advice. My own (rather old) dictionary tells us, unexcitingly, that religion is, variously, 'monastic condition, being monk or nun', 'one of the prevalent systems of faith & worship', and 'human recognition of superhuman controlling power & esp. of a personal God entitled to obedience, effect of such recognition on conduct & mental attitude' (Fowler, 1954, p. 1,029).

A moment's reflection should reveal some of the inadequacies of these definitions. It seems somewhat bizarre to start off with a reference to monasticism, which is absent from at least two of the world's traditional religions (Judaism and Sikhism), and which accounts for only a tiny proportion of religious adherents. Many Buddhists, particularly in the Theravada tradition, are uncomfortable with terms like 'faith' and 'worship', claiming that Buddhist teachings should not be accepted on blind faith, and that the Buddha is not an object of prayer and devotion. Buddhists, equally, find difficulty in affirming the notion of 'a personal God entitled to obedience': God does not feature substantially in Buddhism, which does not usually take its ethics from any supernatural authority.

For a quick definition of the term 'religion' one could fare considerably worse than the above. Certainly its author has identified some of the features that are typically associated with religion: the supernatural, worship, ethics and religious officials. However, as we shall see, these are only a sample of features that are associated with religion, and the author appears to make two basic assumptions about the nature of religion, which are at best controversial: he or she seeks to define religion in terms of the supernatural, and seems to presuppose theistic religion as the paradigm. ('Theism' means belief in a personal God.) What dictionaries overlook is that key concepts – of which 'religion' is one – are often contested. In other words, although it is possible to give a neat dictionary definition for someone who genuinely does not understand the word, there is substantial disagreement among scholars about the exact defining characteristics of the term, and different writers presuppose different definitions.

We shall return to this point shortly. Meanwhile, a word about the importance of defining religion. A formal definition is important for a number of reasons. First, it is necessary for scholars and teachers of religion to define what falls within their domain. There are borderline cases where an organization wants to claim a religious identity, but finds that this is questioned. The Church of Scientology is a case in point: superficially it appears to focus on personality testing, offering its followers improved personal efficiency, and charging substantial sums of money, with the result that its detractors have claimed that it is really a business or company, seeking benefits such as tax advantages that accrue from being classed as a religious organization. Conversely, Transcendental Meditation (TM), and many other 'human potential' organizations, are at pains to deny that they are religions. Although the Maharishi Mahesh Yogi, TM's founder-leader, was a guru in a Hindu tradition, his organization does not call on followers to abandon whatever religion they follow, but offers a better ability to cope with living in the material world. What about the New Age Movement? Are we to regard astrology, Western shamanism, 'deep ecology' or the use of Tarot cards as aspects of religion, or should we distinguish between religion and worldviews, such as occultism and environmentalism? We do not propose to answer such questions here, but to point out that whether one is justified in including them in Study of Religion programmes turns on how one defines religion.

Second, a definition of religion helps the student of religion to do justice to all its aspects. As we shall see, some definitions are limiting, and either leave out important features of religion, or exclude certain worldviews from counting as religions. It has sometimes been said, for example, that Buddhism and Jainism are not really religions because they do not include a creator God in their system of belief. We shall consider later the role that God or the supernatural has in a definition of religion. For the present, however, it should be noted that Buddhists and Jains usually consider themselves to be followers of a religion, signalling that there are other important features of religion that need to be included in the study of the subject.

Third, there are occasions when legal and institutional decisions hinge on whether an organization or community is genuinely religious. In 1986 the Attorney General in Britain challenged the Unification Church (popularly known as the 'Moonies', on account of the name of their founder-leader Sun Myung Moon) to defend its claim to continued charitable status. (In Britain, only genuinely religious and educational establishments can claim such rights, which entitle them to important tax benefits.) The Attorney General's challenge included the claim that the Unification Church was essentially a political and not a religious organization, because of its vehemently anti-communist stance. In the end, the case against the Unification Church was dropped, but if it had gone to court, the definition of religion would have been an important factor in determining the outcome.

Some definitions of religion: Substantive and functional

How, then, should one define religion? The sociologist Peter Berger made a distinction between 'substantive' and 'functionalist' definitions of religion. Substantive definitions seek to define religion in terms of its presumed subject-matter – what religion *is* – while functional definitions seek to define it in terms of what it *does* for those who subscribe to it. We shall consider each type of definition in turn.

An early exponent of substantive definition was E. B. Tylor (1832–1917). Tylor was a pioneer in the field of anthropology: he travelled to Mexico and became particularly acquainted with the Anáhuac region of Mexico, where he became one of the first Westerners to study the Aztecs. In addition to his *Anahuac; or, Mexico and the Mexicans Ancient and Modern* (1861), which recounts his work in Mexico, Tylor's most famous writings include *Researches into the Early History of Mankind and the Development of Civilization* (1865), *Primitive Culture* (1871), and *Anthropology, an Introduction to the Study of Man and Civilization* (1881). Tylor received a knighthood in 1912 for his work and many academic honours, including election as a Fellow of the Royal Society in 1871 and a Doctor of Common Law degree awarded in 1875 by the University of Oxford, where he became the first professor of anthropology in 1896.

As an anthropologist, Tylor was at pains to acknowledge that important differences existed between the worldviews of different cultures, and he wished to ensure that any definition of religion did justice to the variety of the world's religious traditions. Thus, if Tylor had defined religion as 'worship of a creator God who sustains the world', he would not have defined religion, but rather his own brand of spirituality (Tylor was a Quaker). Such a definition would cover the theistic faiths, those faiths that believe in a personal god, but not polytheistic religions or non-theistic traditions such as Buddhism and Jainism. Accordingly, Tylor defined religion simply as 'belief in supernatural beings'. Tylor's work caused him to distinguish between three varieties of religious tradition: *animism* (the belief that natural objects such as trees and rivers are 'alive' with spirits), *polytheism* (the belief in a plurality of gods), and *monotheism* (belief in a single god, as held by Judaism, Christianity and Islam). The term 'supernatural beings', being somewhat wider than 'gods', was thus intended to accommodate a wider variety of religious traditions. Tylor's definition of religion can be labelled 'supernaturalist' as well as 'substantive', since he claimed that the defining characteristic of religion is what lies beyond the physical world, namely a supernatural realm.

A similar type of definition was offered by a contemporary of Tylor, Rudolf Otto (1869–1937). Otto was remarkably well travelled for his time: at various points in his life he visited Palestine, India, Ceylon (now Sri Lanka), Burma, Japan and China, acquainting himself directly with Jews, Muslims, Hindus, Buddhists, Jains and Parsees (Zoroastrians living in India). A number of early experiences in Otto's life prompted him to ask what the essence of religion was. He was profoundly moved by the Coptic liturgy which he heard sung in Palestine; a further significant religious experience was observing Dervishes perform their sacred 'turning' (sometimes inappropriately referred to as dance); again, in a synagogue at Mogador in Morocco (now Essauria) Otto listened to the Jewish liturgy, and was particularly struck by the recitation in Hebrew of the 'Qadhosh' from the Prophet Isaiah: 'Holy, holy, holy, Lord God of hosts; heaven and earth are full of thy glory' (Isa. 6.3). He wanted to know what it was about such experiences that made them religious.

Otto was influenced by two scholars in particular: Friedrich Schleiermacher (1768–1834) and Nathan Söderblom (1866–1931). Schleiermacher had contended that religion was a matter of feeling rather than reason, and consisted of a feeling of 'absolute dependence'. Otto accepted the importance of feeling in religion, but believed that religion could not simply be a subjective internal feeling: there had to exist an *object* of that feeling. In other words, religious experience cannot simply consist of a feeling of helplessness: such a feeling, for the religious believer, is accompanied by the conviction that there is something or someone beyond oneself, who is able to help one.

The question was how one should describe this object of feeling: one could use terms like 'God', 'the divine', 'the Absolute', 'the sacred' or 'the transcendent', but all these terms have their limitations. 'God' is apposite to the theistic religions, and is typically conceived as a person. 'The divine' is too weak a word, covering too much, spanning anything from a sexual encounter to an ice-cream sundae. 'The Absolute' is too impersonal, and is associated with the rationalistic system of the German philosopher G. W. F. Hegel (1770–1831). 'Sacred' is more relevant to religion but encompasses ritual objects, buildings, scriptures, as well as the object of one's devotion. To Otto, 'the transcendent' suggested something utterly beyond oneself, with whom direct communication was difficult, if not impossible.

To solve the problem of how to describe a specifically religious experience, Otto turned to the Swedish theologian Söderblom, who had used the word 'holiness' to encapsulate the activity of being religious. The 'holy' is that which stands apart from, and is to be contrasted with, the 'profane'. The word 'profane' can be easily misunderstood: in ordinary conversation the word has come to connote vulgarity or disgustingness, which is not quite what is intended by scholars who use the term. Perhaps a less misleading term would be 'secular', but the term 'profane' has gained a certain currency in Religious Studies, and it is important to recognize what is meant by it. The word 'profane' has some advantage in indicating that, for the religious believer, when compared with the 'holy', everything in the secular, physical world becomes perceived as worthless, inadequate or illusory – the exact diagnosis varying in accordance with the particular religious tradition.

Otto's most famous book is titled *The Idea of the Holy*, first published in German in 1917 as *Das Heilige* and translated into English in 1923. 'Holy' is a word that tends to have dropped out of common parlance, unless we want to be somewhat rude about someone who is overly religious: we sometimes speak of a 'holy Joe' or a 'holy roller'. Its pejorative connotations perhaps detract from Otto's intended use of the term: its root meaning is 'set apart', and signals the idea that the 'holy' is something which or someone who is set apart from the ordinary world or ordinary experience. In this sense we can speak of a Hindu 'holy man': the holy man marks himself out as different from ordinary people, by adopting a world-renouncing lifestyle and taking up spiritual practices. Christians sometimes refer to the sacrament of the Eucharist as 'holy communion', signalling that the Eucharistic elements, although composed of normal bread and wine, are set apart for special use, and treated in accordance with special rules. To make an obvious point, a host at a party may ask us if we want more wine, which we drink amid light-hearted conversation with our friends, but at a Eucharist nothing like this is permitted: the 'set apartness' of the elements (bread and wine) calls for special reverence and prescribed ritual behaviour, such as prayer, or kneeling at the altar (depending on the Christian tradition); even the remains of the elements are not normally thrown out unceremoniously, but are consumed by the priest.

In addition to the word 'holy', Otto employs a term that is little used outside the study of religion – the 'numinous'. The word is derived from the Latin numen, which can literally mean either 'beckoning' or 'divinity' or, combining these two ideas, 'divine beckoning' or 'divine will'. The fact that it is difficult to translate 'numinous' exactly into English serves Otto's purpose well, since he claims that religious experience is *sui generis* (i.e. of its own distinctive kind), and is not readily explicable in terms of other types of human experience. Thus, religion is to be distinguished in particular from the ethical, the aesthetic and the rational. While gods may make demands on their devotees, religion is not simply an awareness of one's moral requirements; equally, while someone may be moved by one of Bach's arias, this is not the same as being aware of the numinous. Someone who claims to have a compelling proof of God's existence may have discovered an important or interesting fact, but rational proof does not bring with it the experiences and activities that are associated with 'being religious'.

Otto's term 'numinous' has three aspects, which he encapsulated in a now-famous Latin phrase, *mysterium tremendum et fascinans* ('tremendous and fascinating mystery'). The fact that Otto chose to use Latin rather than German is significant, since that language serves to reinforce the 'mysterious' nature of the Holy. The Holy is beyond human comprehension, being 'wholly Other', transcendent, distinct from human beings and from normal empirical human experience. Religious believers who are asked to define God, *brahman*, the Tao or nirvana, find such a task notoriously difficult, if not impossible. It is typical for religions to claim that their focus of devotion or meditation is beyond words; for example the Taoist text, the Tao Te Ching, begins:

The way that can be spoken of
Is not the constant way;
The name that can be named
Is not the constant name. (Tao Te Ching, I, 1)

Hindu philosophers have used the expression *neti neti*, meaning 'not this, not that', indicating that whatever words one uses to describe the sacred, they will never be adequate to sum up its essence. Religions have also often resorted to archaic language to remind their followers of the limitations of ordinary speech. Thus, Hindu brahmins continue to recite their sacred texts in Sanskrit, an Orthodox Jewish service will be almost entirely in Hebrew, and until the Second Vatican Council the Roman Catholic Mass was said in Latin, even though none of these languages are spoken or readily understood by the average layperson. At a Pentecostal meeting, members of the congregation will sometimes 'glossolaliate': this phenomenon, otherwise known as 'speaking in tongues', involves lapsing into an ecstatic form of speech which carries no obvious cognitive meaning. (In some Pentecostal churches, other members will offer to 'translate' glossolaliations during worship.) All this serves to highlight a typically religious idea: that the Holy is ineffable, a 'mystery' beyond human vocabulary.

The second part of Otto's characterization of religious experience is *tremendum*. The religious experiences that are described in scriptures are awesome and overwhelming. The Hebrew prophet Isaiah reported having a vision of God in the Jerusalem Temple (Isa. 6.1-13). The Temple became filled with smoke from the incense burning at the altar, and the foundations began to quake, as a vision unfolded of God in his divine majesty, accompanied by seraphim – six-winged creatures, who surrounded God's throne. One of the seraphim flew to the altar and brought a hot piece of coal with which he touched Isaiah's lips as a symbol of purification. Isaiah heard God's voice commissioning him to serve as one of his prophets, and Isaiah accepted the commission.

A further example that Otto uses (he even quotes the passage in full) is from the popular Hindu text, the *Bhagavad Gita*. The *Bhagavad Gita* describes how the warrior Arjuna encounters the god Krishna, who is an *avatar* (literally 'descent') of the high god Vishnu. According to the story, Arjuna's participation in armed conflict presents him with moral dilemmas, which he discusses with his charioteer. Unbeknown to him, Krishna the charioteer is an *avatar* of Vishnu, the supreme godhead, and his identity becomes evident as the story unfolds. At the climax of the text, Arjuna asks Krishna to reveal his higher nature, whereupon he is given special 'divine sight' in order to behold a tremendous vision of Vishnu containing the entire universe, with thousands of eyes and mouths, facing in all directions, bedecked with jewels, and a brightness that exceeds 'the light of a thousand suns' (Otto, 1928, p. 192).

Although such experiences are depicted as overwhelming, and would no doubt instil terror into most mortals, neither Isaiah nor Arjuna appear to want to flee from these awesome presences, or to swoon from the shock of the confrontation. Isaiah's response is to accept his prophetic commissioning, and the narrative continues with a dialogue between God and Isaiah to clarify his instructions. Arjuna bows down in homage, acknowledging his creaturehood, and expresses his love and devotion to Vishnu/Krishna. These responses indicate the element of *fascinans* in the experience: religious experiences are compelling rather than repelling, drawing the experiencer closer to the Holy.

To someone new to the subject it may seem that Tylor, Otto and others are stating the obvious. Is it not common sense to suppose that religion is about relationships with supernatural beings that allegedly exist beyond the physical realm, and about whom believers claim a reality, an 'otherness' beyond ourselves? One can debate, of course, whether there are such beings – a question that looms large for philosophers of religion. But even if religious believers are deluded in supposing that such beings are real, is it not clearly the case that religion is about acknowledging them, and supposedly establishing relationships with them?

Why can't we simply accept Tylor's and Otto's definitions of religion and be done with it? Those who are unfamiliar with academic study sometimes suppose that it generates unnecessary debate, and that academics never seem content to accept what others say, always raising objections and championing alternative theories. Perhaps academics are too adversarial with and overcritical of each other, but such criticisms can only plausibly be made from the standpoint of familiarity with the debate. Those who assume that religion is belief in or experience of the supernatural would do well to familiarize themselves with the criticisms of Tylor and Otto, and with the alternatives to their accounts.

Deciding whose definition of religion is preferable is no different from the choices we make in other walks of life. Someone buying a used car would be ill-advised to take the word of the first salesperson he or she encountered: a sensible customer will consider the pros and cons of a model, consider what else is on the market, and commission a professional inspection.

How, then, are we to assess the view that religion is to be defined in terms of its subject-matter, that it means belief in or experience of supernatural beings, or the 'numinous'? Some have suggested that Tylor's definition cannot accommodate Buddhism, since Buddhists do not generally believe in a creator God. Although this is true, the Buddhist position on gods is often misunderstood. Buddhism, in the vast majority of its forms, teaches that there are many realms of existence into which one can be reborn, one of which is the realm of the gods. Indeed, Buddhists teach that the Buddha himself, in previous pre-enlightened lives, was born 42 times as a god, among other forms of animal and human existence. The Buddhist gods, however, are impermanent, dying and coming into existence like all other living beings, and they play no role in the creation or sustenance of the universe. They can be prayed to, but offer pragmatic rather than spiritual benefits. In the Mahayana tradition there are many other kinds of supernatural being: *bodhisattvas*, who are enlightened, but renounce final entry into nirvana in order to help others, as well as many buddha figures and less benign beings such as ghosts and demons. In *The Idea of the Holy* Otto draws extensively from Buddhism for his examples, and as an instance of the numinous refers to experiencing a celestial Buddha in his wrathful form. (Buddhas are said to have ferocious as well as benign aspects, in order to show their hostility towards evil.)

A more incisive objection to Tylor and Otto is that their theories are somewhat limited. By emphasizing belief, Tylor tends to suggest that religion is a very cerebral affair. Such a suggestion may be due to the Christian tradition from which he came. Of all the world's religions, Christianity is the one that has laid the greatest emphasis on belief, having formulated creeds and confessions of faith at several significant stages in its history. Christianity has insisted on doctrinal conformity, particularly among its clergy, as a prerequisite for remaining within the Christian fold, and those whose doctrines have seemed unorthodox have faced trial for heresy, and – when found guilty – excommunication, or worse. Other religions, however, have placed less emphasis on belief: for Jews the most important aspect of their religion is the observance of the Torah (the Law, believed to have been given to Moses on Mount Sinai); for the Muslim it is submission to Allah and acceptance of Muhammad as Allah's final messenger. For the Hindu, it is the fulfilment of one's *dharma* (religious, personal and social obligations). Even for Christianity, doctrinal as it is, there is more to being a Christian than believing the right things. As James wrote: 'You believe that there is one God. Good! Even the demons believe that – and shudder' (Jas 2.19). As James is at pains to point out to his readers, faith is not sufficient, but must be backed up by one's deeds.

Likewise, in focusing on the experiential aspect of religion, Otto has clearly identified an important feature. However, experience is only one aspect of religion among several, and one could justifiably claim that Otto tended to pick out the 'high points' of religious experience in the faith traditions that he examined. Otto's examples include Isaiah's vision of Yahweh in the Jerusalem Temple, and Arjuna's theophany, in which Krishna's higher nature was powerfully revealed to him. Most religious followers, however, do not experience these spiritual 'highs', but make much more modest claims about their experiences.

'Functionalist' definitions of religion

These problems with substantive definitions of religion have caused numerous scholars to favour a different way of defining religion, known as 'functionalist'. In the functionalist view, religion is defined not by an essence common to all religions, or by a supernatural object of veneration or aspiration, but rather in terms of what religion does for its followers. Functionalist definitions are particularly favoured in the field of sociology. One prominent sociologist of religion, J. M. Yinger, defines religion thus:

> Religion, then, can be defined as a system of beliefs and practices by means of which a group of people struggles with these ultimate problems of human life. It expresses their refusal to capitulate to death, to give up in the face of frustration, to allow hostility to tear apart their human aspirations. (Yinger, 1970, p. 12)

A number of points are worth noting about this definition. First, Yinger does not deny that beliefs form part of religion: he would agree that Tylor identified something important in this regard. However, for Yinger religion involves much more. Notice that he does not simply talk about 'beliefs' but about 'a system of beliefs': religious beliefs are not assortments of unrelated points, but hang together in a coherent way. Christian belief, for example, is about God's creation, how it was marred by sin, and how God sought to redeem the world through incarnation as Jesus Christ.

Second – and most importantly – Yinger insists that practices are relevant to defining religion: what religious believers do is just as important as what they believe, if not more so. The 'ultimate problems' with which the believer struggles are issues like why we are born into a world, why there is suffering and why there is death. These are not matters for mere intellectual speculation, although philosophers and theologians attempt to provide scholarly answers to such questions; religions offer guidance for life – most obviously in their ethical codes – and spiritual practices to offer strength for living and consolation in sorrow. Religions encourage prayer or meditation, worship and ceremonies, and rites of passage to enable men and women to mark the main life-cycle events such as birth, marriage and death. As Yinger points out, religions offer hope: they never teach that evil, suffering and death are totally pointless, or that there is nothing that can be done to improve the world's predicament. Religions offer sustenance to their followers and encourage them to work for a better world, or for higher goals in some other world.

IS FOOTBALL A RELIGION?

People sometimes talk as if their favourite sport had acquired the status of a religion. An important football match can be described as 'soul-stirring'; fans give it highest priority on a Saturday afternoon; they show unwavering loyalty to their team, and support no rival. As Shirl J. Hoffman (1992, p. 1) points out, sport, like religion, can entail 'conscientious commitment beyond what might be considered ordinary'. A number of sociologists have argued that sports possess many of the salient features of religion, and indeed might even be counted as such.

There can be little doubt that sporting events have certain features that can be regarded as analogous to those of religion. Most obviously, there are the ritual activities: the team entering the playing field, the positioning of the players, the chanting, the cheerleaders' routines and the triumphant lapping of the pitch when an important trophy is won. There is what might be described as 'sacred time': supporters regard match times as sacrosanct, and those of us who are indifferent to football cannot fail to notice how quiet the streets are when a World Cup qualifying match is being played. The cricket or football grounds correspond to the 'sacred places', and are carefully maintained so that they can fulfil their purpose.

Other comparisons involve the values that sports encourage. There is loyalty not only to one's team but to one's town or city, or indeed one's country. One politician has suggested that a test of one's true citizenship is not the religion one espouses, but whether one supports the British or the Pakistan cricket team. The competitiveness of sport underlines the competitiveness which is characteristic of the economy. Hard work and perseverance are essential characteristics of anyone who plays rather than spectates. The sporting 'stars' might be said to correspond to the gods: fans might be said to worship them, displaying their images on posters and other paraphernalia. British footballer David

Beckham even gained recognition in the Pariwas Buddhist Temple in Bangkok, where a foot-high golden image of him was installed among other deities at one of the shrines.

So are cricket, football, rugby, baseball and hockey to be regarded as religions? And what is to be gained from such comparisons? A number of important points emerge. For example, the features associated with religions are not unique to them: allegiance, loyalty, values and ritual activities are not exclusively practised by religious people. Those who are unsympathetic to religion might reflect that ritual activities which appear to serve no obvious utilitarian purpose can also be found in other walks of life. The comparison might suggest that religion, allegedly on the decline, is being superseded by activities such as spectator sports, though religious believers can still take comfort in the fact that fewer British people attend football matches on Saturdays than attend church on Sundays.

It is also instructive to note the ways in which the secular overlaps with the religious life. It is fair to ask what function Beckham's image serves in the Pariwas Temple. At a temple in Wolverhampton which the authors know, images are sometimes introduced simply because the leader happens to like them. These include a Native American Indian chief, and an old woman who appears to be knitting! We have not visited the Pariwas Temple, but it would be interesting to ask what function the Beckham image serves. As Mircea Eliade has argued, sacred space often serves as 'cosmogency', showing the place of humanity within the world and what lies beyond. Since Buddhism endeavours to 'see things as they really are', Buddhist temples have been known to incorporate seemingly improbable images. (One temple with which the authors are familiar includes portrayals of a dog defecating; another features Ninja turtles: all this is part of life!)

Interesting though comparisons between sport and religion may be, we believe that it is unhelpful to conclude that sports should count as religions. Good scholarship aims at clarifying distinctions rather than blurring them. We all know that, if asked one's religion, it would be facetious to respond that it is Manchester United or Crystal Palace! (If readers doubt this, let them try giving such a response on an official document.) Students of religion know too that they can expect to study Buddhism, Christianity and Hinduism, but not volleyball, golf or swimming. The study of religion aims not simply to make a contrast between religion and secularity, but to break down further the various categories of religion that are capable of academic study (such as 'theistic', 'deistic', 'polytheistic'), and to devise further categories relating to religion, such as 'tradition', 'denomination', 'sect' and the like. It is not good scholarship to lump together categories that we know to be different.

Having said this, the suggestion that sports might count as religions calls upon students of religion to test out their favoured definitions of the latter. For example, if one's 'ultimate concern' can be football, then this demonstrates the inadequacy of defining religion along the lines that Tillich suggests. If one adopts a 'functionalist' definition of religion, one might profitably ask whether any sport fulfils all – or even many – of the functions that are typically associated with religion. Does it, for example, deal with the 'ultimate problems of human life' or provide its fans with a 'refusal to capitulate to death, to give up in the face of frustration, to allow hostility to tear apart their human aspirations'? (Yinger, 1970, p. 12). Since when have football clubs told supporters what to expect after they die, or provided rites of passage to mark key events in one's life such as birth, coming of age, marriage and death?

On a 'salient features' definition of religion, it is salutary to note that most of the comparisons between sport and religion relate to what Ninian Smart called the 'ritual dimension', and perhaps the 'experiential' one. It is difficult to determine what its doctrines are: there are no creeds or confessions of faith. Although it may instil certain values, it offers no guidance for specific dilemmas in life. While fans may read avidly about George Best's encounters with women or with alcohol, or about Beckham's relationship with his wife, such stories are gossip, and certainly do not bear any profundity of meaning of the kind associated with religious myth. To conflate myth and gossip would be an even greater mistake than conflating sport with religion.

In sum, we believe that sport serves to test definitions of religion, but any definition of religion that embraces sport requires radical rethinking.

References

Hoffman, Shirl J. (ed.) (1992), *Sport and Religion*. Champaign, IL: Human Kinetics Books.
Yinger, J. M. (1970), *The Scientific Study of Religion*. London: Collier-Macmillan.

If the supernaturalists' definition of religion has been accused of being too narrow, the functionalist definition has been criticized as too wide. Is it not also true of worldviews such as Marxism and humanism, and possibly also psychoanalysis, that they satisfy functional definitions of religion? These worldviews have their beliefs and practices, offer hope to humankind, and encourage them to withstand misery and misfortune. While Yinger seems to capture the range of characteristics that are associated with religion, functional definitions must be treated with caution for this reason: they risk letting in rather too much.

Religion and 'ultimate concern'

Another attempt to define religion comes from the Protestant Christian theologian Paul Tillich (1886–1965). Tillich was born in Germany, gained professorial status in several German universities and became a religious socialist. After Hitler rose to power, he was forced to leave Germany in 1934 and took up residence in the United States, where he held academic posts in several prestigious institutions. Tillich's ideas on 'ultimate concern' are expressed in three weighty tomes called *Systematic Theology*, and also in a volume entitled *Ultimate Concern*.

In *Ultimate Concern*, Tillich offered the following definition: 'Religion is the state of being grasped by ultimate concern' (Tillich, 1965, p. 4; quoted in Thomas, 1999, p. 49.) It should be noted that Tillich did not equate religion with 'ultimate concern' itself, but rather with one's response to it. Ultimate concern for Tillich is something outside oneself, but religion is the inner response of being grasped by it. In this context, he quotes the Jewish shema – the Jews' fundamental affirmation of faith ('The Lord our God is one God'), which was endorsed by Jesus of Nazareth as the essence of the

Jewish Torah (law, or teaching): 'You shall love the Lord your God with all your heart, and with all your soul, and with all your mind' (Mt. 22.37). Tillich's position is an advance on Tylor's: while he agrees that religion presupposes something outside oneself (the supernatural, the religious, the holy or whatever), Tillich acknowledges that being religious involves more than simply belief: belief in God – or, to use Tillich's expression, 'the ground of our being' – involves more than believing an interesting additional fact about the universe. For the religious believer, belief in this 'ground of our being' is not just an extra piece of information to be stored in one's mental filing cabinet: it is something that is compelling, and makes demands on the believer.

Tillich's use of the terms 'ultimate concern' and 'ground of our being' rather than 'God' is intended to make his analysis applicable to a wide variety of religions, not merely Christianity. Thus, a Buddhist could be ultimately concerned with the quest for nirvana; the *advaita* Hindu could point to *brahman* as the ultimate reality, and the philosophical Taoist to 'the Tao', which is held to be an underlying 'flow' that pervades the universe and explains the continuous movement of the complementary but opposite forces of yin and yang.

Tillich contrasts his idea of 'ultimate concern' with what he calls 'preliminary concern' or, one might say, 'relative concern'. The latter, says Tillich, is 'conditioned', whereas the former is 'ultimate, unconditional, total and infinite' (Tillich, 1964, p. 14). What Tillich means is that we pursue relative concerns subject to certain conditions. Take, for example, the student who is studying for a degree: this is certainly an important concern, but many students will abandon their studies if they are offered a good job, if their family life is suffering unduly or if their health begins to suffer. (A few may discontinue for less drastic reasons, such as failing to anticipate the amount of effort and application that is needed!) With regard to our relative concerns, we apply what is sometimes called 'transactional analysis'. We recognize that most of what we do involves a 'trade-off': thus, a student's decision to study for a degree involves weighing up the pros and cons of student life, the effects it will have on one's life outside college or university, the likelihood of success and the benefits it will bring.

Contrast this with someone whose concern for his or her religious faith is truly 'ultimate': the martyr, who makes the supreme sacrifice for religious loyalty. Martyrs are rarely subject to crude assassinations: more often than not they are given the opportunity to recant, or tempted into faith-breaking. However, they perceive their faith's demands as 'unconditional' and view faith-maintenance as substantially more important than self-preservation. Although not himself a martyr, the Protestant reformer Martin Luther expressed the non-negotiability of his faith in his famous hymn *Ein' feste burg*, which continues to be sung in Protestant churches today:

And though they take our lives,
Goods, honour, children, wives,
Yet is their profit small.
These things shall vanish all;
The city of God remaineth.

In other words, for Luther loyalty to his faith was not conditional on life, family, home comforts or material possessions. Tillich points out that the demands religions make on their followers can be overwhelming. Education, wealth or fame are all pursuits that we can abandon at will, but for the religious believer there is something reprehensible about the apostate – the person who gives up their faith. The religious community will often regard that person as a traitor, as someone who has given in to temptation, and possibly as having forfeited the means of salvation or liberation.

Has Tillich satisfactorily defined religion? There are several problems with his analysis. It really seems to apply only to the 'serious' practitioner of religion: monks who renounce the world in order to live in austerity, martyrs who sacrifice their lives, or human benefactors like Mother Theresa of Calcutta, whose life was filled with service to religion. For the vast majority of people, religion may have an important influence on their lives, but only occupies a small part of it. Many Christians go to a church on a Sunday and patronize the occasional garden fete, but their religious life goes little further; faced with a choice between taking a holiday and attending church, most church members would probably opt for the latter. For such people, religion has become a conditional concern, subordinated (in this example) to leisure.

Conversely it is possible to elevate a secular concern to the status of an ultimate concern. The late English football manager Brian Clough was once asked in a television interview what his hobbies were. When he stated that he had none, the interviewer asked if this meant that he was interested only in football, to the exclusion of everything else. Clough agreed: for many football fans, football can be an ultimate concern. Tillich cites as examples political ideologies, such as communism or Nazism, whose goals are viewed by their proponents as supremely worthy of pursuit, and to which all else must be subordinated. Tillich describes such ideologies as 'quasi-religions': they function like religions, but are not genuinely religious; indeed, they are often inimical to religion, and when they are markedly hostile to religion their concerns are 'idolatrous' and even 'demonic'.

How, then, are we to distinguish between a genuinely religious 'ultimate concern', a 'relative concern' that has been elevated to an ultimate one, and idolatrous or demonic concerns? According to Tillich, the 'finite' cannot become a matter of ultimate concern. In the case of political regimes, social concerns and games like football, 'these things shall vanish all': civilizations and political systems rise and fall; football may be popular now, but in a few centuries or less some other form of entertainment may have relegated it to oblivion. By contrast God, the 'ground of our being', is the infinite, enduring throughout eternity.

This means of distinguishing between religions and quasi-religions is unsatisfactory, however. Tillich has already acknowledged that it is possible to elevate relative concerns to the status of ultimate concerns; hence, presumably it is possible for the finite to become a matter of ultimate concern. As we have argued too, it is also possible for adherents of a religion to follow their religion with only relative concern. If the ground for Tillich's distinction is the object of concern – that religion is about the 'ground of our being' whereas secular concerns are about physical, transitory goals – then this does not take us further than Tylor's flawed definition of religion, namely a belief in supernatural beings. Although Tillich undoubtedly has the status of a highly influential Protestant theologian, whatever his merits we do not believe that he has offered a satisfactory definition of religion.

The 'salient features' approach

One further way of attempting to define religion is in terms of its salient features. There are a number of characteristics that are typically associated with religions, and some scholars have suggested that a system of belief and practice might count as a religion if it possessed all or most such features. The best-known scheme of this kind has been provided by Ninian Smart (1927–2001). Smart simultaneously held posts at the University of California and the University of Lancaster, where he established the first Religious Studies department in Britain in the 1950s. He began his academic career as a philosopher of religion, but gained direct acquaintance with Buddhism when he was stationed in Sri Lanka in 1945 with the British Army's Intelligence Corps. There were no Christian clergy to provide religious services for his unit, so Smart asked the abbot of the adjacent Buddhist monastery to perform this role. Smart wrote extensively on the world's religions, and is particularly remembered for defining religion in terms of a number of 'dimensions'.

Because of the inherent difficulty of drawing a line between religion and ideology, Smart preferred to talk about 'worldviews' rather than 'religions'. A worldview is an all-encompassing way of looking at the world and acting within it, and the term is designed to accommodate not only religions but ideologies such as nationalism and communism which, Smart argued, share many of the features that are associated with religions. Smart identified six or seven characteristics that worldviews usually possess: experiential, mythic, doctrinal, ethical, ritual, social and material. These will be discussed more fully in Chapter 6. In the meantime, a brief summary will be sufficient to enable us to understand Smart's approach to defining religion.

Most, if not all, religions have an experiential component whereby followers can communicate with the divine or supernatural, and in some way feel its presence. Religions have a 'mythic', or narrative, dimension: they disseminate stories, which may or may not be literally true, but which inspire and guide their adherents. They have doctrines – teachings about what exists in the supernatural realm, how it interacts with the world, what the human condition is and how it can offer salvation or liberation. Religions invariably possess an ethical system, offering guidance for life and obligations for the believer. There are rituals – prescribed sets of actions to be performed within a religious context. The 'social' dimension refers to the fact that religions or religious communities operate like a mini-society: they have their leaders, decision-making bodies and institutional structures. The 'material' dimension relates to the way in

FIGURE 1.1 *Wat Ong Teu, fortune-telling at a Buddhist temple. Most Buddhist temples in the Far East have fortune-telling facilities. Religion offers guidance for pragmatic as well as ultimate concerns.*

which religions draw on aspects of the ordinary world, transforming it into something non-ordinary or sacred: for example, when a supply of bricks becomes a church, a synagogue or a mosque, it is more than an ordinary building.

TYPOLOGIES OF RELIGION

The study of religion is not the same as the study of religions. The latter focuses on specific religions (Buddhism, Christianity, Hinduism, Islam, Judaism, Sikhism and so on), examining their origins, beliefs and practices. The study of religion is removed from this, focusing on the methods of studying rather than the religions themselves. To the beginner the study of religions might seem more colourful and concrete, and the study of religion more abstract, perhaps even abstruse. Nonetheless, it is important to have a theoretical framework in which to study religion, or we run the risk of collecting unrelated information for no obvious purpose, without making connections or understanding the whole subject-matter.

A number of sociologists of religion have developed Max Weber's Church/sect typology to accommodate the varieties of religious phenomena that can be studied. Roy Wallis (1977, p. 13) has devised the following scheme, of which other sociologists have proposed variants:

A typology of ideological collectivities

	Respectable	Deviant
Uniquely legitimate	Church	Sect
Pluralistically legitimate	Denomination	Cult

Despite its seemingly abstract appearance, the typology is invaluable in several ways. First, it serves to indicate the kind of phenomenon an institution is. There are important differences, for instance, between Christianity (the Church), the Church of England (the denomination), the Jehovah's Witnesses (the sect), and the recent phenomenon of renewed interest in angels (arguably, a cult).

The first benefit of such a typology is that it enables us to position a religious organization. Thus, for example, the Church of England falls under the wider umbrella of Christianity. A sect is a movement that has arisen within a wider organization: thus, the Jehovah's Witnesses emerged from Christianity, but can no longer be accommodated within it. Mainstream Christians regard the Jehovah's Witnesses as heretics, while the Witnesses vehemently contend that Christianity became thoroughly corrupted at an early stage, and can no longer claim to offer salvation. The concept of a 'cult' is more complex, and is contested within the fields of sociology and Religious Studies. The sociologist Howard Becker, who first introduced the term, regarded the cult as something that emerged from outside the dominant religious culture rather than from within. Thus, Scientology is 'cultic': it did not emerge from Christianity, but took its rise from an interest in its founder-leader L. Ron Hubbard and his 'cult book' *Dianetics: The Modern Science of Mental Health*, which was published in 1950.

The typology shows how these phenomena are regarded internally and societally. It is 'socially respectable' to belong to the Christian Church, or to be a member of a mainstream denomination such as the Church of England, the Methodist Church or the United Reformed Church. Rites of passage such as baptisms, marriages and funerals are frequently celebrated in these contexts, and participation is regarded as 'normal' behaviour. By contrast the Jehovah's Witnesses, who are instructed to knock on people's doors to disseminate their teachings, are typically regarded as eccentrics, nuisances or 'cranks'. Scientologists fare little better in terms of public perception: their methods for dealing with human ills are markedly at variance with psychiatry and much of modern medicine.

The labels 'uniquely legitimate' and 'pluralistically legitimate' relate to the internal conception of the various organizations. The Jehovah's Witnesses regard themselves as the sole organization that offers truth and eternal life; indeed their members frequently talk about being 'in the truth' – a term which they regard as synonymous with being a Witness. Such a self-perception is not confined to the sect, however: the Church itself (i.e. the Christian religion as a whole) has typically regarded itself as the only means to salvation. The Latin maxim *extra ecclesiam nulla salus* (no salvation outside the Church) was first introduced by Pope Boniface VIII in 1302, and reflects the position of the majority of Christians throughout the ages.

Such exclusivity is in contrast with the denomination. It would be unusual for a member of the Church of England to claim that salvation could not be gained through Methodism or the Baptist Church. Reasons for belonging to a denomination are more likely to be connected with upbringing, liturgical preferences or congregational life. Similarly, cults tend to be non-exclusive, except in the popular sense of the term. Scientology does not require its members to abandon their existing religion, if they have one. Other cultic phenomena, such as devotion to the Virgin Mary, span numerous Christian traditions, although it is true to say that Protestantism has been eager to ensure that Mary is not regarded as an intermediary to God or an object of adoration.

Typologies of this kind go further than pigeon-holing religious groups as they currently exist. The above schema can help us to understand how religions progress through time. A movement within the Church can initially be accommodated, but, as its beliefs and practices develop, can come to be sectarian. Again, the Jehovah's Witnesses are a case in point. The International Bible Students' Association (their original name) was initially a federation of Second Adventist groups who met to study the Bible. As their criticisms of mainstream Christianity became more pronounced, they became more institutionalized and developed a separate existence outside the Church's boundaries. Sometimes sects can be pulled back into their parent religion, and become denominations. Cases in point include the Seventh-day Adventists, the Quakers and the Salvation Army, who once had a separate ('sectarian') existence, but are now associate members of Churches Together in Britain and Ireland (formerly the British Council of Churches). ·

Like most schemata, the Church/denomination/sect/cult typology has its problems. Now that the study of religions and the societal composition of Europe and the United States extend well beyond Christianity, the use of the word 'Church' is somewhat limited. In the study of religion, the term 'religion' is usually more appropriate, since it has a much wider compass. There are also blurred edges between the categories 'Church' and 'denomination'. How should one regard Roman Catholicism? When the World Council of Churches was formed in 1948, the Roman Catholic Church declined membership, on the grounds that there could be no such thing as 'churches', only 'Church' in the singular, and that the Roman Catholic Church was the one true Church. We shall not attempt to assess this claim here, of course, but merely draw attention to one way in which categories can be contested.

The term 'cult' too is problematic. Becker regarded it as a religious movement outside the dominant religion, while other sociologists, such as Steve Bruce, use the term to designate a loosely knit movement centred around a common interest (such as the Virgin Mary). Outside academia, the term is used pejoratively to designate religious organizations of which one disapproves: popularly, 'the cults' is a synonym for 'new religious movements' – a term much preferred within the study of religion. Some sociologists of religion have embraced the term and endeavoured to develop it further: Rodney Stark and W. S. Bainbridge distinguish between 'audience cults' (where followers have little active involvement apart from buying books and videos) and 'client cults' (where supporters buy services such as holistic therapy, or belong to identifiable communities).

Scholars continue to argue about typologies, their aim being to devise categories that will best enable us to understand religious phenomena. While their debate might seem at a distance from the religions themselves, their schemata are fruitful in enabling us to recognize the salient features of religions, and the ways in which they develop through time.

This method of defining something in terms of characteristic features derives from the ideas of the philosopher Ludwig Wittgenstein (1889–1951). Wittgenstein's entire philosophical writings related to questions about how language worked, and he believed the quest to find some kind of common essence in a phenomenon was misguided. His most famous example was the word 'game'. There is nothing common and peculiar to games, that makes them all games. One might try various suggestions: that games are non-serious, that they have winners and losers, that they have rules, that there are several players and so on, but if one considers the wide variety of games it can be seen that these criteria do not fit them all. Wittgenstein's examples of games include the Olympic Games, chess, noughts and crosses, ring-a-ring-a-roses and a child throwing a ball against a wall: there is no common 'essence' that underlies them all (*Philosophical Investigations*, I, 66). Games have what Wittgenstein called a 'family resemblance'. The members of a family do not all look alike, but there are certain clusters of features that are typically associated with them: their build, their eye and hair colour, their physical features, their mannerisms and so on. Members of the same family rarely share all the family's typical features, but the majority of them will have most.

Applying this analogy to religion, we can observe that most, but not all religions have scriptures: primal religions, emerging from preliterate society, do not. Most religions believe in a creator God, but Buddhism is an exception. Most religions have rituals, but groups like the Society of Friends (the Quakers) avoid ritual, preferring one's devotion to come purely from the heart. Most religions have doctrines, but Unitarianism claims to be 'a faith without a creed'. There is no single ingredient that makes a religion a religion, but it is possible to identify features that are shared by most.

One obvious objection to Smart is whether he has encapsulated *all* the typical features of religion, or whether he has overlooked some. One possible addition might be *scripture*: religions typically have sacred writings, which they endow with special authority. Scripture is not synonymous with the doctrinal, although scriptures sometimes serve as the basis of doctrine, nor are they coextensive with myth or with ritual. It would have been perfectly possible for Smart to have suggested the 'scriptural' as an eighth dimension. Again, what about the aesthetic component in religion? Most religions have their sacred art which spans music, painting, calligraphy, stained glass, movement and dance. Frank Whaling, who has devised an alternative scheme, includes both scripture and aesthetics as categories in their own right (Whaling; in Connolly, 1999, pp. 233–4). Whaling's scheme is an eightfold one, comprising: (1) community; (2) ritual; (3) ethics; (4) social and political involvement; (5) scripture; (6) concepts or doctrines; (7) aesthetics; (8) 'spirituality stressing the inwardness of religion'. It is obvious that Whaling's categories interrelate with Smart's, and indeed Whaling acknowledges his dependence on Smart's scheme.

Other scholars have come up with alternative lists of religions' salient features. For example, Percy Cohen has suggested the following list of 'systems' that operate within religions: cognitive system, moral system, ritual system, symbolic system, affective system, social system. (See Gombrich, 1991, p. 11.) Another attempt at defining religion in terms of salient features comes from the philosopher W. P. Alston, who suggests nine categories:

1   Belief in supernatural beings (gods);

2   A distinction between sacred and profane objects;

3   Ritual acts focused on sacred objects;

4   A moral code believed to be sanctioned by the gods;

5   Characteristically religious feelings . . . in the presences of sacred objects . . . ritual . . . associated with the gods;

6   Prayer and other forms of communication with gods;

7   A worldview;

8   A more or less total organization of one's life based on the worldview;

9   A social organization bound together by the preceding characteristics. (Alston, 1964)

In a recent anthology which I co-edited, we decided to use a nine-fold scheme:

1   Origins and founder-leaders;

2   Key writings and scriptures;

3   Predicament;

4   Worldviews;

5   Lifestyle;

6   Spiritual practice;

7   Societal issues;

8   Organization;

9   Ultimate goal. (Chryssides and Wilkins, 2006, pp. 7–8)

The third and ninth points do not occur in the other schemes enumerated above, and merit brief comment. Our contention was that religions usually identify a serious condition from which humankind must escape (sin, illusion, ignorance), and an ultimate transcendent goal that can be attained by following the appropriate spiritual path (eternal life or salvation, *moksha*, liberation, nirvana). This idea draws on Francis Clark, who pointed out that religions can be encapsulated in terms of their answers to three questions: 'From what?', 'To what?' and 'By what?' (Clark, 1977, p. 9).

How are we to decide between these rival lists of salient features? Perhaps it is not altogether necessary. When devising what are basically pigeon-holing systems, much depends on the purpose to which they are being put. The Chryssides–Wilkins scheme was devised particularly to analyse new religious movements, where it was noted that not all were comfortable with terms like 'doctrine' or 'ritual', or even a popularly used term like 'worship' – hence the categories 'worldviews' and 'spiritual practices'. The important point is that, however we decide to define the salient features of a religion, it should be possible in any such scheme to distinguish a religion from what lies outside the student of religion's frame of reference.

The problem of whether such salient features satisfactorily distinguish religions from other types of activity is the key question. Smart himself believed that communism and nationalism displayed many of the features associated with religion. Communism, for example, has doctrines about the bourgoisie and the proletariat; it talks of experiences like alienation; it has ritual activities such as the May Day parade, and sacred places such as Lenin's tomb. Smart claimed that he preferred to talk about worldviews rather than religions, since he believed that there was not a clear distinction between religions and ideologies. Two concluding comments may be appropriate in response to Smart's position. First, it is characteristic of good academic study to make distinctions, rather than to paper over differences that we know exist. Communism, nationalism, humanism and sports – which some have argued possess the features of religion – are importantly different from Buddhism, Christianity and Islam, and such differences should not be ignored. Second, the real difference lies in the fact that religions normally relate to the supernatural and the sacred, and offer goals that lie beyond the material world. Despite the weaknesses of the earlier scholars of religion who offered substantive definitions, one should not underestimate the role of the sacred or the supernatural in helping to define religion. Religions are characterized by their possession of worldviews, but not *any* worldview makes for a religion: the worldview must relate to the transcendent, and point towards some goal that lies above and beyond the materialistic goals of the present world.

DISCUSSION POINTS

1 What, if anything, do we gain by asking whether football is a religion? How helpful is it to suggest that it might be?

2 In what ways do 'religious' people differ from those who are 'non-religious'? Is there a significant difference?

3 Why should anyone be religious at all? Consider how religious believers might claim to benefit from following a religion.

4 Consider Ninian Smart's 'dimensional' scheme for analysing religion. Are there significant omissions? Are there other possible ways of defining the elements of religion?

5 Practitioners of a religion often claim that they are not following a 'religion' but 'a way of life'. What do you think they mean by this? Is this a helpful phrase?

2

Methodology in religious studies

George Chryssides and Ron Geaves

Chapter Outline

The status of Religious Studies   41
The breadth of Religious Studies   43
Conclusion   62
Discussion points   65

Students of religion will choose one approach to their subject, or they will develop the skills to become a polymath. If the latter, they may read widely from anthropology, sociology, cultural studies, psychology, politics, history, theology and philosophy, as well as reading texts on the major religions of the world. If the student's approach is more narrow, they might specialize in one of the following: translating and interpreting ancient texts; a study of a religious community using the methodology of anthropology and sociology; exploring the religious dimension to a particular contemporary political or cultural phenomenon; or trying to understand human behaviour using the tools of psychology. The latter may find themselves in a theology or a Religious Studies department, but the former may be in a department of Middle Eastern or Oriental studies, or following one of the other disciplines that are relevant to the study of religion.

So one of the key questions we need to ask ourselves as scholars of religion is whether we are merely a multidisciplinary subject, made of several subjects such as those mentioned above that also consider religion to be of interest, or whether there is something unique in the study of religion that offers a methodology, and consequent insights, independent of the above subjects. It is sometimes said that the study of religion is a field of study rather than a discipline in its own right. In this chapter we shall explore this claim and examine the ingredients that comprise the subject of religion.

We need to consider the following questions: Is Religious Studies a separate discipline or a field that draws on a range of disciplines? Does it have a distinctive subject-matter and methods that it can claim as its own, or does it merely combine the methods of the various disciplines that contribute to the study of religion? If the former, it is necessary to elucidate and demonstrate the unique contribution of Religious Studies to the study of religion; if the latter, it is necessary to show the important additions to knowledge contributed by these subject areas and to consider new developments in their methodologies that will help scholars to achieve new insights into religious phenomena.

In the 1970s the philosopher of education P. H. Hirst put forward a theory that there were several 'forms of knowledge'. He meant that there are areas of study that possess distinguishing features, notably characteristic central concepts, a distinctive logical structure and network of relationships, particular ways of testing their truth-claims against experience, and specific sets of techniques and skills to undertake such testing. For example: the study of mathematics is undertaken a priori: it involves pure reasoning and calculation. A mathematician does not measure large samples of triangles in order to prove Pythagoras' theorem: the proof is a theoretical and rational one, which does not need empirical verification. Any diagrams that the geometrician uses are simply visual aids to enable us to grasp mathematical ideas. Because the execution of geometrical figures such as triangles and squares is imperfect, mathematical theorems apply to perfect shapes which, the philosopher Plato argued, only exist in the 'ideal' world, not the real one.

Contrast the above example with chemistry, which largely involves observation, noting how substances behave under particular conditions, and formulating theories or hypotheses that are testable and verifiable. In the sciences, theories have only provisional status. Thus, when a chemist affirms that 'all nitrates are soluble in water', it is conceivable that someone might discover a chemical compound that fails to conform to this hypothesis. If this happens, the hypothesis goes back to the drawing board: it might have to be abandoned altogether, but would more likely require some modification. We would still have rules to explain and predict how nitrates behave in the world. Unlike our imaginary deviant nitrate, however, it is not conceivable that we will ever find a right-angled triangle that deviates from Pythagoras' theorem, for the theorem does not depend on empirical data.

This pair of examples serves to demonstrate the distinguishing features of Hirst's 'forms of knowledge'. First, mathematics and science have different central concepts: mathematics deals with numbers, while the sciences deal with substances. Second, mathematics develops a network of proofs and theorems, whereas the sciences build on a progressive range of empirical findings. Third, as we have seen, mathematics proceeds by a priori reasoning and proof, while the sciences proceed by observation, empirical testing and verification. Fourth, the techniques involved in each area are different: the student of mathematics has to know different numerical concepts and how to manipulate them (plus and minus, fractions, negative numbers, irrational numbers and so on), while students of the sciences have to learn how to observe, test hypotheses, design experiments and interpret results.

In his early essay, 'Liberal education and the nature of knowledge' (1965), Hirst identified seven discrete 'forms of knowledge' with their own distinguishing features: 'mathematics, physical sciences, human sciences, history, religion, literature and the fine arts, philosophy' (in Hirst, 1974, p. 46). It should be noted that 'religion' appears as a distinct form of knowledge in its own right, a claim to which we shall return.

Clearly, there are many more subjects in the curricula of schools and higher education institutions. There are several reasons for this, according to Hirst. First, his scheme is about subjects that make 'cognitive' statements, claims about reality that can be assessed as being either true or false. Physical education, for example, would therefore not count as a form of knowledge, since this involves the development of one's physical skills rather than knowledge about reality. Second, the forms of knowledge can be subdivided further: the human sciences (to take one example) include psychology, sociology, anthropology and several other subjects, so the 'forms' subdivide into 'subjects' or 'disciplines'. Third, forms of knowledge can intertwine, creating interdisciplinary topics: a topic like 'French studies' is a case in point, spanning history, arts, human sciences and religion. Hirst calls such combinations 'fields of knowledge'.

The status of Religious Studies

Hirst's analysis of forms of knowledge raises the question of where the study of religion should be positioned. Is it a 'form' in its own right, with distinctive concepts, networks of relationships, methods of testing its claims, and techniques and skills? Is it a distinct subject – perhaps a subset of the human sciences? Or is it field of knowledge, drawing on a variety of subject areas and forms?

Hirst's category of 'religion' is somewhat unsatisfactory. His original essay was written in 1965, at a time when the study of religion, as distinct from theology, was only beginning its ascent in university faculties, and only two years before the establishment of the Religious Studies department at the University of Lancaster – the first of its kind in Britain. In considering the position of religion, Hirst is thinking mainly of Christian theology, with its key concepts of God, sin, redemption, and so on, although he does note in his later essay, 'The forms of knowledge re-visited' (1974, p. 97), that 'Religious Studies' in its emergent form could be construed as interdisciplinary.

In what sense might religion be regarded as a form of knowledge? Hirst considers whether religion should be excluded from study as 'non-cognitive', since philosophers such as Alfred Ayer and Antony Flew have contended that religious statements are devoid of any cognitive meaning, and only express emotions such as feelings of joy at being alive, awe at the grandeur of tall mountains or delight at the beauty of a sunset. The issue of whether religious claims make sense, or whether they are simply 'mumbo jumbo' as often alleged, has been much debated in the philosophy of religion. Hirst assumes that religious assertions do have meaning, although he also acknowledges that religion is about the world and about people, and not simply about a supernatural being such as God.

There is another way in which religion might be disqualified as a form of knowledge. Religion can be practised as well as studied: indeed, the practice of religion is its primary purpose, without which it could not be studied. A practitioner of a religion may learn things about it: reading the Bible devotionally may yield knowledge about events in human history, or about points of theology. However, that is not the prime purpose of devotional study, which is to inspire and to deepen one's relationship with God. Practised for such purposes, religion becomes more like physical education, where the aim is to develop aspects of one's self, not merely to gain new knowledge about the world.

Hirst's definition of 'religion', however, runs into problems in the light of the emergent religious pluralism of our society. There is some plausibility in arguing that Christian theology is a subject with its own distinctive subject-matter, structure, methods of testing and skills. Christian theology is about God, and seeks to explain Christianity's fundamental tenets as they are defined in its sources of authority, notably its scripture, creeds and ecclesiastical tradition. Theology seeks to explain how God created the world, how sin entered into it and the salvific process by which humanity gained the possibility of redemption. All this sounds plausible enough if we confine our study to Christian theology, but different religions have different key concepts, structures and modes of thought. One could not claim, for example, that God, sin and redemption were central concepts in Buddhism, where notions like Buddha, *bodhisattva*, nirvana, *dukkha* (unsatisfactoriness, sometimes translated as 'suffering') and *dharma* (teaching) have a fundamental role.

The study of religion might be seen as the totality of key concepts which may be drawn from all the world's religions. However, this would be misleading: Christian theology does not draw on concepts like *dharma* and *karma*, but on its own distinctive notions. Indeed, the way in which the study of religion is carried out reflects this. Historically, few if any scholars of religion would claim to study religion in general, intending rather to cultivate expertise in a specific religion, usually one of the six major ones. One way of breaking down the study of religion is to dismantle it into areas of specialism relating to specific religions, or in some instances clusters of religions such as new religious movements, and this is how many scholars work. However, increasingly there are scholars who work on theoretical and methodological issues concerning religion in general, as opposed to studying one religion in particular.

Another option is to regard the study of religion as a field constituted by various interrelated academic disciplines. The study of any religion is likely to involve at least four of Hirst's fields: morality, since each religion has an ethical code to teach; the arts, since religions have their literature, music, painting and sculpture; history, since religions typically tell the story of humanity's plight and struggle through time towards liberation or salvation; and the human sciences, since religions involve people as individuals, communities and sociopolitical organizations.

The breadth of Religious Studies

The study of religion, then, spans a variety of academic disciplines which all contribute to it. The most obvious of these are theology, philosophy, sociology, anthropology and history, but the study of art, iconography, literature, textual criticism, archaeology, geography, statistics, and – more recently – information technology, media studies and cultural studies also inform the study of religion. No student of religion can have expertise in all these areas, but a competent scholar must at least know what they are, what kinds of questions they answer and where one might go for information when studies of religion lead to such areas. We propose therefore to give a flavour of some of the questions relating to religion that are addressed by these respective academic disciplines, though only a brief introduction is possible here.

Theology

We have already discussed theology as the academic subject that has traditionally addressed religion. The theologian is of necessity the 'insider', who attempts to make sense of the key doctrinal features of his or her faith. Unlike the phenomenologist (see Chapter 6), the theologian addresses questions of religious truth, and does so in two ways, first by belonging to a tradition where he or she presupposes the truth of its key doctrines, and second by devising explanations that are themselves believed to be true. For example, a Christian theologian would hold that Jesus Christ died for the sins of the world (a key tenet of Christianity), but would seek to devise an explanation of how this was accomplished, which is also claimed to be true.

It follows that it is not possible to be a theologian in a vacuum. A person cannot simply commit his or her religious beliefs to writing and call the result 'theology'. The theologian writes theology *on behalf of* his or her tradition, since he or she gathers up the tradition and purports to explain it. The word 'theology' is normally associated with the Christian tradition, but there are theologians who speak on behalf of Jewish, Islamic and Hindu traditions, among others. The activity of theology does not only relate to the major parent tradition: there are Orthodox, Catholic and Protestant theologians, each claiming to explain their specific strand of tradition; indeed one can describe a theologian by denomination (for instance United Reformed, Unitarian) or by school of thought (Thomist, Calvinist and so on).

We have already made the point that *the study of religion*, unlike *theology*, is neutral with regard to questions of truth, maintaining 'methodological agnosticism'. There is continued debate in both academic areas as to whether the two subjects are contrasting or complementary. At a practical level, some universities have departments called 'Theology and Religious Studies' (or something similar), thus implying that the two areas fit together; in other institutions there has been a deliberate policy of refusing to combine the two, on the grounds that they must not be conflated. As a student of religion one should remain neutral on issues of truth in theology, but one needs to have at least a working knowledge of the history of theology in the area that one is studying, and of the principal theological issues that divide the different traditions. Thus, the student of religion would not have a proper understanding of (say) Christianity, without knowing something of the history of its doctrines: to understand the practice of reciting the Nicene Creed, for example, one needs at least to know what it is, when it dates from and why it was composed in its present form.

Again, one cannot properly understand the differences between Eastern Orthodoxy and the other two major Christian traditions (Roman Catholicism and Protestantism) without realizing that the Eastern Orthodox do not accept the 'filioque' clause in the creed. Filioque means 'and the Son', and Orthodoxy holds that the Holy Spirit proceeds from the Father only, not from the Father and the Son as the other two traditions affirm, claiming (correctly) that the clause was not in the original version of the Creed but a later addition. The student of religion cannot be expected to know the intricacies of the controversy, although theologians in the various traditions would feel obliged to explain and defend their respective stances. Although the grounds of this controversy may seem abstruse, one of the authors recently noticed a service sheet in a Church of England parish church which set out the Nicene Creed with the words 'and the Son' in italics. This was to alert the congregation that, in the event of an ecumenical service involving Orthodox Christians, this phrase should be omitted. We doubt if many readers noticed this signal, but it makes the point that theology continues to influence religious practice.

Traditional theology has had to face a strong challenge from the social sciences and from religious pluralism on the Christian claim to be the exclusive vehicle for human salvation. Some scholars have asserted that no theological truth exists independent of sociological truth, and that changes in theological thinking are always generated by external social and political change.

An example from outside Christian theology is apt in the present context of religious pluralism. In the first two centuries of Muslim history there was vigorous theological debate about free will and predestination. Parallel to these debates were passionate political concerns over the question of Muslim governance, which revolved around the question of obeying or overthrowing unjust or irreligious rulers. These debates politicized the theological speculation on free will. The ruling dynasties of the Muslim world preferred predestination over free will for very pragmatic reasons. If they were predestined to rule by Allah's omnipotent will, then no human being had the right to overthrow them. On the other hand, human free will provided the justification for rebellion. Governments and rulers have always been able to find theologians, clerics or philosophers to support the status quo, and in this case it was decided in the interests of political stability to prefer predestination over free will. However, such social determinism in forming theological orthodoxy, involving powerful elites, should not blind us to this reality: the emphasis on the omnipotence of the divine will in the Qur'anic revelations would itself have generated intense debate, as believers struggled to comprehend God's word in relation to their own salvation and their relations with the divine.

Christian theology also needs to take into account the accidents of history and the impact of powerful elites in the formation of orthodoxy, set against the struggles of the truth-seekers to understand more fully the implications of the Gospel. This is apparent in the history of the Christian missionary movement, where a direct link can be established between the salvationary message promoted by the missionaries and the concurrent, and equally exclusive, promotion of a particular dominant civilization. The major world power was also the major purveyor of Christian missionary activity. This was true of Spain and Britain, and is now true of the United States. The promotion of Christianity has been linked with particular notions of progress and benefit, because particular colonial powers perceived themselves as divinely ordained to improve the human condition. However, globalization and the postcolonial movement of populations have created multicultural and multifaith societies, especially in Western Europe and North America. Consequently, both theology and philosophy have had to reassess exclusivism in order to deal with increasing pluralism. Moreover, interfaith dialogue in a global society is difficult if one religion insists on an absolute truth-claim in its dialogue with another.

In increasingly diverse populations there are few examples of a 'home' religion being insulated from an 'alien' religion, and it could be argued that genuine multifaith societies would regard all religions on their territory as 'home' religions. Probably few religious believers would claim exclusive access to truth. It is apparent that most of the world's major faiths share certain principles, ethics and teaching on moral issues, even perhaps ideas about the divine, but some might be more exclusivist with regard to salvation. Most believers would probably be exclusivist to this degree: they would argue that their 'home' religion sat at the top of a hierarchy of truth, the best or fullest manifestation of a divine truth. However, religious pluralism in its purest form, best represented by the ideas of John Hick, would suggest that the 'home' religion would provide no benefit as far as salvation was concerned, because the 'alien' religions were equally able to offer salvation to their followers. Of course, these arguments hinge on definitions of salvation. Hick's definition is 'the transformation of human existence from self-centredness to a new orientation, centred in divine reality' (Hick, 1988, p. 366). Hick's pluralist inclusivism applies primarily to the major world faiths; he is more cautious about the position of new religious movements in this regard, and he does not mention indigenous religions. Since Hick's significant contributions, a number of writers have discussed issues of inclusivism and exclusivism in the context of religious pluralism. However, it is notable that in the academic study of religion there is still very little philosophy or theology that is itself pluralistic. Theology on the whole means Christian theology, and philosophy means Western philosophy. For example, the student of philosophy looking at rational arguments for the existence of God is almost certain to encounter the ontological argument of Anselm (1033–1109) and the thought of Aquinas (1225–74), but very unlikely to meet Al-Kindi (d. 866), Al-Farabi (d. 950) or IbnSina (d. 1037), who developed equally convincing ontological arguments for the existence of God and may have influenced Christian thought, especially as IbnSina was a Spanish Moor whose ideas were known in Western Europe.

Philosophy

Philosophy of religion, as its name implies, is an area shared by philosophers and students of religion. Like theology, philosophers of religion address questions of truth, the most obvious and fundamental being 'does God exist?' There are other key issues, of course, like why evil and suffering exist, whether one might expect life after death, and – as previously mentioned – whether religious language makes sense or is meaningless. In philosophy of religion students are encouraged to develop and express their ideas in the light of the various opinions that they encounter; it is a bad philosophy essay that ends with the conclusion: 'We have seen that there are arguments for and against God's existence, so it is a matter of personal opinion.'

Unlike the theologian, the philosopher of religion need not come from a specific religious tradition, although there is an area known as 'philosophical theology' where questions such as those above are considered and answered in a way that enables the writer to defend a partisan theological stance. The philosopher of religion, however, has the privilege of being able to come down on either side of the debate, and some philosophers of religion have been avowed atheists. Antony Flew and J. L. Mackie are cases in point, although Flew recently claimed at the age of 81 that he had begun to reappraise his life-long atheist stance. This shows that a philosopher has the liberty to comfortably reconsider his or her position without repercussions, unlike theologians who may have to leave their denomination if their beliefs change too radically, or even – as in the case of the Roman Catholic theologian Karl Rahner – be suspended from their ecclesiastical position.

History

Someone once described history as 'the sociology of the past'. Just as sociologists seek to explain human events and relationships that occur in the present, historians trace patterns of human activity in the past, and assess their impact on today's world. School students who have had to learn dates of battles and names of monarchs, or traced events on the planet from the 'age of the dinosaurs' onwards, have not truly been taught *history*.

History relates to what is documented. Since the dinosaurs did not leave written records, only their skeletons, they belong to prehistory. History is also about humans, not about animals or the physical environment, so investigation into such aspects of the past belongs to palaeontology. History does not consist of catalogues of dates and events: that is *chronicle*, not history proper. Historians go beyond logging events that we can put dates to: they seek to explain why such events happened, what their significance is and how much credence can be placed on the available evidence.

Take, for example, King Ashoka (c. 265–238 BCE), the third Mauryan emperor. The story goes that after engaging in military combat against Kalinga (present-day Orissa),

Ashoka became distressed at the cost to human life: 100,000 soldiers were killed, 150,000 seriously injured and many thousands taken prisoner. He turned to Buddhism in repentance, and proclaimed religious freedom for all citizens throughout his empire. Unfortunately there are few records dating back to Ashoka's reign: there are pillars throughout India that he erected, and these still provide first-hand evidence of his edicts. However, present-day historians are right to question the legends that have been handed down through time, and it has been asked whether he really converted to Buddhism, or simply facilitated its spread by means of his edicts. Were his motives genuinely religious, or could they have been political?

Historians do not simply pass on accepted facts about the past, but engage critically with the evidence. In the context of religion, historians are particularly reluctant simply to accept the hagiographical accounts of religious leaders, particularly if miraculous deeds are attributed to them. The ideas of the European Enlightenment were particularly influential in the rise of history as a critical discipline. Historians will sometimes affirm that their subject is not an 'art' but a 'science', meaning that it has a definite subject-matter (documented sources of evidence), a rigorous methodology that critically evaluates the evidence, and a respect for the canons of scientific thought, in which the miraculous does not readily find a place. This raises problems for the believer, particularly in the Christian faith, which is essentially founded on the work of a historical figure, Jesus of Nazareth. The relationship between faith and history has occupied the minds of theologians and biblical scholars in recent times. Religious believers may prefer faith to historical evidence: as the line of one Christian hymn puts it, 'faith believes, nor questions how'. They may accept what non-believers find irrational, on the grounds of privileged access, such as divine revelation or the authority of scriptures or the Church. That is their right, but in so doing they are not doing history.

Archaeology

Archaeology features less in the study of religion than it did half a century ago. Archaeological discoveries in the early parts of the twentieth century, especially those in the Middle East and Far East, aroused keen public interest. Howard Carter and Lord Carnarvon discovered Tutankahmun's tomb in 1922; John Marshall discovered Mohenjodaro and Harappa in the Indus Valley in the 1920s; Sir Charles Leonard Woolley excavated the ancient city of Ur of the Chaldees from 1922 to 1934; the Nag Hammadi texts were found in 1945 and the Dead Sea Scrolls in 1947. Such finds from the 1920s to the 1940s had a huge impact, and affected our understanding of earlier books on Hinduism, ancient Judaism and Christianity. Although archaeology remains an important subject in universities, and even though there are still occasional remarkable finds, most of the promising archaeological sites have now been thoroughly explored, and it seems unlikely that we can expect anything on the scale of these earlier breakthroughs.

FIGURE 2.1 *The Dome of the Rock, Jerusalem. © Shutterstock. The site has important historical associations for Judaism as well as Islam. Situated on the Temple Mount, the site of the former Jewish Temple, it is said to be the place where Abraham attempted to offer up Isaac, and also the place to which Muhammad travelled on his night journey.*

Like all disciplines, archaeologists have their specialisms, which are defined by period (prehistoric, medieval, industrial) or by civilization (Graeco-Roman, Egyptian, Mesopotamian). Archaeology sets out to discover and analyse the material remains of human life: the remains can take the form of tools, household objects, houses, temples or tombs. Although archaeological digs have an air of excitement, discovering remains is only the first part of the archaeologist's work. Remains need to be classified and dated, and historical judgements need to be made about them. For example, the discovery of a figurine raises questions about its age, where it originated, what religious tradition it pertains to (assuming it is a religious figure – again, an important question to decide), what role it might have had and how it fits in with the history of (say) Buddhism.

It is unlikely that the student of religion will personally take part in archaeological digs, but archaeological findings help to inform Religious Studies. For example, information about the Qumran community – the source of the Dead Sea Scrolls – gives an insight into a first-century Jewish civilization. The discovery was important to Biblical Studies, since the Scrolls provided scholars with the most ancient versions of Hebrew scriptures. Contrary to popular belief, they do not provide fresh evidence about Jesus of Nazareth, who is never mentioned in them – although the Scrolls do tell us something about the background from which Christianity emerged.

The interest that archaeology provoked in the first half of the twentieth century caused some authors of textbooks on religion to emphasize the origins of religions and to write their accounts of chronology. Indeed it is still common to find books on Hinduism beginning with the discoveries at Mohenjodaro and Harappa, and presenting them as the beginning of Hinduism. This can be misleading, because inferences about the possible uses of ancient materials can be speculative: we do not know whether the 'horned god' that was discovered is a prototype of Shiva or not, or whether the ghats were used for ritual cleansing after pollution. Archaeology discovers artefacts, not theories, and of course the latter can be challenged. Past emphasis on archaeology and on the origin of remains has caused scholars and their students to focus on what is ancient, at the expense of studying religion as a living phenomenon. The subsequent rise of anthropology, however, brought the latter into greater prominence.

Case study: The death and resurrection of Jesus Christ

Some years ago we decided to set students an assignment on approaches to religion, which invited them to select a key event in a religious tradition and to examine how different academic disciplines would approach it. Examples included Moses receiving the Torah on Mount Sinai, Arjuna taking part in the Pandava-Kuruva conflict described in the *Bhagavad Gita*, Jesus' crucifixion and resurrection, Muhammad's night journey and Guru Gobind Singh founding the Sikh *khalsa*. Jesus' death and resurrection is provided as an example.

There are many theological issues relating to Christ's death and resurrection, but the one we have selected relates to 'atonement'. Christianity teaches that Jesus Christ redeemed the world from sin (a key tenet of Christianity), but it is not obvious how one man's death on a cross cancels out the sin of the entire world. The Christian theologian therefore addresses the question of how this was possible. Different theories of atonement have thus emerged during the history of Christian theology. Some theologians have explained the atonement as a 'ransom sacrifice': because of human sin Satan came to hold humanity in his grasp, and required appropriate 'payment' for humankind to be released. This sacrifice was Jesus Christ, who offered the supreme sacrifice, being both divine and human. An alternative account of the atonement was given by St Anselm (1033–1109), who claimed that human sin required the satisfaction of God's 'honour'. Humankind owed God compensation for sin, but was unable to pay it; simply to write off humankind's debt would be inconsistent with God's honour and justice, but through his benevolence he himself paid by becoming a sinless person, thus enabling a human being to pay God the due price of sin. Other theologians, particularly in the post-Enlightenment period, felt that such accounts lacked rationality and proposed a 'moral influence' theory, claiming that the problem of sin needed to be addressed by enabling men and women to improve themselves morally, which was what Christ's teachings and example enabled them to do. Thus the life of Jesus became more important than his death, although his death demonstrated his strength of character, since he refused to compromise his message in order to avoid punishment.

Philosophers of religion have raised questions about miracles. If Jesus really rose again from the dead, this would be something very unexpected in the light of what we know about human physiology. Corpses do not come back to life – certainly not after having been dead for three days. So is it possible for events to happen that violate scientific laws, or is it the case that scientific laws are universal, and by their nature do not allow exceptions? If a law has exceptions, can it really be a scientific law? On the other hand, perhaps divine omnipotence entails that 'with God all things are possible' (Mt. 19.26), and that God is in the privileged position of being able to suspend natural laws temporarily. We cannot take this controversial debate further here, but merely note the issue.

The historian is more concerned with what *did* happen. For many post-Enlightenment historians the fact that something is apparently miraculous is sufficient reason in itself for disqualifying it as an event that really took place. The historian would certainly be concerned to look at the documentary evidence of the resurrection, which includes the accounts of the canonical (biblical) gospels, a few apocryphal gospels and a very small handful of contemporary non-Christian sources. What conclusions might be drawn from these, and do they confirm or refute the key Christian assertion that Jesus rose from the dead? There has been much historical research into the life and death of Jesus, with many competing accounts of what Jesus might have been like, what was distinctive about his message, and whether he was sentenced to death for alleged offences against Jewish or Roman authorities. Such debates show little sign of any agreed conclusions.

Jesus' death raises a number of sociological questions about the rise of a new religion, and the transition of leadership following the founder's demise. The early 'Jesus movement' was originally a Jewish cult or sect that focused on Jesus, then developed into an independent religion. How did such a transition occur, and does it have parallels elsewhere? Sociologists have suggested several models for the development of a new religion. There is an *entrepreneurial* model, suggesting that the founder-leader explored a number of religious ideas and groups and subsequently claimed to improve on them, thus offering followers a better 'product'. The *psychopathological* model suggests that the founder had suffered intense personal stress, which was resolved by the founding of the religion. Another model is the social one, which contends that a new religion is more the work of the social group than the founder himself or herself: the early group turns in on itself, distancing itself from those outside, and hence develops a distinctive life of its own.

Another possibility, developed by sociologist of religion Rodney Stark, is the *natural revelation theory*: the founder-leader begins to ascribe his own observations of the world to God. Consideration of which theory best fits the early development of Christianity must be done in conjunction with a historical approach, since we need good evidence of how the early Church arose, who the early leaders were and what kind of community resulted.

Clearly one cannot go back in time to examine the communities in which Jesus' crucifixion took place, but the anthropologist and ethnologist can investigate present-day communities which mark or re-enact these key events in early Christian history. For example, in the Philippines there are Christian communities who re-enact Christ's Passion by self-flagellation, endeavouring to experience some of the suffering that Jesus endured. The anthropologist can add to our understanding of such groups, although this example raises issues about limits to participant-observation. Ethnographical study could explore minority groups in the West: the Jehovah's Witnesses celebration of the Memorial (this is their term for the communion service which they celebrate annually on the 14th day of the Jewish month Nisan). How the Memorial is celebrated, and the reasons for its distinctive features, have been unduly neglected in academic studies, and these questions present an opportunity for the resourceful student.

An archaeological approach would investigate the possible sites of the crucifixion and burial of Jesus. Unfortunately there is little hard evidence that reputable archaeologists claim to find, although some say they have identified these sites. Roy Wyatt (d. 1999) was an amateur archaeologist who undertook several digs around Jerusalem, and claimed that 'Gordon's Calvary' was the authentic place of the crucifixion. (Gordon's Calvary is so-called because General Alexander Gordon, who fought in the Crimean War, located the site at a high point of the city wall.) Not only did Wyatt also claim to have located the Garden Tomb, but his archaeological 'finds' included Noah's Ark, the Ark of the Covenant, Mount Sinai, the Israelites' crossing point at the Red Sea, sulphur balls from Sodom and Gomorrah and furniture from Solomon's Temple. Unsurprisingly, Wyatt's findings have not been authenticated by the vast majority of professional archaeologists. Though archaeologists have not found positive evidence for these biblical events, their expertise is important, if only to rebut the most suspect claims of the more extreme Christian fundamentalists.

The approach taken by the psychologist of religion might depend on the school of psychology that he or she subscribes to. Freud suggested that the sacrament of the Eucharist, which commemorates Christ's death, was a re-enactment of an ancient event in primal society in which a dominant male had command over the females, then whose sons killed him in order to gain access to the females, and consumed parts of his body. Other psychologists might be more interested in the experiential aspects of early Christianity. What kind of experience had Paul had when he described his vision of the risen Christ, and what explanation might there be? Again, some psychological studies have focused on charismatic leadership, and the types of personality that founder-leaders like Jesus and Paul exhibited.

Sociology

Sociology, as the name suggests, treats religion as a social phenomenon. This implies two aspects: first, examining religious communities as societies in their own right, and, second, considering how religious communities influence and are influenced by society more widely. As we noted in the previous chapter, one possible derivation of the word 'religion' is the Latin *religere*, meaning 'to bind together'. So religion, as Durkheim recognized, can be seen as a social phenomenon.

Some studies of religion have focused on small religious communities. One example (there are many) is John *Lofland's Doomsday Cult* (1966), which was the first substantial academic study of the Unification Church (popularly known as the 'Moonies', and subsequently renamed the Family Federation for World Peace and Unification). The Unification Church was located in California in its early years, and Lofland explored its early development by 'living in'; as the subtitle implies, this is 'a study of conversion, proselytization and maintenance of faith'. At the time Lofland was writing, the Unification Church was virtually unknown, and he preserves the anonymity of this group throughout. His purpose was not to cater for public interest in a controversial religious group, but to undertake a study in the 'sociology of deviance'. Members of new religious movements often behave unlike members of the dominant culture, and thus provide an interesting study in non-conformity. Part of the appeal, too, of studying such groups is that they tend to be small, particularly in their early years, and are therefore easier to study than larger organizations. By studying a microcosm of society, some sociologists hoped to extrapolate from the findings and reach conclusions about wider societal behaviour.

Other sociological studies have tried to relate religion to society by considering what kinds of people comprise a specified religious group. James Beckford's *The Trumpet of Prophecy* (1975) – a study of the Jehovah's Witnesses – is a case in point. Much of his study examines the relationship between Jehovah's Witnesses and social class and mobility. Much earlier than Beckford, Max Weber attempted to find correlations between Protestantism and the rise of capitalism, noting that the majority of countries that accepted the Protestant Reformation achieved greater material prosperity. This was an intriguing problem, particularly since the Protestant Reformers advocated a return to the teachings of the Bible, in which Jesus preaches the virtues of poverty and the dangers of riches. It is not our purpose here to examine the conclusions of any of these sociological writers, but merely to illustrate the types of issue that sociologists of religion address. Much sociological study, particularly in the early stages of the subject's development, tended to be theoretical rather than empirical, and as we saw earlier much early sociological work, by Weber and others, consisted of mapping out concepts such as 'Church', 'sect' and 'cult' (Weber, 1904; Troelsch, 1931).

Although in recent times very few sociologists have attempted to provide overarching theories of religion, Stark and Bainbridge have argued that religion has not declined because it serves human needs (Stark and Bainbridge, 1985). They have provided a compensator theory of religion which asserts that humans seek what they perceive to be rewards and attempt to avoid costs (1985, p. 5). They argue that many rewards are scarce and hard to come by while others, such as immortality, are not available but remain desirable. Religion is thus a form of IOU in order to achieve a compensator, defined as a reward that will be obtained in the distant future or in some context that cannot be immediately verified (1985, p. 6). Regular payments keep the compensator valid. Stark and Bainbridge conclude that:

> So long as human beings seek certain rewards of great magnitude that remain unavailable through direct actions, they will be able to obtain credible compensators only from sources predicated on the supernatural. (1985, pp. 7, 8)

However, scholars of mysticism could argue that mystics have pursued deeply spiritual lives in which they have renounced compensators. In the words of the Muslim female mystic, Rabi'a al Adawiyyah of Basra (d. 859):

> O God, if I worship Thee for fear of hell, burn me in hell,
> And if I worship Thee in hope of paradise, exclude me from
> Paradise; but if I worship Thee for Thine own sake, grudge me
> Not Thine everlasting beauty. (Arberry, 1987, p. 51)

Stark and Bainbridge's theory is derived from traditional monotheistic traditions that offer tangible rewards in an afterlife; however, it is precisely this kind of religious position that finds itself under threat in the Western world. As the authors themselves acknowledge, the future of religion is likely to be found among fringe groups or sectarian movements that provide a more vigorous 'otherworldliness' than conventional religion. Many of the New Age religions and other movements are influenced by 'easternization' in which esoteric teachings focus on *immanence* (the divine within) and *imminence* (the here and now). These states bring immediate experiential rewards rather than creating moral or ethical IOUs for a future existence.

The main criticisms of sociological writings on religion are that they are too Eurocentric, deriving most of their conclusions from the Christian and post-Christian Western world; and that they are in the main reductionist, taking little account of individual or group perceptions of the divine in their analyses and disregarding believers' perceptions of what they do. Influenced still by Durkheim, such sociologists still assume they should focus on what people do rather than what they believe. If one accepts a Durkheimian view, holding that religion is instilled and required rather than something about which one can be rationally persuaded, 'brainwashing' theories can be proposed to explain sectarian allegiance. This view is popularly held, although few academic studies support it.

On the whole the sociologist has not found the diversity of religions and their beliefs to be problematic, but rather the fact that beliefs and practices exist at all. Although the social sciences have moved forward, developing a body of knowledge and epistemology, the heritage of their empirical origins can still be traced in their attitudes towards religion. The pioneers of social science identified a process of secularization in the 1960s which challenged the religious worldview of the West and caused formal Christian worship, registered by church attendance, to go into steep decline. However, the rise of new religious movements, the advent of eastern spirituality in the 1960s and 1970s, and the increasing popularity of New Age religions from the 1980s, all reversed the secularization process, and the sociology of religion experienced a renaissance as it examined the causes of this apparent revival of the sacred. However, little interest was shown in the practices or beliefs of the new religions, and hardly any academic attention was given to doctrine as a motivator of religious growth. Most studies were concerned with the wider social implications of this growth, and were dominated by a functionalist approach to religion.

Anthropology and ethnography

Anthropology literally means the study of humans, and anthropologists study collective human behaviour with particular reference to social hierarchies, customs, ritual behaviour and rites of passage. It is sometimes said that the difference between sociology and anthropology is that sociology is the study of the dominant society, while anthropology is the study of other societies. This contrast is somewhat misleading, since it implies that 'our own' society is the normative frame of reference and is culturally superior. Modern anthropology rejects previous assumptions that Western culture is superior, and that only primal societies offer insights into the origins of culture and religion.

Social anthropologists have moved beyond simply collecting information about non-Western cultures, and today they often work in laboratories or with simulation models. Their work is frequently government-sponsored, examining how cultures respond to technological and social change. Such activities are not really the province of the study of religion, where much work is still being done to understand the religious dimension of cultures, an issue which has sometimes been neglected. Recent studies of Native American and Aboriginal religion owe much to work done in the name of anthropology of religion. In the study of religion attention is often given to minority communities that exist within one's own country, for example the Jehovah's Witnesses, or numerous Buddhist groups that have arisen in the United States and Europe. Studies of such groups are best described not as anthropology, but as ethnography – literally, 'writing about peoples'.

Anthropological study involves attempting to become part of the community, adopting its customs and lifestyle, and participating in its key events. Ideally, the anthropologist needs to learn the relevant language, in order to converse with inhabitants and to understand what he or she is witnessing; but with the movement of faiths across the world this is no longer so necessary for students of religion.

The religious pluralism discussed above has had a major impact on the anthropological study of religion. Traditionally sociology and anthropology divided their territory, with the former investigating modern Western societies and the latter researching traditional or indigenous societies in exotic locations. Typically, the scenario of anthropological studies was the academic entering the location of tribal communities and investigating patterns of behaviour, including religious practices. From this early history of contact with indigenous people, a number of methodological criticisms arose concerning the power imbalance in this relationship. These helped develop contemporary ethnography. Today, ethnographers studying religion are likely to be found investigating the increasingly broad range of religious diversity found in modern societies, including those groups which have relocated as a result of migration.

As far back as 1961 the Swedish Lutheran missionary Bengt Sundkler, who studied Bantu prophets in South African Independent Churches, was challenging the idea of such research as neutral, value-free social science. He called for the values of the investigator to be made explicit in the final writing-up of the project (Sundkler, 1961, p. 16). Fiona Bowie writes that any ethnographers 'who submit themselves to periods of immersion in another culture inevitably take the risk that their own way of looking at the world will be challenged, transformed, and perhaps destroyed' (Bowie, 2000, p. 10). As a result of these concerns many contemporary studies include not only the research, but also analysis of the process of doing the fieldwork, which questions anthropological claims to authority and neutrality of observation. (These issues are explored more fully in Chapters 3 and 9.)

Steven Sutcliffe, writing about his fieldwork in Scotland to explore the origins of 'New Age' religion, suggests:

> I recognise the methodological requirement for scholars to position themselves within their narratives – without, however, taking them over. Related to this point is my interest in working with a 'reflexive' model of Religious Studies as critical research done 'at home', on 'ourselves', in line with critiques in anthropology of the disciplinary preoccupation with studying 'exotic' others elsewhere. (Sutcliffe, 2003, p. 4)

Sutcliffe acknowledges the debt that the study of religion owes to these methodological concerns in anthropology, since it has turned its back on the old paradigm where supposedly neutral observers watched and analysed the 'other' in the name of science. The new paradigm insists that field researchers turn the mirror of 'reflexivity' upon themselves and recognize that they are part of their own research projects. Nirmal Puwar acknowledges this improvement and states that some academics even 'offer in-depth confessional accounts from the field before offering the messy texts of the Other, with a full recognition of the meddling part played by the scholar' (Puwar, 2003, p. 32).

Puwar indicates that globalization has complicated the relationship of observer and observed. No longer can it be assumed that the observer is a Western anthropologist studying an exotic culture. 'Natives in the academy' armed with postcolonial theory are challenging previous discourse from within, and developing new narratives to account for experience. South Asians and others who entered through migration and studied in the universities of Europe and North America are challenging the white bodies as the figures of authority over the study of black bodies, and producing new rules of the game. Creating a sense of discomfort, they are demanding to know why academics want to study the 'other' in the first place. The question of motive needs examination, and researchers should examine themselves for signs of 'Orientalism', the voyeurism of attraction to the exotic, or the desire to transform or protect the vulnerable and marginalized. These patterns maintain the paternalistic relations of colonialism, described by Chow as 'the illusion that, through privileged speech, one is helping to save the wretched of the earth' (Chow, 1993, p. 119).

Anthropological studies have always countered the tendency of traditional enquiry into religion to maintain privileged intellectual elites. It has provided the study of religion with a distinction between 'popular' and 'official' religion, and facilitated study of the layperson's religion. Alternative voices describe alternative beliefs and practices which may challenge authoritative documents, religious leaders such as priests or other hierarchies within institutional frameworks (Thomas, 1995, p. 387). With this focus on 'popular', indigenous, or 'folk' religions comes a different method of analysing text, giving attention to the popular as well as the elite text. Such an approach goes beyond an analysis of content to the way in which audiences use their texts.

Psychology

A further academic discipline that contributes to our understanding of religion is psychology. The early work of Sigmund Freud, Carl Jung (1875–1961) and William James is still much cited. Freud and Jung explored the power of the unconscious in shaping human thought and action, although they expressed diametrically opposing views about religion.

Freud's views on religion are developed in two important works, *Totem and Taboo* and *The Future of an Illusion*. The title of the latter gives a fairly clear indication of Freud's stance. His work stemmed to a considerable degree from J. G. Frazer, who contended that totemism was one of the earliest forms of religion. The totem is an animal or bird – occasionally a plant – that is regarded as the common ancestor of the clan. This totem generates certain taboos, a taboo being 'a primal prohibition, forcefully imposed'. Taboos associated with the totem include prohibitions on incest – having sex within one's clan – and on killing the totemic animal. (Prohibitions on killing the monkey or the snake are often found in primal forms of religion.) Fear of breaking such taboos leads to irrational behaviour and Freud viewed much of religion as irrational or, as he put it, 'neurotic'. Neurotic behaviour is often obsessive: a neurotic might, for example, try all the door handles several times each night to ensure that the house is secure. For Freud, religious ritual was little different. For him it is equally irrational to ritually placate a god, the difference being that religion, acted out communally, is a collective rather than an individual neurosis. Freud held that religious belief was a misguided attempt to control the forces of nature, sustained by a desire for a father figure (God); Freud contended that as humanity progressively fell under the influence of science the illusion (religion) would be abandoned in favour of science.

Jung's attempts to explore the unconscious yielded radically different conclusions. Like Freud, he believed that religion was significantly connected with the unconscious. Much of Jung's work related to dreams, which he saw as having significant parallels with ideas found in mythology. Jung therefore postulated the idea of a 'collective unconscious', a heritage of humankind's spiritual ideas crystallized in myths, folklore, dreams and symbols. The notion of the 'archetypal symbol' derives from Jung, who taught that humankind's collective unconscious generated symbols that were common to several religions and not exclusive to one. Obvious examples of archetypal symbols include the cross and the circle: the circle conveys wholeness, completion and eternity, since it has no beginning or end; the cross, as well as alluding to Christ's crucifixion, connotes the reconciliation of opposites, a unity transcending human consciousness.

Other psychologists of religion have focused on the experiential aspects of religions. Of particular note was William James (1842–1910), who popularized the term 'religious experience'. James was interested in religion as an active element in human life, not merely in its relationship to belief or church attendance, and he explored the nature and significance of key concepts such as awareness of God, faith, conversion, sin, salvation and worship. A central concern to psychologists of religion is whether religion is a sign of mental health or psychological inadequacy. James opposed what he called 'medical materialism' – we now tend to call it 'reductionism' – in which religious experience is simply dismissed as a symptom of mental or physical illness. James acknowledges, for example, that St Paul may have been epileptic (James had a particular interest in the religious experience of founder-leaders, as described in written sources), but James contends that this does not invalidate the authenticity of his conversion experience. He acknowledges that not all religious experience is healthy; and distinguishes between the 'healthy mind' and the 'sick soul'. The former is 'once born', seeing the world as harmonious, and believing that it is possible to overcome evil, while the latter sees evil as predominant, and the world as requiring transformation; the latter tends to need some kind of transformatory experience, and James describes this type as 'twice born'.

Among more recent attempts to study religious experience, the Alister Hardy Research Centre is of note. Originally founded in 1969 at Manchester College, Oxford, the Centre was moved to the University of Wales at Lampeter in 2002. Continuing Hardy's work, the Centre continues to collect reports (mainly British) of religious experiences. The key question it asks is: 'Have you ever had an awareness of a power or presence different from everyday life?' Its studies suggest that as many as one person in three has had a significant religious experience in his or her life. Apparently this is the case even though people seldom mention religious experiences in everyday conversation: this appears to be a modern taboo in our society.

Psychology of religion also tends to be reductionist in its approach and has largely been concerned to explore and explain religious experiences such as mysticism, trance or ecstasy, usually categorizing them as some form of neurological behaviour. This follows directly from the pioneering work of William James, who regarded such experiences as the very essence of religious behaviour (James, 1902). In recent decades, advances in psychology have included mapping the brain and its functions, and increasing knowledge of the genetic system. These developments, using the tools of cognitive science and neuro-theology, attempt to explain religious experience.

Cognitive science seeks to explain the processes whereby human beings gather knowledge of the world. From the very beginning of our existence, even in the womb, we are engaged in gathering information and making sense of the world we have entered. Some forms of knowledge appear to be easier to comprehend than others; for example, learning languages seems relatively straightforward whereas higher mathematical understanding is not. Most cognitive scientists argue that the mind consists of a series of components able to absorb different kinds of knowledge rather than a single, all-purpose knowledge-gathering entity. Since the 1990s scholars have turned their attention to how the mind acquires religious knowledge, arguing that there is no special domain of the mind that acquires, structures, retains and communicates religious ideas, but rather that our ordinary everyday cognitive mechanisms can provide the answer to how religious experience is retained and transmitted.

As cognitive agents, humans are able not only to conceptually organize the data of the senses such as sights, sounds, smells, tastes, objects and events, but also ideas of invisible entities and beings who can be utilized to explain what is not comprehensible in the world. In the realm of the unexplained certain objects are put aside as distinct and labelled as sacred, religious or just different, but nevertheless they remain integral parts of the world of cognition (Anttonen, 2002, p. 25).

These psychological studies raise several controversial issues, not all of which are necessarily best dealt with by psychologists since they cannot be resolved by further empirical work, and hence arguably belong to the province of the philosopher of religion. Such questions include how religious experience relates to the supernatural: does it show that supernatural beings or powers really exist, or are such experiences phenomena that occur only in the mind? How does religious experience differ from, for example, moral experience (feelings generated by conscience) or aesthetic experience (sometimes referred to as experience of the 'sublime')? Is religious experience *sui generis* – that is to say, having its own distinctive quality (literally 'of its own kind'), and hence only ultimately comprehensible to those who follow or experience it? Should it therefore be given its own realm of academic study? Do religious experiences have cognitive status – in other words, do they yield facts about the supernatural – or are they subjective feelings? Lawson and McCauley (1990) argue that however the mind works to understand everyday phenomena is sufficient to explain how it acquires religious knowledge. This contradicts those who have argued that religious behaviour is a special kind of human activity – for example Otto and Berger, quoted above. The question of whether religious believers are mentally healthy or sick continues to be discussed. While it is sometimes popularly believed that religion is a 'crutch' for people who are inadequate, some studies claim to have demonstrated that practitioners of religion have better mental health.

At this juncture it may be worth mentioning the role of parapsychology in the study of religion. Parapsychology is the study of the paranormal – experiences and phenomena that elude explanation in terms of conventional science. In recent times there has been particular interest in experiences relating to death and possible life beyond it. Studies of near-death experiences (NDEs) have been pioneered by the medical doctor Raymond A. Moody. He collected testimonies from people who had been pronounced clinically dead (their brain, heart and lung activity had ceased) but who were resuscitated and subsequently claimed experiences of an afterlife in which they typically travelled through a dark tunnel, were met by a 'being of light' and had a vision of being reunited with deceased family and friends. They were informed that their time had not yet come and were sent back to the world, where they claimed that their lives had been transformed.

Another area of parapsychological study involves people who claim to have experienced previous lives rather than anticipated ones. Ian Stevenson (1918– 2007) at the University of Virginia pioneered such studies, which are now pursued internationally by several researchers. Stevenson's book *Twenty Cases Suggestive of Reincarnation* (1974) is a seminal work in this area, and he studied over 2,000 such cases. He interviewed subjects whose claims to previous existences appeared convincing, but whose knowledge of the relevant people and places in their claimed past could not be readily explained by conventional means (such as reading a history book or having been told about the place and time by an older person). While Stevenson himself did not claim that such cases offer proof of reincarnation, he regarded it as a plausible hypothesis. Studies of the paranormal are controversial and have their critics, some of whom (e.g. Susan Blackmore) have devoted much energy to rebutting claims involving the paranormal. We cannot enter such debates here, however, but merely note their existence.

Neuro-theological approaches

A more conventional scientific approach to religion can be found in the rapidly expanding field of neuro-theology. In recent years a number of books have been published in the United States which argue that religious activities and experiences can be measured as neural activity in the brain. These include: Andrew Newberg et al. (2001), *Why God Won't Go Away: Brain Science and the Biology of Belief*; R. Joseph et al. (2003), *Neuro-Theology: Brain, Science, Spirituality, Religious Experience*; E. Aquili and A. Newberry (1999), *The Mystical Mind: Probing the Biology of Religious Experience*; Matthew Alper (2001), *The God Part of the Brain: A Scientific Interpretation of Human Spirituality and God*; and J. Giovannoli (2001), *The Biology of Belief*. These theories purport to explain why there are common patterns of religious behaviour and experience across cultures which are observable in the field of comparative religion. Most such theories assert that as our understanding of the brain's activities develops through exploration of its underlying structures and mechanisms, so the origins of religious experiences and ritual behaviour will be revealed. The following extract from R. Joseph's book on neuro-theology is typical of this genre, and summarizes the position held by such scientists:

> That the brain underlies all experience of living human beings is an absolute statement. It subsumes all religious phenomena and all mystical experiences, including hyperlucid visionary experiences, trance states, contemplating God, and the experience of unitary absorption into any absolute whether personal or non-personal. (Joseph, 2003, p. 22). Typical of neuro-theology's approach to religion are a number of experiments carried out to identify which parts of the brain respond to religious activity. For example, Andrew Newberg and Eugene D'Aquili at the University of Pennsylvania monitored Tibetan monks and Franciscan nuns using intravenous tracers and imaging cameras. They discovered that a part of the brain known as the posterior superior parietal lobe reduces its activity during intense prayer or meditation. This lobe helps create a sense of separation of the self and the world in order to facilitate spatial awareness. The reduction in activity of this part of the brain leads to perception of the self as endless and interwoven with everything (Newberg, 2001). Others studies have linked a variety of religious experiences to activity in the arousal/quiescent systems of the central nervous system. (Joseph, 2003)

Discussions of neuro-theology among students lead to intense debates about the existence of God. One camp argues that such scientific research eradicates God from the equation and supports an atheistic view of the universe, but others claim that the discoveries only highlight the physical reactions to spiritual experience, and demonstrate that in a physical/mental world even God is experienced through the mind. Another issue raised by these experiments is the universal nature of spiritual experience. Geoffrey Parrinder (1976) and Ninian Smart (1978) both argued that mystical experiences have enough common features, in spite of the differences arising from the multiplicity of religious traditions in which they occur, to be defined as universal. This belief in the universal characteristics of mysticism has been called the 'perennial philosophy', a term first used by Aldous Huxley, an ardent perennialist himself. Recently the debate has been reopened by a series of articles and books, not yet translated into English, by Leonardo Boff, the eminent Brazilian liberation theologian.

This view was seriously challenged by Steven Katz's seminal chapter in 'Language, Epistemology, and Mysticism', the work he edited, where he argued that mystical experience itself is shaped by the doctrines and practices which the practitioner brings to the experience, as well as by interpretation arising from cultural and religious factors (Katz, 1978). So the idea of a universal mystical experience underlying diverse religious expressions is seen as seriously flawed. The experiments of neuro-theology suggest that a reappraisal of this debate is needed.

Postmodernism

The manifestations of postmodernism in the late twentieth century have also presented a new challenge to religions, especially the monotheistic versions with their exclusive truth-claims and meta-narratives based upon linear historical interventions of a caring creator-deity through the mechanism of revelation(s). Postmodernism is defined by Jean-François Lyotard as 'incredulity towards all meta-narratives' (Lyotard, 1984, p. xxiv) or overarching truth discourses. It emerges, in the words of Barry Smart, from Western societies being involved in a process of ever-increasing transformation which can no longer sustain the momentum of progress (Smart, 1992, p. 141). Although the identification of the postmodern condition must be attributed to French philosophers such as Foucault, Lyotard and Derrida, its roots go back to the earlier generation of analysts of Western society, working in both philosophy and sociology, such as Marx, Durkheim, Simmel and Nietzsche.

Although these figures were essentially dealing with an earlier stage of capitalism where manufacturing was creating the conditions for urbanization, they seem to be prescient in regard to the human conditions that would be created by modernity and its eventual metamorphosis into postmodernism. Although Durkheim was to suggest that the traditional ties of close-knit family networks and intimate communities such as existed in rural life would be torn apart by the increased mobility and breakdown of conventional morality leading to uncertainty and loss of direction, it was Marx who seemed to glimpse the postmodern future when he indicated that the constant transformation of the modes of production would lead to a human experience in which 'all that is solid seems to melt into air', quoting Shakespeare's *The Tempest* (Act 4, Scene 1, 1. 150).

In those societies most affected by advances in technology and communication, the rapid pace of transformation leads to loss of all certainties; postmodern culture is heterogeneous, fragmented and pluralist, and any one way of perceiving the world or maintaining a common lifestyle disappears. David Lyon speaks of the 'vertigo of relativity' and the 'vertigo of uncertainty' to describe the condition of individuals in a postmodern society (Lyon, 1999, p. 61). The dark side of rapid progress is a psychological condition of anxiety and doubt. In place of Weber's 'enchanted world', lost in the reign of post-Enlightenment rationality, postmodernism offers endless distraction, fantasy and the 'mobilization of desire' (Jean Baudrillard; quoted in Harvey, 1990, p. 61). The endless pursuit of desire leads to the growth of fantasy and entertainment industries and the 'Disneyfication' of reality, embodied in theme parks. Venturi, for example, argues that Disneyland is the symbolic American utopia (Venturi; quoted in Harvey, 1990, p. 60).

The burning question of the postmodern era must be how human beings can be truly emancipated when the certainties of both science and monotheistic religion begin to fail, and pluralism demands that every truth claim be either abandoned or seen as short-lived, to be renewed or exchanged for another. Postmodernism not only challenges the ability of premodern and modernist forms of religion to remain in existence except as a reaction against the conditions of rapid transformation, it also challenges many prior attitudes towards meta-narratives and their analysis.

Conclusion

The disciplines discussed above do not, of course, exhaust the various academic areas that impinge on the study of religion. One might add the study of modern languages, which enhances anthropological and ethnographical study, and of ancient languages, which can facilitate understanding of a religion's ancient texts. Geography is relevant for understanding the topography relating to a religion: knowing the physical layout of a city like Jerusalem and its surroundings enables a better understanding of the ancient history relating to Judaism, Christianity and (to a lesser degree) Islam. Geography can help explain the way religions spread and the societies in which they are found, for example by identifying trade routes where travelling traders might exchange accounts of their various religions. More modern subject areas like cultural and media studies can raise questions about the way religion is portrayed in the news, on television and in film; and Information Technology both enhances the way in which religion can be studied, and raises issues about how religions can propagate their message by electronic means. Also of interest are music, art, architecture and literature, all of which provide ways in which religions express themselves. The list could readily go on: we leave readers to reflect on which other subject areas relate to religion and make its study truly cross-disciplinary.

Many of the above approaches to religion attempt to explain it in a way that makes the realm of the sacred redundant as a cause of human religious behaviour, and thus could be described as having an impact on the claims to veracity attributed to various religious worldviews by insiders. Among the disciplines described above, the social sciences have provided the study of religion with a number of insights into understanding the relationship between religion and society, and have over the years provided their own discourse into the drawbacks and problems of gathering data in the field, both quantitatively and qualitatively. In particular, they have offered the study of religion the valuable tools of ethnography so that living religious communities may be explored.

Following from the founding fathers of their respective disciplines, social scientists have generally maintained a position of methodological agnosticism or even atheism in their enquiries into religion. The pioneers of sociology and psychology, with the notable exception of Jung, were the product of an era in which modernist attitudes towards the advances of science predisposed them towards a view of religion as moribund. To their rational way of thinking, the apparent irrationality incorporated in bizarre customs cried out for rational explanation. In Durkheim's analysis God was reduced to a reification of human society itself. In his view actions are deemed to be moral because society says so, and it is society that we hear speaking through its representatives, who include religious functionaries. Religion is therefore the collective force of society over the individual, and when we participate in religious rituals we most keenly feel the moral force of society. If Marx saw religion as a social opium, Durkheim perceived it as a social cement, functioning to hold society together through a moral value system, with promises of otherworldly rewards and punishments operating as incentives or deterrents.

In essence, the social science approach to religion insists that it is essential for the scholar to go beyond discovering what the insider might understand concerning their beliefs and practices, and to discern underlying causal explanations as being more 'real' than what believers think are the reasons for what they do. Thus the believer is denigrated to the status of non-ownership of their own motivations, and purely 'religious' causes for human action disappear from the microscope of academic research. In recent years, the well-known words of Rudolf Otto have begun to be taken seriously by sociologists of religion, most notably Robert Bellah and Peter Berger: '. . . for if there be any single domain of human experience that presents us with something unmistakably specific and unique, peculiar to itself, assuredly it is that of religious life' (Otto, 1958). Both have stated that the only way to enter the world of religious phenomena is to accept the idea of the 'irreducible sacred'. Daniel Pals, in his significant contribution to Russell McCutcheon's collection on insider/outsider debates, quotes Berger as saying: 'I would recommend that the scientific study of religion return to the perspective on the phenomenon "from within", that is, to viewing it in terms of the meanings intended by the religious consciousness'. (Berger; in Pals, 1999)

Yet the study of religion has also been the domain of the humanities, which usually employ methodologies that interpret religious data as opposed to causal explanations. Science is often portrayed as the protagonist of religion, and post-Enlightenment science versus religion debates still continue to appear in the media, but in the case of cognitive approaches to religion science is making a claim to explain religious behaviour through understanding the processes whereby human beings acquire knowledge of the world around them. Donald Weibe argues that religion should be extracted from the humanities and become the domain of science. He asserts that the study of religion is merely a pseudo-science and recommends that it should not be left 'to the humanists and religious devotees concerned with their place as public intellectuals in the life of society' (Weibe, 1999, p. 255). He is opposed to the polymethodic study of religion, and believes that the study of religion in universities should be solely confined to scientific research (1999, p. 267). These debates will certainly help to form the way in which the study of religion develops in the future and will generate discussions among scholars from the various disciplines that contribute to the study of religion.

Studies of popular religion have blurred the borders of 'culture' and 'religion', and at this point it is necessary to acknowledge the relatively new discourses of cultural studies, especially with regard to the focus on marginalized voices, in particular those emerging from subcultures, popular culture and countercultures. These can provide the study of religion with important tools for exploring religious transformation and innovation. This is especially true of studies of new religious movements and 'New

Age' forms. The marginalized voices from the borders of religions have until recently been neglected or even disparaged, and need to be reclaimed in order to understand their significance. The most significant of these are the marginalized voices of women, and considerable effort has been made by female scholars to make them heard.

Religious Studies, then, finds itself at a turning-point in its development. It continues, as it has always done since its inception as a subject, to draw upon methods that both explain and explore religious phenomena. However, both methods, the former drawn primarily from the social sciences and the latter from the phenomenology of religion, best articulated by Ninian Smart, have failed to satisfactorily locate the causes of religion or to draw any kind of accurate prediction concerning its future. The phenomenological approach alone, which has attempted to explore religious 'essences', isolates religion from both society and culture, and this self-evidently is not satisfactory. On one hand, it is liable to essentialize religious belief and practice as it remains within the domain of the 'World Religions' categorization; on the other hand, it can lead to a superficial description rather than causal analysis.

The methodological atheism promoted by Berger and its variant, the methodological agnosticism propounded by Smart, are also challenged. There are some, for example Steven Sutcliffe, who challenge the attainability of *epochē*, seen as essential in traditional approaches to phenomenological Religious Studies. Sutcliffe states that the 'moccasin walking' model of 'empathetic' Religious Studies is a 'mystified metaphor' as it is not possible in any meaningful sense to 'get into someone else's shoes' (Sutcliffe, 2003, p. 16). We have seen that new anthropological approaches to fieldwork that incorporate reflexivity blur the borders around emic (insider) and etic (outsider) categories. Anthropologists such as Paul Stoller actually became a sorcerer's apprentice during his fieldwork in West Africa and entered fully into their world of spirits, and was eventually forced to flee from a supernatural attack organized by a practitioner (Stoller and Olkes, 1989). However, even without going this far into the world under investigation it would appear that Smart's distinction between empathy and sympathy can still offer something to the researcher.

The study of religion has always put forward the method of neutral or objective study of religion whether by explaining from the social sciences or exploring through phenomenological discourse. In this it has clearly differentiated itself from theology which in the words of Gavin Flood 'is a kind of writing about religion in which there is no separation between the discourse and its object'. Theology, he states, 'is a reflexive discourse, a discourse about something of which it is itself a part' (Flood, 1999, pp. 19–20). However, it can be argued that the study of religion is also a part of something from which it is not possible to differentiate ourselves. The world of religion as it exists in all its aspects, including its cultural and social manifestations, whether we denounce it or embrace it, is part of our reality. As theology comes to terms with sociological explanations and the discourse of postmodernism, so too should Religious Studies come to terms with a more engaged approach to its subject. Reflexivity and dialogical approaches acknowledge engagement, but more than that may be required.

After the impact of 9/11 and the dangerous thesis of a 'clash of civilizations' dominating the discourse of certain politicians, Religious Studies scholars must surely have something to say. Students, it would seem, rarely come to study religion because they wish to be neutral social scientists or simply to be able to describe religious belief and practice more accurately. Peggy Morgan, in her presidential speech to the members at the Annual General Meeting of the British Association of the Study of Religion in 2003, complained that Religious Studies scholars are rarely asked to provide expert 'opinion' by the media when religion hits the headlines. Perhaps our own lack of engagement and insistence on objectivity has put us on too lofty a platform for the media's prerogative to capture the attention of the public. All too frequently academic research in the study of religion focuses purely on the creation of an academic text, useful only to debates within the subject, focusing on the analytical. Such research avoids the critical, where there is an opportunity for creating change (Zahir, 2003, p. 203). Theologians have always possessed an applied element in addition to their rigorous speculations on the nature of the divine. The most common application of Religious Studies in Britain has been the training of religious education teachers, but without falling into the trap of patronization and 'rescue paradigms' it would seem that it might now be time for Religious Studies to consider the words of Lila Watson, an aboriginal social worker:

If you have to come to help me, you're wasting your time.

But if you've come because your liberation is bound up with

mine, then let us work together. (Watson in Stringer, 1996, p. 148)

DISCUSSION POINTS

1 Is the study of religion best described as 'a discipline', 'a subject' or 'a field of study'? How important is it to decide?

2 Comment on the view that the study of religion should be omitted from the school curriculum in the interests of maintaining religious neutrality in a secular society.

3 Evaluate the theories that identify religion as 'the holy' or 'the sacred'. Is this the subject-matter with which the student of religion should be dealing?

4 In the study of religion, students are rarely asked to read about the archaeology of religion, or to take part in archaeological work. Is this an important omission, or has archaeology now made enough of a mark on the subject?

3

Insiders and outsiders

George Chryssides

Chapter Outline

Can the outsider understand the insider?	68
Can religion be understood at all?	69
Emic and etic concepts	70
Barriers to inclusion	74
Cognitive contamination	77
'Living in' and 'going native'	78
Covert research	81
'Reflexive' research	82
The quest and the landscape	84
Ex-member testimony	85
Stances and stakeholders	86
Discussion points	88

There is no clear answer to the question of how many religions there are in the world. Much depends on how one counts them, but certainly there are many thousands of separate religious organizations. It is therefore inevitable that most of the time the student of religion will be the outsider. The most obvious problem of being an outsider is understanding what insiders say and do. Religious activity is not self-explanatory, especially if a ritual is conducted in a language with which the student is unfamiliar. Ethnographers frequently define their role as 'making the strange familiar and the familiar strange'. It is not known for certain who invented the expression: it possibly goes back to the German poet Novalis (born Georg Friedrich Freiherr von Hardenberg, 1772–1801). The second half of this maxim (making the familiar strange) is a reminder that, when a student is studying his or her own religion, that religion can seem very strange to those outsiders who do not espouse it.

As outsiders we study religions for quite the wrong reasons. The purpose of religion is to enable its followers to make progress towards a supreme goal and to answer life's fundamental questions, not to provide data for researchers. Some scholars will recount that they took up the study of religion as part of their quest for life's meaning, while others report that their study of religions was an attempt to understand people and the variety of lifestyles that they pursue. It is easy for the inexperienced student who is also a believer to suppose that the insider has privileged knowledge of his or her religion. We have occasionally known students who have tried to claim exemptions on the grounds that they have been Sunday School teachers or that they have completed a short course of study within their denomination. While there can be little doubt that some knowledge of one's faith is needed in order to accomplish these tasks, such knowledge may be insufficient for academic study, or demonstrate a different kind of expertise. The study of Christianity certainly involves much more than getting to know the Bible stories that one would teach to children and what a service of worship is like – which is often the extent of a believer's acquaintance. It can be gratifying, after fairly intensive study of a religious community, when its members make remarks like, 'How did you manage to find out so much that we didn't know about?'

Academic study has to be distinguished from a spiritual quest. While some students will report that they have been drawn towards a religion as a result of studying it, there are others who have lost faith as a result of critical enquiry, and perhaps the majority find that their faith is unaffected by their academic work. However, members of religious communities sometimes want students to cross the boundary between academic study and spiritual searching. Sometimes they may wish to proselytize, and sometimes they may attempt – no doubt with the best of intentions – to offer spiritual advice to students. One of our students, who had recently experienced a family death, did not find it particularly helpful when an informant presented her with literature about coping with bereavement. However, such incidents are among the hazards of approaching religions as outsiders.

Can the outsider understand the insider?

Approaching an unfamiliar religion as an outsider frequently presents problems about understanding the ideas and practices that one finds. The intelligibility gap between the believer and a non-believer has caused some scholars of religion to contend that the believer and non-believer can never understand each other.

It is important to distinguish between two different meanings of 'understanding'. I might, for example, say that I cannot understand how someone can accept that Unification Church founder-leader Sun Myung Moon had a vision of Jesus, who instructed him to complete his unfinished work. Such a remark does not mean that I cannot attach any meaning to what they are saying. On the contrary, I understand them perfectly well: in saying that I cannot understand them, I am reporting that I have a serious lack of empathy with their ideas. One must therefore distinguish between inability to accept seemingly strange teachings and lack of cognitive understanding of what such claims mean.

Can religion be understood at all?

It is this second sense of not understanding that has occasioned debate among scholars of religion. Some scholars who stand outside of all religions have taken an extreme position, contending that it is not possible to understand religion at all, since religion is inherently unintelligible. The claim that religion per se is unintelligible is a philosophical position, which may be held on various grounds. There are philosophers who have held that religious claims do not make sense because they are non-empirical, and that only claims that can be verified or falsified by means of our five senses are capable of making intelligible statements about reality. Others belong to a tradition associated with the philosophy of Ludwig Wittgenstein, and have contended that religious language is sui generis – literally, 'of its own kind' – being inextricably associated with the form of life that the religious believer pursues and the language that he or she uses. This position has sometimes been labelled 'fideism', implying that religious language is only capable of being understood from the standpoint of faith, and has been espoused by philosophers such as D. Z. Phillips. Whether or not Wittgenstein would have agreed with the later fideists is a matter of debate, but the fideist's basic position is that religious language is associated with what Wittgenstein called 'a form of life' (Philosophical Investigations, 23). Take the example of a game of chess. Someone who does not play chess may fail to understand why players find it complex and requiring a great deal of study. How can there be so much interesting complexity in two players moving 16 wooden tokens over 64 black and white squares? What do chess players mean when they talk about castling, en passant, or Viennese openings? It is difficult, if not impossible, to understand these concepts without actually playing the game oneself. Analogously, the fideist argues, one cannot understand concepts like God, prayer, sin, or salvation, unless one plays the 'language game' associated with religion.

Just as the non-player may not understand the game of chess, so non-believers do not understand religion and, since they do not understand religion, they do not properly understand what they are rejecting. This could explain why numerous non-believers offer a travesty of religious belief when trying to criticize it. Thus Richard Dawkins offers a summary of the Christian faith beginning 'In the time of the ancestors, a man was born to a virgin mother with no biological father being involved' (Dawkins, 2007, p. 207) – a summary of which most Christian believers would agree does little justice to the doctrines of the Virgin Birth and the Incarnation.

Alisdair MacIntyre, in an article entitled 'Is Understanding Religion Compatible With Believing?', argues that it is possible to understand someone with whom one disagrees if there are at least shared concepts. This, he believes, is not the case in religion, since the sceptic cannot affirm any statement whatsoever that the believer makes about God, sin and salvation. The believer and a non-believer, he contends, seem to disagree *in toto*. Particularly in secularized Western society, MacIntyre argues, there is no longer any specific form of life which is distinctively Christian, and Christians are only distinguished from their secular counterparts by reciting pieces of mumbo-jumbo.

There is now a substantial amount of literature relating to fideism, and hence it is only possible to give a very limited set of observations about the controversy. While there are often serious barriers to understanding another religion, particularly if it stems from a totally different culture, MacIntyre appears to exaggerate the communication difficulties between believer and non-believer. Although the sceptic may have no use for words like 'God', 'sin' and 'salvation', this does not mean that it is impossible to understand their meaning. Even in the case of worldviews that have been largely abandoned, explanation still appears to be possible. Few philosophers claim to be defeated in attempts to understand Aristotelian metaphysics, which underpins the Roman Catholic doctrine of transubstantiation, and it is still possible for present-day philosophers and theologians to understand concepts such as 'substance' and 'accidents', without subscribing to such notions.

Despite the fact that the role of religion may have declined in twenty-first-century Western society, it is simply not true that there is no way of life associated with it. For example, in present-day Britain, the Church of England was bound up with the affairs of the state, with the monarch being its supreme governor, and most national celebrations, such as Christmas and Easter, are very much bound up with the Christian religion, even if these are not necessarily celebrated in an overtly religious way. One further compelling argument against the fideist's position is that, if a religion can only be understood from within, conversion would be impossible, since I cannot convert to a religion unless I have at least a basic understanding of what its teachings are.

Emic and etic concepts

One important aspect of the insider/outsider topic is their understanding of concepts and their use of vocabulary. Just as the aspiring chess player has to learn that the piece next to the rook is called the 'knight' and not the 'horse', so the student of religion needs to be able to employ the correct vocabulary. There are two overlapping sets of vocabulary and ways of describing our subject-matter, often referred to as 'emic' and 'etic'. These have been briefly touched on in an earlier chapter. The former term refers to the insiders' account of a phenomenon – not confined to religion, incidentally – and the insiders' vocabulary that they use to express it. It is sometimes described as 'bottom up' – that is to say, it is the believer who judges what is true and the terminology that is best to describe it. By contrast, the latter is the scholar's account, sometimes described as 'top down', and which is based on critical, scientific analysis of the phenomenon. This outsider approach cannot take the believer's view for granted, and uses scholarly vocabulary to discuss it, some of which may be unfamiliar to the insider. Thus scholars use terms like 'theistic', 'primal', 'apologetic', 'hermeneutic', 'eschatological', 'restorationist', and many more terms that insiders might find bewildering.

At times the insider and the outsider share common vocabulary. Words like 'God', 'religion', and names of religions, such as 'Christianity' constitute shared vocabulary. At times this can cause difficulties, for example when a scholar may need a more precise definition than a believer, or where the meaning of a word is contested. Consider for example the use of the word 'Christian'. The account below is an example of one 'insider' account of what it means:

> Unfortunately over time, the word 'Christian' has lost a great deal of its significance and is often used of someone who is religious or has high moral values but who may or may not be a true follower of Jesus Christ.. . . A true Christian is a person who has put faith and trust in the person and work of Jesus Christ, including His death on the cross as payment for sins and His resurrection on the third day. (Got Questions Ministries, 2013)

The definition of 'Christian' is not merely an 'insider' description, but one of a particular type of Christian insider – the evangelical Christian. Such Christians may well have a point in emphasizing commitment as an important characteristic of belonging to the faith, but it is not the scholar's task to make such adjudications. If the scholar, who may or may not be a Christian, were to accept such a definition, it would seriously hamper the study of the religion. How are we then to describe Roman Catholic and Orthodox believers who also regard themselves as Christian, or those 'nominal Christians' who are willing to check a box on an official form (such as a census form or hospital admission form) stating that their religion is 'Christian' rather than some other descriptor? Acceptance of such a definition would cause all sorts of conclusions that are inimical to the scholarly study of religion.

Issues relating to terminology can be problematic. While we can agree that this insider Christian's definition of 'Christian' is unduly narrow, defining the word for the purposes of research is not easy. While we can agree, say, that Roman Catholics and members of the Church of England are Christians, how are we to describe Mormons, members of the Unification Church, or Jehovah's Witnesses? The opposite extreme to insisting on a narrow definition is the approach by Saint Augustine, in his *City of God*. Faced with the question of how one recognized the true member of God's kingdom (the 'heavenly city'), Augustine concluded that such membership was known only to God, to be revealed at the end of time in the final Judgement. While Augustine may well have had a point theologically, this conclusion will not do for the researcher who is studying Christianity. One must come up with a definition that is clear and not arbitrary, and that possesses what one researcher calls 'predictable content and fixed referents' (Sutcliffe, 2003, p. 29). In other words, I must have a definition that will enable others to predict what I will include under the umbrella 'Christian' and what I will not. There is no single way of solving such definitional problems. I could, for example, state that

I am defining Christian as someone who belongs to an organization that is recognized by ecumenical bodies, such as the World Council of Churches. Alternatively, I could suggest that a Christian is someone who would accept the term as a self-definition. Another approach would be to suggest that the word might be used for those who accept Christianity's traditional creeds, including the doctrine of the Trinity. Or perhaps a Christian is someone who belongs to or attends a church with some regularity.

All these attempts run into problems. Not all churches belong to ecumenical bodies. Several organizations who claim a Christian identity have had this identity challenged by the mainstream. Some organizations that purport to be Christian do not necessarily accept the creeds, and groups such as the 'Jesus Only' Pentecostals are non-Trinitarian. Another way of dealing with the definitional problem is to devise ancillary terminology. Some scholars now talk about 'New Christian' organizations, in contrast with the traditional Christian denominations which undoubtedly can claim a Christian identity.

A further, related issue is whether an organization under study should have a say in determining academic terminology. Members of the new religious movements (NRMs), for example, dislike being described as 'pseudo-Christian', 'pseudo-Hindu', or 'cult members', and indeed the use of the term 'cult' by their detractors is frequently arbitrary. Practitioners of vodou, understandably disliking the popular misconception that they vindictively stick pins into effigies, prefer academic studies, as well as public bodies, to abandon the popular spelling 'voodoo' in favour of 'vodou'. However, one's application of terminology must be consistent. If a term like 'new religious movement' is defined to denote organizations that differ significantly from their parent religion and which have arisen during the past 200 (some would say 70) years, then there can be no special pleading that the International Society for Krishna Consciousness (ISKCON) is not new, on the grounds that it claims to trace its origins back through several millennia. If one accepted this argument, it would equally apply to Mormons, Jehovah's Witnesses, and perhaps other Christian groups who might plausibly claim that their founder was Jesus. If ISKCON devotees wish to reject 'new religion' as an emic self-definition, the scholar may note that, but it cannot be allowed to affect one's scholarly etic definition of NRM.

Explanations of a faith also differ between insider and outsider. Take the case of the ISKCON's account of Krishna. According to ISKCON's teaching, Krishna was responsible for the creation of all life, and lived on earth 5,000 years ago with his consort Radha in the holy city of Vrindaban. He revealed the ancient Indian scriptures to his followers, the most important of which was the *Bhagavad Gita*. Vrindaban fell into disuse until the sixteenth-century CE, when Lord Chaitanya came from Orissa in Bengal to Vrindaban as an incarnation of Krishna and revitalized the movement, thus enabling it to regain its ecstatic devotion (*bhakti*) to Krishna. Because of the long disciplic succession that goes back as far as Krishna, ISKCON is not a new religious movement, but the world's oldest religious tradition.

The scholar cannot take this account at its face value, and must ask some probing questions. How much of this can be backed by historical evidence, such as documentary records or archaeological discoveries? Might this explanation be

FIGURE 3.1 *Ma-tsu (Chinese) Temple, San Francisco.*

contested by other religious groups in India? Does this version of events place the *Bhagavad Gita* correctly within its historical and religious context? Can the scholar write as if ISKCON has truly defined Krishna's and Chaitanya's status within Indian religion? An alternative scholarly account might be that Krishna is – atypically – regarded as the supreme God, but was not a historical figure, and that the *Bhagavad Gita* dates from a much later period, possibly around the second-century BCE. Vrindaban was probably nothing but forest country until the holy man Chaitanya came from Bengal to this area, and established a community who were devoted to Krishna. Chaitanya is the first historically accredited figure who established a disciplic succession of leaders, giving rise to the Gaudia Math tradition, from which ISKCON emerged. Since ISKCON only arose as an independent organization, founded by Swami Prabhupada in New York 1966, ISKCON is a new religious movement, in common with a variety of new spiritual groups that emerged around this time.

The account to which one subscribes depends on whether one is a Krishna devotee or Western scholar (although, to complicate matters further, ISKCON makes its own claims to scholarship, and its exponents would take issue with the scholarly analysis I have outlined above). It does not follow that, because Western scholarship favours the second analysis, that the first should be discarded as worthless. On the contrary, the first account provides a clear indication of an ISKCON devotee's self-understanding, and this is important to the scholar as part of the phenomenon of religion. The maxim, sometimes used by phenomenologists of religion, that 'the believer is always right' does not mean that the believers' understanding of their own history is *ipso facto* true. What it does mean is that the believer is the final authority when it comes to telling us what he or she believes. The scholar is more likely to be the better authority on matters of history, dating of texts and appraising archaeological evidence.

Barriers to inclusion

One frequently used method of researching a religion is for the scholar who is an outsider to adopt an insider role. In order to adopt a participant-observer stance I must first of all secure the appropriate permission to be temporarily part of the religious community under study. In Chapter 9 we refer to 'gatekeepers' and 'gate openers' – key people who belong to or have a relationship with the religious community and who can facilitate one's access to it. Sometimes of course these may not be needed, for example when a religious happening is open to the public. However, even when the scholar has been granted access, such permission probably does not amount to an authorization to explore every aspect of the religious community. Certain events may require special authorization; others may require a level of initiation; and on certain occasions researchers may be barred from participation on the grounds of sex, age, sexual orientation or even colour. Unlike public life, religions do not always offer equal opportunities.

There are a number of barriers that can cause the researcher to be excluded from adopting an 'insider' role. Some of these barriers are insuperable, making research on the religious community or part of it completely impossible, while others are surmountable, but make study more difficult.

(1) *Personal barriers.* The first set of barriers relates to personal attributes. One's gender, colour, caste, age and sexual orientation may prevent one fitting in to a religious organization. A white male student would understandably find it impossible to undertake research on Muslim women, and a 'straight' researcher could find it harder to undertake fieldwork in an LGBT religious organization. In the latter case there may be a feeling of discomfort that one does not fit in well, while in the case of the former a male researcher would be automatically excluded. A black student would be ill-advised to attempt a participant-observer role in a white supremacist group, and we know of one researcher who is a high-caste Sikh, and had considerable difficulty securing acceptance by dalits and persuading them that she was a *bona fide* researcher, and not someone who was infiltrating their community with a hidden agenda. Religious adherents themselves of course do not have access to the entirety of their organization. There may be meetings that are only open to men, women, special interest groups or appointed office-bearers.

(2) *Financial barriers.* Other barriers to entry may be due to cost. Not all religious communities have free entry or ask for a voluntary donation at the visitor's discretion. Some can impose charges for courses or services that might prohibit the average researcher, and may well be beyond the budget of most undergraduates. The Church of Scientology is well known for charging fairly substantial fees for its courses, and progress can be very slow, thus presenting a barrier of time as well as money. In any case, some of the higher Scientology courses are defined as 'confidential', and even if the student were to afford the cost and time involved, there would remain the ethical question of whether one should divulge information that is restricted, once such information has been acquired.

(3) *Legal and ethical barriers.* Occasionally there may be situations where one risks breaking the law, or where there may be ethical reservations about the group's practices. An example of the former recently occurred when one of our researchers was undertaking work on the Rastafari, and was offered *ganja* (marijuana). On another occasion a student undertaking participant-observer research on a New Age group found herself in a situation where the group wanted to perform a sacred dance in the grounds of a Russian Orthodox monastery – probably legal enough, but certain to cause grave offence to the Orthodox community.

(4) *Social conventions.* Some time ago, students who were studying Judaism expressed a desire to be participant-observers at a family sabbath meal. This, of course, was not possible, since bringing in the sabbath is a very intimate family affair, and it would not have been appropriate protocol to invite oneself to it. Sometimes Jewish communities will offer to provide a demonstration Passover meal, in which outsiders may take part, or even invite people outside their community to participate in a real one. Such invitations are at the discretion of the community, and it would be inappropriate for researchers to try to force their way in.

(5) *Rules of the community.* Allowing students to attend an act of worship does not entail that one can participate fully. A Christian Eucharist, for example, involves rules about who may receive the bread and wine. Such rules vary slightly according to traditions and denominations, but students should not assume that it is appropriate to receive the sacrament. The community's rules need to be ascertained and observed: it may be possible for non-members to receive a blessing from the celebrant in lieu of the sacrament itself.

(6) *Imposed exclusion.* Some communities may impose total bars on entry. For example, it is not possible to gain entry to a consecrated Mormon Temple unless one is a member in good standing and has obtained a 'recommend' from one's local bishop. No amount of pleading by an outsider scholar can result in an exception being made.

On rare occasions researchers have reported being banned from attending events. Susan Palmer (2004, pp. 7–12), for example, records that her research on the Raelians did not please the leader, and that he consequently excluded her from any further acquaintance with the organization. Palmer is not alone in having experienced such reactions. Researchers sometimes have a dilemma about publishing their material: if those who hold office in the religion being researched do not like what one writes, might that mean that one's research had come to an end? Should one hold back in order to gain more information about organization? Or should the researcher continue to amass material, and then define a final point at which he or she reveals all, knowing that this is the end of the road?

In some communities there may not be formal exclusions, but their character may make them seem inimical to those who are different. On one occasion I needed to conduct a piece of research involving a Seventh-day Adventist community. On reaching the church it was evident that everyone who was going through the door was black, and although white people were by no means excluded, I could see that I was about to place myself in a situation where I would stand out as being noticeably different. As it happened, the community were extremely welcoming and even offered an impromptu lunch invitation at the end. White members were by no means excluded: in fact, in the congregation which was around 300-strong there were about half a dozen white attendees, at least one of whom was clearly an office-bearer.

In his research on the Amazonian community of Mapià, Andrew Dawson reports that he found three different perceptions of himself as the participant-observer: he calls these respectively the provisional insider, the potential real insider and the counterfeit insider. The provisional insider is someone who is treated as a member of the community for the duration of his or her research. Such researchers will behave as if they belong to the community, but will revert to their normal role on return to the outside. Being a provisional insider might involve 'living in' as part of the community for a predetermined period, or it may mean commuting between life in the community and one's normal domestic existence. Provisional insiders, however, are accepted as members of the community for the duration of the research, and are treated in the same way as normal members.

Not all members of a religious organization, however, are content to let the researcher revert to normal life when outside the community, and one of the hazards of becoming involved with a spiritual community is that there can be pressure on the researcher to take more than an academic interest in the religion, and to become fully committed to it. In this situation the researcher is being viewed as the 'potential real insider': he or she is a potential target for evangelism. There are certainly times when I have felt that a religious community has put me under pressure to give a greater degree of commitment than I would wish. Students who research high-pressure evangelical groups might be well advised to learn assertiveness strategies and be able to disengage when necessary.

There are times of course, when the researcher wants to act differently from the others, and hence it can be helpful to explain one's rules in advance. Some years ago I attended a meeting organized by Maharishi Mahesh Yogi's Transcendental Meditation (TM) organization. After explaining some of the key principles of the practice, and outlining the steps that were needed to be initiated, it became obvious that the attendees were expected to sign up for TM on the spot, without even a break between listening and enrolling. Having explained to the leader in advance that I was merely attending as an observer, I was able to remind him of my observer status at that juncture, and to take my leave. Disengagement would certainly have been much more difficult if I had attended as an interested inquirer, like the others.

Dawson's third category – the counterfeit insider – is the category into which some members might place the scholarly researcher, whom they cannot fully accept as a member of the community. Some members of a community may feel that the researchers are tarnishing their environment, which the community might regard as an oasis of spiritual purity, offering escape from an alien world outside. Particularly if the student looks or behaves differently from the rest of the community, he or she can be made to feel awkward and out of place. This once happened when taking my own students to a temple, in which we were permitted to stay overnight. This privilege was normally only granted to members in good standing. The other residents had come there to perform their own religious rites but, despite the student's impeccable behaviour, we thought we detected glances of disapproval and annoyance. We had come for different purposes, and the pilgrims obviously felt that we were spoiling the spiritual atmosphere of the environment. Our feelings were confirmed when, on a subsequent occasion, students were permitted to visit, but not to stay over.

Cognitive contamination

It can be difficult for the insider to be certain that what he or she is observing is a religious community as it really is. When I attend a religious event, I am not simply seeing its members, but rather the participants plus myself, and my presence may well make a difference to what takes place. This phenomenon is sometimes known as 'observer effect', and it can be likened to Heisenberg's principal of quantum uncertainty: the physicist's attempt to locate the position of an atomic particle can itself alter its position. Similarly, in the study of religion, my presence makes a difference. At the very least I may have occupied a seat that obliges other attendees to select a different one, or added one more number to attendance statistics when the congregation is counted.

Such differences are no doubt unimportant, but what can be more serious is a situation where office-bearers attempt a public relations exercise, perhaps endeavouring to present a controversial religious group in a more favourable light, even withholding information or providing misleading data to the researcher. Differences due to observer effect can be due to the best of intentions. On one occasion I took students on a field visit to observe a Greek Orthodox liturgy. I had explained to them that the entire service would be in Greek, and had provided them with an outline of the order of service, since they would not understand the spoken words. I had also informed them that it was customary for the priest's homily to consist of a very brief retelling of the gospel reading. However, out of consideration for us, the bishop informed the congregation that he would preach in English, and instead of recounting the gospel passage he gave a brief introduction to the key tenets of Eastern Orthodoxy – all very considerate and interesting, but not the phenomenon as it usually appears. The sociologist Peter Berger described this kind of alteration to the phenomenon being studied as 'cognitive contamination'.

'Living in' and 'going native'

One way of reducing the risk of cognitive contamination is to adopt a participatory role over an extended period, either by 'living in' and 'going native'. Such roles help to ensure that the researcher is acquainted with a wider spectrum of a religious community, which is not so likely to be filtered through public relations staff. 'Living in' and 'going native' are not quite the same, although there is considerable overlap between them. 'Living in', as the term implies, involves undertaking fieldwork by living inside the community, experiencing life as a member. This has the obvious advantage of enabling the researcher to practise the religion under study from morning until night, rather than the small sections that one experiences on intermittent field visits. This approach not only allows extended conversations with members of a group, but can provide insights on details like whether certain tasks are reserved for women, what forms of recreation are encouraged and what practices are undertaken that may not be mentioned in the extant literature.

'Going native' is perhaps a slightly unfortunate term, reminiscent of early anthropologists who tried to adopt the lifestyle of foreign cultures that they were researching. However, it implies that the researcher is not merely living with the community as an outside observer, but is prepared to adopt the lifestyle of the group, at least for a limited period. This can entail forms of active participation that may not be anticipated. On one occasion I attended a prayer meeting at which it was clearly expected that each attendee would contribute an extempore prayer. On another occasion members gave their testimony of how they had been brought to the Christian faith, and I was presented with the choice of giving a somewhat unorthodox piece of autobiography, or else appearing to be the odd one out.

Complete or near-complete participation therefore presents a challenge to the researcher. It is not just a question of whether the researcher is altering the religion, but to what extent the religion under study may be altering the researcher. In researching a religious group, to what extent do I modify my own behaviour, and to what extent is this justified? I am conscious that at some gatherings I may dress in different clothes from the ones I normally wear. Partly this is to fulfil a group's expectations, out of respect for them. Partly it is to prevent myself feeling out of place: to find that everyone except oneself is wearing a suit and a tie is embarrassing. Researchers are also more likely to receive cooperation from a group if they demonstrate familiarity with their conventions and can behave appropriately. I have known researchers who have gone so far as to shave off a beard, or in one case grow a topknot on his head in the belief that this gave him better passage in certain Hindu organizations.

Inevitably, the question arises as to how far one should go. A researcher, for example, may be vegetarian or vegan, which poses inevitable problems when it comes to accepting hospitality from a group with different dietary customs. Researchers may be asked to express their views on controversial topics. At a recent Jehovah's Witnesses' Kingdom Hall meeting, a woman asked me what I thought of the newly appointed Pope, and whether I did not think that there was too much ritual and ceremony in Roman Catholicism. Do I express my own views in such a situation, possibly starting an argument and maybe alienating myself from the members? Or should I pretend to share her views, thus becoming guilty of dishonesty? Situations like this raise the question of how much of myself I bring to bear as an outsider to the religious communities that I study. How much should I tell them about my own religious commitment, if I have one? If they ask what I think of their ideas, do I tell them frankly if I cannot accept them? Should I argue with them, or should I react as if I were accepting what I am being told? Sometimes opportunities for socializing with members of religious communities occur, and the researcher is faced with the question of how to respond to invitations, which may range from going to the pub after a meeting to accepting an invitation to someone's home for a meal.

There are no agreed answers on how to deal with these matters. David Gordon (1987) recommends distancing oneself from the religious community under study, even arguing against them when they present ideas that the researcher finds unacceptable. Other researchers – such as Anthony Robbins – believe that this is unproductive, and that it distracts from the process of acquiring data. Inevitably there are pros and cons of attachment and detachment. Gaining and maintaining friendships can help to build confidence and trust, thus assuring one's subjects that information acquired will be used fairly and responsibly, and that gatekeepers will feel more amenable to opening up further doors. Friendships can also enable the researcher to see how members of the religious community behave in their home life, and can provide interesting insights about their interests and their lifestyle. Such opportunities can afford details about aspects of life about which the researcher may not think to ask. In my own relationships with Jehovah's Witnesses, I have been able to learn how they manage to prosper economically despite having part-time or modestly paid jobs, what entertainments they allow themselves, what celebrations they have in place of birthdays and Christmas, how they mark birth, marriage and death, among other aspects of living. However, those researchers who favour detachment can argue that unduly intimate relationships can oblige the researcher to present a religious community in a more favourable light than it really deserves, disregarding data that might embarrass or offend, and ignoring criticisms and observations by detractors. My own position is to adopt a middle road when controversial issues are raised, tending to favour evasion in such circumstances. There does not seem to me to be anything to be gained in arguing against a position that I do not share, when my aim is to gain understanding rather than victory in debate, while at the same time I try to maintain integrity by not openly lying about my own views.

There may, additionally, be practices from which researchers exclude themselves, either through personal conviction or because they seem unduly daunting. The researcher may have to decide how far he or she goes in participating in religious rites. One remarkable piece of research, in which the author virtually became part of the religious group under study, is Karen McCarthy Brown's *Mama Lola*, a study of a vodou group in Brooklyn, New York in the 1980s. Brown not only participated in vodou ceremonies, but underwent a number of initiations, including ritual marriages to Ogou and Danbala, two of the spirits with whom Mama Lola (the medium and group leader) typically made contact. This was done not simply as a means to gain further understanding of vodou, but as a means of coping with personal problems in her own life. Obviously such a degree of intimacy with a religious community is controversial, to say the least, and raises issues both of an ethical and a methodological nature.

One particular issue is how one records the data acquired by such detailed contact with the group. Brown wrote up her research in narrative style, somewhat like a novel, and this raises questions of whether there might be data contamination when Brown reports conversations as if conveying the exact words spoken by the participants. The advantage of reporting one's data in this way is that the research is very readable, detailed and colourful, conveying the spirit of the author's encounters with the group, even if this is at the expense of meticulous accuracy. However, all this raises the question of whether Brown has made creative embellishments in her narrative (and the extent to which this matters) and whether Brown's attempt to bridge the gap between the insider and the outsider results in her effectively becoming an insider herself.

Such close association with the group incurs as a further problem. If one's involvement is fairly constant and over an extended period of time, then the adherents are subject to constant scrutiny, and have little control over what is 'on the record' and what is 'off the record'. Anything they say or do can find their way into the researcher's work. The opposite extreme from Brown is the researcher who wishes to remain plainly an outsider, deciding to have more limited contact with the group under study, defining the relationship carefully, perhaps even entering into a formal contract with the informants as a guarantee of their continued cooperation. (Some university research committees require this before approving a research project.) The researcher then undertakes formal interview work, recording and transcribing the data in order to be able to demonstrate that he or she has an exact record of the information that is offered. Interview work, of course, does not necessarily ensure the absence of data contamination. One religious group that I studied some years ago was also being researched by an academic who conducted interviews in a very formal way. Some members confided in me that such formal interviews made them very nervous, thus raising the question of whether interviewees might withhold information in such a situation, or even provide the researcher with the data that they think he or she expects, rather than giving a frank portrayal of their faith.

Covert research

Another possible way of reducing cognitive contamination is to undertake covert research. Normally it is considered appropriate for students to be 'transparent' in their dealings with religious organizations, but if one researches an organization covertly, omitting to disclose that one is a researcher rather than a convert, one may be more likely to experience a religious community as it really is. The question of how much one ought to disclose is no easy matter. Many religious events are open to the public and do not require researchers either to seek permission to attend, or to satisfy the organization's expectations that attendees are spiritual seekers. Particularly if a gathering is a large one, it may not be feasible or particularly desirable for students to identify themselves to its officials. Although students are sometimes counselled to give 'full disclosure' about their research, such advice is also unrealistic. It is not possible to disclose everything about one's work, and insiders may not be interested in all the details. It may be more realistic to suggest that researchers disclose such details as would enable the community to decide on its willingness to cooperate. Again, this can be problematic. On one occasion I needed to acquire information about a religious organization that had past contacts with the controversial Unification Church. Faced with their reluctance to provide me with the needed information, I decided to tell them that I was researching Christian mission to East Asia, with particular reference to Korea. This was true, although admittedly not the whole truth, but this approach enabled me to be put in touch with the relevant missionary who had met founder leader Sun Myung Moon in the movement's early years, and who proved only too willing to provide me with the details that I needed.

Such situations raise important questions about research ethics. Does the end justify the means, or should transparency always take precedence over one's quest for research data? Is it acceptable simply to be economical with the truth, so long as this falls short of deception? Covert research would almost certainly require the approval of an institution's ethics committee, and such applications would usually be denied at undergraduate level, where work is not expected to push back the frontiers of our knowledge. Understandably, religious institutions tend to resent undercover work being carried out on them, when this has been discovered, although some quite important pieces of research have been undertaken covertly. Examples include Leon Festinger's study of a group to which he gave the pseudonym 'Sananda' and which was published as *When Prophecy Fails* (1956). Festinger and his colleagues set out to study this small group, whose leader prophesied the arrival of spaceships which would take her followers to a higher realm. Festinger's aim was to consider how a group dealt with failed prophecy, and how the failure of prophecy affected faith maintenance. This study was conducted over a period of 18 months, and the researchers' disclosure of their identity would certainly have affected the behaviour of the group, or made the research impossible altogether. Other pieces of covert research have included John Lofland's *Doomsday Cult*, and the work of Robert Balch and David Taylor, published as a number of articles, on the group that became known as Heaven's Gate. All three of these studies have proved to be of tremendous value. Festinger's book is a classic text on prophecy, which continues to influence the study of religion; Lofland's is the first academic study of the Unification Church, giving important insights into its early development in the West; and Balch and Taylor's work charted the history of a seemingly insignificant group that subsequently gained prominent media attention as Heaven's Gate, but was little-known when its members committed collective suicide in 1997.

Covert research helps to ensure that the group under study is not acting up for the benefit of researchers, thus enabling scholars to gain a more accurate picture of its activities. However, such an approach does not surmount the problem of data contamination by the researcher's involvement. On the contrary, since convert researchers act as if they are *bona fide* members of the organization, they are expected to make their contributions to the group in the same way as the others, and this may include sharing decisions about the direction the organization will take. Festinger himself concludes his study by stating, 'Our data, in places, are less complete them we would like, our influence on the group somewhat greater than we would like' (Festinger, 1956, pp. 252–3).

'Reflexive' research

Much of the preceding discussion is assumed that the student is typically the outsider. However, many students and scholars of religion have decided to research their own religion. Ethnographers call this sub-discipline 'reflexive ethnography', but of course reflexive study need not be confined to ethnography: study of one's own faith could, for example, be historical or doctrinal. Studying one's own religion is of course a legitimate activity, but it raises methodological questions of its own. The second part of Novalis' maxim is 'making the familiar strange', and this can pose a very difficult challenge to the believer, whose religion may seem thoroughly transparent, and even possess exclusive claims to truth. How could anything be less than obvious to the unbeliever?

The task of maintaining a critical distance between oneself and one's subject-matter is of paramount importance, and is not easily achieved. It can sometimes be helpful to seek the outsider's perceptions. One Jewish colleague recently told me that he found it difficult to understand the references in the Eucharist to eating and drinking Christ's body and blood, and that he found the idea of consuming flesh and blood cannibalistic. Such comments present an ideal springboard for attempting to explain what Christians are doing at Holy Communion. The precise nature of one's response, of course, depends on the type of research one is conducting. An ethnographic study would entail eliciting responses from other insiders regarding their own understanding of the sacraments, while the researcher who was seeking a more 'official' explanation of the theology surrounding them would be well advised to consult definitive position statements from the main Christian traditions. As mentioned above, the insider-researcher cannot assume that he or she already possesses the needed explanations: at best, one only knows a part of one's tradition.

Researching one's own religion may also afford the advantage of having greater access to gatekeepers and gate openers, particularly if the researcher holds some office within his community. Belonging to the religious community that one is researching also means that there are few issues relating to the limits to participation. It also entails a reluctance to explain it away: it cannot be regarded simply as wish-fulfilment, or as the inevitable consequences of historical forces operating in the past. A practised religion is a living entity, that offers spiritual nourishment to the follower.

Having said this, it is important that the researcher does not confuse academic study with his or her own spiritual quest. While one's spiritual journey may help generate enthusiasm, and academic research may yield a greater understanding of one's spirituality, there can be the temptation to confine one's studies to those aspects that the believer finds spiritually helpful. For example, students who have elected to study pilgrimage might find it an enticing prospect to visit their favourite pilgrimage sites in the name of research, but the importance of objectivity and of maintaining and critical distance cannot be overemphasized. The believer can easily be tempted to confuse hagiography with history, and hence uncritically accept myths about the origins of sacred spaces and stories of apparitions and miraculous healings. Such accounts must always be subjected to the normal canons of rationality and historical criticism, or presented as pieces of 'vernacular religion' – that is to say, that version of the religion that is accepted at the grass-roots level by ordinary believers. It would be inappropriate for the researcher to endorse uncritically those claims made within the religious tradition that are likely to be disputed by the outsider.

This last point highlights a further hazard of insider research. There can easily be a tendency to regard one's own tradition or version of a religion as the normative one, and hence either neglect or inadvertently disparage competing traditions. Believers' knowledge is often confined to a small slice of their own tradition, and they may not know its wider history, its theology, surrounding debates, how other traditions differ or even what happens within the neighbouring congregation. The insider needs to recognize what is local and what is universal.

Reflexive research once again raises the question of whether researchers need to declare their stance in their written accounts. While the phenomenologist's approach suggests the bracketing of one's assumptions, and the desirability of studying religion from a wholly neutral standpoint, it is plain that the insider and outsider respectively occupy different stances, which may have an important bearing on their methodology and possible bias. Since the insider's reflexive study forms part of his or her methodology, it is therefore important for researchers undertaking such study to declare their stance, and to discuss its bearing on their work.

The quest and the landscape

We have explored some of the problems inherent in insider and outsider stances. However, different types of insider can find themselves inside different aspects of religion. Spiritual seekers who have not put their roots down in any particular religious organization might be said to be 'inside religion' or even 'inside spirituality', meaning that are amenable to following a religious or spiritual path, and are sympathetic to the idea of a spiritual journey. The seeker might subsequently decide to place himself or herself 'inside' a definite religious tradition, such as Christianity or Buddhism. What 'inside' amounts to can be a matter of personal decision. There are those who claim to be Buddhists for example, but who do not belong to any particular Buddhist organization: their Buddhism simply consists of reading pieces of Buddhist literature, feeling a rapport with some of its teachings and perhaps trying to put some of these into practice in the daily lives. There are also different types of Buddhism to be 'inside', and its Theravada and Mahayana forms have their varieties and subdivisions. Additionally one can be inside monastic orders, or simply a lay follower.

Being inside a specific religious tradition or organization may or may not increase one's understanding of other traditions that fall under the same religious umbrella. As Helen Waterhouse points out, belonging to the Soka Gakkai may place oneself within an organization that has been marginalized by other Buddhists, and probably does not serve as a key to understanding those other more 'mainstream' forms of Buddhism (Waterhouse, in Arweck and Stringer, 2002, pp. 66–7). Being inside one of the Christian Free Churches certainly enables the follower to understand the basics of the Christian message and at least the best-known Bible stories. However, Protestant Christians typically find that they have a decided lack of rapport with Eastern Orthodoxy, often reacting very badly to its elaborate liturgy and its heavy reliance on ancient tradition. Conversely, Orthodox Christians tend to find Protestant worship over-casual and lacking in structure and reverence. Religious affiliation can be like being inside a series of overlapping circles: the believer can be 'inside' Christianity, but outside Eastern Orthodoxy and inside the Salvation Army.

There are further subdivisions. A religious organization may have different levels of initiation: laity, elders, deacons, priests, and so on, the precise designations and associated powers and duties varying according to the organization. The laity are noted for having different levels of commitment and, perhaps associated with this, different levels of knowledge about their faith. There are those who only attend at special festivals, those who come regularly on the religion's holy days, but do nothing else, and there are insiders who appear to make their religion their life's work, almost to the exclusion of all else. Within an organization, too, there are different shades of opinion. Most religions have their conservative members, who dislike any kind of change. At the other end of the spectrum, there are the radicals and reformers who are pressing for change. Both types of member may be part of their own special interest groups. In twenty-first-century Christianity, the issue of role of women has generated a complex variety of attitudes, and a proliferation of pressure groups, ranging from the Movement for their Ordination of Women, to Forward in Faith, which seeks to preserve the priesthood for men only, to uphold traditional moral values, and to retain the denomination's traditional forms of liturgy.

The boundary between inside and outside is also a blurred one. I have mentioned the 'seeker', who may be exploring a variety of expressions of religious belief, suspecting that someone somewhere might be able to provide the truth, but not yet having found the religious community that will prove to be satisfying. A further stage on from seeking is the waverer – one who feels attracted to the faith in question, but is still wondering whether to make a decision to join. Somewhat further on is the one who is taking instruction in a faith – the acolyte, the catechumen, or whatever name of this person goes by within the organization: such a person has decided to make a commitment, but still requires fuller instruction and fuller acceptance by the community in question, and may not yet be fully authorized to participate in all the community's rites. Then again different members of the organization have different levels of maturity and knowledge, different degrees of commitment and different levels of attendance. Inside the religious community one finds staunch and solid members, whose commitment is a lifelong unwavering one. By contrast, there are insiders whose faith has gone lukewarm, and doubters who may even be reappraising their commitment. There are waverers on both sides of the fence: just as one can waver about whether or not to come in, one can be undecided about whether to come out of an organization.

Ex-member testimony

This last category – the ex-member – is of particular interest in the study of NRMs, where they tend to be particularly vocal, and are often given privileged popular credence, in the field of new religions. In the popular literature about 'cults' this kind of testimony frequently purports to offer an exposé of the organization that the ex-member has left, with graphic accounts of life inside the organization, accusations of brainwashing, and sometimes an amazing escape story of how the member managed to gain his or her freedom and return to 'normality'.

The majority of scholars are wary of the atrocity tales that are told by ex-members. James Beckford (1978) suggests that their accounts may not be straightforward narratives about coming out of a religious organization, but may be highly influenced by – even negotiated with – family, friends, media impressions and anticult organizations. Understandably, ex-members may wish to devise explanations for their entry, allegiance, and ultimately their exit, which absolve them of responsibility, making use of explanations such as 'brainwashing', 'mind control' and indoctrination.

This privileged credence to ex-member testimony is sometimes justified on the ground that ex-members have seen both sides of the picture: they have been insiders, and are outsiders; furthermore the ex-member purports to have seen the light and realized the true nature of the organization he or she has left. Such claims should not be accepted uncritically, however. It is not only the ex-member who can tell both sides of the story: the same is true of converts, who can equally claim that they have been once outside the movement, and now have 'seen the light': 'But now in Christ Jesus you who once were far away have been brought near . . .' (Eph. 2.13). Ex-members may often be embittered, bearing a grudge against the movement and its leaders, and keen to discredit it. The researcher will obviously listen to the testimony, both of the disillusioned apostate and the enthusiastic convert, but of course both types of testimony must be critically evaluated. The new convert may well see nothing but good in the new religions that he or she has found, and may have failed to notice important factors that may subsequently lead to their exit. Both types of member may be subject to false memory syndrome, and hence their testimonies must be compared with other information ascertained by the researcher. Sometimes the ex-member may not so much be recounting bad experiences within an NRM, but rather re-evaluating his or her experiences. This can be somewhat like buying a new gadget: my previous laptop may have seemed all right while I was using it, but once I have upgraded to a new one I can more clearly see the shortcomings of the old model!

Nonetheless, the ex-member has an important perspective to bring to bear on the study of a religious organization. The ex-member is sometimes able to provide information that current members are reluctant to disclose, or sometimes information to which they do not have access – particularly, as sometimes happens, when the ex-member held a fairly high position within the movement. There have been occasions too when groups of members have broken away from an organization to form their own schismatical movement. This kind of apostasy can yield interesting information about a religious organization. Since schisms tend to be acrimonious, both parties can be prone to divulge information that has hitherto not come into the public domain.

Stances and stakeholders

In the light of this discussion, instead of talking about insiders and outsiders, it is probably better to identify various stances that are adopted by different stakeholders in religious communities. Further, just as there are varieties of 'insiders', there are many types of 'outsiders' with an interest in religious communities. There are critics, some of whom are ex-members of organizations, sometimes seeking to disseminate negative information about the religious group that they have left, and perhaps assisting others whom they believe are trying to exit from the organization. Several of these ex-members have become organized, forming their own organizations, with their own publications and networks. There are also the media, who attempt to inform the public about religious matters, but who cannot always be relied on to provide totally accurate information. Particularly in matters relating to NRMs the reader can normally expect somewhat negative reporting.

Public authorities also have a certain interest in religion: this interest may range from town planners who will have to consider applications to build religious premises, to the police force who may from time to time need to be informed about special forms of behaviour within the religious groups. Politicians too may have occasion to comment on religious groups, sometimes on account of lobbying on behalf of, or sometimes in opposition to particular religious communities. Employers also are stakeholders in religion, particularly in multicultural communities in which employees belong to different faiths, and may have different requirements regarding holy days, dietary practices and restrictions that their faith may impose on certain activities. Finally, there are students and academics, whose work itself does not necessarily involve the practice of religion, but who are attempting to ensure good standards of understanding of a range of worldviews, and to place these in the public domain.

The religious landscape is indeed complex, and – once again pursuing geographical metaphors – the task of the scholar of religion is often one of 'mapping', noting and charting the points of interest within people's religious lives. Deciding what is a manifestation of a specific religious tradition, and how these various groups derive from and relate to each other, are all part of the scholar's work. Equally, examining the various ways in which one can practise religion within a specific tradition (such as meditation and contemplation, gender-specific groups, special interest groups, reforming and campaigning bodies) is all part of the study.

WHICH SIDE ARE YOU ON? OLCOTT'S BUDDHIST REVIVAL

Colonel Henry Steel Olcott (1837–1907) is frequently portrayed as the first Westerner to embrace Buddhism and as initiating a Buddhist revival in Sri Lanka. Olcott was a military officer who had fought in the American Civil War and subsequently became a successful lawyer. He came to accept Buddhism as a result of reading its scriptures, which had newly become available in English. He decided to travel East, accompanied by Helena Petrovna Blavatsky (1831–91), with whom he had founded the Theosophical Society in the United States in 1875. They arrived in Bombay in 1879, and went on to Ceylon (now Sri Lanka) the following year.

Olcott believed that the Christian missionaries had done considerable damage to Buddhism, and that the Buddhist monks had insufficient knowledge of their tradition. Olcott sought to revive Buddhism, and in 1881 he compiled a *Buddhist Catechism*, setting out what he regarded as Buddhism's basic teachings. He subsequently travelled to London to see the Secretary of State for the Colonies, and as a result Buddhists were allowed to act as registrars in Ceylon, and were exempted from taking Christian oaths in law courts. Buddhist festivals became recognized as public holidays, and Olcott designed a distinctive Buddhist flag, which can be seen worldwide in many Buddhist temples.

Olcott believed that Buddhism had become debased and superstitious, however, and he wanted to restore it to its former glory. He was particularly scornful of the Sacred Tooth relic, housed in the Temple of the Tooth at Kandy, and generally regarded a splinter from one of Gautama the Buddha's teeth. Olcott may have misjudged the popular attachment to the relic, for his description of it as 'ignorant superstition' and his suggestion that it was merely a piece of deer's horn caused grave offence. The Sinhalese Buddhist leader Anagarika Dharmapala went so far as to describe Olcott as 'an enemy of our religion', and additionally contended that his Catechism presented a pantheistic worldview, an incorrect account of the nature of nirvana, and was 'absolutely opposed to Buddha's doctrine' (Prothero, 1996, pp. 97, 167).

Olcott's Buddhist revival may not have pleased many of the Sri Lankan Buddhists at the time, but he pioneered a new form of Buddhism that proved much more popular with Westerners – one which placed much more reliance on sacred texts, which stressed monastic practices such as meditation, and which jettisoned many of the traditional folk practices which were popular with many Asian Buddhists. Was Olcott an 'insider' seeking to reform the religion and give it a renewed expression, or was he an 'outsider' – a Western intellectual who lacked a proper rapport with the indigenous Buddhist community? Who has the right to decide?

Further reading

Almond, P. C. (1988), *The British Discovery of Buddhism*. Cambridge: Cambridge University Press.

Blackburn, A. M. (2010), *Locations of Buddhism: Colonialism and Modernity in Sri Lanka*. Chicago and London: University of Chicago Press.

Prothero, S. (1996), *The White Buddhist: The Asian Odyssey of Henry Steel Olcott*. Bloomington and Indianapolis: Indiana University Press.

DISCUSSION POINTS

1 Identify an aspect of a religion to which you belong, or with which you are familiar (e.g. a ritual, a sacred object or a custom). Why might it seem strange to an 'outsider', and how might you make its strangeness familiar?

2 This chapter has argued that one's type of commitment to a religion affects how one perceives one's own religion and that of others. To what extent should this oblige us to declare our religious commitment when we write about an aspect of religion?

3 The chapter identified different categories of insider. Are some better placed than others to achieve the goals of their religion (*moksha*, nirvana, salvation, etc.)? Does this vary according to religion?

4 How does the student of religion deal with competing claims about who are genuine followers of a religion?

4

Does size matter?

George Chryssides

Chapter Outline

Early attempts at quantifying religion	92
The Victorian Census of 1851	93
Religiosity then and now	96
Where are Britain's Christians?	99
Allied to attendance, membership seems to fare little better	103
What is being measured?	107
The world's fastest-growing religion?	111
Collecting one's own statistical data	120
Conclusion	124
Discussion points	125

To the beginner, it may seem that the study of religion is a 'soft' subject, standing at the other end of the curricular spectrum from the 'hard' sciences that deal with hypothesis testing, empirical observation, experimentation and calculation. However, a number of factors have caused scholars within the last century to talk about the 'scientific study of religion'. As we have seen, the study of religion in the West has moved from being Christian-centred and focused on theology, history and textual analysis: the awareness of and increasing contacts with other World Religions have created a wider centre of attention, and the rise of new religious movements has widened the subject's scope even further. As we have already shown, fieldwork entails empirical observation, a characteristic of the sciences, and sociological, anthropological and ethnographical approaches do more than observe forms of human behaviour, but also offer classifications, theories, explanations and data processing, the last of which not infrequently involves collecting and manipulating statistical data. Students of religion, therefore, who think they have escaped from mathematical calculations could be mistaken: while students of religion can decide the extent to which their work involves number-crunching, the use of number continues to be a key part of the subject. Although some students may feel that they are unlikely themselves to collect or process numerical data, they should bear in mind that they will almost inevitably come across statistical information from other researchers and religious organizations, and that they will need to be able to evaluate critically such data.

It was the Unitarians – a small and relatively unknown denomination in Britain, now on the decline – who contributed substantially to the establishment of the Manchester Statistical Society in 1833. Similar organizations were set up in London in 1834, and in Bristol in 1836. Statistics were important in the understanding and political organization of society, since it was recognized that it was only through quantitative data that one could ascertain the real nature of Britain's social problems. The first British Census took place in 1801, and until that date no one even knew for certain the size of Britain's population – a key factor in planning the economy, and indeed in ascertaining the amount of provision of religious buildings that was needed. Richard Price (1723–91), one of the early Unitarian clergy, helped to set up The Equitable Society in 1762, which used the newly discovered science of statistics to calculate life assurance policies on proper actuarial principles: although insurance had been available since ancient Roman times, its costs and risks had been determined largely by guesswork until the advent of statistics. Alongside his religious and political writings, Price published a work on this topic entitled *Observations on Reversionary Payments* (1769). Present-day students of religion, of course, are not expected to have Price's breadth of interest: in any case, in the eighteenth century there was much less by way of written literature in theology, politics and statistics, and hence less need for specialism. However, statistical information remains important in the study of religion, for a variety of reasons.

First, from the point of view of religious organizations themselves, keeping track of one's degree of allegiance bears clear importance. Just as a business firm needs to know how it is faring in the marketplace, so a religious organization benefits from knowing whether it is on the ascendant or in decline, in order to determine its evangelization and organizational strategies. Clearly religious organizations have teachings and practices that are non-negotiable, since religions typically claim to possess truth, but there are non-compromising ways in which a religious community can promote its message: perhaps an advertising campaign might help; or perhaps, if it seems to have lost its appeal to a younger generation, more youth activities or 'trendier' forms of worship might help to regain lost adherents. A community that is thriving can equally benefit from statistical information: a nearby Christian evangelical church, known to the present author, recently signed a contract for over a million pounds to build new premises on a prime site. Despite Christianity's emphasis on faith, the decision was not taken simply as a result of prayer or blind trust in God, but on the basis of hard statistics, collected each week, on attendance and financial contributions. Although one comes across stories of faithful devotees who have taken 'leaps of faith' and committed themselves against all odds to ambitious projects, most religious organizations act on the basis that faith does not absolve their followers from careful planning, including the use of financial and statistical information.

The planning of religious organizations is not done in a vacuum. Communities who claim to need new premises generally have to persuade local councils to grant permission for building work. It is therefore important for town and city planners to have reliable information about the sizes of communities in order to determine whether it is appropriate to erect a new temple or mosque, or whether a community's needs are already well catered for by existing provision. Even seemingly mundane issues, such as parking and traffic flow, are not determined by faith or by guesswork; religious communities need to persuade local councils that new premises will not create unacceptable traffic problems. The International Society for Krishna Consciousness (ISKCON) at Bhaktivedanta Manor, in the small village of Letchmore Heath, caused a large-scale legal case, following villagers' objections to traffic congestion on festival days. Much of the evidence on either side involved statistical information relating to numbers of attendees, numbers of vehicles and the degree to which traffic flow would become more acceptable if a different approach route were created. ISKCON finally won their case, but if they attributed their success to Krishna, this was not to the exclusion of good evidence and hard statistical facts.

Legal decisions, then, can turn on religious statistics. The present author was recently asked to be an expert witness in a case where a Jehovah's Witness had been killed in a traffic accident, which appeared to be the result of a lorry driver having committed a traffic offence. The Witness's family were the plaintiffs, seeking compensation. The lorry driver's solicitors argued, perhaps predictably, that an important contributory factor in the Witness's death was that his family would not permit a blood transfusion. The plaintiff's rejoinder was that Jehovah's Witnesses were a sizeable group of people, not a minuscule handful of eccentrics, and that drivers should be aware of the diversity of road-users, and not assume that standard medical treatment would be given to all. One key question, on which my own expertise was sought, was whether it was more or less likely that one would encounter another driver who was, say, a Buddhist, as compared with a Jehovah's Witness. Intuitively one might have been inclined to think that there are bound to be more Buddhists around than Witnesses, since Buddhism is one of the world's major religions, and Britain is a multicultural, multifaith society. However, the available statistical information showed otherwise: the British 2001 Census indicated that 152,000 British residents returned 'Buddhism' as their religious affiliation, whereas the 2002 *Yearbook of Jehovah's Witnesses* indicated that there were 213,595 attendees, nationwide, at the Annual Memorial service, a major event in the Witnesses' calendar. On the basis of these statistics it could therefore be argued that one is roughly 40 per cent more likely to encounter a Jehovah's Witness in Britain than a Buddhist. Indeed, the case in favour of the Jehovah's Witnesses could be further strengthened by pointing out that the two statistics are not comparing like with like: the number of Buddhists in the British census was determined by householders simply filling in a form; by contrast, to become a statistic in the Jehovah's Witnesses' yearbook one had to do something active, namely spending an evening at a service of worship.

A further reason for keeping track of the relative sizes of religious communities relates to academic study. In a subsequent chapter (Chapter 7) we raise the question of whether the numerical strength of a religion enabled it to qualify as a 'World Religion'. All other things being equal, we would normally expect the size of a religion to be reflected in the amount of research carried out by scholars, as well as the amount of space given to it in an educational curriculum. Thus Christianity, being the dominant religion, is required to occupy some 90 per cent of the British school RE curriculum, and in some universities it is virtually 100 per cent of undergraduate study. However, there may be sound reasons for according a seemingly disproportionate space to minority religious groups. For example, their social significance may exceed their size, as in the case of Islamic resistance movements such as Hizbullah and Al Qaeda. Where a religious group has a tiny following it may lack a voice, fail to gain a fair hearing publicly, and become the object of misunderstanding or even discrimination: where this occurs, it is important for academics to enable a small group to gain 'empowerment' by helping to remove public misunderstandings and prejudices. It is worth remembering, too, that the world's largest religions started life as the world's smallest ones, and therefore the significance of studying a small group may only become apparent after several decades. In the 1970s, sociological studies by Robert W. Balch and David Taylor of a then obscure group known as Human Individual Metamorphosis (HIM) may have looked unlikely to yield any public benefit; a quarter of a century later, the group – then known as Heaven's Gate – gained worldwide notoriety for its 39 suicides in San Diego in March 1997. Balch and Taylor's earlier studies have therefore proved invaluable for understanding a small religious movement, about which little was known.

In the early days of sociological study of new religious movements, their smallness was precisely the reason for undertaking academic study. A small new religion was a microcosm of society more widely, and afforded a manageable way of shedding light on how humans behaved in association. Phenomena such as charismatic leadership, persuasion, recognition of authority, rule-governed behaviour, making the transition from loose organization to institutionalization, dealing with conflict (internal and external), deviance, and seeking legitimation are equally found in new religious communities and in wider society. The more feasible small-scale study, it was argued, could help to shed light on human behaviour in society more widely.

Early attempts at quantifying religion

Writing in 1879, James Freeman Clarke, one of the pioneers of the study of World Religions, collated a number of sources that estimated the numbers of adherents to the various religions. On his own admission these are only guesses, the difficulty of estimation being compounded by the fact that the world's population was itself unknown at that time. The lowest and highest estimates that Clarke cites are as follows:

Religion	Lowest estimate	Highest estimate
'Brahmas'	111,000,000	133,000,000
Buddhism	222,000,000	320,000,000
Christianity	120,000,000	369,000,000
Jews	4,000,000	6,000,000
'Mohammedans'	110,000,000	252,000,000

Source: Clarke, 1879, p. 146.

Note: It should be noted that 'Brahmas' and 'Mohammedans' are Clarke's terms; the latter, in particular, would not be used today in the study of religion, since it is considered inappropriate by Muslims, possibly implying that they worship Muhammad.

It may be interesting to compare Clarke's table with a present-day collation of estimates of religious affiliation. The table below is compiled from a variety of sources listed on the website <adherents.com>. Even with much more advanced methods of collecting data, it will be apparent that there are still sizeable variations in estimates. Preston D. Hunter, the webmaster of this site, deliberately does not evaluate his sources, but merely reports them.

Religion	Lowest estimate	Highest estimate
Buddhism	250,000,000	500,000,000
Christianity	1,500,000,000	2,200,000,000
Hinduism	600,000,000	1,400,000,000
Islam	1,300,000,000	1,340,000,000
Judaism	14,000,000	18,200,000

Source: www.adherents.com, accessed 9 June 2013.

The Victorian Census of 1851

In Britain, one early attempt to collect statistics relating to religious allegiance was the great Victorian Religious Census of 1851. Unlike Clarke's sources that 'guestimated' religious allegiance worldwide, the Victorian Census was an attempt to obtain firm statistical data, using statistical and actuarial techniques that had been developed over the previous hundred years or so.

The Victorian Census was a government-sponsored attempt to ascertain the amount of church accommodation available in England, Wales and Scotland (Ireland was not included), and what proportion of the population attended public worship. The date of 30 March 1851 was set as the Sunday on which the census would be conducted. Participation was voluntary, but most congregations responded – 34,467 in all. An enumerator was appointed by every congregation to count the numbers of people who attended worship. In addition to numbers of attendees, information that was sought included the name of the congregation, the denomination, the date of the building's completion and consecration, the amount of space available, the average attendance for 1850 and the congregation's endowments. Spaces on the return form allowed for statistics on morning, afternoon and evening services (some churches had three services in the day, although most had two), and for the numbers in the general congregation and in the Sunday school. Anyone over the age of 10 was to be counted as a church attendee if they were part of the congregation.

Out of the 34,467 congregations that submitted a return, 2,524 failed to provide information on seating; 1,394 did not submit attendance data, and 390 gave no information on either. Additionally, some of the statistical data in the returns was inconsistent: some clergy apparently were not good at arithmetic! The request to provide attendance data for the previous year was hardly a realistic one: few, if any, churches did regular attendance counts and recorded such information, so responses to this question were 'guestimates'. Notwithstanding these deficiencies, however, this was a very good response, and the 1851 Victorian Census remains a unique landmark in gauging church attendance at the time.

Every survey has its strengths and weaknesses, and commentators frequently draw attention to some of the inadequacies of the 1851 Religious Census. One problem relates to the Sunday on which the survey was conducted. The 30th of March was the fourth Sunday in Lent – Mothering Sunday – which is a minor Christian festival. It is possible that this attracted a slightly increased attendance, and it should be borne in mind too that, in any case, the population knew well in advance that a census would be taken on that Sunday. The advance warning may have inflated the numbers, and it is even possible that clergy specially encouraged their congregation to be present and be counted. The choice of Mothering Sunday was slightly unfortunate, not simply because it is a minor festival, but because it could have had the effect of skewing attendance patterns. In Victorian times, it was not simply a day to be kind to one's mother: servants were typically given a day off to visit their mothers, and this may have caused them to travel to a different place, and perhaps attend worship there – or perhaps fail to attend, if they were accustomed to attending simply because their master and mistress required them to do so. Additionally, Mothering Sunday is traditionally the day in which Christians attend their 'mother church'; in other words, if one regularly attended a small church that had been created by a parish church's mission, it was common practice for members to attend at the parent church on that Sunday. These factors could have caused geographical movements that did not truly reflect typical patterns of church attendance.

A further criticism relates to the fact that most churches had multiple services. There was no accurate way of knowing how many of the congregation attended more than once; their heads were simply counted irrespective of whether they had been at church before on that day. This means that there is likely to have been some double-counting, although Horace Mann, who wrote the Census Report in 1853, devised a formula for dealing with the problem. He assumed that only half of those attending an afternoon service, and one-third of those attending an evening one, had not worshipped previously on that day. His formula, however, was only a way of scaling attendance down to a more plausible statistic: it is still a guess.

There also remains the question of whether small congregations might have been missed in the course of the census. Because of the country's parish system, it would be easy to locate every Church of England, Church of Wales and Church of Scotland congregation. Methodists, Non-conformists and the Society of Friends (the Quakers) were included, as were Jewish congregations, who made their returns, of course, on the previous Saturday. However, could one be sure that one had included each small independent tabernacle or gospel hall? It could legitimately be argued, of course, that such congregations must have been very small in number, and hence the numbers of attendees would have been a mere drop in the ocean, barely affecting the overall pattern of religious attendance on Census Sunday.

Despite these criticisms, it is possible to draw some important conclusions from the census results. Overall, somewhere between 47 and 51 per cent of the British population attended a place of worship on Mothering Sunday 1851. This is perhaps not as many as one might have imagined; if one thought that the Victorian era was a golden age of church attendance, then the census results disabuse us of such myths. We can also draw conclusions about geographical trends in attendance, although here one has to exercise some care: there was a heavy rainstorm in Nottinghamshire on that day, and it is possible that this had an unduly adverse effect on attendance. The places where attendance was low by comparison were London, the industrial parts of Lancashire, the West Riding of Yorkshire and the Black Country in the West Midlands. It was higher in Scotland than England (although Scotland had a poorer return rate).

It is also possible to compare denominations and to detect patterns. The Church of England amassed 50.3 per cent of attendance in England, with the Methodists gaining second place at 24.3 per cent. All localities contained more than one denomination; Non-conformity was stronger in the north than in the south, and dissenting congregations were more abundant in industrial areas than in rural ones. Roman Catholicism was stronger in Lancashire than elsewhere, and tended to be prevalent in localities with prominent Roman Catholic landowners, and in areas of Irish immigration. The Victorian Religious Census therefore enables us to extract much more information than simply a global statistic about church attendance.

Of course, more than 150 years later, we have much better knowledge of how to collect statistical information, but considering the state of the art in statistics at that time, the census provides extremely useful if not totally precise data. The survey measured the measurable: double-counting apart, 'bums on pews' are clearly identifiable. In principle, the Victorians could have chosen other methods of surveying religious affiliation, such as asking people's declared allegiance. (At that time, the questionnaire was not yet in use. Sir Francis Galton (1822–1911), who invented the self-administered survey, first made use of it in a publication in 1874.) However, asking people how often they attend worship can give rise to exaggeration or invoke faulty memory; actually observing how people behave is a much better method of measuring human behaviour. Of course, counting heads does not tell us the extent to which religion affected the lives of the attendees, or what their real reasons might have been for being present. Some may have been attending through habit, and going through the motions of ritual enactment; servants may have been present because the lord of the manor required it; the lord and lady of the manor may have been there because attendance reinforced their social status. Every survey has its scope and limits, and the Religious Census did not set out to measure religious commitment and motivation. What it does give is a useful set of conclusions about levels of attendance, and denominational and geographical trends – data which are of high significance. We should not be too hard on the Victorians for their methods of conducting the census.

Religiosity then and now

With over 150 years of experience at data collection, methods have been refined, and many more surveys conducted – although no one has attempted to conduct another nationwide religious attendance survey by individual headcounting. Surprisingly, no official government survey of religious affiliation was carried out until 2001, when an optional question on religious affiliation was included in the ten-yearly British Census. Other surveys had of course been carried out by pollsters, and statistical information was available from specific religious organizations. Such research was piecemeal, however. It was conducted with the agenda of the researchers in mind, sampling was small-scale in comparison with the population as a whole, and was prone to sampling errors. Religious organizations have collected data in different ways, and hence it was difficult to obtain an overall picture of Britain's religious landscape.

It would be wrong to suppose that the 2001 Census was without its problems. One major preliminary problem was the issue of whether the government should be collecting such information at all. Religion, some argued, was a personal matter, and information collected in a census readily correlated answers with their respondents: the state could easily find out which specific citizens were Jews, Christians, Muslims or whatever. No doubt memories of the atrocities of Nazi Germany sprang to mind.

Statistics are not cold clinical numbers on pages that are consigned to inaccessible archives: they are there to be used, and a hostile government could readily introduce discriminatory measures against Jews or Muslims, if it so wished – as indeed one or two British political parties seek to do. Despite such fears, however, the recognition that the 2001 Census would be the only opportunity to undertake a nationwide religious survey for another ten years won the day.

For those who were unhappy about divulging their religious affiliation, the question was made optional. When the census data were collated, it was found that 7.48 per cent of the British population had declined to answer this question. It is impossible to tell whether these non-respondents skewed the picture of Britain's religious landscape, or whether they spread themselves proportionally over the spectrum of Britain's faiths. Although it is preferable to maximize responses, any survey has its scope and limitations, and a 92.52 per cent response rate remains one that many pollsters would envy.

Survey questions need careful thought and preparation. An inexperienced student may think of the seemingly obvious question, 'What religion do you follow?' Little reflection is needed to conclude that this will not do. A questionnaire designer must consider the likely responses that this will elicit. A general open-ended question could cause some respondents to name a broad 'World Religion' – 'Christianity', 'Hinduism' or 'Islam'. Other respondents might wish to be more specific, identifying themselves as 'Church of England', 'Quaker', 'Krishna consciousness'. If different respondents provide different types of answer, problems of collating the data occur. If some refer to the generic religion (Christianity, Hinduism, Islam), there is no way of telling which particular version they subscribe to. Conversely, if respondents are specific, questions can arise as to which specific religious organizations belong to a generic category. For example, should someone who writes 'Unitarian', 'Mormon' or 'Jehovah's Witness' be counted as 'Christian'? There are no clear answers to such questions.

The ensuing methodological question about the census was whether the religious question should be open-ended or closed-ended. Those who favoured an open-ended question could argue that this enabled religious adherents to define themselves in their own terms, and that doing so was a fundamental right. The counterargument – as is obvious from the preceding paragraph – is that open-ended self-definition would generate data that simply could not be collated, thus negating the whole purpose of a census question on religion. Accordingly, the argument for a closed-ended question won the day, and the British population was asked to declare whether they were: Christian, Buddhist, Hindu, Jewish, Muslim, Sikh, Other or No Religion. (It may be worth noting that the ordering of religions was not wholly alphabetical. It is possible that 'order effects' can influence the results of a survey: perhaps the appearance of Christianity in first place helped people to select it as the 'default' form of religious allegiance.)

The category 'Other' secured a reasonable compromise between allowing open-ended answers and defining closed categories, although it presented a dilemma for some religious adherents. For example, some Unitarians defined themselves as 'Christian', while others, encouraged by their General Assembly, considered themselves distinct from mainstream Christianity and wrote 'Unitarian' as an explanation of 'Other'. Since Unitarians declared their allegiance in different ways, there is therefore no accurate way of determining the strength of this denomination through census statistics.

The 'Other' category created the opportunity for people to devise new or non-serious religions and thus attempt to 'put them on the map'. In 2001 some people started a worldwide email campaign, urging people to declare their religious commitment as 'Jedi' or 'Jedi Knight' in censuses in Canada, Australia, New Zealand and Britain. There was a popular belief in Britain that if over 10,000 citizens declared their religion as 'Jedi', then Jedi would become an 'official' religion. As a consequence, approximately 70,000 respondents identified themselves as 'Jedi' in Australia (0.3% of the population), 53,000 in New Zealand (0.12%), 20,000 in Canada (0.05%) and 390,000 in Britain (0.7%).

The 'Jedi' phenomenon is interesting for a number of reasons. The result did not demonstrate, as some believed, that Jedi had now become a genuine religion. One needs more than a census result for this to be the case. One would have expected to hear of the Jedi's doctrines, their religious practices, their organizational structure and the other features that one normally associates with religion. Obviously one would not expect this in the census returns, but certainly one ought to find it in other contexts. Although the census data give us the statistics, the statistical information is not accompanied by underlying explanations. It is more likely that the respondents were attempting to defy authority, to make fun of the census, to express enthusiasm for Star Wars, or out of curiosity to see whether it might be possible to create a hypothetical new religion. In Britain, religious organizations do not need any government recognition in order to count as genuine religions. Unlike numerous other countries, there is no need to prove that one has (for example) a minimum number of followers in order to obtain state benefits, such as registration as a charity. (In Austria 16,000 members are required for government recognition; in Macedonia it is only 100.)

It is sometimes argued that the Jedi phenomenon made the census unreliable. Statistical data can seldom achieve total precision, particularly on the scale of a national census. In all probability, the Jedi respondents did not seriously skew the census' picture of British religion, since it is unlikely that staunch followers of well-accredited religions would have been persuaded by the Jedi campaign. Even if the Jedi respondents all came from the same genuine religion, their responses would have made little difference to the overall national picture. However, notwithstanding the fact that 390,000 British citizens may have falsely declared their religion, John Pullinger, Director of Reporting and Analysis at the National Statistics Office, argued that the campaign may have actually enhanced the quality of the census information more widely. He argued that it may have encouraged younger citizens, particularly those in their late teens and twenties, to submit a return, and thus to create a more comprehensive picture of the British population (National Statistics, 2003).

One final point on the Jedi phenomenon is important in connection with information-gathering: how does one process such responses? One approach might be to discard obviously facetious answers: thus, in New Zealand the census statisticians classified such answers as 'answer understood, but will not be counted'. Australia initially categorized Jedi responses as 'not defined', but later decided to declare a Jedi statistic. In Britain, the Jedi were given a code (896), since it was decided that a substantial body of recognizable answers should merit inclusion with the rest of the data. It emerged that there were marginally more self-professed Jedi than respondents who wrote 'heathen' or 'atheist'. Perhaps one should not judge the seriousness of a claimed worldview; after all, there exist some very real religions that many regard as bizarre.

Where are Britain's Christians?

Thus far we have focused on one (perhaps insignificant) detail of Britain's 2001 census, but there are wider, more substantial issues that merit discussion. The fact that Christianity emerged in Britain as the most popular of the world's religions was no surprise, but much more surprising was the strength of professed allegiance – a staggering 71.6 per cent. It is certainly obvious that such a vast proportion of Britain's population do not attend church on a Sunday. Other studies that have been carried out indicate a very low commitment to membership or Sunday attendance. According to Peter Brierley's authoritative *UK Christian Handbook*, only some 10 per cent of Britain's population were actually members of a Christian denomination in the year 2000.

As Steve Bruce points out, attendance is more difficult to measure: Peter Brierley gives the statistic of 9.55 per cent as the proportion of adult church attendees as a percentage of Britain's total adult population, but such a statistic is problematic for a number of reasons. First, what does it mean? Is this the proportion that attended on any one Sunday, or is it the proportion that are deemed to attend regularly? 'Regular attendance' could be construed, for example, as attending twice – or even once – a month; hence a count of worshippers attending (say) every second Sunday is going to be double that of those who attend faithfully every single week. Second, there is the question of how attendance is measured. As Bruce points out, there are various ways in which this can be done: appointing independent enumerators, eliciting congregational or denominational returns or conducting a survey in which members of the public are asked about their religious behaviour. These respective methods may well yield significantly different results. Having enumerators, as in the Victorian Census, would be prohibitively expensive, while asking clergy or members of the public may not yield accurate data. Although one might suppose that clergy would tend to exaggerate congregational attendance, Bruce claims, surprisingly, to find the opposite: they are more likely, he thinks, to bemoan dwindling numbers than to try to impress researchers about their popularity. The kinds of questionnaire and interview surveys carried out by sociologists probably continue to provide the best available information.

Case study: Where is Britain's Christian'population?

The 2001 British Census revealed that 71.6 per cent of Britain's population were prepared to declare themselves to be 'Christian'. This surprised many people, since only a much smaller proportion (between 4 and 10%, depending on one's measure) attend church on a Sunday with any regularity.

However, in his book *Counting People In*, Richard Thomas presents the following statistics on how the British celebrated Christmas in 2001.

Question: Which activities will you participate in this Christmas?

Activity	Percentage of respondents
Exchange presents	94
Have a special Christmas Day/Eve meal with your family	80
Decorate inside/outside your home	80
Have a turkey over the festive season	74
Buy Christmas crackers	66
Have an advent calendar	51
Listen to/view the Queen's speech	51
Buy a Christmas tree	49
Make a special donation to charity over Christmas	49
Attend a carol service	41
Make a Christmas cake/pudding	40
Attend nativity/Christmas service	35
Attend religious service on Christmas Day/Eve	26
Visit a pantomime	25
Have a crib in your home	14
Pray at a crib in church	13
Spend it with friends but without your family	13
Work on Christmas Day	10
Have Christmas abroad	4
Spend Christmas alone	4
Do not celebrate Christmas	1

Source: 'Survey of Christmas plans', from Richard Thomas (2003).

Thomas argues that we should draw a distinction between participatory membership and what he calls 'associate membership'. Participatory membership is the kind of affiliation that is measured in the statistics for church attendance. Only a small proportion of British people feel drawn towards participatory membership, as is witnessed by the low attendance statistics. By contrast, however, the vast majority of the population observe the major Christian festivals of Christmas and Easter by giving presents, consuming seasonal food and taking part in a public holiday. Even the churches enjoy participation at these times: the statistics in the table indicate that roughly half the population attend a church service during the Christmas season; however, Easter is regarded as the high point of the Christian year, and the Church of England uses its Easter attendance as the definitive figure by which to compare its year-by-year progress. One might also add that other festivals such as St Valentine's Day, Mother's Day and Hallowe'en have associations with the Christian calendar.

Why should not the popular ways of celebrating these festivals count as evidence of religious observance? Many members of the clergy deplore these popular ways of celebrating Christmas and Easter as signs of the 'commercialization' of Christian festivals, complaining that they obscure the 'real meaning' of the Christian message. In the academic study of Christianity, such elements tend to be ignored; if asked, I imagine that many scholars would perceive popular observance of such festivals as folk practice rather than genuine religion. Certainly it is true that, in terms of Christianity's ultimate goal, eating a Christmas pudding is unlikely to help to provide the means of salvation, whereas according to traditional teaching the Church is the 'ark of salvation' and therefore belonging to the Church is necessary to becoming part of the body of Christ, who offers eternal life which was made possible through his incarnation, which the festival of Christmas emphasizes.

However, religions offer a variety of benefits to their followers, encompassing the pragmatic, the ethical and transcendental, and which exist at a variety of levels. Because Christianity has tended to emphasize its doctrinal dimension more heavily than other major religions, and because its character tends to be congregational rather than individual, it has tended to measure its success in terms of numbers attending congregational worship, where they are afforded the opportunity to hear the Christian message. However, religious observance is capable of being observed at an individual or a social level, as well as congregationally. Elementary textbooks on Hinduism will typically mention how the festival of Holi is celebrated by having a party at the temple, lighting a bonfire and throwing coloured dye. There is not an evenness of treatment in how allegiance to different religions is measured. It would be interesting to see statistical information on the proportion of Hindus who attend a *kirtan* (congregational service with singing) for example, and the proportion that practise their religion in other ways.

Even though church attendance has declined during the past few decades, Christians might take comfort from some of the statistical data given above. For example, there is almost unanimous recognition that it is a special day, and 99 per cent of people observe it in some way or other. There are as many people who attend carol services as make Christmas cakes or puddings. More than half of Britain's population have Advent calendars – although it might be interesting to know how many of them use them as reminders of the Christian season of Advent, and how many simply use them to count down the days to Christmas. Carol services are much more popular than pantomimes, nearly one person in every seven has a crib in their home, and nearly one in eight prays at a crib in church.

Like any statistical survey, this one has its limits, and leaves unanswered questions. For example, what is the overlap between those attending carol services, nativity/ Christmas services and Christmas Eve/Christmas Day services? Simply adding up the three statistics would give a total of 102 per cent, so clearly a significant number of respondents placed themselves in two or more categories. Our understanding of Christmas church attendance would have been enhanced by a question eliciting information about the proportion of respondents who attended any one of these events. Of course, the survey does not elicit information on people's motives for going to church at Christmas, or whether they appreciate the 'true meaning' of the festival – but then again statistical information on regular church-going tends not to explore motivation and understanding either.

The survey does not explore the proportion of respondents who are not professing Christians. In Britain's multifaith society it has become common practice for adherents to other faiths to join Christmas celebrations, and hence these statistics cannot be said to provide totally accurate information about how the population is expressing a Christian identity. Despite these limitations, however, this statistical information is a useful antidote to those sociologists of religion who continually inform us that Christianity is fast declining.

Exact precision may not be possible, but a number of studies of church attendance have confirmed that only a small proportion of Britain's population attends on a Sunday. One such study yields the following results:

Church attendance, England 1989	
Non-conformist	1.25 m
Church of England	1.14 m
Roman Catholic	1.30 m
Total Christian	3.71 m
Adult church attenders as % of adult population	9.55 %

Source: Peter Brierley, 'Christian' England. London: MARC Europe, 1991. Cited in Bruce, 1995, p. 39.

Older people will often claim that churches were full in their youth, but that attendance has declined. Such claims may intuitively seem likely, but social scientists and statisticians cannot simply thrive on impressions, and need hard data to substantiate such claims. It is important therefore to look at comparative statistics. Again, Bruce has collated a number of surveys that have been made of attendance over past decades:

Allied to attendance, membership seems to fare little better.

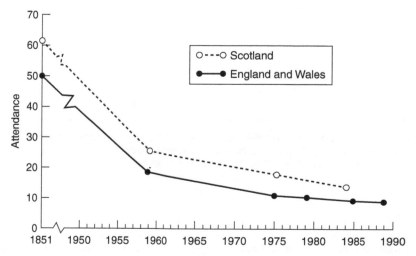

FIGURE 4.1 *Adult Church attendance, Britain, 1851–1989.*

Sources: Peter Brierley, *Prospects for the Eighties: From a Census of the Churches in 1979* (London: Bible Society, 1980); Peter Brierley and Fergus Macdonald, *Prospects for Scotland: From a Census of the Churches in 1984* (Edinburgh: The Bible Society of Scotland, 1985); Peter Brierley, *Prospects for the Nineties: Trends and Tables from the English Church Census* (London: MARC Europe, 1991); *British Parliamentary Papers, 1851 Census, Great Britain, Report and Tables on Religious Worship* 1852–3 (repr. Irish University Press, 1970); *British Parliamentary Papers, Religious Worship and Education, Scotland, Report and Tables* (London: HMSO, 1854).

Bruce, 1995, p. 40.

As we noted above, social scientists need to go beyond the mere presentation of data. We need to consider explanations and formulate possible hypotheses. One possible suggestion that was popularly made in the 1960s was that many Britons were attaining higher standards of education and were becoming aware of intellectual objections to the Christian faith. Such a hypothesis was fuelled by the appearance of books like *Honest to God*, written by John A. T. Robinson, who was then Bishop of Woolwich, and who called into question traditional notions of God as a personal being. The question of how Britain's religious climate changed in the 1960s cannot be explored in any depth here, but we can examine the statistical evidence that has been amassed about religious beliefs in Britain. Again, Bruce collates a number of surveys across past decades:

Christian Church Membership, Britain, 1900–90

Year	All Protestant		Roman Catholic		All Christian
	Total (m.)	Total (m.)	Total (m.)	Ratio	% of adult population
1900	5.4	2.0	7.4	100	30
1930	7.1	2.8	9.9	133	29
1950	6.1	3.5	9.6	129	25
1970	5.2	2.7	7.9	107	19
1990	3.4	2.2	5.6	76	12

Note: For comparability, the 1970 and 1990 Catholic figures are for mass attendance on an average Sunday. As the proportion of 'observant' Catholics has steadily declined over the century from over 80 per cent to less than 40 per cent, 1900, 1930 and 1950 data have been left as the total Catholic population. If they had also been adjusted, the decline in percentage of total adult population who are church members would be slightly but not significantly less dramatic.

Sources: Peter Brierley, *A Century of British Christianity: Historical Statistics 1900–1985 with Projections to 2000* (Research Monograph 14; London: MARC Europe, 1989); Robert Currie, Alan D. Gilbert and Lee Horsley, *Churches and Churchgoers: Patterns of Church Growth in the British Isles since 1700* (Oxford: Oxford University Press, 1977); Peter Brierley and Val Hiscock, *UK Christian Handbook 1994/95 edition* (London: Christian Research Association, 1993).

Bruce, 1995, p. 37.

Belief in God, Great Britain, 1940s–2000 (%)

Beliefs	1940s	1947	1981	1990	2000
There is a personal God	43	45	41	32	26
There is some sort of higher power, spirit or life force	38	39	37	41	21
There is something there		n.a.	n.a.	n.a.	23
I don't really know what to think		16	16	15	12
I don't really think there is any sort of God, spirit or life force		n.a.	6	10	15
None of these		**n.a.**	**n.a.**	**1**	**3**

Note: n.a. 5 not asked.

Sources: Gill et al. (1998); *Opinion Research Business* (2000).

Interestingly, a number of surveys have confirmed that belief in a god between 1990 and 2000 stands at roughly 70 per cent – slightly less than the percentage who defined themselves as Christian in the 2001 census.

Sociologists of religion are faced with the perplexing problem of trying to make sense of apparently incompatible data about religious conviction and allegiance. Unfortunately we cannot pursue such debates here, but merely show the possible discussions that the data open up. One hypothesis that can be excluded is the suggestion that Christianity's apparent decline is due to the substantial immigration of the 1950s and 1960s. According to the 2001 Census, only 7.34 per cent of the population defined themselves as Buddhist, Hindu, Muslim or Sikh. Although these figures are not insignificant, they do not account for the much more substantial drop in church membership and attendance. By the same argument, the rise of new religious movements and the New Age phenomenon does not account for the shortfall: only a further 4.10 per cent claimed to be 'Other' – the sole category by which New Agers were able to identify themselves.

Sociologists have advanced a number of theories to account for the phenomenon of Britain's changing faiths. A popular one is the 'secularization thesis'. The theory is a complex one, and has different forms. The secularization thesis goes beyond the straightforward observation that church attendance and membership have declined. Bryan Wilson defines secularization as 'the process whereby religious thinking, practices and institutions lose social significance'. The theory is that the Church no longer exercises its influence over communities to the degree that it did in former times. The past half-century has seen an increase in 'urbanization' and demographic changes that have resulted from it: Britain is no longer a country with geographically defined communities that are centred on a parish church. Even a church spire – once the highest point in a locality – now tends to be dwarfed by skyscrapers. Scientific and technological advances, stemming from the European Enlightenment, have caused people to look for rational rather than supernatural ways of understanding the world: as Weber put it, we are experiencing 'disenchantment of the world'. Men and women look to science and technology to solve the earth's problems, rather than relying on divine aid. Secular ideologies now rival religious ethics: writers such as Karl Marx, Jeremy Bentham and John Stuart Mill produced moral theories that were based on humanity and society rather than divine authority. As far as rules for life are concerned, members of Western societies tend to look to secular ideologies rather than refer to the Bible: human rights declarations, civil liberties, equal opportunities and so on are now prevalent in our thinking.

Secularization theory exists in different forms. Writers such as Steve Bruce claim that we can expect the secularization process to continue, with the result that Christianity will virtually die out by around 2030, while others claim that we can expect a coexistence between secularized and religious people. The 'disappearance thesis', whose principal proponent is Bruce, largely relies on the assumption that recent trends in religious allegiance will continue at approximately the same rate. If we examine Bruce's table of Christian church membership in Britain from 1900 to 1990 it is possible to reason that, if the Christian churches in Britain are losing between 3 and 3.5 per cent of the country's population each decade, then the proportion will reduce to around 6 per cent by 2010 and 0 per cent by 2020.

Is such a conclusion warranted? Clearly, this will only be the case if this present trend continues in the same way. However, human behaviour cannot be predicted with strict mathematical certainty. It is possible that we are seeing a 'bottoming out' of formal church membership, perhaps at around 10 per cent of the country's population, and that what is happening is a 'de-identification' from mainstream Christianity. As we noted, the 50 per cent of the population who attended church in 1851 may not all have been present for religious reasons, but may have been fulfilling social expectations. Now that social expectations have changed, it is possible that the less committed members have dropped out, leaving a somewhat depleted membership, but a more committed nucleus of adherents. A further possibility is that a religious revival might occur: religions have their peaks and troughs, and Christian allegiance may have hit a rock bottom, only to re-surface with renewed vigour. In recent years, a number of congregations have claimed an increase in attendance and membership.

In a few paragraphs within a chapter on statistical data, we cannot open up a topic on which many books have been written, and on which the jury is still out. Students who are interested in pursuing the secularization debate can profitably consult the writings of Harvey Cox, Bryan Wilson, Steve Bruce, Thomas Luckmann, Peter Berger and Rodney Stark, and – more recently – Paul Heelas, Linda Woodhead and Christopher Partridge, which are listed in the bibliography. We can usefully note, however, that 'secularization' is not a state of affairs that admits wholly to numerical measurement. We can attain reasonable statistical precision on membership and attendance, but how can we measure the degree to which religion has 'lost its hold' on people, or the extent to which people rely more on science than on religion? Thomas Luckmann has pointed out that 'secularization' is not a single monolithic phenomenon, but incorporates a cluster of disparate concepts, some of which are measurable, and some of which are not. Luckmann therefore questions whether the concept itself is really a useful one at all.

Luckmann's objections impinge on a number of issues on which further statistical data can help to shed light. Secularization is certainly not a single process, as we find it in present-day Western society. Religiosity varies according to one's gender and social class, for example, and different denominations have experienced different patterns of development in recent years. Thus, women are more likely to attend church than men, and manual workers are marginally less likely to attend than non-manual (Bruce, 1995, pp. 43–4). Roman Catholicism and the more charismatic versions of Christianity are experiencing increase rather than decline. Despite institutional decline in the majority of denominations, religious experience is a phenomenon which has aroused interest in recent times, and which can be subjected to statistical measurement and analysis. Alister Hardy, the founder of the Religious Experience Research Centre, now based at the University of Wales in Lampeter, concluded that one person in three has undergone at least one experience that they were willing to classify as 'religious'. (This is a surprising result, since we seldom hear people talking openly about their religious experiences.) Since the 1970s, much publicity has been given to Near-Death Experiences (NDEs), and what these might tell us about the possibility of life after death. There are those who have claimed visions of angels in recent times: this too can be, and has been, subjected to statistical analysis (Heathcote-James, 2002). There is a huge complexity of data that impinges on the secularization debate, and to which numerical analysis is relevant.

Whether or not 'secularization' is useful as a concept, it is worth remembering that data on religion – as with most other subjects – can be qualitative as well as quantitative, and that both types of data have their role. Students who instinctively endeavour to avoid anything numerate can take refuge in the thought that the student of religion is not obliged to collect and process statistical data, or do complicated mathematics. However, one needs to be aware of existing statistical data, and the ways in which that data sheds light on issues in religion. At the other extreme, it is possible to overemphasize the role of numbers and statistical data. This is no doubt evidenced in our present societal concern with quality assurance ratings and league tables. There is a maxim that, if you cannot make the important measurable, you make the measurable important. It is tempting to suppose that, because ideas and theories cannot be given mathematical precision they are therefore woolly, vague and mere matters of impression. While it is true that one cannot be precise about the extent to which religion has a hold over people's lives, or whether people pursue a religion for pragmatic or spiritual benefits, such issues are nonetheless real, and worthy of discussion.

What is being measured?

The preceding discussion demonstrates that membership, formal initiation, professed allegiance, attendance and spiritual activities are different from each other, and people who qualify as a statistic on one of these criteria may not necessarily do so on the others. For example, in England it is common for someone to state that they are 'Church of England' on admission to hospital, when the relevant paperwork asks for one's religious affiliation. Such a profession may have a 'default value': there is no other religious affiliation that appeals more to the patient. At best, the patient may be staking a claim to have his or her rites of passage (a funeral, if the medical treatment is unsuccessful) carried out within the context of the stated religion. (In England, everyone who lives in a parish is entitled to a funeral at the local parish church.)

Professed allegiance may be nominal, and hence statistics on allegiance can differ markedly from those of attendance or membership. Membership may seem a concept that is easier to measure than adherence. However, measuring membership is not without its problems. A few religious communities are not membership organizations, while others may have degrees of membership. Mainstream Christianity distinguishes between those who have been baptized, those who have undergone confirmation, and those who formally belong to a congregation. Other organizations make distinctions

FIGURE 4.2 *St Michael the Archangel, exterior (Church of England).*

like 'full member', 'part-time member' and 'associate member', or maybe even a category such as 'friend'. A full member may be someone who works full-time for their religious organization, either sharing its spiritual life as part of a community, or employed full-time in the organization (waged or unwaged). Associate membership can mean a variety of things including distance membership, a formal declaration of sympathy with the organization's aims, or simply acquiring a membership card, perhaps with a view to obtaining discounts when purchasing goods and services. Some organizations such as The Family International (formerly the Children of God) devised their own distinctive categories of membership: The Family talks about 'charter members', meaning those who live in community, agreeing to abide by The Family's 'Charter' (a detailed code of practice). The notion of being a 'sympathizer', which has occasionally been used in assembling statistics of religious affiliation, is problematic since the concept ranges from the neophyte, who has still to attain deeper levels of commitment, to someone who may not necessarily share the aims of a community but is nonetheless prepared to offer support when it becomes a victim of persecution or discrimination. Indeed, a sympathizer's real allegiance may even lie outside the community with which he or she expresses sympathy.

If all this seems untidy and potentially confusing, the difficulty is compounded by the fact that religious organizations may either exaggerate or downplay membership statistics, or even change their methods of measurement. Exaggeration may occur where an organization wishes to convey an impression of popularity. The Discordians – a small organization with an almost exclusive online following – nonetheless claims that *everyone* is a member, without knowing it! The so-called Ice Cream Church – one of the cyber-churches, which is probably only active in cyberspace – boasts 4,000 members at the time of writing: presumably this figure relates merely to the number of visitors to its website.

IDEOLOGIES

The website www.adherents.com, which provides statistical information on over 4,200 religions at the time of writing, provides a 'league table' indicating their overall numerical strength. Surprisingly, in the ninth position comes 'Juche' – a movement for which little information is available. The movement has 23 million members – a larger following than Judaism or Jainism – and is described as 'North Korea's state religion' or as 'Kimilsungism', after North Korea's leader, Kim Il Sung (1912–94). It is also known as ChucheSasang (meaning 'self-reliance') or Chuch'e. It is practically unheard of because it is confined to North Korea, a country that is hardly renowned for open contacts with the outside world, although it has been speculated that Juche ideas influenced the politics of Indonesia, and the regimes of Nicolae Ceausescu in Romania and Pol Pot in Cambodia.

Whether Juche should count as a religion is debatable. It is based on the Marxist communism that has prevailed in China and the former Soviet Union, although it renounces its Marxist-Leninist roots. It is sometimes regarded as a form of Stalinism, since it did not accept the USSR's anti-Stalinist revisions in 1956. It is opposed to the supernaturalism that typically forms part of religious allegiance. According to Juche, supernaturalism is a form of belief that is encouraged by the ruling classes for their own cynical ends. Kim Il Sung takes the example of lightning: scientific thought has established that lightning is an electrical discharge from clouds, but primitive humanity held that it was wrathful communication to humanity from supernatural forces. He has argued that it was in the interests of the ruling classes to keep their subjects in a state of illusion, so that they would be less critical of their oppression, and not harbour vain hopes that their subservience and poverty in their physical lives would be compensated by a life after death where their fortunes will be reversed.

In place of such supposed illusion, Juche teaches the importance of transforming the material world. It is professedly based on a scientific understanding of humanity, viewing humankind as 'substance' as well as consciousness. Philosophers have typically emphasized the human mind, thought and ideas, and Juche terms this way of thinking 'idealism'. (This is not used in quite the same way as the term 'idealism' has been used in Western philosophy.) Substance and consciousness should thus be seen as in dialectical opposition to each other, and this opposition needs to be resolved in some higher synthesis. In simpler terms, this means that there is a very marked contrast between the world as it is (substance/being) and the world as we might conceive it to be, in its ideal form (consciousness/thinking). Men and women are therefore constrained to transform the world into this ideal, resulting in independence and victory. The fundamental principle of Juche is 'self-reliance', a term that is sometimes given by way of translation of the name. As Kim Il Sung taught, 'Humanity is the master and decides everything.' This self-reliance applies to three principal areas, as defined by Juche: politics, economics and national defence.

The purpose of this case study is not so much to expound the ideas of Juche, but to highlight what an ideology is. Philosophy offers a way of understanding the world, defining what entities exist (substance, values, supernatural beings and the like), how we can know them, and how they can coexist. Philosophy of religion typically asks how (or whether) one can know that there is a God, and if so, how God's existence can be reconciled with a world that contains evil and suffering. Such debate tends to be theoretical, and does little if anything to change the world. An ideology by contrast is an organized, systematic collation of ideas that can be used by its supporters to change human society. Recent Western examples of ideologies include utilitarianism – the doctrine, made famous by Jeremy Bentham and John Stuart Mill, that one ought to promote the greatest happiness of the greatest number. Both Bentham and Mill were social reformers, and saw their philosophy as a means of providing a basis of values and of transforming society without presupposing religious belief. Another ideology – one which ran alongside religion, rather than sought to displace it – was fascism: Hitler's policies were based on the notion of the supremacy of the Aryan 'master race'. Hitler, however, remained a Roman Catholic.

Is it possible to separate ideology from religion? Should Juche be counted simply as an ideology, and hence left out of the league tables of religions? Should it be counted as a subset of communism? Or should it be given the status, as the Christian theologian Thomas J. Belke suggests, of 'North Korea's state religion'? There are certain elements that might seem to suggest that Juche has a religious identity. There has arisen a kind of foundation-myth that Kim Il Sung's son, Kim Jong-Il, who assumed leadership after his father's demise, was born on Mount Paekdu, where mythic deities have been said to arise. Many homes across the country have framed pictures of Kim Il Sung and Kim Jong-Il; they are regarded as father-figures who offer inspiration and protection against evil. Loyalty is expected, and expressions of irreverence or disloyalty are punishable offences. The leader is honoured with an elaborate monument at Kŭmsusan Memorial Palace, which thousands of supporters visit daily to pay their respects and to lay wreaths, and North Korea has even devised its own distinctive calendar, in which year one begins in 1912, Kim Il Sung's birth year.

Belke claims that Juche is espoused by 100 per cent of the North Korean population, but other sources claim to find supporters of Buddhism, Christianity and Ch'ondogyo (a syncretistic Korean religion). Support for Ch'ondogyo has been estimated at between 12.5 and 14 per cent of the population, Buddhism at between 1.6 and 2 per cent, and Christianity at around 0.8 per cent (Goring, 1994; Ash, 1998). Goring gives a 1992 statistic of 68 per cent as 'non-religious'. Juche certainly defines the practice of religion in North Korea: the fact that American evangelist Billy Graham was permitted to visit Pyonyang in 1992 and preach there is evidence that religion is not totally suppressed. Belke argues that the separation of politics and religion reflects a Western mentality, and that we should not discount Juche as religious simply on the grounds that it emphasizes the material rather than the supernatural, and venerates human rather than divine figures.

It is certainly true that in the Far East, the Confucian legacy of ancestor veneration causes deceased heroes to be venerated within the context of religion. It is quite common in Vietnam, for example to find pictures of Ho Chi Minh (1890–1969), who was prime minister and subsequently president, in Buddhist temples, although he also has his own state monument in Ho Chi Minh City (formerly Saigon).

There is no one 'correct' way of presenting religious statistics relating to North Korea and Juche. The case study highlights the fact that statistical information is often meaningless without accompanying explanation and analysis. In particular, it requires the student of religion to decide what counts as a religion (a theme of a previous chapter), and whether it is completely possible to distinguish between the religious and the ideological.

References

Ash, R. (1998), *The Top 10 of Everything 1999.* New York: D.K. Publishing.
Belke, T. J. (1999), *Juche: A Christian Study of North Korea's State Religion.* Bartlesville, OK: Living Sacrifice Books.
Goring, R. (ed.) (1994), *Larousse Dictionary of Beliefs and Religions.* Edinburgh: Larousse.

At the other extreme, an organization may have reasons to appear to minimize its membership, for example if it has to pay a regular per capita levy to its headquarters. One Unitarian congregation known to the author previously listed 101 members, but after experiencing some financial problems, recognized that reducing its membership roll could save some *per capita* levies. Accordingly the membership list was scrutinized, and it was noted that numerous people on the list did not attend, did not live locally and did not contribute financially. Such people were designated 'associate members', and the membership reduced from 101 to 66 – a notional reduction of 33 per cent, thus saving the congregation nearly £400 a year. Yet despite this declared reduction in membership, congregational life continued exactly as before, with exactly the same levels of activity, including Sunday attendance. The fact that Unitarianism appears to have declined numerically in the past decade or so (8,000 members in 1992, and 4,900 in 2003) may be due at least partly to other congregations adopting a similar practice, although no doubt death and resignation also played a significant part.

The world's fastest-growing religion?

In the light of the above discussion, it may be tempting to conclude that statistical information is unreliable or misleading. One might call to mind the well-known aphorism, 'You can prove anything by statistics.' Those who have listened to politicians arguing about the incidence of crime or about the state of the economy will recognize that opposing parties will claim simultaneously that crime is increasing and decreasing, or that unemployment is rising and falling. Indeed the way in which statistics can be massaged, manipulated and misleadingly presented caused one author, Darrell Huff, to write his popular book, *How to Lie with Statistics.*

We have already touched on issues relating to the size of religious communities, and how statistics about membership can be massaged in order to fulfil their needs. Statistical information, however, provides a diachronic as well as a synchronic picture of religions: that is to say, it can measure change in size through time as well as portraying size at any given time. In measuring growth, however, great care has to be exercised, and in order to illustrate this I want to examine a question that is frequently asked, and frequently given different answers: 'What is the world's fastest-growing religion?'

In order to collect some data on this question for this chapter, I decided to type the phrase 'fastest-growing religion' into a search engine as a keyword. There were 115 hits, but remarkably few discussions of the question that had any academic merit. One hit was a bulletin board, where a woman posed the question 'What is the world's fastest-growing religion?', stating that she needed information for a statistics essay that she was writing. She received numerous replies, mainly citing Islam, but also including Christianity, Buddhism, wicca, Satanism, atheism or transhumanism (http://answers.yahoo.com/question/index?qid=1006051218682). Apparently the practice on this board is for the 'asker' to select what he or she regards as the best answer, for which the participant receives cumulative points. The favoured answer was from a member who produced a long string of media quotations extolling the virtues of Islam, such as Hillary Clinton's remark that 'Islam is the fastest-growing religion in America, a guide and pillar of stability for many of our people . . .' (*Los Angeles Times*, 31 May 1996, p. 3). Not only did this answer miss the mark by referring to America when the questioner had asked about the world, but neither he nor any other respondent cited a single statistic. Before declaring this respondent's contribution to be the best answer, the questioner ought to have noticed his profile, which endorsed a quotation from the Qur'an. One critical question should have been whether she was receiving unbiased information. However, she was satisfied with his answer, and regarded her question as having been closed. One wonders what grade she received for a statistics essay without statistics!

Another web author, this time actually using some statistical data, makes the following comparisons involving the Latter-day Saints (LDS – the Mormons), the Jehovah's Witnesses (JWs), the Bahá'í, and the Church of Scientology (CoS), and confidently concludes, 'And the winners are – the Witnesses!'

LDS	1986–99	4.4 %
JWs	1988–99	4.9 %
Bahá'í	1963–85	10.0 %
Bahá'í	1985–94	4.0 %
CoS	1977–94	2.4 %
CoS	1994–9	3.7 %

Source: Anon, 2005.

Presumably the conclusion is reached on the basis of the average annual growth rate – which for clarity's sake should have been presented to readers in a separate new column.

In fairness to this author, he or she points out that the growth rate is not a straightforward average obtained by dividing the growth rate by the number of years. Growth rates are 'compound': that is to say, a religion that grows at a rate of (say) 10 per cent increases by 10 per cent in the first measured year, and then by a further 10 per cent of the previous year's membership plus 10 per cent, and so on progressively. Thus, assuming a steady growth rate, an initial membership of M and a growth rate of 10 per cent would display the following pattern.

Year 1	M
Year 2	M + 10% × M
Year 3	(M + 10% × M) + 10% × (M + 10% × M)
Year 4	(M + 10% × M) + 10% × (M + 10% × M) + 10% × (M + 10% × M) + 10% × (M + 10% × M)

and so on. Students may remember from their school days a mathematical formula normally used for calculating compound interest on money, which is expressed thus:

$$x = 100((F/S)^{(1/y)}-1)$$

x is the percentage growth rate; y is the number of years; S is the start number; and F is the final number.

If all this sounds complicated, it goes to show how carefully statistical information needs to be processed. At this stage we are only dealing with GCSE standard arithmetic: we have not attempted to engage in statistics or data processing as academic subjects!

Despite the fact that the web author recognizes that growth is compound, it should be obvious that the Jehovah's Witnesses should not be declared the world's fastest-growing religion on the basis of the evidence given. One obvious problem is that the comparative statistics relate to different time periods; it is also rather strange to present two time periods for the Bahá'í and the Church of Scientology, but only one for the Latter-day Saints and Jehovah's Witnesses. (Which time period is the better indicator of current growth?) Another concern is that the author ignores the fact that different religious groups measure their allegiance in different ways. The Bahá'í count any child born to Bahá'í parents as a member of the faith, while other religious organizations do not: the Jehovah's Witnesses (as discussed below) provide a range of statistics, some of which include children and some of which do not; the Church of Scientology probably only counts those who have done their courses, or who have signed an associate membership form.

FIGURE 4.3 *Hassan II Mosque, Casablanca.*

Clearly we need to examine proper numerical estimates given by, or on behalf of, the relevant contenders. Claimants for the title 'fastest-growing religion' include not only Islam, but Bahá'í, Scientology, Buddhism, Soka Gakkai (a Japanese Buddhist organization) Pentecostalism, Latter-day Saints (Mormons) and Jehovah's Witnesses. Let us examine their respective claims.

1   *Islam* Islam is generally agreed to be the world's largest religion after
     Christianity, having 1.4 billion followers, currently growing at a rate of
     2.9 per cent per annum according to Bruce Robinson (www.religioustolerance.
     org/growth_isl_chr.htm) – higher than the world's population growth rate of
     2.6 per cent.

2   *Scientology* According to another source, Scientology increased from
     5,437,000 members in 1977 to 7 million in 1992; during the period 1950–92,
     some 15 million copies of L. Ron Hubbard's *Dianetics: The Modern Science of
     Mental Health* were sold, and the Church of Scientology boasted 143 Class IV
     'orgs' (organizations, i.e. local centres) and 230 'missions' in 107 countries and
     31 languages by 1998.

3   *Buddhism* Presumably the claim that Buddhism is the 'fastest-growing
     religion' relates to the substantial uptake by Westerners over the past century.

According to a recent article on Buddhanet.net, Buddhism expanded at a remarkable rate in Australia in the early 1990s. According to Commonwealth Government Census statistics, the author claims there were 80,837 Buddhists in Australia in 1986. In 1991 the number had risen to 139,847 – an increase of 74 per cent. By 1996 the number had again increased, this time to 199,812 – a growth of 43 per cent from the 1991 statistic, and a growth of 247 per cent over the decade. Although the growth rate had apparently slowed down, the author believes that this still makes Buddhism the fastest-growing religion in Australia. (The author could have made his claim sound even more impressive by stating that the 1996 figure was 148% greater than the 1986 figure: the Buddhist population had more than doubled within a decade.)

4 *Bahá'í* In his *Sects, 'Cults' and Alternative Religions* David Barrett points out that the number of Bahá'ís worldwide in 1963 was a mere 400,000; by 1985 this rose to 5 million. This is an increase of 1,250 per cent in 22 years, an average growth rate of 56.8 per cent. A more recent statistic (adherents.com, Preston, 2006) indicates that worldwide there are 7 million Bahá'ís : if so, this represents an increase over the 1963 figure of a staggering 1,750 per cent – very impressive! The Bahá'ís' average annual growth rate over these 43 years works out at 40.1 per cent per annum. One can see why the Bahá'ís claim to be the world's fastest-growing religion.

5 *Jehovah's Witnesses* One Jehovah's Witness researcher describes the organization as 'one of the world's fastest-growing religious groups' (Wah, 2001, p. 161). The Jehovah's Witnesses publish very precise statistics annually, which they take considerable care to collect. The following are culled from the *Yearbook of Jehovah's Witnesses* from 2002 to 2006. (Each Yearbook presents statistics for the previous year, so the latest five-year span for which statistics are available at the time of writing is 2001–5.)

	2001	2002	2003	2004	2005
Baptisms	263,431	265,469	258,845	262,416	247,631
Congregations	93,154	94,600	95,919	96,894	98,269
Memorial attendance	15,374,986	15,597,746	16,097,622	16,760,607	16,383,333
Average publishers*	5,881,776	6,048,600	6,184,046	6,308,341	6,390,016

* A publisher is a Jehovah's Witness who undertakes house-to-house evangelism.

Presented as percentage increases or decreases over the previous year, we can calculate the following:

	2002	2003	2004	2005	Percentage increase from 2001 to 2005
Baptisms	10.77	22.5	11.38	25.63	26.00
Congregations	11.55	11.39	11.02	11.42	15.4
Memorial attendance	11.45	13.20	14.12	22.25	16.56
Average publishers	12.84	12.24	12.01	11.29	18.64

* A publisher is a Jehovah's Witness who undertakes house-to-house evangelism.

Despite one or two statistical setbacks that are obvious above, the overall trend seems to be a substantial increase.

6 *Pentecostalists* One writer has described the Pentecostalists as 'the fastest-growing Christian movement after World War II' (Crim, 1989, p. 564), and Harvey Cox alludes to an estimate that there is an increase of some 20 million members annually. Estimates of the total number of Pentecostalists vary, but one Pentecostalist writer claims a 1998 world membership of 450 million. If we accept this estimate, the annual growth rate could be argued to be substantially higher than Cox suggests: since the rise of Pentecostalism is usually dated from 1906 (the date of the so-called Azusa Street Revival), the movement must have increased by 4.5 million members annually to achieve this total.

7 *Soka Gakkai* and *Latter-day Saints* The back cover of Philip Hammond and David Machacek's *Soka Gakkai in America: Accommodation and Conversion* describes the book as the 'first ever US study of the fastest-growing religion in the world', although no statistical data are given. Several websites make similar claims for the Latter-day Saints: for example, the US News and World Report states that 'Mormonism is the fastest growing faith group in American history' and 'if present trends continue there could be 265 million members of the Church of Jesus Christ of Latter Day Saints (LDS) worldwide by 2080' (cited by Christian Broadcasting Network, 2007). However, the report does not specify any parameters for 'present trends'.

So what is the world's fastest-growing religion? The answer is that the question is meaningless until one specifies both the time period that is to form the basis of comparison, and also what we mean by adherents or members. Are we counting children as well as adults, 'active' members (in which case we would need to specify what 'active' meant and how one recognized it), only those who have undergone an initiatory rite of passage (baptism, *amrit*, 'taking refuge' in Buddhism's *triratna*), self-declared followers (as in the 2001 British Census), those who are formally recognized as members by their religious community or what? Growth could also be counted in terms of congregations: Mormons, for example, will sometimes point to the remarkable increase in numbers of new Mormon temples as evidence that they are growing the fastest. The truth of the matter is that different religious organizations measure allegiance in different ways and at different points in time. Unless we are able to compare reliable statistics, all of which measure the same thing, and over the same period of time, one cannot talk about fastest-growing or fastest-declining religions. Statistical data simply do not exist to enable such a comparison. This conclusion no doubt comes as a disappointment to those religious groups who claim to be the fastest-growing, as well to those students who like to have firm answers to questions that initially seem straightforward. In the study of religion however, straight answers are not always possible, or desirable.

The fact that the preceding discussion failed to elicit a firm answer, compounded by the competing claims of different religious organizations, may cause the student to wonder whether gathering statistics relating to religion has any significant value. If one's questions are ill-framed or ill-conceived, then clearly gathering statistical information is unhelpful. However, where we clearly define the information we are seeking, and ensure that we know what our statistics are measuring, then – as we argued at the beginning of the chapter – statistical information can be invaluable to the scholar and to religious communities alike.

DESIGNING A QUESTIONNAIRE

Students are often keen to undertake interview and questionnaire work. While this has its place, it can be extremely time-consuming, and it is therefore important to ensure that it serves a useful purpose and that the information gained is valid and reliable. Two initial questions are worth asking: (1) What important information would a questionnaire elicit that is not covered in the relevant literature? (2) Has some other scholar already undertaken a similar survey on which one could draw?

A questionnaire needs

A definite aim

Decide what you need to know, and remove everything else. (Do you really need to ask someone's age, for example?)

Predetermined sampling techniques

Results will be seriously skewed if you redefine your sample half way through the survey, or if you randomly select a few extra respondents simply to make up numbers.

Predetermined methods of analysis/coding

Consider how you will process your results, and anticipate possible answers. For example, if you ask 'What is your religion?', what do you do if respondents give 'Christianity', 'Mormonism', 'Church of England' and 'Unitarianism' as answers?

An idea of possible conclusions

It is not 'cheating' to guess that a survey may confirm a favoured theory, so long as the questioner is open to the possibility that the reverse might happen. Academic work involves 'hypothesis testing', and one therefore needs a hypothesis to start from. Remember that research is conducted to find out whether something is the case, not to prove that it is.

Recognition of issues in research ethics

Research involving human participants often needs the approval of an ethics committee these days. It is advisable to check. In particular, a researcher will probably need to demonstrate that a questionnaire and interview work does not inconvenience people, waste their time or touch on unduly sensitive areas.

An appropriate sample

While writing this section, the author passed a store that claimed, 'Eight out of ten customers think the store offers better value than any of its competitors.' A footnote explained that this claim was based on a survey of customers inside the store. This sample was hardly appropriate: presumably those who did not believe the statement went elsewhere!

Piloting

A small group of friends or colleagues can help to pilot your questionnaire. This will identify ambiguous or problematical questions. It will also enable you to advise your respondents how long it will take to complete. We should not tell respondents that something will 'only take five minutes' if it really takes half an hour.

Impeccability

A questionnaire should look good. It should be free of misprints, incorrect spellings and faulty punctuation. You will find that there is a better response rate if you look truly professional and are seen to take a pride in your work. Closed-ended questions are probably better for questionnaires, while open-ended ones are better for interviews. Questionnaire respondents may find it hard work if they are called upon to write mini-essays, while interview subjects often like to expand on and qualify their answers. Open-ended information is more difficult, although not impossible, to process. Processing involves coding your questions and responses, and analysing them appropriately; it may be helpful to use a software program like Excel to process your data.

Consider what kind of information you want to elicit

A broad question like 'What religion do you subscribe to?' is likely to produce crude data. What does 'subscribe' mean? Is it asking for one's self-defined religious allegiance, whether one is on some membership list, whether one practises a religion (another vague notion) or whether the respondent attends his or her place of worship regularly (however that is defined)? A survey can ask questions about backgrounds, roles, attitudes, behaviour, or some combination of these, and it is important to decide what precise data one needs. Much better than the above question would be something like the following:

- Would you describe yourself as: Buddhist / Christian / Hindu / Jewish / Muslim / Sikh / other (please specify)?
- How often do you attend your place of worship? Most days / once a week / once a month / less than five times a year / never
- Do you hold any office in your religious organization (e.g. treasurer, teacher of children)? Yes / No. If yes, please specify
- Which of the following sources keep you informed about current religious affairs? (Please indicate more than one, if appropriate.) Newspapers / radio / television / the internet / publications from my religious organization / other (please specify)

Notice how the various questions seek to elicit these different types of information.

Some questions NOT to ask

Apart from unduly intrusive or embarrassing questions, the following types of question should be avoided.

Multiple questions

Avoid trying to elicit more than one piece of information at a time, for example 'Do you attend a place of worship, and do you find it beneficial?' (Make this two separate questions.)

Leading questions

Allow informants to give their own opinions, rather than suggest them. A question like, 'Do you think you should move with the times by ordaining women?' is clearly a loaded one, and predisposes respondents to give an affirmative answer.

Presuming questions

'Do you find there are enough opportunities to socialize at your place of worship?' presupposes that socializing is an important consideration. Maybe it is not, and perhaps it is; but it is the researcher's task to check this out, if this line of questioning is important.

Hypothetical questions

'If you were disabled, how amenable would you find the premises of your place of worship?', if put to people without disability, might well give rise to misleading information. If I am not disabled, do I really know all the problems a disabled person might encounter? (Of course, if the researcher is testing whether able-bodied people are unduly complacent about disabled facilities, the question might be more appropriate.)

Questions with too many negatives

'How strongly do you disagree with the view that women should not be ordained when there are not yet any signs that the entire Church will accept their ministry?' is plainly confusing, and hence is likely to elicit unreliable responses. Keep questions as straightforward and intelligible as possible, and use your pilot study to check that you have done this.

Respondents are giving up their time voluntarily to assist us with our research. It is therefore important to show due respect for them. If they do not want to respond, that is their choice. They must not be coaxed into answering; they may decline to answer specific questions, or indeed to withdraw at any time – and without having to give their reasons.

Collecting one's own statistical data

So far we have examined statistical information that already exists in the public domain, but we can also add to the available data by creating our own, and some students feel a need to collect their own statistical data using surveys, questionnaires or interviews. Careful thought needs to go into such ventures: simply to jot down a few questions and find 20 students in the campus refectory is easy enough to do, but surveys of this kind are unlikely to yield useful or reliable data. Even a shoddy piece of questionnaire work of this kind takes time: an afternoon or a day is needed to devise even simple questions, talk to people and note their responses and then process the results. It is salutary to remember that the large opinion poll companies, such as Mori and Gallup, normally use samples of 1,000 respondents or more, and even then have been known to come up with incorrect results. A number of considerations are therefore appropriate before contemplating undertaking one's own personal surveys.

First, because questionnaires and interviews involve working with human subjects, such activities often involve ethical considerations, and may even require formal permission from an ethics committee. Questions may sometimes be intrusive, or relate to sensitive issues: while it may be interesting to ascertain people's attitudes, say, to abortion, broaching the subject unexpectedly in an interview or questionnaire might well be inappropriate. Some target groups may be vulnerable, an obvious example being Holocaust victims, who may well have been traumatized by their experience and may not wish to be reminded of their trauma by talking to researchers. Holocaust victims raise another issue regarding interview work: since they are an ageing group of people, rapidly diminishing through death, the sheer amount of Holocaust research that has been conducted can result in a target group becoming saturated by researchers. The researcher must guard against a group becoming overused for research purposes. Also included in the category of 'vulnerable' subjects are children: at the very least interviewing minors requires parental consent, and in some situations it may even require that one's police record is checked. All research on human subjects takes up people's time. More often than not, religious communities are only too willing to spend time with staff and students, but in return one must ensure that respondents' time is not simply being wasted, which it will be if the way we collect information is invalid or unreliable.

All this raises a basic question about interview work: does it need to be done at all? While students may think that survey work is a welcome change from book-based research, it may well be that research on a similar topic has already been done by academic researchers. It should be borne in mind that academic researchers have often spent years accumulating and interpreting data, often with funding, research assistants and sophisticated computer software for data processing. There is no point in reinventing the wheel with one's own amateurish quick survey, when it is possible to draw on work that has already been done by others. Even if one is sure that a survey has not already been carried out by established scholars, one must ask whether supplementing book-based research with empirical work will really add to the existing body of knowledge. Sometimes inexperienced students believe that empirical surveys are expected of them: when asked to write research proposals, it is not uncommon for students to declare that they will not only consult relevant books and articles, but that this will be complemented by fieldwork, interviews and questionnaires: it is almost as if one had asked them to write down as many methods of information-gathering as they could think of!

Where interviewing or questionnaire work is conducted, however, two key considerations are paramount: *validity* and *reliability*. A survey must be valid: that is to say, it must accurately measure what it sets out to measure. For example, if one's aim is to ascertain the extent to which churches use ethical investments, a survey of the opinions of rank-and-file members would not be valid. (Do they know how their congregation's monies are invested? Are their views reflected in church policy? Greater validity might be attained by surveying church treasurers, or by examining annual accounts.) Again, if one wanted to elicit Christian views on investment, it would not be valid to confine oneself, say, to the university Christian Union, which may reflect one distinctive Christian stance; surveying the Christian student population would, likewise, be invalid, since it is possible that students give more thought to such issues than other churchgoers, and therefore do not reflect Christian attitudes more widely. Achieving a sample of Christians in general might be too tall an order for the average student researcher: greater validity can of course be attained by narrowing one's focus, and if one's aim was to ascertain only the attitudes of the college's Christian Union, then questioning its members might be appropriate.

Reliability involves conducting one's research in such a way that the results are capable of replication. A survey is unreliable if someone is likely to obtain quite different results using the same means. Interviewing an opportunity sample of 20 people may seem easy, but how can we be sure that a second group of 20 would give similar responses? Our group of 20 might be atypically likeminded; we may have found them because they have all come from the same event, or are together because they share similar opinions.

Survey work cannot be conducted with any degree of validity or reliability without knowing the different types of sample that can be used, and making a conscious decision as to which is appropriate. First, there is the *random sample*. The unwary may believe that if they approach a variety of people without any preconceived means of selection, then this is a random sample. In all probability, it is not. Selecting people in a shopping mall on a weekday does not yield randomness: such a sample would have a definite bias towards shoppers, possibly women, and leaves out most people who are in full-time employment, people who are ill in bed, and nightshift workers, among others. Picking names randomly from a phone book targets telephone subscribers, leaving out anyone who is not on the telephone (some people still fall into this category), and those who are ex-directory. (The use of telephone lists also raises ethical questions: is the researcher intending 'cold calling', either by telephone or by ringing someone's doorbell, and is this acceptable?) It is best to accept that the notion of randomness is too problematic, and to claim that one's sample is of another variety.

Slightly more achievable is the *representative sample*. A representative sample reflects the spectrum of people who are found either in the public at large, or within one's target group (e.g. Muslim women, 'born again' Christians, animal rights campaigners). To be properly representative, one's sample should reflect the proportions of sexes, ages, marital status, incomes, social classes, indeed all the major categories that are typically applied to people. Readers have probably had the experience of being approached in the street by a market researcher, asked (for example) their age range, and then been turned down for the interview: the market researcher has no doubt already attained his or her quota of people in that age band. In order to achieve a truly representative sample, one must first have appropriate demographic data: the researcher needs to know the relative proportions of men and women in society (it is not quite 50–50: the male–female balance is 48–52, to be precise), the proportions who are single / married / living together / separated / divorced / widowed, the range of income distribution and so on. Such information can be readily found in standard reference works such as *Social Trends* (ONS, 2006), and the difficult task is creating a sample that accurately reflects all these variables.

Much easier to obtain is the *opportunity sample* (sometimes known as the 'convenience sample'). As the name implies, this type of sample consists of a number of people who present themselves as opportunities for interview. A researcher who attends a religious meeting – having obtained appropriate permission, of course – might take the opportunity to interview some of the attendees. Even easier might be one's own fellow-students after a lecture. Such samples may not be typical of any wider population: the religious meeting might consist of a Muslim community with very specific interests and views; one's fellow-students may not reflect the attitudes of the student population more widely. Despite these obvious limitations, it could be claimed that using an opportunity sample yields useful data: it may be of interest to know what one specific religious group or student class thinks of an issue. (Student module evaluation only surveys one small group at a time, and this is precisely its merit: the tutor receives feedback specifically about that module, which is probably more useful than reading a global survey of student evaluation of classes throughout the institution.)

A further type of sample is the *snowball sample*. This involves starting with a small group of people in a defined category (e.g. parents of members of new religious movements), seeking an interview with them, and then asking them to recommend others whom they know fall into the same category. The snowball sample is particularly useful where it is initially difficult to find a significant number of people who fall into the required category. Perhaps the researcher initially knows only a couple of parents; but parents of members of new religious movements (NRMs – popularly but inappropriately known as 'cults') tend to know each other, and thus can provide the relevant introductions. One has to bear in mind, though, that a snowballed sample may not be a representative sample: if the first parents who are approached belong to an anti-cult organization, they will be likely to know and to recommend others who have similar attitudes towards NRMs. The student who wants a range of opinion will need to find clusters, and to 'snowball' from examples in different categories. Snowballing can be used in conjunction with other types of sample.

Yet another type of sample is the *cluster sample*. This can be used where the researcher knows that there exists a range of attitudes or perspectives on a particular topic. The previous example – NRMs – is a case in point, since there are a number of categories of interest groups. There are current members, ex-members, members' parents and evangelical Christians who would criticize NRMs' theology rather than their practices. This list is not exhaustive: the reader can no doubt think of other categories of people who have concerns in this field, and the researcher might also decide to split some of these broad groups further. For example, not all ex-members are necessarily bitter about their life in an NRM; hence it might be appropriate to define a cluster of hostile ex-members and another cluster of non-hostile ones. The cluster sample of people who assume the defined positions does not have to reflect the proportions of the population more widely (that would be a representative sample), since the aim is to elicit the different viewpoints of the different stakeholders, not necessarily to ascertain the respective proportions of people who hold them.

The *focus group* also needs some comment. Although it is seldom explicitly discussed in the methodology of the study of religion, scholars often find themselves talking to religious practitioners in small groups, and the technique remains an option for students who want to gather data. Originally referred to as 'focused interviews' and 'group depth interviews', the focus group normally consists of between seven and ten people whom the interviewer invites to a group discussion on account of their common interest in a specified topic. Members of the focus group should not previously know each other. It is usual to use a number of different focus groups on the same topic, in order to identify trends in opinion: it is possible that a single group may take their cue from a dominant individual. The facilitator (or moderator) defines the purpose of the group discussion, having prepared some open-ended questions: it is common practice to start with fairly broad issues and narrow these down, as appropriate, to specific ones. It is normal to record and transcribe the interview, enabling the researcher to identify common words, themes and sentiments, and sort them into categories.

The advantages of a focus group are that it is relatively easy and quick to conduct, and incurs little cost to the organizer. It can bring out issues that may be previously unknown to the researcher, who has the opportunity to probe and follow them up. The researcher, however, needs excellent interviewing skills and good familiarity with group dynamics. As most students and teachers know, group discussions can easily wander considerably off target, and in a focus group the facilitator needs to steer a careful balance, keeping the discussion on track while ensuring that opinion is not suppressed. Allied to this point is the inevitable problem of ensuring that one or two highly opinionated participants do not dominate the discussion, and that reticent members get a chance to express their views. There is a danger too that the interviewer may inadvertently give cues that certain types of response are more welcome than others. Although the focus group has its advantages, it has limitations too: in particular, it cannot elicit individual opinion, and the sample group may not be representative of opinion more widely. There can also be practical difficulties in ensuring that an appropriate group of people all become available at the same time and place.

Conclusion

We have covered a considerable amount of ground on religious statistics, and it will be useful to sum up at this point. First, we believe we have demonstrated the falsity of the popular maxim: 'You can prove anything by statistics.' This is simply false: statistics cannot possibly prove that more people attend church now than a century ago, that Buddhism is the most popular religion in Britain, or that most new Scientology recruits are minors. Statistics are not infallible: like any other group of researchers, statisticians can make mistakes, and statistical findings can be presented in slanted or misleading ways. However, provided that statistics are valid and reliable, they can provide useful precision to the study of religion, and can serve to confirm or deny our more subjective impressions. It is not normally a requirement for students to collect and present their own statistical information – usually an enormously time-consuming task – but familiarity with statistical methods enables the student to assess critically the statistical information provided by other researchers. Finally, we noted that the study of religion involves both qualitative and quantitative data. Both have their place and they interact with each other, and it would be wrong to suppose that one or the other had superiority.

DISCUSSION POINTS

1 What are the problems of identifying the 'fastest-growing' or 'fastest-declining' religion (or religious organization)? Is the problem that the statistics for meaningful comparisons are not available, or is the entire quest an unproductive one?

2 Is it possible to define an 'active member' of a religious community? If not, what criteria can usefully be employed to measure the numerical strength of religious organizations?

3 In the 2001 UK Census, 71.6 per cent of the population defined themselves as 'Christian', 14.8 per cent as having no religion and 3.0 per cent as Muslim. In 2011 the UK Census revealed that 59.3 per cent self-defined as Christian, 4.8 per cent as Muslim and 25.1 per cent as having no religion. How should we explain this change? Has the British population lost its historical faith, or might there be other factors involved?

4 Can a religious organization ever be too small to be worth considering for academic study?

5

Key figures in the study of religion

George Chryssides

Chapter Outline

Early explorers	128
William Jones and the East India Company	130
Christian missionaries	132
The legacy of the East India Company	133
The European Enlightenment	137
Hegel, Feuerbach, Marx and Freud	138
William Robertson Smith (1846–94)	141
The World's Parliament of Religions and developments in Buddhist studies	143
E. B. Tylor (Sir Edward Burnett Tylor)	146
Emile Durkheim and early anthropology of religion	148
Max Weber	150
Modern anthropology	152
Conclusions	153
Discussion points	156

The study of religion has been continuing for little more than a century and a half, and it is therefore remarkable that the subject has come so far in such a short period. When we bear in mind that foreign travel was limited, and that the texts of the world's religions were in unknown languages, progress has been astonishing. This chapter aims to trace the origins of Western religious scholarship, and to introduce a number of key players in its history. Approaches to the study of religion today are considerably different from those adopted in the nineteenth century and the first half of the twentieth, and one may therefore be justified in evaluating the enterprise.

The study of history has several functions. First, it serves to contextualize our present situation: knowing our past can help us to understand how things have come to be as they are. Second, it is sometimes said that studying history 'helps us learn from our mistakes'. Readers may consider the extent to which this is true of military and political history, but certainly in the study of religion scholars have introduced theories and methods that seemed plausible, but which, having been debated and criticized over time, are no longer acceptable. The phenomenologists suggested that we should bracket our personal assumptions, empathize with religions that are not ours, and see them as they really are, but we must consider the inherent problems rather than glibly assenting to such an approach. This issue will be raised later.

Before serious academic study of religion began around the mid-nineteenth century, information was limited and unreliable, but a number of sources were available. In earlier centuries there were explorers who charted geographical territory, there were Christian missionaries, and there was the military expansion of the then superpowers, Britain, France, Spain and Portugal. The resulting occupation of eastern and Latin American countries meant that those countries' religions came to be studied. Archaeology later provided material and textual evidence of lost civilizations, and the nineteenth century witnessed the beginnings of translation work on eastern texts. The study of religion involves more than simply logging information, of course, and as we shall see much energy was channelled into two areas: methodological issues, generally relating to classification schemes; and speculation about what discoveries about religion revealed of its origins and function. This chapter covers a considerable area of ground; in the space available it cannot hope to be complete, but it aims to paint in broad brushstrokes the main landmarks in the subject, and identify the key issues.

Early explorers

From the late thirteenth century, various explorations by the Spanish, Portuguese, Dutch, French and British opened up new territories, and paved the way for studying the religions of indigenous peoples. Simon de la Loubère, who was sent by Louis XVI to Siam (now Thailand) in 1693, made some early observations about Buddhism. He hypothesized that the religion had come to Siam from Ceylon rather than India, and that the Chinese 'bonzees' (devotees of the Buddha) derived their doctrines from the Siamese.

The early discovery of Buddhism by Westerners raised a number of questions. The religions of different Far-Eastern countries did not look alike: anyone who visits Buddhist temples in the Far East cannot fail to notice that a Theravadin shrine with Shakyamuni (Gautama) Buddha as the focal point differs markedly from a Ch'an (Zen) temple, which will typically be much more elaborate, with some other *buddha-rupa* as the centrepiece, and possibly without any image of Shakyamuni. Should they both be regarded as aspects of Buddhism? Followers of the Buddha spoke of buddhas who existed before Gautama, who is now typically regarded as the religion's historical founder, and Indian scriptures spoke of the Buddha as an *avatar* ('descent') of the high God Vishnu. Did Buddhism exist before Gautama? Also, from which country did Buddhism originate before spreading throughout Asia? Some early writers such as William Jones and Horace Hayman Wilson advocated a 'two Buddha' theory: one was a historical figure who was regarded as the Vishnu-*avatar*, while the second was Gautama. On the question of the geographical origin, it was noted that the Buddha was depicted with curly black hair and it was surmised that he originated in Africa, possibly Ethiopia.

Explorers, colonizers and missionaries were early pioneers who helped to open up the study of eastern religions. The Jesuit missionary Louis le Comte wrote of the Buddha in 1697 that 'all the Indies have been poysoned with his pernicious doctrine', declaring that the religions of Siam, Tartary (formerly the Central Asian territory from the Black Sea to Tibet), Japan and China were one. Explorers included Vivien de Saint Martin (1802–97), a cartographer who wrote a treatise on the geography of North Africa. (He is mentioned by Jules Verne.) His travels in Asia enabled him to claim to have determined the route of the Aryans when they invaded India. Other discoveries served to reinforce ideas about the origins of religion more generally. In 1914 a number of cave paintings were discovered in the Dordogne area of the Franco-Spanish border. These appeared to depict huntsmen pursuing their prey, but curiously the paintings were located deep inside the caves, rather than displayed for public view. A painting at La Grotte des Trois Frères portrays an animal figure with a human face and antlers.

The European colonization of Asia and Africa helped to advance the study of World Religions. Of particular importance was Napoleon's expedition to Egypt, which included a number of scholars and scientists who discovered much about ancient Egyptian culture and religion. This was the first systematic attempt to study a culture, and paved the way for later archaeological expeditions, the best known of which was the discovery by Howard Carter and Lord Carnarvon of Tutankhamun's tomb in 1922. Excavations were also carried out in Masala, providing evidence of first-century Jewish sects. Other archaeological work related to Mesopotamia, where the ancient city of Nineveh was discovered as well as evidence of Sumerian culture. The focus on Mesopotamia was of particular interest to scholars of the Judaeo-Christian scriptures, affording evidence of a culture that existed side by side with that of ancient Israel. Archaeological finds included some important ancient texts, such as the *Egyptian Book of the Dead*, and the *Mesopotamian Epic of Gilgamesh*.

Other archaeological expeditions unearthed information about eastern religions. Stone pillars bearing the 'Rock Edicts' of the Indian King Ashoka (third-century BCE) were discovered, providing evidence of the spread of Buddhism, which Ashoka's rule encouraged. John Marshall's excavations in the Indus Valley in the 1920s revealed some of India's prehistory, which extended back as far as 3500 BCE. The civilizations he discovered at Mohenjodaro and Harappa indicated that an advanced culture had existed long before the Aryan invasions of 1500 to 1000 BCE. The twentieth century witnessed the excavation of a number of important sites in Asia: Angkor Wat in Cambodia, Borobudur in Indonesia, and the Ellora and Ajanta caves in India, revealing evidence of the spread of Buddhism. These sites have been preserved for both scholars and the general public.

Archaeology makes its contribution, but has its limitations. Archaeology provides objects rather than theories and explanations, and the purpose of the paintings at Dordogne is a matter of conjecture. Scholars typically inferred that they were connected with magic, perhaps about improving one's prospects in hunting. Such conclusions reinforced the notion that the roots of religion lay in magic – a theory to which we shall return. Archaeology, too, can only discover substantial and durable objects. We cannot excavate music, although musical instruments can be found: until the technological era there was no way of preserving actual sounds. Even musical notation is relatively new – it was devised around the fifteenth-century CE in Europe. Stone artefacts are more likely to survive than wooden ones; consequently, any religion that expressed itself in wood is less likely to have bequeathed any of its relics. Archaeology tends to provide evidence of dead religions, and of course the study of relics has to be supplemented by the study of religion as a living phenomenon. It is to the study of living religions that we now turn.

William Jones and the East India Company

The British colonization of India heralded a growing acquaintance with India's religions. The East India Company was formed in 1600 with the aim of promoting trade with South Asia, South-East Asia and India, and helped to consolidate British rule on the Indian subcontinent. The best known of the civil servants who pioneered the Western discovery of eastern faiths was William Jones (1746–94). Jones was born in London, schooled at Harrow, and undertook higher education at University College, Oxford, where he became proficient in several ancient languages: Latin, Greek, Hebrew, Aramaic, Persian and Sanskrit. He commenced studies in law in 1770 and departed for India, where he became a judge in Calcutta in 1783. Jones' interest in Hinduism was partly professional and partly a pastime. He was responsible to the Governor of India, Warren Hastings, who had initiated the translation of the ancient *Laws of Manu*, and who had promulgated a judicial plan in 1772 to govern India by its own laws. Jones' role was to study the ancient Indian law code, to translate it, and to clarify and codify the *Dharma-Shastras*. (Jones was not the first to attempt this: he had predecessors in Alexander Dow, Nathaniel Brassy Halhed and George Costard.) Jones' approach was not exclusively text-based; he consulted Indian pundits, seeking their understanding of the ancient law code.

In 1784 Jones became the first president of the Asiatic Society and editor of the journal *Asiatick Researches*. In the same year he completed a study titled *On the Gods of Greece, Italy and India*. This work claimed to show historico-religious connections between the ancient Graeco-Roman pantheon and the forms of deity that were worshipped in India. He viewed the religions of India as polytheistic, and in common with a number of writers of that time and later, he adopted an evolutionary approach to religion. Perceiving Hinduism as polytheistic, he regarded it as a stage on the evolutionary scale, which would culminate in the acceptance of Christianity as India became civilized. Jones' study of the *Vedas* (the earliest Indian religious texts) suggested to him that there existed an original monotheism in India: the *Rig Veda*, for example, asserts that 'the Real is One, though sages name it variously' (*Rig Veda*, 1, 164:46). This original monotheism, he thought, had become corrupted, causing Indian religion to degenerate into worship of a plethora of deities.

Coupled to Jones' 'original monotheism' theory was his belief that important parallels could be found between the Bible and ancient Hindu texts. For example, the story of *matsya-avatara* – the manifestation of the great God Vishnu as a turtle – occurs within the context of a great flood, confirming the biblical story of Noah, who enabled his family and a plethora of animal species to survive this disaster. Both events are associated with law-giving: on God's behalf Noah prescribes the first law code, principally relating to food laws, and Jones suggested that Noah was to be equated with the Hindu law-giver Manu. One principal difference, however, between the *matsya-avatara* story and that of Noah is the timing of the events: Hinduism presupposes a much longer time period between the flood and the present day. This showed, Jones believed, that although the stories related in the Indian tradition confirm those of the Bible, the points that do not conform indicate that the Indian timescales need reappraisal, or that some of the stories themselves are simply myths. Jones referred to the 'fertile and inventive genius' of the writers of Indian scriptures, and of the 'mystic religious allegory' of the Radha-Krishna stories.

Jones thus showed considerable respect for the Indian religious tradition, but it might be fair to say that his respect was primarily for the aesthetic merit of the Indian texts. He liked the hymns to the deities in the *Rig Veda*, but they were poetry rather than theology, and he regarded their ideas as primitive in contrast with Europe's emphasis on reason and science. He did not condemn Hinduism, but he viewed it as a retrograde form of spirituality, and his writings employ such terms as 'heathen' and 'idolatry' with reference to the Indian tradition. Indeed, the very quest for clarifying and codifying Indian law implied that he perceived the Western legal system as preferable to the traditional Indian law codes.

Despite these criticisms, Jones is nonetheless important in pioneering the study of the Hindu tradition. Although not an academic by profession, he aroused an interest in Indian philosophy and religion, and was the first to undertake a serious study of the tradition that became accessible to others. It is a telling tribute to Jones that his statue can be seen today in St Paul's Cathedral in London.

Christian missionaries

There were other Westerners whose encounters with Hinduism were less favourable than Jones, but who were nonetheless early pioneers in opening up Western understanding of other religious traditions. Christian missionaries have played an important part in the development of the study of religion, even though their evaluations of other religions have been somewhat negative. Although missionizing from the West has taken place since the fifteenth century, substantial written accounts of other faiths only began to emerge in the early nineteenth century. Of particular importance are William Carey (1761–1833), William Ward (1769–1823) and Joshua Marshman (1768–1837), commonly known as the 'Serampore Trio' on account of their collegial work in Bengal as Baptist missionaries. Carey is the best-known of the trio. He wrote in defence of missionary practice, while Ward wrote much more substantially on the religion of the 'Hindoos'. Ward's principal work was his *Account of the Writings, Religion and Manners of the Hindoos* (1811), later expanded to four volumes as *A View of the History, Literature and Mythology of the Hindoos* (1818). Ward's account is detailed and is copiously illustrated to depict Hindu deities, customs and practices. Being a missionary in contact with the local people, his account of Hinduism comes from its grass-roots, by contrast with the more text-based accounts of other writers of his time. Ward also undertook some translation of Hindu scriptures, and commented on them.

Ward was not impressed by Hinduism, either in its written form or its practical expression. In contrast with William Jones' cautiously positive evaluation, Ward described the *Puranas* as 'filth'. (The *Puranas* are the Hindu scriptures that include Krishna's erotic escapades with the milkmaids of Vrindaban.) He regarded the *Laws of Manu*, which Jones attempted to codify, as immoral, since they sanctioned adultery and other vices. To Ward the Hindu gods represented and condoned vice, and were worshipped as idols. Among the practices Ward singles out for condemnation were the caste system, *sati* burning, polygamy, child marriage, infanticide and *antarjali* (the practice of exposing the bodies of the sick on river banks). Ward's assessment of Hinduism could scarcely be more negative. He writes:

> '. . . if the vices of lying deceit, dishonesty, and impurity, can degrade a people, then the Hindoos have sunk to the utmost depths of human depravity'. (quoted in Sugirtharajah, 2003, p. 82)

Ward concluded that only divine providence could have subjected such a large country as India to the governance of a small island like Britain. The Hindus needed the Gospel in order to be purged of their vices and superstitions.

Of course, no present-day student of religion would be permitted to write about Hinduism – or any other belief system – in the way in which Ward did, although such examples can still be found among the writings of religious 'outsiders'. But these were early days, and Ward at least did his readers the service of providing detailed information about Hindu scriptures and practice. Ward's work was read in the West by writers such as Ralph Waldo Emerson and Henry Thoreau, who were able to propagate more conciliatory accounts of Eastern faiths and commend their positive features.

Not all Christian missionaries had such a negative view of Hinduism. John Nicol Farquhar (1861–1929) was sent to India in 1891 by the London Missionary Society. After studying at the University of Aberdeen Farquhar went to Oxford, where he came under the influence of Müller and Monier-Williams. Farquhar's years in India led him to write prolifically on Indian religions, especially Hinduism, and after returning to England he became Professor of Comparative Religion at the University of Manchester. His writings include *The Age and Origin of the Gita* (1904), *Gita and Gospel* (1906), *The Crown of Hinduism* (1913), *Hinduism: Its Content and Value* (1920a), and *An Outline of the Religious Literature of India* (1920b). Of these writings the most influential, and the most discussed, is *The Crown of Hinduism*.

Farquhar contended that the older, exclusivist, Christian approaches to other religions were harmful, and he rejected the idea that Christianity should displace religions such as Hinduism. Other faiths did not consist of heathens in total darkness, he believed, but rather people who were imperfectly striving towards an ultimate truth and salvation. Farquhar advocated a more empathetic understanding of Hinduism than that of William Ward, and he laid emphasis on Jesus' words about the Jewish teachings of his time: 'I have not come to destroy the law, or the prophets: I am not come to destroy, but to fulfil' (Mt. 5.17; KJV). He argued that just as Christianity was the culmination of Judaism, so the other faiths of the world were imperfectly searching for the final complete truth which could only be found in the Christian faith. Farquhar wrote, 'In Him [Jesus] is focused every ray of light that shines in Hinduism. He is the Crown of the faith of India.' Farquhar was very much influenced by the evolutionary theories of his time, viewing Hinduism as the religion that was still at the infant stage, waiting to grow into Christian completion. To quote Farquhar: 'The author of the Gita would have been a Christian, had he known Jesus' (*Permanent Lessons of the Gita*, 1903, p. 31; quoted in Sughirtharajah, 2003, p. 95).

In common with the other evolutionists of religion, Farquhar saw evidence for Christianity's superiority in Hinduism's apparent polytheism, in contrast with the former's 'purest spiritual monotheism'. Additionally, Farquhar held that the Christian Bible was a superior book, having greater power to transform human society. Christianity was an organized religion with a clear historical foundation, and which recommended service to humanity rather than Hinduism's ideal of the *sannyasin* (world renouncer). Thus, although Farquhar was less vitriolic in his critique of Hinduism, he still saw it as superstitious, idolatrous and morally inferior.

The legacy of the East India Company

The East India Company and the Royal Asiatic Society did much to propagate the study of Indian religions. One important bridge between colonial interest and academic study was made by Horace Hayman Wilson (1786–1860). Wilson initially studied medicine in London and came to work as a surgeon in Bengal for the East India Company. Wilson was extremely versatile: he was conversant with metallurgy, and provided advice on coinage to the mint at Calcutta. His interests extended to India's ancient languages, and he became Secretary of the Asiatic Society of Bengal. He translated Kalidasa's lyrical poem *Meghaduta* ('Cloud Messenger'), and compiled *Select Specimens of the Theatre of the Hindus* (1827), an anthology of Hindu drama, consisting of his translations of six classical Indian plays, and a synopsis of a further 23. Hayman Wilson was one of the founding members of the Royal Asiatic Society. He prepared the first Sanskrit-English dictionary with the help of Indian scholars. His *Mackenzie Collection* (1828) was a catalogue of Indian manuscripts collected by Col Colin Mackenzie, some of which are now located in the British Library. When the Boden Chair of Sanskrit was established in Oxford in 1831, Hayman Wilson was appointed as its first holder. He initiated the University's collection of Sanskrit manuscripts, now housed at the University of Oxford's Indian Institute.

Wilson's interests lay in wider Indian culture, but his pupil Monier Monier-Williams (1819–99), who succeeded him, focused his Indological interests on religion. Like his predecessor, Monier-Williams was acquainted directly with Indian culture: he was born in Mumbai (previously known as Bombay) and having travelled widely on the subcontinent studied and subsequently taught in the East India Company's College until the Indian Mutiny of 1857. After two years at Cheltenham, Monier-Williams competed fiercely with Friedrich Max Müller for the Boden Professorship. Monier-Williams' success was largely attributable to his more conservative views. Müller was acquainted with the authors of *Essays and Reviews* – a controversial anthology edited by Benjamin Jowett in 1860, which promoted the highly controversial advances in German liberal biblical scholarship – and had intended to contribute an essay on World Religions to a proposed sequel. Monier-Williams had different objectives: being more conservative, he wanted Christian missionaries to learn Sanskrit in order to debate with Hindu *pandits* (scholars of philosophy and religion) about their scriptures, and he explicitly professed the wish that all of India should be converted to Christianity.

Although the vast majority of twenty-first-century scholars would have serious reservations about Monier-Williams' objectives, his contribution to the study of Indian religions was considerable. His approach was linguistic and empirical: one major contribution to scholarship was his Sanskrit–English Dictionary, which gave further impetus to textual study. Monier-Williams made the first translation of *Shikshapatri*, an ethical code attributed to Lord Swaminarayan, and which continues to be used by Swaminarayan devotees. (Swaminarayan (1781–1830) was an Indian guru who taught in Gujarat.)

Although Monier-Williams wrote principally on Hinduism, his writings extended to Buddhism, Jainism, Zoroastrianism and Islam. His *Hinduism* (1877) proved popular, despite the fact that it is not easy to read. Monier-Williams endeavoured to present

FIGURE 5.1 *Hindu shrine, Pushkar, India.*

Hinduism as a living religion, as well as one that is based on ancient scriptures, and he described pilgrimages, festivals and the various forms of Hindu deity. His account of Hinduism tends to favour *advaita vedanta* – philosophical non-dualism – which he held to be the philosophy propagated by the *Vedas* and the *Upanishads*. On this view, there is no ultimate distinction between individual soul (*atman*) and the divine (*brahman*): in the words of the *Chandogya Upanishad*, *tat tvam asi*, which is Sanskrit for 'You are it' (i.e. the divine). Monier-Williams viewed *jnana marga* as the normative form of Hinduism: this is the spiritual path of wisdom, pursued by holy men who renounce the world to engage in meditation. *Karma marga* (the path of good deeds) and *bhakti marga* (the path of devotion) constituted 'popular Hinduism', he contended. This slant on the Hindu religions has continued to exert its influence on popular textbooks and on the way Hinduism tends to be taught, although it has since been challenged.

Monier-Williams' Christian bias is evident in much of his work. He described Hinduism, Buddhism and Islam as 'the three chief false religions' (in Carpenter, 1900) – a characterization that would not be accepted from today's students of religion. However, it is important to note that this description was an advance on some of the earlier Christian missionaries' evaluations of 'non-Christian' faiths. At least Monier-Williams was prepared to describe them as 'great'; he was conceding that they had significant merit, although lacking complete truth. In this regard he rated them more highly than missionaries such as Reginald Heber, whose famous hymn contains the lines: 'The heathen in his blindness / bows down to wood and stone.' Monier-Williams avoided the term 'heathen' in his writings.

Monier-Williams' rival Friedrich Max Müller (1823–1900) was arguably the greatest contributor to the study and translation of Hindu and Buddhist writings. He oversaw the translation of the 50-volume *Sacred Books of the East* – a collection that is still used by students of eastern religions. Müller was responsible for the first scholarly edition of the *Rig Veda*, which he started in 1861 and completed in 1877. Also of importance was T. W. Rhys Davids (1843–1922), who founded the Pali Text Society, and whose work principally involved the translation of Theravada Buddhism's scriptures. Theravada Buddhism was generally regarded as the primordial form of Buddhism (a view that still prevails in the majority of textbooks on Buddhism), and Davids' emphasis led scholars to focus on Buddhism's Theravada rather than its Mahayana forms. A number of other translations were responsible for producing English editions of Mahayana texts, which became incorporated in Müller's *Sacred Books of the East*.

Müller did much more than provide translations of eastern texts. He used the method of comparative philology to provide insights into the origins and development of religion. Müller's comparative philology involved comparing three sets of languages, which he believed corresponded to three great races of people: the Turanians (including the Ural-Altaic), the Semites and the Aryans. Müller believed that careful examination of the languages yielded the conclusion that these three races were originally a unity, but had come to diverge through time and occupy different parts of the globe. Müller did relatively little study of the Turanians, and his main specialism was the Aryans. His comparisons focused on the names of deities, similarities between mythologies and parallels in religious terminology. For example, the name of the sky god in the *Vedas* is Dyaus Pitar: since the letter 'd' typically mutates into a 'z' or a 'j' in Middle-Eastern vocabulary, 'Dyaus' becomes 'Zeus' (the name of the ancient Greek principal deity). Similarly, 'Dyaus Pitar' can readily be paired with 'Jupiter' (the principal deity of ancient Rome). An obvious example of a common myth is the one noted by William Jones, the story of the flood: the Book of Genesis recounts the story of Noah's ark (Gen. 6.1–9.17), while Hindu scriptures tell how Vishnu's *matsya-avatara* avatar (the fish *avatar*) saved humanity from a watery disaster (*Mahabharata* 3.185); and there is likewise an ancient Babylonian flood-myth, recounting how God created the world from a watery chaos.

The European Enlightenment

Much of the study of religion was influenced by the ideas of the European Enlightenment. It is not possible in a short space to draw out the details of this somewhat loose eighteenth- to nineteenth-century phenomenon, but it is helpful to note a few key notions that were current in Europe in this period. The first of these was empiricism, a school of philosophy claiming that all our knowledge is based on sensory perception. This entailed a rejection of blind faith, and indeed a questioning of all supernatural explanations and concepts. Sensory observation was – and remains – a key feature of scientific thinking, which was then in the ascendant: scientists base their theories and explanations on observables, and do not admit religious or super-empirical hypotheses in their attempts to understand the world. Empiricism and scientific thinking require the rejection of ideas of supernatural intervention. Although there are religious believers who claim to have experienced divine healing or witnessed a miracle, science works on the assumption that nature is uniform and seeks to define natural laws that admit of no exceptions, not even by divine intervention.

One important theory stemming from the Enlightenment was evolution, which has already been mentioned in connection with Jones' analysis of Hinduism. Although evolutionary theory is frequently associated with Charles Darwin, he only applied a prevalent way of thinking to biology. With the rise of the Enlightenment in Europe, it was not uncommon to see society in general as progressing from the simple to the complex, from primitive credulity to the rational and scientific. Evolutionary thinking swiftly came to be applied to religion. Some thinkers, such as Auguste Comte (1798–1857), regarded religion itself as a manifestation of the primitive, contending that there were three stages in human development: the religious, the metaphysical and finally the scientific (Comte, 1830). Other thinkers – for example the Christian missionaries – did not take the view that religion would be superseded by science, but rather that the true religion (by which they meant Christianity) would triumph over the practices and worldviews of the benighted heathens. Slightly later than Comte, Herbert Spencer (1820–1903) in England wrote much in defence of evolutionary theory. Evolution was therefore part of Europe's *zeitgeist* rather than the insight of one single thinker like Darwin. Before the Enlightenment period, Christian scholarship tended to focus on Christian theology and Biblical Studies. Scholars had noted that different gospels appeared to give different accounts of events in Jesus' life, or arrange them in chronologically different ways. Andreas Osiander (1498–1552), for example, produced a *Harmony of the Gospels* in which he assumed that where two accounts of apparently the same event contradicted each other, two different though similar events had occurred. Thus Jesus is portrayed variously as feeding a crowd of 4,000 and of 5,000 people. Both accounts were correct, according to Osiander, since these were two separate incidents (Mk 6.35–44; Mk 8.1–9).

The scientific attitude of the Enlightenment rejected the harmonizers' approach. The study of history, like the study of the physical world, had to be scientific: it adopted a definite methodology, examined the empirical evidence, and raised critical questions about source material, such as where it came from, and the extent to which it could be regarded as reliable. Of particular importance in opening up critical questions about sources was the work of two German scholars, Karl H. Graf (1815–69) and Julius Wellhausen (1844–1918), who argued that the Pentateuch (the first five books of the Jewish and Christian Bibles, known to the Jews as the Torah) was not divinely dictated or the work of a single author (previously assumed to be Moses), but was a composite work with at least four identifiable authors whose work had been collated by a redactionist.

New Testament studies underwent a comparable revolution. The early rationalists who challenged the views of the old-style harmonizers were Hermann Samuel Reimarus (1694–1768), J. S. Semler (1725–91) and H. E. G. Paulus (1761–1851). Their approach included a questioning of the miraculous elements in the biblical narrative; where the Bible recounted a miracle, they reasoned, it was likely that an event occurred with a perfectly natural explanation, but that such an event became embellished and imbued with miraculous elements. Thus, when Jesus was said to have fed the crowd of 4,000 or 5,000, it was more likely that he had provided 'spiritual food' through his teachings; later embellishments caused his preaching to be translated into a miraculous healing story. Commentators came to question whether there was always a historical base for the miraculous stories that the gospel writers recounted. One of the first to adopt this radical approach was D. F. Strauss (1808–74), whose key work was the *Life of Jesus Critically Examined*. Strauss was the first New Testament scholar to use the term 'myth' with regard to the gospel accounts. The figure of Jesus as portrayed in the gospels was the product of Christian messianic interpretation, he thought, and many (although not all) of the stories written about him were attempts to illustrate this theological position in narrative form. In particular, Strauss was significantly influenced by the philosophy of Hegel, and saw Jesus as the man in whom the infinite Spirit actualizes itself in the finite.

Hegel, Feuerbach, Marx and Freud

Something needs to be said about the influence of Georg Wilhelm Friedrich Hegel (1770–1831) at this juncture. Hegel was a German idealist philosopher – that is to say, one who emphasized the superiority of the non-empirical over the empirical. The term 'idealism' relates to the word 'idea' rather than 'ideal', and originated among philosophers who argued that the ideas of the mind constituted ultimate reality, rather than objects in the empirical world, which were mind-dependent. Hegel's starting point was that everything in the world was in a state of change. Such change, however, was not random but unfolded in accordance with a 'dialectical' pattern. Every concept, he contended, generated its opposite: for example, if one thinks of 'being', this implies 'non-being'. Being and non-being are in contradiction, however, and such contradictions require resolution, or need to be overcome. Hegel used technical vocabulary for such pairs of contradictions: Being and non-being are the 'thesis' and the 'antithesis', and they need to be resolved in a 'synthesis'. In the case of Being and non-being the synthesis is 'becoming', but this synthesis itself generates its opposite and thus becomes the new thesis that generates a new antithesis requiring yet another synthesis, and so on. This process of crab-like movements from thesis to antithesis to synthesis is known as 'dialectic'.

Hegel perceived the entire universe as being subject to this dialectical process. Events in the world are manifestations of the finite, but in the finite its antithesis the Infinite is progressively manifesting itself. Thus human history is progressing to a point where all its changes and contradictions will be resolved – the final manifestation of the Absolute or Spirit. Hegel claimed to perceive this dialectical process operating through the history of religion which he divides, unsurprisingly, into three stages. First there is the religion of nature, in which God is conceived as less than Spirit. There are three subdivisions in this first stage: (1) magic, or 'immediate religion'; (2) 'religion of substance' which is exemplified in Chinese religion, Hinduism and Buddhism; and (3) the religions of Persia, Syria and Egypt, in which God is regarded as the good and the 'undifferentiated individual'. This first stage is polytheistic. The second stage is that of 'spiritual individuality'; there is a single God, who is Spirit and an individual person: this is exemplified by the religions of ancient Judaism, and Graeco-Roman religion. In this phase the divine stands apart from the human, demanding obedience and sacrifice in order to be propitiated. The final stage is that of 'absolute religion', which Hegel equated with Christianity. In the first two stages, Spirit is immanent and transcendent respectively, but in the third stage the immanent–transcendent contradiction is resolved in the union of the Infinite and finite, which is manifested in the incarnation of Jesus Christ. Likewise, the contradiction between divine unity and plurality is resolved in the Christian doctrine of the Trinity, in which God is the triune three-in-one. This is not to say that all Christians have experienced Christianity's absolute truth; in order to attain this one must view the Christian faith in pure conceptual form: philosophy must unite with practice to achieve the perfect expression of the Absolute Spirit.

All this is difficult material, even for the specialist student of philosophy. However, although Hegel did not offer new data to inform the study of religion, his speculative theorizing on the subject proved highly influential both to Christianity and to the study of religion. Hegel had his supporters and his critics, and each took the academic study of religion in different directions. It should be noted that Hegel's notion that there are progressive stages in the development of religion paved the way for the somewhat later evolutionary approaches. It hardly needs to be pointed out that Hegel placed Christianity on top, regarding it as superior to its competitors, all of which were presumed to be less developed.

  Hegel's ideas were taken a stage further by Ludwig Feuerbach (1804–72). Hegel had contended that matter was inferior to Spirit, but Feuerbach emphasized the importance of matter and of the empirical world. His most famous exposition of his ideas is found in *The Essence of Christianity* (1841), which was translated from German into English by George Eliot (1853). Feuerbach believed that the human's ideal aspirations were reason, will and love. Since most humans did not behave totally in accordance with these three ideals, they experienced alienation and consequently projected their aspirations to a metaphysical realm. God was therefore not someone or something with any ultimate reality, but rather humanity's creation in an attempt to re-appropriate its essence. As Feuerbach put it, 'man is God to man'.

  Feuerbach's ideas were appropriated in turn by Karl Marx (1818–83) and Sigmund Freud (1856–1939). Marx used Hegel's dialectic as a means of understanding the class struggles inherent in human history. Pre-industrial society entailed a dialectical opposition between landlord and serf, causing revolution. The new society that emerged generated its own dialectical tensions, this time between bourgeoisie and proletariat, with the bourgeoisie exploiting the workers by owning the means of production and alienating workers from the true rewards of their labour. This state of affairs could only lead to revolution, followed by the utopia of the classless society. Marx, together with those of his collaborator Friedrich Engels (1820–95), expressed these ideas in their *Communist Manifesto* (1848).

  Much has been written on what Marx meant, why his predictions of future revolutions were not fulfilled and how subsequent communist leaders developed his ideas. Our concern here, however, is with the role that Marx assigned to religion. Marx did not view religion as offering a solution to humankind's problems. These problems lay in the here-and-now, and it was important to address society's this-worldly state, rather than look to some hypothetical other-worldly realm for an ultimate solution. Religion, Marx taught, could actually be harmful for the workers: instead of supporting the revolution against the bourgeoisie, they would be more likely to accept their lot in their present lives if they believed that there was spiritual hope in some afterlife. Religion therefore slowed down the revolution, and acted as a false comforter to the oppressed. As Marx put it in his famous dictum, 'Religion is the opium of the people' (Marx, 1843).

  Sigmund Freud gave a similarly negative evaluation of religion, but from a different standpoint. Being the founding figure of modern psychoanalysis, Freud was anxious to show what it was about the human mind that gave rise to religious belief. He is best known for two short but significant works on religion: *Totem and Taboo* (1913) and *The Future of an Illusion* (1927). In an earlier essay entitled 'Obsessive Actions and Religious Practices' (1907) Freud argued that religious ritual activity closely resembles obsessive behaviour, in which one behaves in accordance with a set of fixed unwritten rules that serve no obvious purpose. One example that Freud gives is of a patient who obsessively noted the serial numbers of every banknote that passed through her hands. He found this to be connected with a past incident in which the patient asked her lover to change a five kronen piece. He promised never to part with the coin, since he had received it from her; however, because five kronen coins are indistinguishable she had no means of verifying whether his promise was serious or whether he had kept it. Freud argued that obsessive behaviour frequently represents some previous experience of which the agent is unaware.

There is no sharp distinction, Freud claimed, between neurotic behaviour and religious ceremony, which is similarly circumscribed with highly prescriptive rules serving no obvious purpose. *Totem and Taboo* claims to provide the explanation of such behaviour. The book's sub-title is *Resemblances between the Psychic Lives of Savages and Neurotics*, and it simultaneously purports to explain the origins of religion and the causes of its continued practice. Freud's answer was that religious worship is a relic of deference to one's ancestors. Since ancestors are no longer alive to be shown respect, acts of deference become suppressed in one's unconscious and re-emerge in a displaced form. Once religion is understood in this way there can be no reason to continue its practice, just as there is no reason to note meticulously every banknote one handles. The title of Freud's *The Future of an Illusion* (1927) is self-explanatory: the illusion is of course religion, and once it is recognized as such it will be abandoned in favour of science, for to act in accordance with scientific thinking serves an obvious set of purposes.

Feuerbach, Marx and Freud did not uncover any new data concerning religion, but they offered important explanations of religion which continue to be debated. Their accounts are often labelled 'reductionist': that is to say, none of them believed that there existed any transcendent reality to which religion alluded. Instead, religion is to be 'explained away': it is all illusion, being nothing more than a response to alienation or repression, or else wishful thinking or obsessive behaviour.

William Robertson Smith (1846–94)

Other scholars were more positive towards religion. One such figure was William Robertson Smith (1846–94), a scholar whose name is little known but who is nonetheless a pivotal figure in the study of religion. William Robertson Smith was a Scottish Free Presbyterian minister whose influence extended to biblical scholarship, social anthropology and the psychology of religion. Although his writings have fallen into neglect, they were read both by Sigmund Freud and Emile Durkheim, who drew on them considerably and allowed them to shape their thinking. A precocious youth, William Robertson Smith entered the University of Aberdeen as a student at the age of only 14. He studied mathematics and natural philosophy (primarily physics) before embarking on studies in divinity, specializing in Hebrew and Semitic religions. At the age of 24 he was appointed to the Chair of Hebrew at Aberdeen Free Church College.

Smith was profoundly influenced by the ideas of the European Enlightenment, believing that scientific rational methods should be applied to the Bible. Smith was asked to contribute entries to the current edition of *Encyclopaedia Britannica*, then embarking on its third edition. His contributions included articles on 'Bible' and 'Sacrifice'. It was his entry on 'Bible' that caused a stir. Although Smith preferred to use the term 'historical criticism' to 'higher criticism', he supported the view that had emerged from scholars in Germany and Holland, that the Bible was not an inerrant book and could not straightforwardly serve as an infallible guide to the history of Israel and its surrounding nations. The Bible, he argued, contained myths relating to the founding of a nation; prophets did not predict some far-distant future, but offered social and political comment on current affairs; and they did not explicitly predict the birth of Jesus Christ, events in his life or his death. Angels were not necessarily substantial beings: their presence in parts of the Bible could be attributed to 'conscious poetic art'. Some books were written by multiple authors: for example, Smith distinguishes two authors of the Book of Isaiah.

Although these ideas are widely accepted among present-day biblical scholars, they seemed outrageous in a society that had been accustomed to thinking of the Bible as an infallible book, divinely dictated, which pointed in its entirety towards Jesus Christ's atoning sacrifice for humankind. Smith was taken to task by the Presbytery of Aberdeen, who began a prolonged and acrimonious heresy trial. When allowed to address the presbytery, Smith did not try to persuade them that his ideas were true, but rather that tolerance should be extended to scholars like himself, who should be free to explore such emergent ideas of biblical scholarship. The outcome of the trial was that Smith was formally admonished in 1880, and the following year he was deprived of his professorial chair. In 1883 he moved to Cambridge, where he continued to develop his ideas and to write.

Smith's principal writings were *The Old Testament in the Jewish Church* (1881), *The Prophets of Israel* (1882), *Kinship and Marriage in Early Arabia* (1885), and *The Religion of the Semites* (1889). The last title was particularly important, since Smith explored the relationships between the Israelites and the Babylonians, Assyrians, Phoenicians and Syrians, commenting on their mutual trade and their political alliances. He examined the role of Jewish sacrificial rites and their place in Hebrew religion, as well as the cosmogonies of the surrounding nations, making particular reference to the contrast between Israelite monotheism and the polytheistic worldviews of Israel's neighbours. Because of these interests, Smith is sometimes described as the father of social anthropology (a title sometimes reserved for Durkheim): his focus was not so much on individual prophetic leaders, but on interactions and religious rites within the ancient societies. Sigmund Freud was particularly interested in, and developed Smith's ideas on, sacrifice.

All the time, Smith remained a practising Christian and did not see these new intellectual ideas as in any way undermining the Christian faith. In fact, in *The Religion of the Semites* he extolled the superiority of the Jewish prophets (whose status was endorsed by Christianity) over Muhammad. Although much influenced by the

Dutch Protestant scholar Abraham Kuenen (1828–91), he regarded the latter's views as 'naturalistic' – 'reductionist' in our terminology. In other words, he believed that they removed the supernatural from the explanations of religious history and society, regarding scriptures as merely human inventions. Smith believed that one's approach should be rational, but not 'rationalistic'.

The World's Parliament of Religions and developments in Buddhist studies

Some mention should be made of the World's Parliament of Religions, held in Chicago in 1893. The event was organized to coincide with the 400th anniversary of Christopher Columbus' 'discovery' of America in 1492, which was to be marked by an Exposition featuring the world's technological, commercial and cultural achievements. It was felt that humankind's religious achievements should not go unmarked, so the World's Parliament of Religions was proposed to run alongside the Exposition. Plans were delayed, and the Exposition and the Parliament came adrift from the centenary by one year. The Parliament was an unprecedented gathering of some 7,000 people who represented all the world's major religious traditions, as well as some of the minor ones. The word 'Parliament' was slightly misleading, since it suggests an official body empowered to control and decide on behalf of the world's religions. Strictly speaking it was not a parliament, but a large interfaith gathering which aimed to promote inter-religious understanding, bringing together a wide range of scholars from different traditions to speak on the present state of their respective religions and the light they might shed on other traditions and on current affairs. Max Müller was one of the invited speakers, but was unable to attend in person: he sent a paper, which was read during the 20-day gathering.

The Parliament had an important impact on Buddhist scholarship. Paul Carus (1852–1919), a publisher as well as one of the speakers, was highly impressed by Soen Shaku (1859–1919), the Rinzai Zen master and Abbot of Kamakura's Engakuji Monastery, who attended the event. Carus wanted to commission material on Zen Buddhism from Soen Shaku, who in turn recommended his pupil Daisetz Teitaro Suzuki (1870–1966). Soen Shaku returned to the United States in 1905 together with three pupils, including Suzuki, who proved to be a prolific writer on Zen. His three-volume *Essays in Zen Buddhism* (1927–34) proved to be one of the most important and influential pieces of writing on the subject. Suzuki's writings were of interest not only to students of religion but to spiritual seekers, and his work was as influential on the development of Western Buddhism in the West as it was on Western Buddhist scholarship.

The first translation of Buddhist scriptures in Roman characters was done by the Danish scholar Viggo Fausboll (1821–1908), who translated the *Dhammapada* into Latin (1855). Other translators, more helpfully, used their own spoken languages.

Eugène Burnouf (1801–52), under whom Max Müller studied in his early career, translated Pali texts into French, together with his colleague Christian Lassen (1800–76). Burnouf's *Essai sur le Pali* (1826) effectively initiated the academic study of Buddhism.

In the meantime Buddhist studies were developing through the translation of Buddhist scriptures, largely due to the work of T. W. Rhys-Davids (1843–1922) and his wife Caroline A. F. Rhys-Davids (1857–1942). T. W. Rhys-Davids previously worked for the Archaeological Commission and was involved in the excavation of the town of Anaradhapura in Ceylon (now Sri Lanka). He wrote a series of articles for the *Royal Asiatic Society Journal* (Ceylon Branch) during the period 1870–2. After a brief career in law he returned to Buddhist studies, becoming Professor of Pali at the University of London, a post which he held from 1882 until 1904. The following year he was appointed to the Chair of Comparative Religion at the University of Manchester. The Rhys-Davids' translation work was exclusively on Theravada scriptures, and this tended to reinforce the still-prevalent idea that Theravada Buddhism is the normative form of the religion.

The Western acquisition of knowledge of Tibetan Buddhism provides an interesting case study. The first documented Western traveller to Tibet was the Jesuit missionary Ippolito Desideri (1684–1733), who walked from Delhi to Ladakh, where he stayed from 1716 to 1721 when he was called back by the Vatican authorities. Desideri stayed at the famous Sera monastery and studied Buddhist scriptures. Csoma de Koros (Sándor Körösi Csoma, 1784–1836) later arrived in Ladakh. De Koros was a Hungarian scholar whose purposes were academic rather than evangelistic; being a philologist by way of specialism, his emphasis was on the origins of Tibetan religion. His contribution to Tibetan studies was impressive, causing him to be known as 'the father of Tibetology': he learned Tibetan, studied under Buddhist lamas, and compiled a Tibetan–English dictionary, a grammar and a compendium of Buddhist terminology.

Brian Houghton Hodgson (1800–94) worked for the East India Company, and lived in Kathmandu from 1821 to 1843. Hodgson came to know the Buddhist monks there and purchased a total of 88 scriptures, which he sent to Paris to be translated by the celebrated scholar Eugène Burnouf (1801–52). (Hodgson also had an interest in Nepalese wildlife and discovered several new species, about which he wrote.)

Another writer of this period deserves brief mention: Helena Petrovna Blavatsky (1831–91), one of the founder-leaders of the Theosophical Society. In her *Isis Unveiled* (1877) she claims to have spent ten years of her early life travelling the world, finally reaching Tibet about 1858. This claim is generally regarded as spurious, although it continues to find support in some of the 'Body Mind and Spirit' literature that features prominently in bookshops. It is certainly true that she set out in 1878 with the Theosophical Society's co-founder, Henry Steel Olcott, travelling in India and Ceylon. The Theosophical Society facilitated the publication of Blavatsky's writings and was instrumental in popularizing the study of World Religions, although it promoted its own agenda of discovering a secret core that underlay all of them.

The best-known early account of Tibetan Buddhism was by Laurence Austine Waddell (1854–1939) and was titled *The Buddhism of Tibet, or Lamaism* (1895). In 1972 the publishers (Dover) re-titled the book *Tibetan Buddhism: With Its Mystic Cults, Symbolism and Mythology*, since the word 'Lamaism' was considered inappropriate by both later scholars and practitioners of Buddhism. Waddell was an army medical officer who attained the rank of colonel: from 1885 to 1895 he was stationed at a small colonial post at Sikkim, where he came into contact with Tibetan Buddhists. Waddell attempted to enter Tibet, but was disallowed until he became part of Younghusband's 1904 expedition. The Buddhist communities soon came to regard Waddell as an incarnation of the Buddha Amitabha, affording him, in the words of the later scholar Donald Lopez, 'a posture of control over and contempt for his informants'. Waddell was instrumental in propagating the view that Tibetan Buddhism was a corrupt form of the religion, a view that continues to prevail among some Western writers, for example Christmas Humphreys in his popular Penguin paperback *Buddhism* (1953). Waddell described Tibetan Buddhism as degenerate, consisting of 'devil worship' and 'polydemonist superstition', and he also made some inappropriate comparisons with Christianity, describing one Tibetan rite as 'the Eucharist of Buddhism' and a Tibetan lama as a 'doctor of divinity'. Despite the weaknesses of Waddell's approach, however, his writings provide some very detailed first-hand information about Tibetan Buddhist history, doctrine and practice.

Some time later, the French mystic and traveller Alexandra David-Néel (1868–1969) explored Tibet. She began her career as an Orientalist at the Sorbonne in Paris, but came to acquire a spiritual interest in eastern religions. She travelled to India and Ceylon in 1891. After writing her *Buddhism: Its Doctrine and its Methods* (1911) she departed for India again, and from there made a 2,000-mile journey on foot to Tibet, disguised as a beggar. There she met the thirteenth Dalai Lama and various Buddhist scholars including Lama Kazi Dawa-Samdup (1868–1922), with whom she studied Buddhist doctrines. She also became fluent in Tibetan. Her other writings included *My Journey to Lhasa* (1927), *Initiates and Initiations in Tibet* (1931a), *Magic and Mystery in Tibet* (1931b) and *The Secret Oral Teachings in Tibetan Buddhist Sects* (1964). Despite her pioneering work, David-Néel tends not to receive the same scholarly recognition as other Tibetologists. This is no doubt because her writings mingle scholarship with travelogue and accounts of her personal spiritual search.

Also worthy of mention is W. Y. Evans-Wentz (1878–1965), who studied at the Universities of Stanford and Oxford, subsequently travelling to Colombo where he collected a number of Pali manuscripts which he donated to the University of Stanford. In 1918 he began a tour of India, where he met a number of religious celebrities including Lama Kazi Dawa-Samdup, who was a lecturer at the University of Calcutta as well as a Tibetan lama. Although Evans-Wentz receives the credit for the English translation of the *Tibetan Book of the Dead*, which was published in 1927, he was not a fluent Tibetan speaker and in fact Dawa-Samdup did most of the translation, using Evans-Wentz as his 'living dictionary'. Evans-Wentz published further material on Tibetan Buddhism, including *Tibet's Great Yogi, Milarepa* (1928), *Tibetan*

Yoga and Secret Doctrines (1935) and *The Tibetan Book of the Great Liberation* (1954), and presented a much more positive view of this strand of Buddhism, in contrast to previous exponents. His translations are read as much by spiritual seekers as by students of religion.

This case study of Tibetan Buddhism serves to illustrate some of the problems inherent in the academic study of religion. It illustrates the way in which source material was discovered, and also highlights the problems inherent in the blending of primary sacred texts, scholarship, personal spiritual quests and travelogue, which commonly occurs in this particular area of Religious Studies. This case study raises important questions of how one's religious stance affects the way one expounds and evaluates a religion, and the degree to which spiritual commitment skews academic study. Even today there are Western scholars of Tibetan Buddhism who simultaneously pursue the religion as their spiritual path. There are writings too which are undoubtedly forgeries, like the novels of T. Lobsang Rampa (1911–81), who claimed to be a Tibetan lama but turned out to be a surgical fitter and the son of a Devon plumber! All this illustrates the need for very critical evaluation of one's sources.

E. B. Tylor (Sir Edward Burnett Tylor)

Field work and theorizing needed combining, and the nineteenth century saw the beginnings of sociological and anthropological approaches to religion. One early pioneer was Edward Burnett Tylor (1832–1917). As a young man, Tylor developed the symptoms of tuberculosis and went to America in the hope that a different climate would improve his health. From America he went to Cuba in 1856, where he met the archaeologist Henry Christy. They became friends and Tylor accompanied Christy to Mexico, where they made a study of ancient Toltec culture. The expedition provided the basis for Tylor's first major work *Anahuac; or Mexico and the Mexicans Ancient and Modern* (1861). Tylor's travels also took him to continental Europe.

Tylor's reputation as a leading anthropologist was made by his second book, *Researches into the Early History of Mankind and the Development of Civilization* (1865). The book treated humankind as having a single common history with stages of progressive development, from 'savage' society to civilization. As far as religion was concerned, Tylor contended that it had its origins in 'animism', the belief that entities in the natural world are inhabited by spirits and thus 'animated'. Entities most commonly associated with spirit animation are trees and rivers: dryads inhabit trees, nymphs plants and lymphs expanses of water. Tylor held that such beliefs arose from a variety of experiences that were not fully understood in primitive society, such as dreams, trances and hallucinations. From this primitive stage humankind progressed to polytheism, which largely grew out of ancestor veneration. Totemism was – and in some parts of the world remains – the practice of having a tutelary deity or guardian spirit to protect the tribe. As humanity matured further, polytheism gave rise to monotheism: out of a pantheon of deities, one typically emerged as the dominant god (most frequently it was the sky god), leading to the belief in one single supreme deity. Tylor's thesis was further developed in his *Primitive Culture* (1871).

Tylor's evolutionary model of humanity's religious development was later challenged by R. R. Marett (1866–1943), another early anthropologist, who was Reader in Social Anthropology at the University of Oxford from 1910 to 1936. Marett believed that Tylor set out an overly rational evolutionary model; a much-cited quotation is 'Savage religion is not so much thought out as danced out' (Marett, 1909, p. xxi). Marett meant that early practitioners of religion were actors rather than thinkers and devised rituals and myths in order to achieve desired ends, such as making crops grow and enlarging their tribe.

Marett questioned whether the earliest stage of religion was animism and proposed an earlier period, which he labelled 'animatism'. This term describes the belief that special people, spirits and objects are imbued with a special power. The Melanesians of the Pacific called it *mana*, the Africans *mulungu* and the Native Americans *orenda*. This power has been described as 'spiritual energy', imbuing its owner with power. Thus a warrior may be regarded as having power in battle because of an amulet, and not merely on account of his physical strength.

The evolutionary theories of Tylor and Marett were questioned by Andrew Lang (1844–1912). Lang was a folklorist and had read reports of 'high gods among low races', which appeared to provide counter-evidence to the notion that belief in a supreme god indicated an advanced state of religious development. Lang's ideas ran counter to the evolutionary theories of his time; however, being a popular writer rather than an academic, his ideas were not taken as seriously in academic circles as Tylor's or Marett's. Later Wilhelm Schmidt (1868–1954), a Roman Catholic priest and ethnologist, lent support to Lang's critique. Schmidt's research had encompassed Tierra del Fuegans of South America, the Negrillos of Rwanda, and the Andaman Islanders of the Indian Ocean, as a result of which he wrote his 12-volume *Der Ursprung der Gottesidee*, 'The Origin of the Idea of God' (1912–55). Schmidt's theory was that these disparate cultures all believed in a God who had revealed himself to humanity at different times and places, but that this belief had become tarnished through time. Like Lang, Schmidt's account called into question evolutionary theories of religion, and incorporated Christian notions such as the Fall.

One important milestone in the study of religion is James G. Frazer's (1854–1941) *The Golden Bough*. This monumental work was first published in two volumes in 1890, and later expanded to 12 between 1911 and 1915. Subtitled *A Study in Comparative Religion*, these volumes recount myths and religious practices from a variety of European and Middle-Eastern cultures, and trace their connections with present-day religious and folk customs. The book's title relates to the sacred grove at Nemi, near Rome, where according to the myth there was a tree guarded by a priest who would murder any intruder. Anyone able to pluck a branch from the tree was entitled to engage in combat with the priest and, if successful, usurp his position. The story gives the flavour of the book's contents: Frazer collects and classifies these myths, relating them to key themes, the principal ones being trees and tree-spirits, fertility, taboos, kingship and priesthood, sacrifice, death and immortality, and magic.

Frazer did no fieldwork and undertook little travel, confining himself to the European continent, principally Greece. Frazer and others are sometimes labelled 'armchair theorists' by their detractors, but it should be remembered that travel was not as easy then as it is today, and Frazer's work is the result of some remarkably thorough literature-based research. He was particularly influenced by E. B. Tylor's *Primitive Culture* (1871), and was a friend of William Robertson Smith.

Frazer perceived an evolutionary connection between magic, religion and science. There were two types of magic, he contended: homeopathic or imitative magic, and contagious ('sympathetic') magic. The first type (homeopathic) works on the principle of 'like effect, like cause', and involves ritual activity which mirrors the desired outcome: for example, a sacred dance in which the participants leap in the air might be believed to mimic the upward growing of crops. Sympathetic magic presupposes that one thing that has been connected with another continues to maintain a connection. One well-known example is the cutting of a braid of hair from someone's body; ownership of the braid is sometimes believed to give its owner power over that person. Frazer contended that such beliefs and practices are primitive and based on faulty reasoning: he frequently uses the term 'superstition' interchangeably with 'magic'. Frazer often uses terms like 'the savage' and 'barbarous society' in his portrayals of such activities.

Magic, however, is an attempt – albeit a primitive one – to gain control over parts of one's world. As it becomes evident to its practitioners that it is ineffectual, men and women seek better ways of controlling their environment; in particular they seek to enlist supernatural support. Here, Frazer believed, we have the beginning of religion in activities like prayer and sacrifice. As humankind progresses, however, it eventually sees that science proves more effective as a means of controlling one's environment than magical ritual or petitions addressed to supernatural beings. Thus Frazer emerges, like many of his contemporaries, as an evolutionist.

Emile Durkheim and early anthropology of religion

Emile Durkheim (1858–1917) remains a key figure in the study of religion. A sociologist, he is often said to be the founder of the French school of sociology. A significant proportion of Durkheim's work focused on religion, and his book *The Elementary Forms of the Religious Life* (1915) was highly influential. Durkheim is sometimes referred to as a 'structural functionalist', meaning that he emphasized the structures of religion and the functions it performed. Durkheim's theory, in a nutshell, was that religion was essentially a social phenomenon. He wrote:

> The general conclusion of the book which the reader has before him is that religion is something eminently social. Religious representations are collective representations which express collective realities; the rites are a manner of acting which take rise in the midst of the assembled groups and which are destined to excite, maintain or recreate certain mental states in these groups. So if the categories are of religious origin, they ought to participate in this nature common to all religious facts; they too should be social affairs and the product of collective thought. At least – for in the actual condition of our knowledge of these matters, one should be careful to avoid all radical and exclusive statements – it is allowable to suppose that they are rich in social elements. (Durkheim, 1915/1971, p. 10)

To the uninitiated this may seem a statement of the obvious. Who could deny that religion is a group activity, involving like-minded people assembling together to perform collective rites? However, to focus on the social function of religion is first to reject the view that religion is a matter of individual experience. Scholars such as Tylor had defined religion as 'belief in supernatural beings' – something that might be done individually rather than collectively. Second, Durkheim believed that such a definition of religion distinguished it from magic. Magic, he claimed, was a set of activities performed by individuals; where magic involved a number of consultees coming to the magician for help, such assemblies of people merely involved temporary ties, which were discontinued after the magical rites had been performed. Although subsequent researchers such as Radcliffe-Brown, later challenged the idea that magic was not communal, Durkheim's theory was a rejection of those approaches to religion that identified the magical as a pre-religious human state.

Like some of the pioneers of the study of religion, Durkheim was an 'armchair theorist' rather than a field worker. He travelled little, and only learned about other societies at second hand, by reading. Durkheim was particularly interested in 'primitive' society, and in particular Arunta aboriginals of Australia. He based his writing mainly on the work of the anthropologists Baldwin Spencer and Frank Gillen, whom J. G. Frazer had commissioned to undertake an Australian expedition. Durkheim chose to focus on one specific case study of a religion, in order to explore it in depth, and he believed that the Arunta provided an example of religion in its simplest, most primitive form. The Arunta could therefore shed important light not only on the origins of religion, but on the origins of human thought more widely. The Arunta exemplified totemism, and Durkheim concluded that since the totem symbolized God, God was a personification of the clan. In this way religious belief and practice bound their society together, legitimated it and gave it cohesion.

FIGURE 5.2 *Synagogue interior, Vilnius, Lithuania. The word 'synagogue' literally means 'meeting place', underlying the concept of religion as a collective activity. The* bimah *has central position, being the rostrum from which the Torah is read. The screen behind the candles covers the Ark, where the scrolls are housed.*

Max Weber

Max Weber (1864–1920) is of key importance, not simply in the sociological study of religion, but in sociology more widely. His best-known writing is *The Protestant Ethic and the Spirit of Capitalism* (1904–5), in which he analysed the relationship between economic prosperity and acceptance of the ideas of the Protestant Reformation. Weber was more of a theorist than a fieldworker, but as a theoretician he put forward a number of ideas that have proved seminal in the study of religion.

It was Weber who introduced the notion of 'secularization': the idea that religion has lost its hold on humankind in scientific industrial society. Modernization, characterized by scientific advance, was part of the process of 'rationalization', by which events in the world could be explained in terms of rational, scientific theories, rather than by resorting to supernatural explanation. In Weber's terms, Western society was experiencing 'the disenchantment of the world'; in other words, the world could no longer be regarded as controlled by mysterious supernatural forces. Thus religion became consigned to the margins of human significance: it had come to lose its importance in explaining the world. Much subsequent argument has followed from Weber's secularization thesis, focusing particularly on the issues of what precisely secularization is, whether it is a useful concept and whether it is a phenomenon that is actually being witnessed. (See Chapter 4.) It is worth noting that Weber's analysis of society was not an evolutionary one: Weber rejected evolutionary theory, and was merely drawing attention to a process of societal change. Modernization, he taught, led to disenchantment and to increased societal bureaucratization: Weber did not imply that this represented a leap to a higher evolutionary echelon; merely that this was the way human affairs were going.

Two other topics on which Weber wrote are particularly relevant to the study of religion. One is charismatic leadership. Religions frequently start with a founder-leader who attracts people by virtue of his (occasionally her) charisma: he has personal magnetism, which accounts for his followers' allegiance. He has not been appointed to his office, and the obedience his followers give him is entirely voluntary. When the leader dies a void is created, which needs to be filled. Weber enumerated a number of ways in which this can be done: a search process, presumed supernatural revelation, nomination by the leader during his lifetime or hereditary succession. As the movement gains momentum, prescribed practices and the beginnings of hierarchical bureaucratic organization set in: Weber called this 'routinization'. Finally, the movement undergoes 'institutionalization', becoming a formally established organization, perhaps with a formal constitution and appointed office-bearers, and often becoming incorporated as a legal entity.

Of course, not all emergent religious organizations go through these three stages in a neat and consistent way. Weber realized this, and devised the notion of 'ideal types' to meet this potential criticism. An 'ideal type' is not ideal in the sense of being perfect, nor is it an average type. It is, rather, a theoretical model which in all probability does not accurately describe any one particular religious organization, but is an approximation, possibly accentuating certain features, in order to facilitate understanding of the phenomenon.

We noted earlier how some of the pioneers produced typologies, to enable classification of different forms of religion. Weber made his mark on this subject too, proposing a distinction between 'church' and 'sect' – a distinction that continues to influence the study of new religious movements in particular. The term 'church' designates the dominant religion: it is the religion into which most citizens are born, and there is an automatic right to belong. It tends to accommodate societal values and goals and gives ceremonial backing for key civic events, such as a coronation. By contrast, the sect is small; those who belong are more likely to have joined out of conviction than by being born into it. The sect does not automatically provide backing for societal values, and often it rejects and openly criticizes them: a good example is the Jehovah's Witnesses, who regard the world as being under Satan's rule, and who do not participate in the process of electing politicians.

Weber's church/sect typology has been criticized and elaborated over time. His student Ernst Troeltsch (1865–1923) suggested a third category, which he called 'mysticism', to account for those who pursued a more individualistic quest for spiritual experience, while Howard Becker (1899–1960) introduced the term 'cult' to serve the same purpose. The appropriateness of the term 'cult' is much debated; while some sociologists retain the term, it is not favoured in the study of religion, principally because of its pejorative connotations. Later sociologists, such as J. M. Yinger (1916–2011), Bryan Wilson (1926–2004) and W. S. Bainbridge have produced other classificatory schemes; Wilson and Bainbridge have focused particularly on new religious movements.

Modern anthropology

The present-day study of religion combines theoretical and empirical research, and the study of anthropology and ethnography now assumes a high importance. The pioneer of anthropology, as we now recognize the subject, was Bronislaw Malinowski (1884–1942). After acquainting himself extensively with the literature, Malinowski spent a total of two years (1915–16 and 1917–18) in the Trobriand Islands of Papua New Guinea. The results of his research are contained in his *Argonauts of the Western Pacific* (1922), which was one of the numerous volumes that he published. His method of studying the islanders was to live with the people – Malinowski lived in a tent for the entirety of his stay – to learn their language, and to participate actively in their customs and rituals. His approach was detailed and holistic: unlike earlier pioneers of anthropology he did not simply focus on rituals and rites of passage, but aimed to gain an overall picture of the society. Of particular interest to Malinowski was the *function* of customs and rituals, and their interrelationships with their society's myths. In this regard his approach contrasted with those earlier writers who had adopted an evolutionary approach to religion and viewed 'primitive' societies as shedding light on the origins of religion. Accordingly, Malinowski did not direct his attention to magic and fertility; indeed he rejected the previously held assumption that primal societies were inhabited by 'irrational savages'. As he observed, the Trobriand Islanders were as astute as Westerners when it came to agriculture and trade. Malinowski perceived a distinction rather than an evolutionary continuity between magic and religion: magic, he thought, deals with areas of life where results are speculative; religion, by contrast, consists of activities that are habitual and traditional and in particular it provides psychological support to its adherents, especially in the face of death.

'Going native' or 'living in', as such methods are sometimes called, are rarely straightforward or easy. We shall discuss the problems the later phenomenologists encountered when recommending 'empathetic understanding' and trying to 'walk in other people's shoes' as a method of studying their religion. Societies are complex, and made up of a wide variety of people: male and female, young and old, laity and religious officials, and so on, with greater and lesser levels of education and understanding of their tradition. Some may be easier to empathize with than others, and it is not possible to completely enter into the thought-patterns and way of life, even of those with whom the researcher feels the greatest rapport. There are limits to participant-observation, and where researchers participate there is not likely to be the same degree of engagement or purpose that one finds in one's research subjects. Malinowski's diaries reveal that for a significant proportion of his time in the Trobriand Islands he felt frustration and lack of rapport. At one point he records in his diary, 'I am living outside of Kiriwina although strongly hating the niggers' – an astonishing, although honest, statement.

Malinowski's candid remark illustrates well the point that anthropologists cannot completely 'go native', although he tried to adopt the lifestyle of the Trobriand Islanders. It would be more accurate to see the anthropologist as someone who is on the margins of the community he or she is researching. He or she is the outsider posing as the insider, the stranger and the friend, the one who is studying a phenomenon that appears strange, and trying to make it familiar. How far one goes in entering into the society that one is researching remains a matter of debate among anthropologists and ethnologists. Remaining aloof may prevent the researcher from gaining empathetic understanding, while becoming over-friendly may limit the researcher's critical faculties, making him or her too ready, for example, to accept the community's account of its own history.

For the majority of Western students, fieldwork is more likely to be conducted near home, rather than at more exotic locations such as Papua New Guinea. (Chapter 9 discusses fieldwork in greater detail.) Western religious communities have their distinctive beliefs and practices, and their own internal network of interrelationship among members. Some may go as far as living apart from the rest of society, while others may keep their contacts with wider society to a minimum. Certain Buddhist communities fall into the former category, while organizations like the Jehovah's Witnesses minimize contact, for fear of falling prey to the standards of the world, which they believe is ruled by Satan. Western religious communities are more likely to speak English and live in the society with which the student is familiar – even if the religious group chooses to withdraw from it. Investigating communities from the inside constitutes ethnographical study, and is undertaken by participation-observation combining with interviewing.

Conclusions

Anyone who began his or her study of religion in the 1960s or earlier should be able to recognize from this overview of the history of scholarship how basic introductions to World Religions came to be written as they were. They tended to be historical, starting off with the presumed roots of religion in magic and animism, and moved through ancient Egypt to the archaeological finds in Mohenjodaro and Harappa to the Aryan invasion and the sacred texts of the *Vedas*, the *Upanishads* and the *Bhagavad Gita*, with perhaps some reference to reincarnation, the caste system and village practices. The treatment of Buddhism tended to be historical-philosophical, with little reference to present-day grass-roots practice. All this reflects the way archaeological and textual studies blended with a fascination for origins and evolution. The Western predilection for translating and interpreting religious texts can partly be explained by the way in which the Christian religion has been taught in Western universities: study of the Bible, supplemented by ecclesiastical history and systematic theology. The lack of travel facilities and the scarcity of immigrants militated against fieldwork, which only really took off in the second half of the twentieth century. Today the student of religion can expect to combine the traditional historico-philosophical accounts of religions with practical fieldwork, examining how the more doctrinal and intellectual aspects relate to religions as they are practised. Some institutions now go so far as enabling students to undertake placements, where they live or work in a religious community for a brief period in order to gain first-hand acquaintance with its lifestyle and practices.

While continuing to subscribe to the biological theory of evolution, most scholars would now reject any schema which graded religions on an evolutionary scale, as writers like Tylor and Frazer were prone to do. The later phenomenologists of religion, who will be considered in Chapter 6, justifiably challenged the idea of these evolutionary systems, emphasizing the need to suspend one's own value-judgements. Regarding the quest for the origins of religion, few scholars would proffer a global explanation. Terms like 'primitive' are rejected in favour of 'primal' – the latter term serving to highlight the point that the religions of agrarian societies are relatively untarnished by the missionary activities of the world's major faith traditions. There is a tendency now to extol the virtues of primal religions, viewing them as possessing an equally coherent worldview to those of the major faiths, and perceiving them as more in tune with nature than those of industrialized societies. Anthropologists and ethnologists endeavour to view them empathetically, and by contrast with the earlier pioneers do not confine their interests to rituals and rites of passage.

Classification schemes are still under discussion. This is partly because terms like 'theism', 'monotheism', 'polytheism' and 'atheism' emanate from a Western context, and do not neatly fit religions such as Hinduism and Buddhism. It is also because new religious movements, being vast in number, need to be organized in such a way as to make academic study feasible. This is no easy matter: terms like 'cult' are pejorative; all three elements of 'new religious movements' defy easy definition; 'New Age' lacks a clear referent and is not a term that spiritual seekers readily use to refer to themselves; and to what is 'alternative religion' an alternative? There is still much scope for continued methodological debate, as well as enhancing one's knowledge of the religions themselves.

Future trends in the study of religion may well see attempts to reconcile the marked differences between 'textbook' religion and religion as it is practised. Much of the literature, particularly in regard to the traditional religions, still tends to emphasize

FIGURE 5.3 *Wolverhampton Buddha Vihara. The figurines represent Buddhist monks, indicating that the accompanying offerings are for them.*

the historical and intellectual components. There are disparities, too, in the ways different religions are treated in academic study. For example, there is an unevenness of treatment between Hinduism and Buddhism in Western scholarship. Students of religion become much more aware of folk practices in the former than in the latter, where they are largely ignored or dismissed as 'pre-Buddhist', or in Melford Spiro's terminology 'apotropaic' (lying aside from the mainstream). This is no doubt because there has not been a clear divide between scholars and seekers in this area, and Western intellectuals who have discovered Buddhism have done so largely because of the literature they have read in their Western environment. Studied outside the countries where it is practised, it comes across as 'the religion of reason' and, if not preferable to Christianity, at least a close second. More work still needs to be done in order to present Buddhism, as well as Christianity, as a folk religion.

This chapter has covered a lot of ground. Because of the intertwining of different disciplines, and because certain key figures have contributed to the study of religion in several ways, it has not been possible to give a neat chronological overview of the history of scholarship. Inevitably there have been omissions: for example, the discussion has tended to focus on scholars of the past, rather than on living academics. We have said relatively little about the psychology of religion – a field which has been neglected in recent times, but is now beginning to enjoy a revival – and hence given little space to important figures such as E. D. Starbuck, William James and Carl Jung, all of whom had a much more favourable view of religion than did Freud.

Over the past two centuries the study of religion has made many important strides. It has become critical, refusing to accept the traditional assumptions of the faiths it has studied, seeking to analyse their writings rather than to harmonize apparent inconsistencies. It has endeavoured to separate history from myth, and to draw on the methods of history as a science with a proper methodology. Archaeology, sociology, anthropology and ethnography have all played their roles in building up pictures of religions of the past and present. Sociological study in particular has raised questions about classification schemes and thus provided a set of tools with which to discuss religion. There is still a lack of clear agreement among scholars, highlighting the point that in academic study there is no view too sacrosanct to challenge, and demonstrating the endeavour of scholars to continue striving towards the truth.

DISCUSSION POINTS

1 Since scholars continually change their ideas, what purpose is served by studying figures whose ideas have been largely abandoned?

2 Consider the advantages and disadvantages of studying (a) texts, and (b) people.

3 What do you see as likely future trends in the study of religion?

4 Has the study of religion made progress through time, or have its methods merely changed?

6

Phenomenology and its critics

George Chryssides

Chapter Outline

The origins of phenomenology	159
Phenomenology and religion	161
Religion as 'power'	162
Mircea Eliade	165
'The believer is always right'	167
Ninian Smart's 'dimensional' approach	171
Some criticisms	175
The lessons of phenomenology	181
Discussion points	182

Islamic countries are becoming increasingly zealous for Islam and we are witnessing a troubling growth in the extreme militant strain of Islamic belief. More and more countries in the Middle East are becoming run by Islamic regimes. When this happens, it can be readily seen that Islam is not just a religion, but a way of life. In fact, in Islamic countries, the Muslim faith is interwoven with politics, justice, social behaviour, culture, etc.

REACHOUT TRUST, 2006

Aquick surf of the internet will find a host of statements like the above, and others that are even more hostile to Islam. Influenced by various sectors of the media, a significant proportion of the public have come to regard Islam as a militant faith, committed to *jihad* – frequently translated as 'holy war' – and with 'backward' values such as the oppression of women, and barbaric sanctions such as lashing or limb-amputation for crimes such as adultery and theft.

It is not our purpose here to try to set the record straight about Islam, important though that may be. The important point to note is that, only too frequently, accounts of a religion can tell us almost as much about the author as they do about the subject-matter. Most obviously, we can detect from the above that the author is not a Muslim; in fact, a reading of the extract in its wider context quickly indicates that he is an evangelical Christian, who regards his own faith as superior to that of the Muslim. He is clearly perturbed by Islam, and in particular what he perceives as recent militant developments, and he regards these militant aspects as part of the Muslim faith. The author's contrast between 'religion' and 'way of life' also betrays a view that religion should not be overly campaigning, or bound up with political systems, and perhaps that ideals like social justice should not be on a religion's main agenda. Perhaps too we can detect a fear that Islam, which he believes increasing numbers of countries are officially embracing, will take over the world.

In fairness, the article cited is not intended as a piece of academic writing, but students – and their teachers – can easily write inadvertently about themselves, rather than about their subject-matter. One common, although seemingly insignificant, word is 'we': it is not uncommon to read a student essay on Christianity that starts off by describing Christian practice, but lapses into phrases like 'when we recite the Creed'. The word 'we' immediately lets the writer's colours show: the student is a Christian. So why should this worry us? After all, do not religions often teach that we should have the courage of our convictions, and that we should stand up and be counted? What scholars and students do in the role of practitioners is their personal choice, of course. A student may be a Sunday School teacher, a monk, a prayer leader or whatever, outside the classroom, but it is a convention of academic study that one strives not to let one's colours show. A piece of advice that we often give to our students is that they should write so that we cannot tell whether they are Buddhists, Christians, Hindus, Muslims or atheists. What they write about is not themselves, but the subject-matter, and this needs to be treated fairly and impartially.

It may seem strange to say that the study of religion (as distinct from the philosophy of religion and theology) is not concerned about religious truth. (The issue of truth in the study of religion will be explored further in Chapter 11.) We are not in the business of deciding whether there is a God or not, or whether key religious figures are really prophets, *avatars* or messiahs. We endeavour to listen to the practitioners who make such claims, but methodologically we sit on the fence. The study of religion has frequently been understood to employ methodological agnosticism. The present author recently met a member of a new religious movement who believed that the founder-leader of his organization was the present-day Messiah. He offered to teach me a set of spiritual exercises that would help me discover whether or not this was so. 'Do you not want to know whether the Messiah is now here on earth?' he asked. He seemed surprised to be told that the study of religion did not involve an evaluation of truth-claims. I explained that he subscribed to a worldview which I was prepared to listen to and to endeavour to understand, but that scholars typically distance themselves from their subject-matter. It was not my task either to endorse his doctrines or to criticize them, and studying religion left unresolved questions of religious truth. Of course, outside my role as a scholar of religion, I could consider his offer of spiritual help: that is a personal matter, and of course many religions offer spiritual practices and paths to salvation, sometimes claiming that a special prophet, *avatar* or messiah is now on earth.

The notion of neutrality is part of a phenomenological approach to religion. Once it is pointed out, the notion of neutrality in the study of religion may seem obvious to the majority of students of religion. It may seem to them unnecessary that such a seemingly straightforward idea can become bound up with complex philosophical and methodological theories, and enshrined in difficult jargon. It may also come as a surprise that, once this apparently simple idea is explained in this complicated way, the theory no longer secures acceptance among scholars. What follows may therefore seem a slightly tortuous journey, but whatever we think of phenomenology the discussion can at least help to shed light on some of the issues that confront us when we try to study religion academically.

The origins of phenomenology

There is no one body of doctrine that is shared among phenomenologists. For some, phenomenology constitutes a philosophical theory of knowledge; for others it is a method; and for some it simply connotes a state of mind in which to approach one's subject-matter. The first scholar to use the term 'phenomenology' was P. D. Chantepie de la Saussaye (1848–1920) in his *Lehrbuch der Religionsgeschichte* ('Handbook of the History of Religions', 1887). De la Saussaye endeavoured to analyse data pertaining to the history of religions, classifying their characteristics into 'common manifestations': for example worship, prayer and sacrifice, sacred objects such as stones, trees and animals. The concept of 'comparative religion' stemmed from the idea of such categories; although the emerging scholars of World Religions who belonged to de la Saussaye's era did not make direct comparisons between religions, these categories ran across the spectrum of the world's religions, and facilitated systematic study of them.

The principal ideas underlying phenomenology are generally traced back to Edmund Husserl (1859–1938), who introduced two key terms commonly associated with it: *epochē* (bracketing one's assumptions), and *eidetic reflection* (apprehending an object's form). His ideas are expressed in two principal writings: *Philosophy as Strict Sense* (1910–11) and *Ideas: General Introduction to Pure Phenomenology* (1913). Husserl's philosophy starts from the idea that perceiving something requires two components: consciousness (*noesis*), and objects of consciousness (*noema*). This is best illustrated by an example. (The one that follows is ours, not Husserl's.) I am seeing a red car. For this to be possible, I need to be present, experiencing it (the *noesis*), and the car needs to be there in front of me (the *noema*). If I am unconscious – perhaps in dreamless sleep – my psyche is not engaged to apprehend the car; likewise, if the car is not there in front of me (perhaps it is locked in my garage, or lent to a friend who is driving it miles away), again no perception of the red car can happen. There may be occasions when I think I see something, but am mistaken: I might have a vivid dream involving my red car: in that situation there is *noesis* but no *noema*.

So far, this may seem patently obvious, apart from the introduction of the terms *noesis* and *noema*. However, Husserl takes these points a stage further, and asks us to reflect on what is happening when we make a seemingly straightforward perceptual judgement. I have described my car as 'red', and in doing so I have applied a universal category to it. In some sense, the attributed colour manifests a universal redness, and thus I am prepared to give the description 'red' to many other cars, and many other objects – carpets, shirts, books and so on. The redness I attribute to my car also differs from its appearance. Does my car look wholly and homogeneously red? Anyone who has tried painting a picture that includes a red object will know that simply colouring in its area with red paint gives a very unconvincing and unrealistic result. The artist needs to allow for different amounts of light on different parts, for its shine, and for other objects that become reflected in it. The appearance of the car will therefore change, in accordance with its changing ambience, the amount of daylight and a host of other factors. Yet I still refer to it as my 'red' car. It is still a red car, even in pitch darkness, when it is impossible for anyone to perceive its colour.

My perception of the car is affected not only by the car's environment, but by myself. The state of my sensory organs will make a difference to my perception of it. Suppose I were red/green colour-blind, for example: I might then claim to perceive a green, or maybe a brown car. Again, the concept 'red', although seemingly straightforward, is something that I have learned to use. I have been taught where the boundaries lie between red and orange, red and maroon, and red and pink. Our colour demarcations are not predetermined for us; we create them according to our needs. It is well known, for example, that some African tribes use different words for different shades of green. Thus, the judgement that something is red is made by the perceiver, influenced by his or her upbringing and social environment. Nonetheless, despite these considerations, Husserl contended that we still in some sense apprehend a universal redness that we apply to the same object under different conditions, and to other objects that merit similar categorization. We have what he called 'eidetic intuition' – that is to say, we are able to apprehend the 'form' ('eidetic' relates to the Greek word *eidos*, meaning 'form') or basic reality of redness, which in some way transcends its manifestations. The example I have chosen is deliberately a banal one, in order to illustrate how complex an apparently simple act of perceiving is. Consider how much greater intricacy is involved when we describe a more complex phenomenon: describing an accident, recounting an item of news, or – of greatest relevance here – explaining someone else's religion.

Husserl's quest was – as the philosopher Antony Flew puts it – a quest for a 'non-committal description of the features of subjective experience' (Flew, 1971, p. 217). If my seeing a red car is dependent on the contingencies I have discussed, how can I be certain that I am seeing the red car? Is there some way of describing my experience which is 'incorrigible', in other words incapable of being proved wrong if certain factors do not hold (such as the state of my eyes, the ambient light)? How much of the redness is actually in the car itself, and how much is contributed by myself and by the car's environment? And is it possible to 'get at' this inherent redness and describe what it is like, apart from its experienced manifestations? How do I get to the *eidos* – the true 'form' of redness?

The quest for certainty has been a perennial one in the history of modern Western philosophy, going back at least as far as René Descartes (1596–1650), who is known for his famous dictum, '*Cogito ergo sum*' ('I think, therefore I am'). Descartes' argument, in short, was that whatever else can be called into question, at least I can affirm my own existence with absolute certainty. Descartes continued his argument by supposedly proving God's existence and arguing that God, being benevolent, would not permit him to fall into error when perceiving 'clear and distinct ideas'. Subsequent philosophers were not so comfortable in introducing God as the guarantor of certainty, and the British philosopher John Locke (1632–1704) distinguished between 'primary' and 'secondary' qualities in objects. He argued that colours, tastes and smells, for example, were contributed by the perceiving subject (secondary qualities), being relative to the state of one's senses, while shapes and sizes were inherent in the object (primary qualities). Thus, if I eat a large green apple, the taste and the greenness reside in me, while the largeness and the (approximate) roundness reside in the apple. George Berkeley (1685–1753) later questioned whether the distinction between primary and secondary qualities was a tenable one, pointing out, for example, that the perceived size of an object depends on the observer's standpoint: thus distance and perspective will influence whether we perceive objects as large, small or medium-sized. It was Immanuel Kant (1724–1804) who subsequently made the distinction between noumena and phenomena; the former being the ideas in the mind, and the latter being the properties of the perceived object. Because we can only be aware of what is in our minds, not what is outside them, he concluded, we can only be aware of noumena, not phenomena, and therefore the 'thing-in-itself' is something that will constantly elude us. Obviously, it is unsatisfactory to compress some 300 years of philosophy into a paragraph, but it provides some flavour of the kinds of problem with which philosophers were struggling, and the debate that the phenomenologists were continuing.

Phenomenology and religion

All this may seem somewhat abstruse, and we must now endeavour to demonstrate its relevance to the study of religion. The principal exponents of the phenomenology of religion are generally held to be Nathan Söderblom (1866–1931), Rudolf Otto (1869–1937), Gerardus van der Leeuw (1890–1950), Joachim Wach (1889–1955), Mircea Eliade (1907–86) and most recently Ninian Smart (1927–2001), who is sometimes said to have been the last of the phenomenologists. The earlier phenomenologists' quest was to find an essence of religion. By this they sought, not a set of common beliefs and practices that spanned the world's religious traditions, but rather that which was quintessentially religious. As with the redness of the red car in our previous example, their question was: What is the distinctive feature that is shared by all religions, by virtue of which we are able to apply the term 'religion'?

The most obvious candidate might initially appear to be belief in, or awareness of, 'God'. Yet a moment's reflection will show that the concept is not shared by all the world's religious traditions. Most obviously, it does not feature in Buddhism. Contrary to popular stereotyping, Buddhism does assign a role to the gods: they are part of *samsara* (the cycle of birth and rebirth), but they are impermanent, play no role in the world's creation and sustentation, are not addressed in prayer or worship and play no part in bringing living beings any nearer to the goal of nirvana. Similar comments can be made about Jainism and Taoism, which accommodate gods, but do not usually assign them any importance. One might try somewhat wider concepts than 'God', such as 'the divine', 'the supernatural', 'the transcendent', 'ultimate reality', the Absolute, 'power' or 'the sacred'. We shall give the last two separate treatment, since these were particularly favoured by van der Leeuw and Eliade respectively. The others are either vague, or are more like abstract philosophical concepts. 'Divine' is less specific than 'God', but does it include angels, *devas* or saints, and what about human emperors, to whom divinity has often been ascribed? It is still not obvious that Buddhism and Taoism can comfortably share any 'divinity'. 'Supernatural' is even more problematic as a term: Buddhism has its supernatural figures such as *apsaras*, *bodhisattvas* and *dakini*, among others, and Taoism encompasses beliefs and rituals associated with a plurality of deities. Jains believe in a multiplicity of *jina*, literally 'conquerors' – human beings who have attained perfect knowledge and mastery of themselves, and who are free from the cycle of birth and rebirth. The problem is not finding seemingly 'supernaturalist' components in Buddhism, Taoism and Jainism, but whether such concepts of the supernatural have much in common with those of the theistic religions. There also remains the question of whether the term 'supernatural' allows too much to be included as religion: ghosts, genies and fairies could count as 'supernatural' beings, but are seldom objects of devotion, and are scarcely associated with what one normally considers to be religious. In Chapter 1 we argued that 'the divine' was too weak a word, since it covered too much, spanning almost anything. 'The Absolute' was too impersonal a concept, being associated with somewhat abstruse Hegelian philosophy. 'The sacred' proved to be more germane, although it denoted material objects as well as beings to whom devotion is due.

Religion as 'power'

A further attempt to identify a distinctive feature of all religion is Otto's concept of the 'holy' or the 'numinous'. A summary of Otto's ideas was given in Chapter 1, and it is unnecessary to repeat our exposition here. The experiences of the holy that Otto cites – Isaiah in the Jerusalem Temple, and Arjuna apprehending Krishna's higher nature as Vishnu in the *Bhagavad Gita* – are powerful experiences, and we argued that one limitation of Otto's analysis is that few rank-and-file religious believers are party to such tremendous theophanies. Nevertheless, to Otto these experiences are indeed powerful ones, and the notion of power manifests itself in a variety of ways in religion, as Gerardus van der Leeuw went on to explore. Van der Leeuw's central position on the phenomenology of religion is expressed in his *Religion in Essence and Manifestation*, first published in English in 1948: the original 1933 German title translates simply as *The Phenomenology of Religion*. Van der Leeuw regarded the notion of 'power' as the central feature of religion – not mere physical power, which all humans possess to a greater or lesser degree, but a power that transcends any natural force that can be brought to bear in the world.

Van der Leeuw's ideas can perhaps be best explained by looking at a specific example: the one I have selected for discussion (my example, not van der Leeuw's) comes from Jewish scripture (2 Sam. 6.1–8). King David has been crowned as King of Israel and has occupied Jerusalem, establishing it as his capital city. One remaining objective is to conquer the Philistines, and to recapture the Ark of the Covenant. The Ark of the Covenant (not to be confused with Noah's Ark!) was the portable shrine set up by Moses some centuries earlier and was Yahweh's sacred tabernacle, containing the scriptures of the Torah and the two stone tablets on which Moses had inscribed the Ten Commandments under Yahweh's dictation. Two men were chosen to carry the cart containing the Ark up to the city, and in the course of the journey the oxen stumbled, whereupon Uzzah – one of the cart-bearers – reached out and grabbed hold of the Ark in an attempt to steady it. This act intensely angered Yahweh, who immediately struck him dead for irreverent behaviour.

From a secular human standpoint it may seem outrageous that Uzzah was struck down for apparently trying to be helpful. After all, the object he steadied was simply a wooden box, made by human hands out of ordinary materials. Why should it be given any more special treatment than other seemingly more valuable objects that were no doubt transported to Jerusalem, such as gold and jewellery? Van der Leeuw's notion of 'power' can help shed light on this seemingly strange incident. Van der Leeuw refers to the concept of *mana*, a term used by Melanesians for 'the Infinite'. The Christian missionary R. H. Codrington first drew attention to the notion, in a letter to the scholar Max Müller. Codrington explains it thus:

> It is a power or influence, not physical, and in a way supernatural; but it shows itself in physical force, or in any kind of power or excellence which a man possesses. This *mana* is not fixed in anything, and can be conveyed in almost anything; but spirits . . . have it and can impart it . . . All Melanesian religion consists, in fact, in getting this *mana* for one's self, or getting it used for one's benefit. (Codrington, 1891; cited in Bettis, 1969, p. 57)

This special power has a supernatural origin; in theistic religions it is God who possesses this ultimate power, known as *mana* to the Melanesians, but frequently called *ruah* (Hebrew) or *pneuma* (Greek), usually translated as 'spirit'. (The Book of Genesis, the first book of the Jewish-Christian Bible, states that it is through God's Spirit that the world is created, and the Holy Spirit is the third person of the Christian Trinity.) Other power-bearing concepts in other religious systems include the Tao, *rta* (the principle of order in ancient Indian thinking), and *archē* (primal unity in Greek thought). 'The power' is inescapable: while one can attempt to combat opposing physical power, this kind of supernatural power cannot be resisted. The Hindu notion of *atman* is yet another of van der Leeuw's examples: *atman* is the soul or the self, which in Hindu thought is held to be one and the same as *brahman*, the divinity that sustains the world. Van der Leeuw refers to a passage in the Hindu scripture, the *Bhagavad Gita*, where the god Krishna tells Arjuna, the warrior who is faced with a moral dilemma about an impending battle: 'If the slayer thinks he slays and the slain that he is slain, they both fail to understand; the one slays not and the other is not slain' (Bettis, 1969, p. 69). In other words, since the soul is eternal, the cosmic law that no one can ultimately die is one that no earthly power is capable of overthrowing. The same can be said of the law of *karma*: according to Hindu, Buddhist and Sikh thinking, all our actions sow seeds, the appropriate fruits of which we shall all eventually reap, and, however much we may try to resist, there is no escape from these consequences.

This 'power' can reside in special objects, and van der Leeuw uses the term 'fetish' to describe these. A fetish is a surrogate object that is treated as having similar powers to that which it represents; thus some men are sexually aroused by women's shoes, which act as a substitute for the female body. In a similar way, an object such as a painted stone can serve as the residence of the deity, and a totem pole can be venerated as the emblem of the tribe. Van der Leeuw includes the Ark of the Covenant as an example of a fetish in this sense: despite being a human artefact, it becomes the house of God, and is to be treated accordingly. Sacred power can also be enshrined in special people: religions typically appoint their 'religious specialists' such as the prophet, the priest, the shaman or the exorcist, to whom due deference is appropriate.

These observations link with another important concept: the taboo (*tabu*). Associated with the sacred object is a warning for unauthorized parties to 'keep off'. In most Christian denominations, it is the priest ('minister' in the Protestant tradition) who has the exclusive power to consecrate the bread and wine in the sacrament of the Eucharist. These 'elements' (as they are called) are held to have potency: they are primarily to be conceived of as the 'means of grace', but in the wrong hands or in the wrong context they could be potentially harmful. One fear, although perhaps not so common in the twenty-first century, was that a consecrated host (the official name for the communion wafer) taken from a Mass, could become the object of popular superstition: the host, being the body of Christ, has sometimes been alleged to bleed, as Christ's body did on the cross. The Churches therefore consider it important to exert control over who dispenses the sacrament, who receives it and what is done with it. To receive a Eucharistic wafer and put it in one's pocket would, in van der Leeuw's analysis, be a violation of a taboo, and steps would most certainly be taken to ensure that it was not allowed to be taken out of the premises unconsumed. The violation of a taboo is regarded as having serious consequences, which are often automatic rather than imposed. Thus, Uzzah did not have to stand trial for his misdemeanour in touching the Ark: he was immediately struck down by God.

It follows, van der Leeuw argued, that sacred power generates a corresponding human response. One important response is avoidance. In the Jerusalem Temple, the Holy of Holies – its central shrine – was strictly out of bounds for all except the High Priest, and even the High Priest was only allowed to enter the sacred place once a year, on the Day of Atonement. The Christian Eucharist is to be avoided by the unauthorized – the precise criteria vary according to different Christian denominations, but appropriate conditions must be satisfied for participation, such as belonging to the Church, confession of sin and perhaps previous fasting. Some Christians hold that they should not 'communicate' more than once in the same day, lest the sacrament should appear too ordinary. Yet the avoidance is not the kind of avoidance that one would make of something utterly horrible. The sacred power generates awe and amazement: the Christian talks of 'amazing grace', and is invited to 'draw near with faith' rather than to remain distant from the sacred.

Mircea Eliade

We mentioned earlier that phenomenology is not a single body of doctrine, and Mircea Eliade's phenomenology differs from that of Otto and van der Leeuw. For Eliade, the central concept in the study of religion was 'the sacred', which is roughly equivalent to Otto's 'holy' or 'numinous' and van der Leeuw's 'power'. However, Eliade held that the religious consists not so much in the object itself, but in the way one relates to it. The sacred is thus not so much another world that lies beyond the present world, but a way of relating to this world, of organizing it and understanding it.

Eliade, like Otto, makes a fundamental distinction between two concepts: the sacred and the 'profane'. Viewing the world as profane entails seeing it as essentially empirical, discernible through sensory experience and 'one-dimensional'. It can be controlled for our own purposes, which are economic or sense-gratifying. By contrast, the religious attitude to the world is one of awe or wonder, and sees something 'out there' manifesting itself in space and time. Someone with this attitude sees himself or herself as not having control over the cosmos, but being controlled. In this respect religion differs from magic: a magician is one who claims to have special powers that enable him or her to control aspects of the universe which lie beyond the normal capabilities of other mortals.

The sacred manifests itself in time and space. It is not a different world of which we catch a glimpse when we lift our eyes away from the profane world. On the contrary, religion uses aspects of the empirical world as ways of being attuned to the ultimate meaning of the cosmos, creating images and symbols which reflect the essence of the sacred. Because religious believers want to live as close as possible to this centre of the universe, they typically build 'houses' to resemble the house of the gods. ('The house of God' is a typical phrase in the Jewish and Christian faiths.) This sacred space typically serves as a kind of 'cosmogeny': its construction, and what takes place within in, reflects humanity's position within the overall scheme of things, and the actions that are performed recapitulate the actions of God or the gods. For example, an Eastern Orthodox church is constructed so that worshippers enter at ground level, thus reflecting the belief that humanity's place is under God's surveillance and authority. In the dome on the roof is pictured the 'Christ *pantokrator*': Jesus Christ, the judge of all. Christ looks down on all – a reminder that our actions are judged by God. This idea is sometimes reinforced by a large eye that is depicted at the front: this is the eye of God who, being omniscient, sees everything. In between the ground level and the dome are icons: pictures of the saints and the Virgin Mary. The saints are now dead, but they are still an important aspect of the Church ('the communion of saints') and they are capable of interceding on one's behalf. Thus iconographically the saints and the Virgin Mary are portrayed in a medial position between heaven and earth. At the front of the Orthodox Church is the iconostasis (literally, an 'icon stand') – a wooden screen that separates off an inaccessible area to which only the priests may gain access, and during the liturgy the priest will traverse to and from the area behind the iconostasis, to make supplications on behalf of the people, and – most especially – to bring out the sacramental elements for them.

Just as sacred space is a reflection of the divine abode, so sacred time serves to re-enact divine activity. Most religions observe a liturgical calendar, which enables followers to re-enact the divine activities and participate in them. Religions tell of the beginning of creation, the lives of divine or semi-divine beings on earth, how they created sacred history ('myth'), and how they interrelated with humankind and helped to bring them to the spiritual goal. In Hinduism there are cycles of cosmic time – the *kalpas*, subdivided into *yugas* (ages) – which define the periods of the earth's creation through to its destruction. These are mirrored in the religion's myth, and re-enacted in its sacred calendar. Thus the Hindu festival of Holi, a spring festival, marks the world's creation and reminds followers of the cosmic order. Distinctions of gender, age and caste are disregarded on that day, serving as a reminder of the disorder that would otherwise prevail. In Christianity, the Passion of Christ is often re-enacted between Palm Sunday (the Sunday before Easter) and Easter Sunday. Followers will process with palm branches, re-enacting Jesus' triumphal entry into Jerusalem; services during the week will focus on the incidents attributed to Jesus during that period; on Maundy Thursday believers may participate in the Last Supper (the Eucharist), sometimes incorporating a foot-washing ceremony to reflect Christ's washing of the disciples' feet before their last meal. On Good Friday, some churches will mark the 'stations of the cross', keep an all-night vigil, echoing the 'watch' on Jesus' tomb, and of course Easter morning reflects the belief in the resurrection. All this enables the Christian not simply to be reminded of stories that are recounted in scripture, but to become part of the Easter story, appropriating its meaning and blessing for themselves.

FIGURE 6.1 *St Michael the Archangel (Church of England), Rushall: interior. The high altar is the focal point. Different colours denote the point of the liturgical year: the pulpit fall is red for Palm Sunday, but statues are covered over since it is Lent.*

'The believer is always right'

The ideas of phenomenology simultaneously serve two functions for the student of religion. First, at a mundane level, they offer insights in how to explore and write about religion. The student who simply recounts that Hindus throw purple dye at each other at the festival of Holi does no more than describe folk custom: this is not an account of religion, until he or she relates it to the supernatural, perhaps showing how it re-enacts the activities of the gods, and the ways in which human actions relate to the divine.

The phenomenologist also draws attention to the need to strive for objectivity in the study of religion. As students of religion, our aim is not to endorse, to criticize or to change the religious practices that we come across. Our role is that of the neutral observer, or at most the participant-observer. In the course of academic study it is inevitable that we come across much of which we disapprove: perhaps attitudes to women, war and peace, the treatment of animals. There are many controversial issues on which one might campaign outside the classroom, but which are not to be championed in academic writing. The scholar of religion aims to achieve empathetic understanding, and to build a 'bridge of understanding' between himself or herself and religions that may frequently seem foreign. In an attempt to create this bridge, recourse is needed to the believer: as we have argued above, any account of a religion must be about its exponents, their beliefs and practices, not about ourselves.

Building a bridge of understanding between oneself and the believer entails listening to the believer's explanations, accepting them as part of the phenomenon that one is studying. This notion has led at least one writer to encapsulate phenomenology in the maxim 'The believer is always right' (Sharpe, 1977, p. 81). The maxim requires some critical examination, however. Can the believer really always be right? Does he or she never make mistakes within the context of his or her religion? Sharpe's maxim serves to emphasize the point that believers' explanations have privileged status above those of the outsider. To take a simple example, some students on a recent field visit to a Buddhist *vihara* asked one of the monks about *pindapat* (the alms round), and were told that an alms bowl was not a begging bowl. The informant explained that monks are not beggars, since the latter actively ask for donations, and want money rather than food. By contrast, a Buddhist monk will only wait at someone's house, and move on silently if no food is forthcoming; it would certainly be inappropriate to offer money. Nonetheless, one student somewhat rudely insisted that, since Buddhist monks were expecting free food, monks doing *pindapat* were therefore begging. Such a response was inappropriate: the monk had clearly distinguished himself in an important and valid way from the eastern beggar, and unless we have reason to believe that our informants are lying to us (a most infrequent occurrence), their accounts have a privileged status over any competing ones that we, as students, may have.

This brings us to the question: cannot believers tell us falsehoods? Informant testimony may not be deliberately false, but informants cannot know everything about their faith, and from time to time they may get things wrong. Another example will illustrate this. Outside my university environment I am an amateur church musician. On one occasion I was due to play at an unfamiliar church at Pentecost. The vicar handed me a list of hymns, all of which seemed quite inappropriate, being about the Trinity rather than the Holy Spirit. (Trinity Sunday follows Pentecost by one week.) Should I have taken the view that 'the believer is always right'? Of course not; the vicar was pleased to have the mistake pointed out in time, and we found the right list.

On that occasion I was not there as a student of religion, but of course if I had been present on a field visit, I might well have taken a less interventionist role, waiting to see what would happen. I have witnessed occasions where an officiant at Christian worship has mistaken the Sunday in the liturgical calendar, and it can be argued that it is an interesting part of the phenomenon of Christianity that this can occasionally happen.

The second, more substantial contribution of Otto, van der Leeuw and Eliade is their attempt to answer the question, 'What is religion?', which we considered in Chapter 1. Their respective accounts are 'supernaturalist', relating religion variously to the 'holy', the 'numinous', supernatural power and the 'sacred'. It would be inappropriate to open up yet again the issue of defining religion. For our present purposes, however, it is useful to point out the potential weakness of their type of answer. Focusing as they have on the supernatural, they all seem to point to profound experiences that few rank-and-file believers have felt. How many Jews and Christians have experienced a theophany in a synagogue or church? How many Hindus have seen Vishnu's highest form when visiting a temple? These phenomenologists appeared to focus on such rare spiritual 'highs', leaving out the typical religious consciousness of the average follower. Furthermore, it should be noted that the approaches of Otto, van der Leeuw, Eliade and other phenomenologists are 'confessional': they assume that there really exists a 'numinous', a 'holy', a 'sacred' or a 'power' which the believer can access. What has happened to the methodological neutrality that the phenomenologist has advocated?

ENGAGED SCHOLARSHIP

Scholars of religion often claim to strive for impartiality and objectivity, even if this is an ideal rather than a reality. However, should we always seek to understand religious phenomena, without passing value judgements or seeking to change things?

Not infrequently, scholars are requested to intervene in religious matters. On a recent occasion the present author was contacted by a firm of solicitors. A Jehovah's Witness had died in a road accident, and the other driver had claimed that his refusal to accept a blood transfusion amounted to contributory negligence, and hence that he was at least partly to blame for his death. I was asked if I would be an expert witness and provide a report, outlining the Jehovah's Witnesses' position on blood, and whether giving and receiving blood were absolute prohibitions. At that time (around 2002) it was alleged that the Watch Tower organization had changed its position regarding blood – an idea to which the media gave momentum, but which was largely untrue. Additionally I was asked for statistical information. How likely was one to encounter a Jehovah's Witness on the roads? Was the average British driver more or less likely to come across a Jehovah's Witness than, say, a Buddhist? My checking of statistical data confirmed my impression that there are more Jehovah's Witnesses than Buddhists in the country, and that they were a significant religious minority, and worthy of consideration.

On discussing the matter subsequently with colleagues, I was surprised to learn that quite a few who had equal expertise in the field told me that they never offered their services in this way, believing that their proper aim was impartial investigation and not active support. My rejoinder was that if I had not provided an expert opinion, someone else might have been sought who had less empathetic understanding of the Witnesses. There are many self-styled 'cult experts' around, who are only too ready to provide opinions on radio and television when some 'cult controversy' arises. Should I really be content to leave important decisions to them?

Studying religion involves something akin to the Heisenberg principle. Heisenberg was an atomic physicist who held that it was impossible to investigate the position of atomic particles without altering that position. It is rather like sending a rolling ball to discover the position of a second ball: the first ball cannot locate the second without displacing it, at least slightly. At a very minor level, I am conscious that the Witnesses' published statistics for Memorial attendance would be one person less if I had not attended as a participant-observer in the past. More significantly, to write about the Witnesses is to go some way towards changing the way the reader – and perhaps the public more widely – may perceive them. Academic writing seeks to dispel ignorance and to correct misconceptions.

Academics often talk about 'empowering' communities that we study. We are indebted to them for much of our livelihood. If they are unwilling to co-operate with academics who study them, our knowledge will be significantly poorer. As researchers, we gain prestige and indeed our livelihood from our study of them. Many members of the communities we study undertake to speak to our students, enable them to undertake fieldwork and act as unpaid providers of information for student assignments. It is therefore appropriate that scholars and students of religion should 'put something back' into these communities and offer some reciprocal benefit. One minimal expectation is that we should not remain in a university's ivory towers, but disseminate our knowledge to improve people's understanding and to inform public debate.

Does this mean that we should always feel constrained to plead the cause of the religious organizations we study? In common with a number of colleagues in other institutions, I recently received a message from the Church of Scientology. Their perceived problem was that the internet's search engines did not give Scientology's websites a sufficiently high ranking in their league tables, causing internet surfers to accept their opponents' rather hostile information in preference to their own. Their request was two-fold: I might care to contact the technical staff at Google to protest about this, and I might also insert some additional hyperlinks from my own website to theirs. (The number of hyperlinks pointing to a website increases its ranking.)

On this occasion I was not so co-operative and, perhaps unsurprisingly, neither were any other colleagues who received a similar request. So what was the difference? After all, the Church of Scientology has also hosted our students and provided them with information. Whatever one's opinion about the respective merits of Jehovah's Witnesses and Scientologists, surely both have a right to fair and accurate media portrayal? My response was influenced by several factors. First, I did not know enough about how search engines rank internet material to decide whether a gross injustice had occurred. Second, the first request was for impartial information; although the firm of solicitors clearly expected that my report would help their case, expert witnesses are expected to provide information that is fair and accurate, to the best of their knowledge, and if there had been exceptional circumstances in which Jehovah's Witnesses permitted blood transfusion, I would most certainly have mentioned this. By contrast, the Church of Scientology was seeking support: they were campaigning, and inviting me to align myself with their cause.

One particularly contentious issue is the acceptance of sponsorship or hospitality from religious organizations, especially controversial ones. Should one accept an invitation to join a fact-finding expenses-paid trip abroad, or should one adopt the policy of a colleague who specializes in new religious movements, and who tells me that she will never put herself in a position where she benefits in any way from such organizations? The sponsored overseas visit may be the quickest and most efficient way of information-gathering, and funding from external sources may be difficult to find. In any case, if a scholar goes on a fact-finding visit, surely the information is the same, whoever is funding the visit? Those who criticize academics who go on such expenses-paid trips may justly point out that finance can skew research: those religious organizations which have the funds are more likely to be able to commission research than poorer groups who do not. There is also the fear that those who accept funding and hospitality may find themselves compromised. It is more difficult to refuse to speak on behalf of a religious organization if one is beholden to them, and the scholar may feel constrained to accept the organization's version of controversial issues.

In this matter, two considerations remain paramount: the pursuit of knowledge, and the integrity of one's research. If the researcher feels compromised by a religious movement, then he or she has probably acted inappropriately. Whatever one's level of engagement, the scholar must remain able to weigh up different points of view and, when appropriate, present material that diverges from the account that adherents might wish to hear. Some time ago I received an invitation to take part in a radio interview about Nostradamus. I had not realized that the presenter was highly impressed by Nostradamus' prophecies, and she was clearly disappointed with my criticisms that his prophecies are vague and inconsistent. The discussion was a healthy one, though, enabling different viewpoints to be expressed and examined.

Perhaps more significantly, religion in recent times has emerged once again as a significant factor in public life which strengthens 'social cohesion'. In Britain, hardly a week goes by without media attention or political activity concerning a religious issue. It seems to me that when religion 'goes public' it needs another approach to be added to the confessional (theology) and the agnostic (the study of religion). High-profile media coverage can distort public perceptions and influence government decisions. The scholar of religion has a role to play in these debates, hopefully providing a more informed perspective that can redress the imbalance.

Ninian Smart's 'dimensional' approach

It is at this point that Ninian Smart (1927–2001) should be introduced. Although much of Smart draws on van der Leeuw's writings, his phenomenology differs from that of the earlier phenomenologists, in that he does not presuppose the existence of any supernatural being or power. Smart adopts a stricter methodological agnosticism:

although one can disagree about whether there exists a god or supreme power, the people who practise their religions undeniably exist, with their associated worldviews. Smart's phenomenological approach entails 'structured empathy': in other words it does more than simply describe, by attempts to organize the phenomenon, using appropriate scholarly apparatus. Smart's six or seven 'dimensions' provide one basic way of structuring religion for academic study.

Phenomenology has been deeply influential in the study of religion, enabling a contrast between the way in which religion is studied academically, and the 'confessional' approaches that are characteristic of the instruction that takes place within religious organizations and seminaries. At a basic level, phenomenology entails avoiding any criticism of a religion that is under study, any pejorative characterizations of it (e.g. with the use of words like 'idol', 'superstition', 'Mohammedanism'), or the application of vocabulary which does not properly belong to the religion under discussion: for example, early scholars of Buddhism wrongly described a 'Buddhist church'. False comparisons are also ruled out, such as 'Nirvana is the Buddhist equivalent of heaven'. It may be necessary, of course, for the purposes of scholarly analysis, to use 'etic' as well as 'emic' categories. Ideally, one should write about religion so that one's colours do not show: we are writing appropriately when it is not apparent whether we are Buddhist, Christian, Muslim, or whatever, or nothing at all! (As previously mentioned, when discussing a religion we should not lapse into a statement like, 'We believe that . . .', even if we are writing about our own religion.)

In outlining his phenomenological method, Smart insists that one fundamental quality of the student of religion is *empathy*. As Smart writes, '. . . we should not judge a person until we have walked a mile in his or her moccasins' (Smart, 1995, p. 6). Smart is quoting a Native American proverb, and the word 'moccasins' rather than 'shoes' reminds us that – unless a reader is a Native American – we must try, as far as we are able, to 'get inside' the follower of a religion that is alien to us, and to understand and feel what the experience must be like. This entails adopting a non-confrontational and non-judgemental stance: we seek to understand, not to criticize, stereotype or misconstrue. However, empathy is not the same as sympathy – a common misunderstanding. We may not necessarily approve of everything we come across in the name of religion, but we must try to understand *why* people follow the religion they do. Bracketing one's assumptions does not mean that, at a personal level, we do not have those assumptions and value-judgements.

Unlike sympathy, empathy is not a feeling of rapport but an analytical tool, and it is therefore not a matter of cultivating 'positive vibrations' about a religion, or being able to imagine what it must be like to be one of the various practitioners that comprise each religion. This would be an impossible task. Smart commends 'moccasin-walking', but one cannot experience what it is like to be a follower of another religion, or even to be another follower of one's own. To give one example: when Pope Benedict VI was elected Pope in 2004, he said, 'Dear brothers and sisters, after the great Pope John Paul II, the cardinals have elected me, a simple and humble labourer in the vineyard of the Lord.' People often say that being given an honour is a 'humbling experience', but is this how Pope Benedict felt, or did he feel pride at having aspired to Roman Catholicism's top job? We do not know. We have no idea what it must be like to be elected Pope: papal office is one of many pairs of moccasins that we will probably never be able to try on. Religions have many different varieties of follower, and we cannot hope to understand them all. Islam includes Muslim women who cover their faces in public with a veil, workers who may be trying to reconcile their faith with a secular environment, adolescents who suspect that they may be gay and Al Qaeda suicide bombers. They are all Muslims, but it would be hypocritical to suggest that we 'know how they feel'. However, this is not what the phenomenologist recommends. What I need to acquire is an ability to understand their worldview, and to make sense of it non-judgementally.

In order to understand these different worldviews, we need to discover what their various components are, how they are structured and how they interrelate. Smart therefore talks of 'structured empathy' and his 'dimensional' scheme, which we touched on in Chapter 1, is an attempt to achieve this. Smart's scheme initially involved six dimensions; he later added a seventh.

First, the *experiential*. Most followers of religions do not have the dramatic religious experiences like St Paul's on the Damascus Road (Acts 9.1–19), Isaiah's in the Jerusalem Temple (Isa. 6) or Arjuna's theophany of Krishna's higher nature (*Bhagavad Gita*, 11). These high 'numinous' experiences appear to be reserved for a privileged few. However, many religious adherents would claim to be aware of some kind of divine or supernatural presence at least occasionally, for example in prayer, worship or meditation.

The *mythic* – also called the 'mythological' or the 'narrative' – is often misunderstood. 'Myth' is an item of technical vocabulary among scholars and differs from the popular meaning of something that is popularly believed but false. Perhaps it is unfortunate that the term carries the connotations derived from its popular use, but for better or worse it is the technical vocabulary that scholars have adopted, and is unlikely to be changed. Whatever else followers of a religion know, they will be familiar with their myths. No Jew is unfamiliar with the story of how Moses led the Israelites out of Egypt through the Sinai desert where he received Torah, or how they entered the promised land of Canaan. Every Buddhist knows the story of Prince Siddhartha Gautama renouncing the luxurious life of his palace, taking on the lifestyle of a world-renouncing ascetic, and finally gaining enlightenment by sitting under a pipal tree in Bodh Gaya in North India. No Christian could fail to know the story of Jesus' birth, ministry, crucifixion and resurrection.

Some of the features of these stories may be historically true, some may not, and adherents to a religion may differ regarding the literalness with which such pieces of narrative are believed. However, for the scholar as for the believer, their real importance lies not so much in their historicity as in their meaning. Their function is to inspire, to offer guidance for living, and sometimes to legitimize religious practices such as the Jewish Passover, Buddhist meditation, the Christian Eucharist, the Sikhs' wearing of the *khalsa* symbols and so on.

We turn now to the *doctrinal* dimension. Christianity attaches a high degree of importance to doctrines, having formulated creeds and confessions, particularly during its early history and – in Protestantism – at the time of the Protestant Reformation. Other religions do not necessarily formalize doctrines in this way, but they do have typical teachings. Thus Muslims typically believe that the Qur'an eternally existed in heaven and was given to Muhammad, the final prophet, by the Angel Gabriel (Jibreel). Hindus, Buddhists and Sikhs typically believe in rebirth. Jews generally hold that Moses received the Torah on Mount Sinai, and characteristically expect some kind of messianic age.

The *ethical* dimension is an important component of religion. Most religions teach that there is something radically wrong with the world and the individuals in it. Accordingly they have devised their ethical systems, while usually acknowledging that good conduct in itself will not lead to salvation or liberation. Jews acknowledge the Torah, interpreted by the Talmud, as the supreme source for guidance in the moral life. Christians have the teachings of Jesus, and gospel passages such as Jesus' Sermon on the Mount may be particularly singled out as encapsulating his ethical teachings. For the Muslim, the Qur'an offers not only prescriptions for human behaviour, but also a means of ordering society. Islam focuses on the community as much as on the individual. Hindus have the *Dharma Shastras*, which dictate a way of life to be lived according to one's caste. Theravada Buddhists would look to the *Dhammapada*, which contains the Buddha's seemingly simple instruction: 'Do good; avoid evil; cleanse your own mind' (*Dhammapada*, 163), although Buddhists would agree that this is more easily said than done.

The *ritual* dimension is based on the fact that religions have their rites and ceremonies. A ritual is a set of rule-governed repetitive actions that have no obvious practical effect on the physical world. To the outsider it may not seem quite obvious why someone should receive a small piece of bread and a small sip of wine from a priest, sit cross-legged in meditation for hours on end, tie pieces of thread around a tree or sing *bhajans* in front of a holy book. To understand the meaning of a ritual can be a difficult and complex matter, and believers themselves may have different understandings and explanations.

Then there is the *social* dimension of religion. Smart's alternative expression 'the institutional dimension' is perhaps less misleading, signalling as it does that religions work as institutions, with some kind of organizational structure. Some religions have a very tight and clearly identifiable structure. Roman Catholicism displays a very high level of organizational complexity, with a clearly identifiable hierarchy, rather reminiscent of the 'line management' that one finds in international business companies: the 'infallible' Pope at the top, assisted by his College of Cardinals, archbishops, bishops, priests and laity. At the other end of the scale, there are forms of religion that are loosely structured. Examples are branches of the *Sangha* – the Buddhist monastic community – who are accountable to no higher authority. They are autonomous, with no central authority controlling them or regulating their practice.

We turn now to the last of Smart's dimensions: the *material* dimension. Most religious believers do not directly encounter supernatural beings in the way that Moses, Isaiah and Arjuna are believed to have done. The second best, therefore, is for believers to have something in the physical world which mediates the supernatural, and in order to achieve this religions use aspects of the material world. Mircea Eliade wrote that 'sacred always manifests itself as something non-ordinary', but claimed that anything could be set apart in order to disclose the sacred. The material dimension incorporates sacred objects that are used within a religion, and 'sacred spaces' that followers revere.

A sacred space may be of two types. It may be a place where a key event in a religion's history is believed to have taken place, such as Bodh Gaya, where the Buddha is said to have gained enlightenment, or it may be a place created by the religion for its rites and ceremonies, such as a church, mosque or temple. Sometimes the two types of sacred space are combined: for example, the Church of the Holy Sepulchre is said to mark the location of Jesus' crucifixion and subsequent burial, and hence combines the sacred location with a set of premises designated for religious purposes. The materials from which religious premises are constructed are ordinary, but in an important sense they become transformed when they are made sacred. One's behaviour must be appropriately modified in order to demonstrate that one is inside a sacred space. Removing shoes, taking off headgear or putting on a head covering (whichever is expected), bowing, genuflecting, making the sign of the cross on one's person, are all marks of reverence that are expected within certain sacred spaces.

It is not merely physical buildings that become transformed in the context of religion: material objects can also become special. Take, for example, the bread and wine that are used during the Christian sacrament variously known as the Mass, the Eucharist or Holy Communion. The bread and wine are physical substances, made according to human recipes, but placed within the context of a communion service the bread and wine become transformed into sacred food. The priest or minister declares them to be 'the body and blood of Christ', and they are treated differently from conventional commodities.

Some criticisms

No scholar ever has the last word, and we need to examine briefly why phenomenology has largely been abandoned. One of the most forceful recent attacks on phenomenology comes from Gavin Flood in his *Beyond Phenomenology: Rethinking the Study of Religion* (1999). Flood questions the legitimacy – indeed the very possibility – of postulating a detached self that separates itself from the subject-matter, so that the latter can be viewed in its true essential form. Flood argues that such a view presupposes that the self is a rational entity (*res cogitans*), separate from the world and from other people, similar to the philosopher René Descartes' conception of the self. Descartes' view of the self as mental substance, mind distinct from body, and self standing in contrast to others, has been under a cloud for a considerable time in contemporary philosophy. It has been argued, as indeed Flood argues, that it is the very nature of the self to exist 'dialogically'. The Jewish philosopher Martin Buber (1878–1965) became renowned for his concept of the 'I–Thou' relationship. The 'I', he contended, can only exist in relationship: it needs a 'Thou', which may be either another human being, another animate object or a thing. What would it mean for 'me' to exist without anything to relate to, to perceive or to communicate with? Could there really be an 'I' that is pure consciousness, that is conscious of nothing at all?

Furthermore, religion itself is an inter-subjective phenomenon. Once we become participant-observers – a role that is frequently essential to students of religion – we become part of the phenomenon. It is not feasible for us to become detached observers who 'sit out' on the performance in the interests of amassing data in some objective, detached way. Indeed, for many students, even *being* part of the phenomenon, assuming the dual role of researchers and practitioners, is a common scenario. To talk about a 'bridge of understanding' appears to assume that the religions that one studies are on the 'opposite side' from oneself. For much of the time, this may be so: if one is a religious believer, one is usually committed to one single religion, and, since one typically studies several religions, most of the time one will be studying religions that are not one's own. Yet, at least some of the time, a student may legitimately be studying his or her own religion. Whether the 'insider' or the 'outsider' has a better stance from which to study religion is a much-debated issue, and there are potential problems in studying a religion as an insider. However, for the purposes of the present argument it is sufficient to note that insiders as well as outsiders study religion, and do so effectively; for them there is no bridge to be built or additional empathy to be acquired.

Flood makes the further point that phenomenology fails adequately to take language and meaning into account. Take, for example, the Christian concept of the Trinity. Proponents of other faiths have often construed the Christian as affirming the existence of three gods, and hence concluded that Christianity is not wholly monotheistic. Different Christians at different times and places have offered different ways of understanding the concept of the Trinity: for example, three different modes of existence like water existing as ice, liquid or steam; St Patrick used the analogy of the shamrock, construing it as three manifestations from the same root; in my youth I was taught that God was like three parts of an egg: shell, albumen and yolk. Not all these analogies are necessarily appropriate and, as Flood cautions, one has to be careful about assuming that believers themselves always have privileged superior knowledge. (The 'egg' analogy, although commonly used, seems to militate against the teaching that God is 'without body, parts or passions', and seems to 'divide the substance' – an ancient heresy!) The point of this example is not to open up an age-old debate, but rather to demonstrate that different individuals attach different interpretations

FIGURE 6.2 Arati *at the Hare Krishna (ISKCON) Temple, Birmingham. Students adopt a participant-observer role.*

and meanings to what appears to be the same concept. Indeed, since I cannot get inside someone else's mind, I cannot know for sure whether someone is conceiving a concept in a way similar to, or different from, myself.

Of course we can share meanings, otherwise communication would be impossible. However, as Flood points out, meanings are culturally conditioned, and any attempt to explain a phenomenon by prising off a culturally conditioned meaning is likely to result in a 'thin description' of the phenomenon to be studied. To illustrate this point, I often show students a video clip of part of a Quaker meeting. Most of them have never attended such a meeting, and most do not even know what it is: they therefore do not have presuppositions. When asked to describe what they see, everyone is able to recount the visual and audible phenomena: a room with about 20 people, sitting in silence in a circle, around a table on which there is a vase of flowers. After a while, a young man gets up and starts to speak in a somewhat unprepared, hesitant way. So far, so good: but this kind of 'innocent' description, without presuppositions and without background information, is unhelpful precisely because it leaves out the background explanation, the appropriate vocabulary and its shared meanings. For example, most students (understandably) fail to notice the expression 'giving ministry', which is the Quaker term for the Spirit-inspired promptings that give rise to the impromptu contributions from the congregation. But in order to understand the phenomenon we are seeing we need a lot more than this: once we start to talk about the Protestant Reformation, the Puritans, a religion that comes from the heart, the absence of ritual objects and symbols, the lack of clerical attire and the deliberate policy of not wearing one's 'Sunday best' at a Quaker meeting, we begin to understand what is happening. It is clothing the phenomenon with explanation, rather than paring off preconceptions, that provides the key to understanding it.

There is another sense in which one cannot separate oneself from the phenomena one is studying. As someone who was brought up in the environment of Protestant Christianity, I realize that this has created a bias for which I need to compensate. I have therefore endeavoured to ensure that my studies in Christianity pay due regard to Christianity's three major traditions, which also include Roman Catholicism and Eastern Orthodoxy, and have accordingly done reading and fieldwork in these two traditions as well as my own. However, my choice of books to read and people to talk to has inevitably been my own, and even if I have taken up other people's suggestions for reading and fieldwork, the decision whether or not to accept such recommendations has been mine. In an important sense, then, any account of Christianity which I give – however seemingly unbiased – is bound to be based on my own personal, spiritual and intellectual history. There has always been one person around when I have studied Christianity, and indeed any other religion, and that is me! Some other scholar who writes on the same subject-matter will inevitably have read different material and discoursed with different informants from mine. I have only seen my own slice of the world's religions; other scholars and students have inevitably seen different slices.

This kind of observation lends support to the more general postmodern criticism of phenomenology. Postmodernist thinkers such as Jacques Derrida (1930–2004) and Jean-François Lyotard (1924–98) argue that there is no objective reality ('phenomenon') that can be correctly viewed by bracketing one's subjectivity. On the contrary, there are only subjects, each of whom can do no more than report their own subjective stance. What a writer can do, therefore, is simply to identify his or her background and standpoint, so that readers know 'where he or she is coming from', and can if necessary redress the imbalance by consulting sources that are written from a different standpoint.

From this discussion, there appear to be two extreme positions: on the one hand, the phenomenologist claims to be able to bracket assumptions and see the phenomenon objectively, as it truly is; on the other hand, there are those who aver that there can only be complete subjectivity. Is there some middle position between these opposing stances? One such attempt is by James L. Cox, in his *Expressing the Sacred:*

An Introduction to the Phenomenology of Religion (1996). Cox draws substantially on phenomenology, acknowledging the importance of *epochē* and empathy, and the existence of an objective phenomenon that exists independently of the self. At the same time, Cox suggests a 'dialogical' model for investigating religions. Cox's methodology is based on the activity of Christian mission, where the missionaries' understanding of other faiths was shaped by encounters with their exponents. The scholar thus endeavours to develop *epochē*, but subsequent dialogue with exponents of the religion under scrutiny acts as an important check on how religious activities such as rites, ceremonies and festivals are to be described, what they are called and how they relate to other phenomena in their society.

Cox identifies nine steps in describing religious phenomena.

Performing epochē

In part this entails an attitude of mind, which avoids making value-judgements about the subject-matter. It also involves a 'methodological agnosticism' in which one neither endorses nor rejects the religious phenomena under scrutiny. Cox acknowledges that this is an ideal which can be aimed at, although probably not perfected.

Empathetic interpolation

This term is borrowed from Ninian Smart. The observer attempts to 'enter into' the community to be studied. This involves not only observation, but also understanding. It includes understanding the relevant languages, the cultures in which the religious phenomena are situated and the associated symbols and ritual activities. At this stage, one provides explanations (as in the example above of the Quaker meeting); such interpretation is gained through dialogue with believers, and by studying the salient literature. Understanding comes by degrees, and therefore there is imprecision about stating that empathetic interpolation is to be undertaken. Such interpretation must be recognizable to the believer, without endorsing the beliefs and practices.

Maintaining epochē

'Entering into' the community does not amount to conversion. Hence the researcher must continue to distance himself or herself from the community while entering into their practices and seeking to obtain explanations that they would recognize. The researcher should be able to recognize the community's feelings and convictions, but without sharing them personally. Smart describes this as 'expressive bracketing'.

Describing the phenomena

Cox acknowledges that there is no uncontentiously 'pure' way of describing a religion or religious community. The researcher must select his or her data; however, the selection ought to reflect the relative importance attached to its various aspects by its adherents. This is done, as Cox puts it, by 'creative interaction': one checks one's understanding and emphases with the members of the community, but one needs to decide creatively how one will portray it.

Naming the phenomena

Providing an account of a religion involves learning the appropriate vocabulary. Some of this will be derived from the community itself ('emic' terminology) – for example, the use of terms like 'giving ministry' in connection with the Quakers. Another element of vocabulary will be scholars' terminology ('etic' terminology), which may or may not be intelligible within the community: Cox cites as example 'myths', 'rituals', 'sacred practitioners', 'scripture', 'art' and 'morality'. Pejorative, vague and distorting vocabulary should be avoided: examples cited by Cox include 'primitive', 'pre-literate' and 'superstition'.

Describing relationships and processes

It is not sufficient simply to name the phenomenon and place it into typological categories such as 'myth', 'ritual' and the like. Such elements of religion are interrelated. For example, the Hindu festival of Holi commemorates the myth of Hiranyakashipu, celebrating how he was overcome by Vishnu descending in the form of the Narasimha (the lion-man *avatar*). The myth is also reflected in Hindu art, which is frequently displayed in temples. As well as noting the intertwining of these different categories, the student of religion needs to be able to see them in cultural and historical context. Myths and festivals evolve over time, and can vary from place to place.

Constructing the paradigmatic model

The scholar will have become acquainted with a range of aspects of a religion, as well as significant differences between different traditions and differing ways in which the religion is practised by its proponents. What is it that holds these different forms and aspects together? Cox provides the example of Theravada Buddhism, for which he suggests that the core factor that runs through it is the perceived need for detachment from the world in the quest for enlightenment, and the way in which monasticism provides a means for world-renunciation. In Chapter 1 we considered the broad questions of 'From what?', 'To what?' and 'By what?' as tools for understanding a religion's main purpose. All-pervasive questions like these can help us to develop paradigmatic models for understanding a religion.

Performing the eidetic intuition

'Intuition' in this context does not mean an inspired hunch: it denotes seeing into the essence of something. At this eighth stage, the scholar attempts to understand the nature of religion itself, which stands above its manifestations in particular religions. For example one might conclude, like Eliade, that the aspects that comprise religion provide the pivot between the sacred and the profane. This is not the same as defining the term 'religion': it involves insight into the essence of what religion is.

Testing the intuition

In academic study, theories are not accepted uncritically, but must be tested and challenged. Having reached a conclusion about what the essence of religion is, one must test it out against the features of religion, and against specific religions that we have considered. Supposing we agreed with Eliade, would his identification of religion's essence encapsulate everything from the Quaker meeting to an elaborate Buddhist ceremony? Would we find such an essence in Marxism? If not, does this serve to confirm or refute his theory of religion? Would we find this essence in the folk customs associated with festivals such as Christmas? Again, is it an advantage or a disadvantage if it does not? Attempting to see the essence of religion is vitally important for the study of religion, in order to identify our subject-matter and to determine the role of phenomena that form part of any religion that is studied.

The lessons of phenomenology

The discussion of phenomenology has been fairly lengthy, but it is not fruitless. Although phenomenology has fallen under a cloud, it still affords a number of valuable insights into the way in which religion is to be studied. First, the phenomenologist draws attention to the fact that there is an important approach to religion that is neither theological nor sociological, but seeks to understand religion in its own right, without explaining it away as a psychological delusion or a means of maintaining social stability and control. Second, even if strict neutrality is an ideal rather than something completely achievable, our attention is drawn to an important way of examining religion which is neither confessional nor derogatory: our studies as students of religion do not endorse the worldviews that are studied, but do not seek to discredit them either. Third, Smart's 'structured empathy' points to a need to examine a range of features associated with a religion, not just one or two, or those features that are superficially obvious. Studying religion involves not only simply listing these, but also relating them to each other by means of a paradigmatic model. Fourth, we have seen the need for employing appropriate terminology – emic and etic – drawing on the vocabulary of the tradition being studied, as well as the technical jargon developed by scholars. Finally, the study of particular religions enables conclusions to be drawn about the essence of religion itself, and one's understanding of what is distinctively religious enables the scholar to identify what falls within the scope of his or her study, and what can be safely left outside.

DISCUSSION POINTS

1 Examine Ninian Smart's statement that '. . . we should not judge a person until we have walked a mile in his or her moccasins' (Smart, 1995, p. 6). To what extent do you think it is (a) possible, (b) desirable, to attempt 'moccasin-walking' in the study of religion?

2 The phenomenologist is purportedly attempting to create a bridge between 'I' and the religion I am studying. Consider whether this is a helpful way to model the relationship between 'me' and the believer.

3 According to phenomenology, scholars of religion should 'bracket their assumptions'. What assumptions are we likely to bring to bear on the study of religion? How are they manifested?

4 Part of the phenomenologists' quest was for an 'essence of religion'. How feasible is such a quest? Can there be such a thing as 'religion' that is manifested in each way in which it is expressed?

7

Colonialism and postcolonialism in the study of religion

Ron Geaves

Chapter Outline

Colonialism	185
World Religions	187
The origins of the term 'World Religion'	189
Levels of religion	192
Buddhism	195
Hinduism	198
Postcolonialism	200
Globalization	201
Conclusion	208
Discussion points	209

The study of religion in recent decades has been highly influenced by the theorists of cultural studies, political science and cultural anthropology as religion resurfaced in the twenty-first century as a significant player in a globalized society, sometimes competing with the notion of the nation state itself as the way in which the world is constructed. Despite various claims by some sociologists of religion in various periods of the twentieth century that religion will decline in influence under the forces of modernity and secularization (Bruce, 2002, 2003, 2011) the twenty-first century arrived with religion playing a significant part in debates on society. Arguably these were driven by the politicization of Islam, the role of religion in ethnic and tribal conflicts, for example, the Balkans, Sri Lanka, and Burma, the significance of Protestant Christianity in the United States' declaration of war against 'terror' after 9/11, and a new balance of power after the fall of Communism and the collapse of the Soviet Empire. Confucian values were seen to re-emerge again in mainland China and the continent of Africa has become a battle ground between both Muslim and Christian missionaries, exploding into ethnic/religious conflicts in Sudan and Nigeria. The following chapter will explore the significance of a number of postcolonial theorists on the study of religion and the way in which European colonialism has impacted on the study of religion. However, this is a book on the study of religion as opposed to how religion is dealt with as an aspect of cultural studies, political science or sociology of religion where the critique of reductionism is often applicable.

Religions have felt the impact of transformations that have taken place globally as a result of several dramatic forces impinging on both traditional and modern societies; these can be described under the banners of globalization and modernity, resulting in secularization, mass migration, the breaching of political, economic and cultural frontiers (Lehmann, 2002, p. 409), and various conflicts. All of these create pressures on religions that can lead to mutations resulting in fundamentalisms, including religious violence, possible decline or revivals, identity formations, gender debates, ethical debates, restructuring of state and religious relations, and conflicts over what constitutes authentic belief and practice, to name only a few points of pressure amidst many. Today the pace of globalization with accompanying mass movements of people and ideas has undermined traditional centres of authenticity and recreated structures where the authentic variations are not only plural, but are located both at the historic centres of religions and at the margins.

Thus the challenges facing religions are many and the consequent effects on societies have seriously impacted on the old adage that religion is in decline that was expounded among sociologists from the time of Emile Durkheim (1976, 2nd edn) and which remains staunchly defended by Steve Bruce. However, secularization, defined as the loss of religious life (public or individual) is not the only pressure point for the study of religion. Scholars of religion(s) have not only followed intensely the transformations taking place within religions, but have themselves been called upon to redefine their methodologies and even their understanding of what constitutes religion itself. Lehmann points out that globalization unpacks 'local cultural identities' leading to 'multifarious local identities and criss-crossing frontiers, so that *diversity comes to rule more than ever in local spaces* [my italics]' (p. 409). Kim Knott speaks about the complexity of 'interconnections' and asks the question what 'theoretical and methodological resources are available for tackling these interconnections?' (2002, p. 23) and points out that the scholar as well as the subjects of study become part of this interpretive process, interacting with each other in a dialogical framework of interaction (23). The intensity of change leads to a shifting in the balance of studies from the vertical (historical studies) to the horizontal (slicing across a religious phenomenon in the present), a shift that involves a renewed focus on the anthropological and the sociological at the expense of the theological. The concern over the methodology of study has led to debates over the relationship between 'orthodox' and the 'popular' forms of religion, the boundaries between religious and ethnic identity and even problematizes how religious labels are constructed. How safe is it to call 'Hinduism' by that name? How is the label constructed? Who constructed it and why? What is a 'World Religion'? Who declares that a religion is a 'World Religion' and who stands to gain from joining the club? Some scholars have felt that the label 'religion' itself is problematic as a separate category of study and that religion is only a constitutive formation of 'culture' and therefore should not have its own distinctive departments of study (Fitzgerald, 2000).

It is Kim Knott who alerts us to the significance of the colonial and postcolonial on the study of religion when she writes 'the study of religion has developed substantially since the late nineteenth century in response to colonial expansion and interest in different places, peoples and religions' (2000, p. 15). This chapter will therefore examine the changes in religions themselves as listed above and the transformations to the study of religion(s) as a discipline through the lens of the impact of colonialism and the subsequent postcolonial period.

Colonialism

Colonialism was more than the simple expansion of influence of the European powers through trade, mass migration of people and direct conquest. The European powers colonized more than territory as they created empires across the globe. Ashis Nandy (1983) examines the psychological problems that arise from colonialism, for both the colonizer and colonized, arguing that the construction of selfhood is intrinsically interwoven with race, class, and religion under colonial regimes and that even the attempts by colonized nations to free themselves only succeeded when the European cultural and political frameworks were used in the struggles for independence. This deculturalization arose because European colonialism was able to subjugate not only through advanced technical and economic resources, but because the colonizers successfully promoted a cultural subservience of the colonized. The overriding narrative and self-justification of European colonialism was presented as the extension of civilization, whereby imperial stewardship would transform the 'lesser' cultures of the world through an intellectual and moral reformation of 'coloured' peoples of the world. Christianity was used to theologically demonstrate that the process was divinely ordained, a natural ordering in which colonizer and colonized occupied a social and economic role within the imperial venture. Nandy was influenced by the work of the French poet and activist Aimé Césaire (1955) who calls the colonial enterprise 'thingification' where subject races are merely 'things' to be 'improved', 'reworked', 'remodelled' and if necessary recalibrated, discarded, junked or treated as obsolete, redundant or anachronistic. Césaire argues that the process involves a dehumanizing of the colonized but has a similar impact on the colonizer. In this chapter we shall see that the European colonial enterprise had profound implications not only for the categorizing of religions but the shaping of the study of religion itself.

As an Indian scholar, Nandy focuses on the Indian experience and presents Gandhi's ability to unify indigenous Indian religious traditions and politics into a resistance movement that provided an alternative to aping the values and norms of the colonizer, thus breaking with the imposed norms of Western culture and driving a hole into the ideology of colonialism. In this significant analysis, the Gandhian movement can be understood as an attempt by educated Indians to achieve independence on their own terms. Nandy's analysis has implications for the struggles of indigenous religious and tribal communities in South America, New Zealand, Australia and Northern Canada and may provide insights into the turmoil that appears to exist in many parts of the Muslim world. However, it should also be noted that Gandhi was also trained in British Law, and was able to cross the borders of two worlds successfully. With one he mobilized the masses, with the other he manipulated the colonial authorities. Gandhi was able successfully to cross or even transcend borders and pointed the way towards cultural, political and religious hybridity.

Arguably the most influential text in this field and surely compulsory reading for any student engaged in the study of an 'eastern' religion is Edward Said's *Orientalism* (1977). Said puts forward the thesis that the colonizers culturally reinvent the 'East' and offer it back to the colonized as the accurate 'view' of themselves. In other words the 'Orient' is a construction in which the 'Oriental' is only permitted to see through the 'gaze' of the Occidental. Said's quintessential text had an immense impact on the field of postcolonial studies, especially in the study of literature and provided the intellectual inspiration for scholars from the former colonized nations. Said focuses on the 'othering' of the Orient through a focus on European relations with Islam and today there is a strong critique by Muslim activists and scholars of Western scholarship of Islam as being 'Orientalism'. However, Said's work has not been without its critics. The claim in *Orientalism* that no European or American scholar could 'know' the Orient was considered highly controversial. In a comprehensive listing of the weaknesses of Orientalism as defined by Said, George Landow states:

> If someone knew Persian or Tamil grammar, the history of Islam or Hinduism, or the societies of Saudi Arabia, Egypt, or Bangladesh, he or she already belonged to the devil's party. They were corrupted by what Said defined as Orientalism. (2002)

Any attempt by scholars of eastern religions and culture to argue otherwise became almost impossible as to do so labelled them as 'Orientalists'.

It has also been commented by Gayatri Spivak (2001) and others that the book neglects China, Japan, and South East Asia, and has very little to say about India, focusing almost entirely upon the Middle East. Arguably the borders of the Orient begin at India, at least in the study of religions, where Christianity, Islam and Judaism share a common monotheistic worldview that is very different to that found in Indian religions and further eastwards. Said appears to argue that cultural appropriation was something that the West did to the East without acknowledging the Occidentalism through which the East views the West. Spivak argues that other forms of cultural domination have to be taken into account. Indian scholars, in particular, are likely to point out that Islam was culturally imposed on many places through the expansion of the Arab and other Muslim empires.

World Religions

The label 'World Religion' is more than problematic as it might appear. The task of the student of religion is to challenge such labels and understand how they come to be constructed. What makes a religion a 'World Religion' is not straightforward. If we apply the criteria of the number of adherents then Christianity, Islam, Hinduism and Buddhism would certainly qualify but Judaism and Sikhism would not be included. There are certainly Far-Eastern religions such as Taoism or Confucianism that have more followers numerically but do not appear as the 'big six' in British or Scandinavian school curricula, for example. School curricula are usually devised on the basis of the size of religious communities that are present in the country and therefore we can state with some certainty that the 'World Religions' as defined in Britain are more accurately 'British World Religions' and the same would be true in other nations where multiculturalism demands the study of several religions to further integration.

A 'World Religion' needs to be more than simply *a religion of the world*. Any religion that has a presence anywhere at all is, by definition, a religion of the world. This includes the 'big six' as well as minuscule groups such as the Way of Truth Bible Association, based in Walsall, England, which until its recent demise had only two members. A 'World Religion' also needs to be more than a religion *that has spread across the world*. Increased global communication and social mobility have caused members of many – perhaps most – religions to be distributed worldwide: this is almost as true of indigenous tribal religions (such as the African Yorubas or Australian aboriginals) as it is of mainstream Christianity.

Faced with the problems inherent in using numerical strength as a measure of whether a religion is a 'World Religion', one might suggest that it is the *chronological span* that is decisive. Such a criterion might distinguish a religion from a new religious movement, which is often said to be characterized by substantial allegiance from first-generation converts. Such a suggestion would certainly admit the 'big six' as acceptable candidates for academic study as 'World Religions'. Scholars would certainly have to add Zoroastrianism to the list of religions to be studied, since Zoroastrianism is probably the world's most ancient religious tradition, and, since Zoroastrians do not permit conversion to their faith, there are no first-generation converts to it. On a 'chronological span' criterion, Sikhism (having arisen in the fifteenth century) would have less of a claim for inclusion than the other more ancient traditions, and Bahá'ísm would at best be a very borderline case. Cao Daism would be 'out', and primal religions would be 'in'. Added to this is the problem of deciding what to do with present-day religions that claim to be revivals of ancient traditions, such as modern Mithraism, Paganism and Celtic spirituality.

Allied to the notion of chronological span is the *influence* exercised by a religion. The longer a religion has been in existence, the more likely it is to exercise its influence on other faiths and to generate new expressions of spirituality that develop into independent religions. Thus Judaism provided the common heritage for Christianity and Islam; Islam provided the cradle for the Bahá'í faith; the brahmanical tradition which is now known as Hinduism produced Buddhism, Jainism and Sikhism. Zoroastrianism had a profound influence on Judaism in the first-century BCE (or maybe slightly earlier) and hence on the emergent Christian faith; it was one of the faiths known to Muhammad, and may well have had some bearing on the inception of Islam. On the 'influence' criterion, more recent religions would not qualify, since they have significantly less time to make their impact felt. Bahá'ísm would certainly be excluded, and Sikhism remains a doubtful candidate: it has scarcely had a global impact, although it has given rise to several Sikh-related sects such as the Ravidasis, the Nirankaris and some new religious movements such as Healthy Happy Holy (3HO).

Influence relates to a religion's *mission*. There is an important difference between a religion that spreads worldwide through the dissemination of its members throughout the globe – the rise of 'diaspora' communities – and a religion that attracts new converts through evangelizing and proselytizing. In a discussion of Hinduism, Timothy Fitzgerald argues that regarding Hinduism as a 'World Religion' is highly problematic. He argues that for something to be regarded as a 'World Religion' it must do more than simply spread worldwide; it must offer a universal message for the whole world's acceptance, rather than a localized ethnic community, thus transcending cultural boundaries. The import of this line of argument is to propose a typology of religions that distinguishes between 'ethnic religions' and 'World Religions'. Fitzgerald contends that the hallmark of a World Religion is that it has scriptures in which its principal teachings are encapsulated, and missionaries who will take its message beyond the frontiers of its country of origin.

The point about scriptures certainly identifies a feature that is common to the 'big six', as well as to the Bahá'í : all of them have their distinctive scriptures, and, as has been argued in a previous chapter, the study of scriptures has been a key factor historically in securing academic interest in them. However, we have also noted that recent decades have seen a growing interest in primal religions, and it has been argued that traditionally scholars have tended to privilege 'religions of the book', thus undervaluing the ones that rely on an oral tradition, and express their spirituality in less permanent forms. It also remains true that there are religious communities who possess scriptures, but to whom scholars do not typically accord the status of a World Religion. Examples are the Church of Scientology, who defined their own canon of 'scripture' in 1996, consisting of founder-leader L. Ron Hubbard's philosophical and religious writings, and the Family Federation for World Peace and Unification (formerly the Unification Church), whose leaders have defined which versions of Sun Myung Moon's speeches are authoritative, and whose key writing *Divine Principle* serves as a main text.

The notion of mission and the possession of a universal message remain problematic. It is certainly true that a religion like Santeria, followed by an African former-slave diaspora in Latin America, and which offers communication with ancestors and deities, lacks a universal message, while mainstream Christianity seeks to bring the world to Jesus Christ, whom Christians proclaim to have died for the sins of the entire world, offering universal salvation. It is doubtful, however, whether all of the 'big six' purport to offer a universal message. Christianity, Islam and Buddhism certainly do, although since Buddhism teaches that one has many lives to live, there is less urgency in Buddhism to follow the *dharma* (teaching of the Buddha). All these three religions have propagated themselves worldwide, attracting new followers in many diverse cultures. The same cannot be said for Hinduism and Sikhism, however. Apart from a few movements such as the International Society for Krishna Consciousness, Brahma Kumaris and Sahaja Yoga (there are a few others), Hinduism tends to exist outside India as a diaspora, and Westerners seldom join indigenous Hindu temples. Hinduism tends to adopt a tolerant view of other faiths, typically claiming that 'all paths lead to God' – hence its reluctance to proselytize and persuade others to abandon their faith in favour of Hinduism. Both Hinduism and Sikhism are particularly associated with geographical locations: India in the case of Hinduism, and the Punjab in particular in the case of Sikhism, which militates against the claim that these are 'World Religions'.

Under the scrutiny of such analysis only Christianity, Islam and Buddhism would fulfil all the criteria of a 'World Religion'. They each possess the *numerical strength,* global *influence* and a universal *mission* global in scope. Sikhism and Judaism are too small, Hinduism is too regional and although it has spread around the world it is primarily through Hindu migration.

The origins of the term 'World Religion'

Thus a number of scholars in the study of religion have become uneasy with the World Religion's approach as it regards the divisions between religions as unproblematic and does not investigate the processes whereby such construction of a 'World Religion' were created. Although the term 'World Religions' was in regular use within Religious Studies in British universities by the middle of the 1960s, its historical use does not go further back than the twentieth century. One of its earliest usages in a title of a book was in 1916 when William Paton published *Jesus Christ and the World's Religions*. In 1938 E. O. James' book *Comparative Religion* contained a section entitled 'The Rise of the World Religions' and in 1952 Finegan published *The Archaeology of World Religions*. However, by the mid-1960s a plethora of scholars who could be argued to be the founders of the contemporary study of religion in the second half of the twentieth century were employing the term. For example, Geoffrey Parrinder published *What World Religions Teach* in 1963 and the influential Ninian Smart changed the title of his *A Dialogue of Religions* published in 1961 to *World Religions: A Dialogue* when reprinted in 1966.

These book titles go some way to showing that the use of the term 'World Religions' was a mid-twentieth-century construct to some degree created by university professors in the study of comparative religion. The term 'comparative religion' had itself appeared in the nineteenth century along with the first university chairs in 'comparative religion' being established in the late nineteenth century, for example, the famous German Orientalist Max Müller was awarded a professorship in comparative religion at Oxford University in 1850. William Paton's *Jesus Christ and the World's Religions* published in 1916 alerts us to the role of Christian missionaries in the study of the world's major religions and indeed the study of 'comparative religion' would come to be criticized in the second half of the twentieth century as too tainted by favourable comparisons of Christian doctrine with that of other religions. Even as early as 1624 Herbert of Cherbury was arguing in his work *De Veritate* that the judge of a religion's truth-claims corresponded to the truth or falsity of its doctrines as measured against Christian truths. In the eighteenth century this continued with other religions, especially those encountered in the East, being defined by reference to Western categories such as monotheism. Indeed Hinduism would be reinvented as Brahmanism, while other versions of the vast and diverse ancient tradition were ignored. By the beginning of the nineteenth century, the religious traditions of the world were being examined to determine their constituent parts, sacred texts, ritual practices, core doctrines and structural organizations to form 'isms', for example Hinduism, Buddhism, Jainism, Taoism, Sikhism and so on. Where religions did not fit such categorization they were deemed as outside the fold, for example, African traditions were defined and marginalized as 'not a religion' (Chidester, 1996) until Geoffrey Parrinder (1949) was to argue effectively for a primordial monotheism that underpinned most African religions.

It was during the period of European colonial domination of the Orient that most of the individual World Religions from that region were labelled under the categories that still exist in the World Religions approach. The interest in 'comparative religion' paralleled the colonizing of the East, which effectively privileged those religions whose countries came under British, French and Dutch colonial rule. Thus Hinduism and Buddhism in particular attracted Western scrutiny, but not the traditional religions of China, Japan and Korea. The strong interest in Islam can also be attributed to its geographical proximity to the Mediterranean, and the fears which this generated in the medieval period. As soon as the European powers expanded their influence and territory they met Muslim empires in the Middle East, North Africa, Central Asia and India.

The expression 'World Religion' may not therefore be a particularly appropriate one, but merely a 'construct', an artificially devised term, whose boundaries and application are somewhat nebulous, and to argue, as does the anthropologist Pnina Werbner (2002) that to some degree, the labelling of the world's religions through identifying their constituent components is part of the process of colonization, and is also a feature of the subaltern position of colonized peoples. Pnina Werbner notes in her study of Muslims in Manchester that 'in their performative rhetoric, the people we study essentialise their imagined communities in order to mobilize for action' (Werbner, 2002, p. 234).

THE STUDY OF HINDUISM

The study of Hinduism is problematic and challenging in a number of ways. As an ancient religion with no single founder and a bewildering array of sacred texts, Hindus display considerable cultural plurality which may be described as a 'mixing' with other faiths but in fact reflects the encompassing nature of Hindu traditions and a prevailing mood of inclusivism. The fact that Hindus may venerate Jesus at Christmas time or possess religious posters of the Sikh Gurus and the Buddha in their homes does not necessarily signify a syncretic mix of two or more religions but rather that Hindus 'layer' religious narratives instead of replacing one 'truth' with another.

In recent years, the labelling of a cluster of various traditions originating in the Indian subcontinent as 'Hinduism' has been challenged by various scholars. It has already been noted that the term 'Hinduism' was not ascribed by those who practised the religion. It was a label given by outsiders, first by Muslim conquerors and then the British, and only referred to a geographical location; namely the people who lived on the other side of the River Indus. The label of 'Hinduism' was first used among Westerners in the eighteenth century and the earliest known reference to it being used by a 'Hindu' was in 1816 when uttered by the nineteenth-century reformer Ram Mohan Roy who was himself considerably influenced by Western theology. Richard King points out that it was not until the nineteenth century that the term 'Hinduism' became a label to refer to an apparent 'unified, all-embracing, and independent religious entity' (King, 1999, p. 100). King effectively argues that the British, with their privileged colonial position in India were in part responsible for the creation of 'Hinduism' as a single World Religion (1999, p. 100).

If King is right, then any study of Hinduism must take into account the construction of contemporary academic approaches to the religious life of South Asia and the degree to which 'Hindus' themselves have been influenced by such perceptions. In short, the label 'Hinduism' requires deconstruction. King mentions two ways in which Western colonization has impacted on the construction of modern understandings of Hinduism. The first is through the emphasis on certain Sanskrit texts translated into European languages and perceived to contain the core of 'Hindu' doctrine. The second is the degree to which the study of 'Hinduism' has reproduced the disciplines that have historically developed in Western study of the Judaic-Christian religions (King, 1999, p. 101).

The two strands are intrinsically connected but a third stream of Western cultural phenomenon, increasingly significant since the early nineteenth century enters the mix and profoundly transforms the European gaze at the Hindu 'other'. King mentions that one of the enduring images that has imposed itself on the imaginations of Westerners is the characterization of Indian religions as mystical (King, 1999, p. 96). It had not always been so. J. J. Clarke reminds us that the first love of the Orientalists was in fact China. In the eighteenth century India was perceived as backward, superstitious, lacking reason and a civilization in decay. The qualities of Indian religions did not appear to match the sensitivities of the Enlightenment and it was only with the rise of Romanticism that attention was diverted to India. Clarke argues that the rationalists of the eighteenth century imposed upon Confucianism, the concept of an 'ideal polity governed by wise and philosophically educated rulers' while the poets and idealists of the nineteenth century created the idea of 'a more holistic and spiritually driven culture' (Clarke, 1997, p. 60). The teachings of the *Upanishads*, in particular, appeared to offer a counter to the materialistic and mechanistic philosophies of the Enlightenment. However, the Romantics were not only in rebellion against the ideas of the previous century. The 'mystic East' also represented a spirituality that appeared to be absent from much of Western Christianity since the Protestant Reformation and which paralleled the renaissance of all things medieval among the Romantic artists and writers. The post-Romantic movements, embodied in the counterculture of the 1960s were to pick the same distortions of Indian religions, celebrating them as possessing the magic, spirituality and mystery apparently lacking in Western Christianity. If the Orientalists and Romantics of the nineteenth century brought Hinduism back to Europe repackaged in the framework of their own idealism, the youth countercultures of the second half of the twentieth century completed the process. The former only translated the texts, the latter invited the gurus. Our understanding of 'Hinduism' and the way we study it has to be placed in the context of the meeting between East and West in a colonial and postcolonial context.

Reading

Clarke, J. J. (1997), *Oriental Enlightenment*. London: Routledge.
King, R. (1999), *Orientalism and Religion*. London: Routledge.
Nesbitt, E. (2004), *Intercultural Education*. Brighton: Sussex Academic Press.

Levels of religion

It is not only in the way religions are constructed as discrete entities with fixed borders between them, identifiable by their key characteristics that was to some degree part of the colonial venture on the part of European states, but also the way that certain aspects of the religions were privileged over others. Whether explicitly or implicitly the colonial powers were Christian and Christianity became the 'ideal type' for measuring all others against. Religions that had ancient sacred texts, 'spiritual' historic founders, ethical traditions that could be measured against Christian teachings, were eligible to join the 'World Religions club' and to be studied by European scholars, religions that had none of these elements were more likely to be categorized as 'superstition' or 'backward'. In the post-Darwinian world of the second half of the nineteenth century when colonialism was at its peak, scholars of the time applied evolutionary theory to their categorization of religions, with aboriginal or 'native' religions at the bottom of the scale, labelled as 'primitive' religions and Christianity at the top. The academic interest in World Religion began with the study of religious texts in ancient languages, thus privileging the 'book' religions, especially monotheism which was perceived as the pinnacle of religious development. The consequent impact on the categorization of religions would shape *inter-religious* dialogue throughout the twentieth century, but there was an effect on intra-religious privileging where certain forms of religious phenomena within a 'World Religion' were perceived to be more 'worthy' of serious scholarly enterprise than other forms.

In his classical text, *Sufism*, first published in 1950, A. J. Arberry writes that Sufism had gone into decline by the end of the Middle Ages as a result of degeneration from its mystical origins to a corrupted form of religion consisting of tomb worship and a number of popular practices prevalent among rural people (Arberry, 1956). He states:

> It was inevitable, as soon as legends of miracles became attached to the names of the great mystics, that the credulous masses should applaud imposture more than true devotion; the cult of saints, against which orthodox Islam ineffectually protested, promoted ignorance and superstition, and confounded charlatanry with lofty speculation. (1956, p. 119)

Although it is possible to challenge Arberry's main thesis by demonstrating that a number of Sufi mystics and their subsequent institutional orders have continued to appear in various parts of the Muslim world until the present time, of more importance to the theme of this chapter is the distinction that Arberry appears to be making between levels of religion: with a 'high' mysticism, on one hand and 'low' popular beliefs and practices, on the other (1956, p. 121). Arberry criticizes later Sufism for its lack of rationality, claims of miraculous powers, use of charms and amulets and associates it negatively with 'cabbalism and witchcraft'. He appears to suggest that this division is most apparent in rural areas where 'every village or group of villages acquired its local saint, to be revered and supported during his lifetime, worshipped and capitalised after his death' (1956, p. 121).

As a result of this focus on mystics and their poetry by Oriental scholars versed in ancient languages, the study of Sufism has seemingly suggested that Sufism itself was a long extinct tradition that flourished in Persia, Turkey and North Africa during a particular period of Islamic history and was represented by exceptional men and women who achieved high mystical awareness and expressed in ecstatic poetical forms (Geaves, 2000, p. 3). Living Sufi traditions, such as those prevalent in the Indian subcontinent, and practised by millions of adherents were therefore perceived as a form of religion that was left over after the decline of the classical tradition. Such an approach to Sufism not only distorts the living reality and complexity of contemporary Muslim belief and practice but it provides us with the problem of a value judgement being made between so-called high and low forms of religion.

Islam consists of a tendency towards both this-world and other-world hierarchies, a reliance on human intermediaries in this world and a hierarchy of spirits in the other, the development of perceptual symbols or images rather than the abstract word which in turn leads to a multiplicity of ritual and mystical practices, and finally loyalty towards personalities rather than a formal set of rules (Gellner, 1968, p. 130). Gellner goes on to argue that the urban literate and egalitarian Islam is represented by seminary (madrasa)-trained clerics (*ulema*) and is to some degree identical throughout the Muslim world

FIGURE 7.1 *Sufi leaders and Muslim dignitaries process in the streets of Manchester on the occasion of Muhammad's birthday (Milad i-Nabi). Such processions take place wherever sufficient numbers of South Asian Muslims have settled in British cities.*

and can be defined as orthodox, whereas 'the hierarchical, less puritanical, emotionally and sensually indulgent Islam of the saints, holy men etc is more fragmented' (1968, p. 130).

Gellner bases his observations on the argument that rural Muslims whether from the tribe or village require spiritual intermediaries between themselves and a remote deity because illiteracy renders the abstract reasoning of theologians and trained *ulema* and even the revealed voice of the deity itself are beyond them (1968, p. 133). He suggests, however, that rural Muslims require the sacred for settling disputes and defining the norms of village or tribal life. For this reason, hierarchical, charismatic religious personnel are essential (1968, p. 134). He concludes that the relationship of this religious elite with their followers is one of intense personal loyalty rather than obedience to a set of principles or rules and that this is liable to expose the villagers or tribesmen to accusations of heterodoxy (1968, p. 135). On the other hand, the city dweller is more likely to be literate and therefore the literate trained *ulema* can best function as mediators of scripture (1968, p. 135). Thus a division is placed between the orthodox, urban, literate *ulema* representing the teachings of the Qur'an and the heterodox, rural, illiterate but charismatic Sufi sheikhs providing a direct mediation between their followers and an immanent deity.

Thus Muslim beliefs and practices are divided into various orthodoxies described as 'scripturalist' Islam, and a remainder which Asim Roy argues is perceived as a 'shadowy and bottomless pit of "folk" or "popular" Islam usually denigrated by members of the orthodoxies as contaminated or corrupted by contact with local or indigenous forms of non-Islamic religions' (Roy, 1998, p. 5). Roy is aware that this kind of dichotomy not only plays into the hands of various orthodoxies but is also influenced by their polemic or didactic writing since the nineteenth century (1998, p. 34). Pnina Werbner also suggests that the division between a folk tradition and an 'official' religion in the work of Orientalists and sometimes seen in the studies of anthropologists has been influenced by the discourse of various Islamic reform movements who have been critical of Sufism (Werbner, 1998, p. 5).

Islam is not the only religion to have raised debates concerning value-laden labels of 'high' and 'low' being given to the rich variety of beliefs and practices that coexist in any tradition that has succeeded in establishing itself in the world and existing over a large period of historical time and across significant stretches of geographical distance. Buddhism, too, although its study, similar to Sufism, has been marked by a focus on doctrine and interpretation of sacred texts, has caused some scholars to be dismayed by the difference between a scholarly portrait of the religion and the beliefs and practices found by observers of indigenous Buddhists in various localities around the world.

Buddhism

A contemporary visitor to the Buddhist nations of South-East Asia would certainly be surprised if they expected to find the doctrinal Buddhism of academic texts. Although the Theravada School dominates the region, there is little evidence of a doctrinally orthodox tradition focused purely on the teachings of the historical Buddha. Adherents to Buddhism worship at shrines to Hindu deities and frequent locations associated with fertility, usually considered to be the abode of local deities or spirits. Donald Swearer reminds us that since the earliest beginnings through to the present, South-East Asian Buddhism has been both diverse and eclectic. He states:

> the area covered by present-day Burma, Thailand, Vietnam, Cambodia and Laos defies rigid classification. Both archaeological and chronicle evidence suggest that the religious situation in the area was fluid and informal, with Buddhism characterised more by miraculous relics and charismatic, magical monks than by organized sectarian traditions. (Swearer, 2002, pp. 119, 120)

In Mahayana forms of Buddhism, especially in its Tibetan manifestations, the above is even more apparent. A vast body of popular customs and beliefs coexist alongside Buddhism, sanctioned by the practitioners and it would be simplistic to make a dichotomy between the religion of the monk and the popular practices of the rural people. Techniques of divination, worship of local deities, propitiation of demons, seasonal festivals, sacralization of the land, especially mountains, household gods and particular pre-Buddhist cosmologies all figure largely in the day-to-day life of the laity. But as stated by Per Kvaerne, monks actively participate in the activities that take place outside the monastery, while simultaneously studying Mahayana philosophical systems and practising Tantra within the confines of the monastery (Kvaerne, 2002a, pp. 199, 200). Buddhism in China has integrated a number of practices that it shares with other Chinese religions such as Taoism or Confucianism. Many of these predate all three religions and can be traced back to the Shang dynasty (circa 1500–1050 BCE) and the Chou dynasty that replaced it in 1050 BCE. Many of the practices were associated with divination and were motivated by pragmatic concerns. Overmyer

FIGURE 7.2 *The Jade Emperor Pagoda, Ho Chi Minh City, Vietnam. The temple is part Taoist/Confucian and part Buddhist. Outside the temple, the priest makes offerings to spirits. Eastern religions do not always neatly fit the categories devised by Western scholars.*

explains how the Shang interpreted the patterns of cracks in oxen or sheep bones, after inserting heated bronze into bored holes. Petitions were made concerning weather, illness, harvests, fertility and administrative decisions. Sacrifices of flesh and grain were made to spirits of the air while libations of fermented spirits were offered to the spirits of the earth.

What is undeniable, is the degree to which they remain a part of the everyday religious life of the Chinese, practised by millions that claim allegiance to Buddhism, Taoism and Confucianism even those traditions that were more concerned with soteriology in their doctrines and practices. However, it is important to note that the quest for immortality is found in Chou engravings as early as the eighth-century BCE (2002, p. 266), thus the pragmatic concern for health and longevity overspills into the hope for immortality that becomes a quest to transcend the world.

One of the most useful categorizations of Buddhism is proposed by Melford Spiro who utilizes a fourfold division of Nibbanic, Kammatic, Apotropaic and Esoteric (Spiro, 1970). Spiro's Nibbanic Buddhism refers to the final goal of the Buddha's message, that is nirvana. Thus the practitioners of this aspect of Buddhism focus on the means of liberation from this world by close observance of Buddhist doctrines as enshrined in sacred texts believed to the teachings of Gautama Buddha or other enlightened luminaries. The ideal practitioner will be the world-renouncing monk who acknowledges that Buddhist end-goals can be achieved only by total rejection of the world (1970, pp. 31–65).

Kammatic Buddhism is defined as a religion of proximate salvation, that is a shift in the soteriological goal from the absolute nirvana to that of better rebirth. In a sense, the practitioners of Kammatic Buddhism, more likely to belong to the laity than the order of monks, have accepted the proposition that the planes of nirvana and samsara are eternally distinct and separate. Although the monk may endeavour to attain nirvana, most Buddhists see themselves passing innumerable lives in samsara. Consequently, they are concerned with ethical, moral and religious behaviour which will make samsara as pleasurable as possible, or at least reduce its level of suffering. For many Buddhists, although intensely aware of the nature of *dukkha* (suffering, unsatisfactoriness), much of samsaric life is *thukkha* (pleasure) and to be pursued. Rather than the knowledge required by the pursuer of nirvana, the practitioners of Kammatic Buddhism focus on meritorious action in order to achieve their desires rather than the former's attempts to eliminate desire (1970, pp. 66–91).

Apotropaic Buddhism is not concerned with either nirvanic liberation or better rebirth. On the contrary, it is concerned with pragmatic elements in everyday life such as health, longevity, fertility, drought, floods and other natural forces that can bring either disaster or prosperity. Furthermore it assumes that these requirements for daily well-being can be controlled by magical means that enlist either the assistance of benign or keep away the malign influence of supernatural beings through the intercession of specialist practitioners or ritual activity. The everyday world is assumed to be filled with dangerous spirits and beings from whom protection is essential (1970, pp. 140–61).

Spiro's final category of esoteric Buddhism refers to a number of sects, that although soteriological in their motivation, are not purely Buddhist but rather draw upon syncretic meetings with other Chinese, Indian or indigenous religions. The practices of esoteric Buddhism are not normative as in the other categorizations but require initiation. Spiro argues that these sectarian movements also transform the soteriological intentions of exoteric Buddhism away from the future (final nirvana or better rebirth) to the present and immediate (1970, pp. 162–87). Spiro's esoteric Buddhism generally describes the type of Buddhism usually described as Tantric.

Hinduism

Scholars of Hinduism have also created a number of category systems to describe the complexity of the living religious traditions that make up the strands or layers that comprise the whole. Sharma has noted that the study of popular Hinduism presents problems for the researcher who is faced with 'an inextricable relationship between the 'multiplicity' and diversity of ritual practitioners' that function within the vast variety of local cults and pan-Hindu practices (Sharma, 1970). Several studies have attempted to categorize this complex relationship by suggesting that cults develop strategies of authentication that move them from a 'Little Tradition' to a 'Great Tradition' (Singer, 1972) or from local Hinduism to all-India Hinduism (Srinivas, 1952).

Srinivas refers to this process in Hinduism as 'sanskritization' but it is important to understand that Srinivas is not referring to the Sanskrit language but to a process whereby a marginalized 'mobile group' in Hindu society introduces changes of custom, ritual, ideology or lifestyle to bring themselves closer to the mainstream of Hinduism (Srinivas, 1989). However, Srinivas, a highly educated member of a Brahmin intellectual elite, seems to be suggesting that lower castes or deprived sectors of Hindu society can achieve parity or respectability by incorporating aspects of Hindu religious doctrine such as *varnashramdharma*, *samsara*, *dharma*, *pap*, *punya*, and *moksha* more usually associated with higher caste groups. Srinivas' sankritization theory has been criticized by a number of anthropologists and sociologists but remains an important contribution in the process of classifying and categorizing Hinduism's diversity and complexity. It would appear, certainly, that Srinivas is saying that if a tradition within Hinduism has gained credibility or popularity throughout India then it has been sanskritized. A closer look at Srinivas' ideas will reveal the categorization of religious phenomena as either 'high' or 'low'. It is advisable to look out for descriptions of South Asian religious traditions as contrasts between 'elite', 'official', 'orthodox' or 'intellectual' as opposed to 'folk' or 'popular'. As with Srinivas, there may be elements of elitism that are associated with particular groups within the tradition that have a vested interest in promoting their values over and above the claims of others. This

FIGURE 7.3 *Village Temple, Pushkar.*

may be to do with class or caste distinctions or a feeling of superiority that arises from feeling that a more exclusive access to truth is possessed by various self-proclaimed orthodoxies. The above categories often bear a relation to societal divisions. Tarachand states:

There have always been two distinct strata of society in India, the one higher and the other lower; the first small in numbers but in possession of highly developed religious, social orders and institutions. The second, comprising the great mass of the people who occupy a humbler rung in the cultural ladder. The first provides the intellectual and aristocratic and the second the folk element in India's culture. (Tarachand, 1963)

Several scholars have tried to make sense of this layering without falling into the trap of making value judgements such as 'high' and 'low' or 'primitive' and 'folk' as opposed to 'orthodox' or 'official'. One of the earlier attempts to achieve this categorization, was developed by Mandelbaum in which he categorized Hinduism as having three complexes: Pragmatic, Dharmik and Transcendental (Mandelbaum, 1966). Simon Weightman connected these three complexes in Hindu belief and practice to three distinct but overlapping motivations, survival and improvement in this life, the acquisition of merit and therefore a better rebirth and finally salvation or liberation (Weightman, 1978, pp. 38–42). Roger Ballard introduces new and valuable categories Panthic and Qaumic not found in Weightman or Mandelbaum's classifications. Qaumic is used by Ballard to describe the more recent phenomenon where a group of people use a set of religious ideas and activities to close ranks as a community and advance their common social, economic and political interests (Ballard, 1996, pp. 25–8). The Panthic describes any religious movement where a group of followers organise themselves to promote and follow the teachings of a spiritual master, living or dead. The overriding motive is usually concerned with closer proximity or experience of the Divine through mystical union (Ballard, 1996, pp. 16, 17). Discerning students will notice the similarity between Spiro's classification of Buddhism and the above classifications of Hinduism.

Postcolonialism

Said and Spivak move us on from colonialism to postcolonialism and the emergence of new world order that challenges the conception of the nation state fundamental to the colonial mentality. Postcolonial too is far more than merely the reorganization of the geographical and political world after the decline of colonialism. The term 'postcolonial' does extend 'colonialism' to encompass all culture and political life that remains affected by the imperial process to the present day. Postcolonialists see the world through the 'lens of a continuity of preoccupations throughout the historical process' that was started by the European imperial expansion (Bill Ashcroft et al., 1989). Yet Postcolonialism (also Postcolonial Studies, Postcolonial Theory, and Postcolonialism) is also a significant interdisciplinary academic discipline containing methods of intellectual theorizing that analyse, explain, and respond to the cultural legacies of colonialism and all forms of imperialism, to the human consequences of controlling a country for the economic exploitation of the indigenous people and their resources. Postcolonialism is a theoretical position which has offered scholars of religion significant insights into contemporary religion(s).

Globalization

Postcolonialism is also connected to the concept of globalization. Ohuabunwa describes globalization: as the process of the intensification of economic, political, social and cultural relations across international boundaries. It is principally aimed at the transcendental homogenization of political and socio-economic theory across the globe (1999, p. 20).

Fafoyora states that it deals with the 'increasing breakdown of trade barriers and the increasing integration of World market' (1998, p. 5). MacEwan defines globalization as the spread of capitalism (1990) but Akindele et al. (2002) point out that with the collapse of the Soviet Empire in the late 1980s and early 1990s a global economy that is primarily structured and governed by the interests of 'Western behemoth countries' became ascendant. Consequently, capitalism as an economic system now dominates the globe more than at any other time in history. Those who perceive the global spread of capitalism as positive argue that it breaks down cultural barriers, promotes free-market economics, liberal democracy, good governance, gender equality and environmental sustainability. Not everyone agrees and the critics insist that along with the rapid transformation in information technology it leads to the homogenization of ideas, cultures, values and even lifestyles (Ohiorhenuan, 1998, p. 6) and the 'deterritorialization' and 'villagization' of the world. Yet it would seem apparent that global capitalism and homogenization of cultures could be the colonial enterprise in a new and even more virulent form.

In this context Gayatri Spivak developed and applied Michel Foucault's concept of *epistemic violence* to describe the destruction of non-Western ways of perceiving the world, and the resultant dominance of the Western ways of perceiving the world, introducing the theoretical positions of *subaltern*, *essentialism* and *strategic essentialism* into the fray. The term subaltern is crucial to colonial and postcolonial theory as it identifies those who exist outside the dominant power structures of either the colony or the colonial power because of social, political or geographic discrimination. Methodologically it provides a tool to retell history from below and builds upon the cultural hegemony work of the Marxist theorist Antonio Gramsci. It is equally influenced by Jacques Derrida's theory of deconstruction which is used to interrogate the assumptions of Western thought by reversing or displacing the hierarchical 'binary oppositions' that provide its foundation. Deconstruction challenges the privileging of identity based upon someone believed to have the truth. It does expose the error of such truth claim-based hegemony but rather constantly and persistently looks into the structural processes whereby such truths are produced. The term *essentialism* refers to the dangers of perception that lie in reviving subaltern voices that oversimplify the cultural identity of heterogeneous social groups, and, thereby, create stereotyped representations of the diverse identities that compose a given social group. The term *strategic essentialism* denotes a temporary, essential group-identity used in the praxis of discourse among subaltern groups as a way of advancing their cause and opposition to hegemony. Dipesh Chakrabarty (2000) builds upon Sivak's work proposing that Western Europe simply be considered as culturally equal to the other cultures of the world, that is, as 'one region among many' in human geography.

ESSENTIALISM IN WORLD RELIGIONS

An essentialist position within the context of the study of religions is usually taken to be located in the work of a number of significant figures with their roots in liberal Protestantism, for example John Hick, Ninian Smart and Wilfred Cantwell Smith who have adopted a pluralist position based on the idea of an existing 'essence' that unites all the world's major faith traditions, despite the evidence of diversity. Kenneth Surin and others have criticized this position and argued that the pluralism of Hick and Cantwell Smith itself represents a mode of cultural production which is historically, socially and politically constituted. He points out that pluralists depend upon an unspoken religious position which relies on a Kantian-type distinction between a 'noumenaltranscendent focus common to all the religions' and the culturally conditioned and hence 'culturally specific' phenomenal images which are a schematization or concretization of the Real.

In the context of South Asian traditions, essentialism takes on other dimensions linked to the social and economic conditions of the significant diasporas that now exist throughout the world and creates problems of representation. It is the problem of essentialism that often underlies these difficulties of representation. Feuerbach (1841) argued that each religion contained an essence and the early phenomenologists provided a methodology for identifying and classifying essences in particular religions. The fear, then, is that religions may be presented as series of ideal types that do not represent the complexity of lived religious experience. Consequently, a number of criticisms of the World Religions approach to the classification of religions have been made from scholars from within the study of religion and from those who specialize in religious education in schools.

A part of the problem lies with understandings of South Asian religions derived from borrowing the prevalent methodologies for studying Christianity. The original study of other traditions or even comparative religion was often undertaken by Christian scholars anxious to demonstrate that their own tradition's truth-claims were paramount. They often adopted the methodologies used for the study of Christianity to explore other faith traditions, and a division was made between the study of correct doctrine (theology), textual criticism (Biblical Studies) and history. This methodological compartmentalization appropriates a tradition into the hands of scholars whose systematization and categorization will not reveal the fact that religious conviction is often messy and idiosyncratic, but particularly in the context of South Asian traditions which did not generally draw upon the discourse of Christian exclusivism or compartmentalization until colonized. Veiko Antonnen, for example, states 'Scholars of comparative religion should not be hunting for the religious sacred according to prototypes given by Jewish, Christian and Islamic religious traditions' (Antonnen, 1999, p. 12).

In addition to this, it was during the period of European colonial domination of the Orient that most of the individual World Religions from that region were labelled under the categories that still exist in the World Religions approach. Both Hull and Jackson have argued that this was a reification process which was deeply flawed by the colonial power relationship. This raises serious questions as to the ownership of a religious tradition and unequal power relations. The point of concern here is that the same unequal power relations still need to be examined in the context of scholarship and the arena of religious education, where migrant faith communities are being presented. The historical processes by which a variety of Indian religious traditions have been labelled as discrete and separate, with clearly demarcated borders between them, must be part of the study of religion rather than a priori fact. It may well be that the more rigid differentiation of the traditions now prevalent in parts of India itself, and manifested as various forms of communalism, is not only a consequence of a variety of political struggles for self-identity, but has come about through contact with Western models for perceiving religious and cultural reality. Yet it is not only colonizing powers that find it convenient to essentialize in the interests of creating discrete communities, identified and divided from each other in the interest of government. To some degree, the labelling of the World Religions through identifying their constituent parts is part of the process of colonization, but it is also a feature of the subaltern position of colonized peoples. Pnina Werbner notes that 'in their performative rhetoric, the people we study essentialise their imagined communities in order to mobilize for action' (Werbner, 2002, p. 234). Mushirul Hasan refers to this process in the context of South Asian Muslim developments in the early nineteenth century when he notes that theologians, publicists and itinerant preachers called upon the notion of solidarity within the community and utilized Islamic symbols to encourage religious revivalism and Muslim nationalism (Hasan, 2002, p. 9). Other religious communities have behaved in a similar manner to create self-images, for example the Hindu Mahasabha, the RSS and various *Khalsa* movements. Self-essentializing is then, as in Werbner's definition, 'a rhetorical performance in which an imagined community is invoked' (Werbner, 2002, p. 234). Thus a number of scholars in the study of religion have become uneasy with the World Religion's approach as it takes the divisions between religions as unproblematic and does not investigate the processes whereby such constructions as a 'World Religion' were created.

Reading

Antonnen, V. (1999), 'Does the sacred make a difference? Category formation in comparative religion', in Tore Ahlback (ed.), *Approachng Religion, (Part 1)*. Abo: Scripta Instituti Donneriani Aboensis XVII:1, p. 12.

Geaves, R. A. (2005) 'The dangers of essentialism: South Asian communities in Britain and the "World Religions" approach to the Study of Religions', *Journal of Contemporary South Asia*, Special Edition – Teaching Across South Asian Religious Traditions, 14(1), March: 75–90.

Hasan, M. (2002), *Islam in the Subcontinent: Muslims in a Plural Society*. Delhi: Manohar.

Hull, J. (1995), 'Religion as a series of religions: a comment on the SCAA Model Syllabuses', in V. Baumfield, C. Bowness, D. Cush and J. Miller (eds), *The SHAP Working Party on World Religions in Education: Syllabus to Schemes – Planning and Teaching Religious Education*, pp. 11–16.

Jackson, R. (1995), 'Religious education's representation of "Religions" and "Cultures"', *British Journal of Educational Studies* XXXXIII(3): 272–89.

Surin, K. (1990), 'A politics of speech: religious pluralism in the age of the McDonald's Hamburger', in Gavin D'Costa (ed.), *Christian Uniqueness Reconsidered: The Myth of Pluralistic Theology of Religions*. New York: Orbis Books.

Werbner, P. (2002), *Imagined Diasporas among Manchester Muslims*. Oxford: James Currey.

Two other scholars need to be introduced in our examination of postcolonial theorists who have some bearing on the study of religion in the twenty-first century. The first is Homi Bhabha who attempts to throw some light upon the 'liminal' negotiation of cultural identity across differences of race, class, gender and cultural traditions (1990, 1994). Globalization has brought with it mass migration of people, reversing the tide of population shifts of the colonial era. Postcolonialism has been marked by large migrations from the colonized to the colonizers. This has not only challenged understandings of what constitutes nationhood and national identity in Western European nations, it has changed the religious landscape completely. No longer can Islam, Hinduism, Sikhism and Buddhism be studied as foreign religions when they form part of the European and North American religious landscape. Postcolonial debates over 'nationalism' have become concerned with the limitations in conceptualizing these overlapping, migratory movements of cultural formations. Bhabha's concern with the liminal attempts to theorize these 'in-between' categories of competing cultural differences. Thus Bhabha essentially argues that cultural identities cannot be ascribed to pre-given, irreducible, ahistorical cultural traits that define ethnicity. 'Colonizer' and 'colonized' cannot any longer be viewed as separate entities that define themselves independently. Bhabha introduces the possibility of the 'liminal' space as a 'hybrid' site that witnesses the production of cultural meaning. It is a short step from Bhabha's challenging of the myths of constructing the nation to Benedict Anderson's (1991) influential analysis of nationhood as 'Imagined Communities' and Talal Asad's (1993, 2003) and other anthropologists' extension of the theorization of postcolonialism from nations to religious formations. Finally we need to give some consideration to another influential South Asian Arjun Appadurai who specializes in sociocultural anthropology, globalization, and public culture and writes more explicitly on religion than the previous theorists (1974, 1977, 1981, 1983, 1986). Appadurai believes that the nation state is at a critical juncture but argues positively for the impact of global migration levels and new information technologies that will deterritorialize identities formed in old national narratives. He looks forward to a culturally hybridized world created by the growth of diverse diasporic public spheres and the global movement of images, finances, technologies and ideologies. He also persuasively argues against one-dimensional understandings of globalization and secularization, linked to the impact of modernity, suggesting that area-focused case studies have shown that globalization does not necessarily result in homogenization or Americanization but rather in a more complex dynamic between the local and the global (1995). In particular he is excited by the impact of contemporary media and migration creating 'ruptures' and instabilities in the creation of subjectivities in diasporic public spaces (e.g. Pakistani cabdrivers in Chicago listening to sermons recorded in Iranian mosques). He challenges critics who describe a modern world based on growing rationality, shrinking religiosity, secularization, increasing commoditization and regulation, and the loss of play and spontaneity. Appadurai counters that there is evidence that new religiosities of every sort are not dead at all, but have even been encouraged by global media and networks (1996, p. 7). He argues that imagination is now the property of collectives, creating 'communities of sentiment', groups that imagine and feel things together (1990) building upon Benedict Anderson's understanding that 'imagined communities' do not require face-to-face human contact any longer as electronic capitalism has produced forms that exceed both the potential of the printing press to bond communities and nation states, working transnationally and internationally. These communities carry the potential of moving from shared imagination to collective action.

Sverker Finnström notes that is now common for anthropologists to include historical accounts of colonialism in their ethnography, leading to a more interdisciplinary approach. This will impact on the study of contemporary religion as it begins to absorb the various theoretical positions outlined above in the study of the resurgence of religion in the twenty-first century. The above theorists tend to see religion as an aspect of culture but a note of warning is necessary. Finnström notes that the 'imagined' elements of group identity arising from colonial and postcolonial states exploiting various tribal, ethnic or religious traditions in the past overlooks precolonial history and places too much stress on imperialism as the sole cause of local identity formation and cultural traditions. In other words it is guilty of a form of reductionism often found in social sciences when dealing with religious identity formation.

Finnström cites the example of the cultural anthropologist Richard Fox who had argued for the impact of colonialism on the formation of Sikh *Khalsa* orthodoxy (Fox, 1985). Finnström acknowledges that it is fruitful to explore the colonial and imperial impact on the development of eighteenth- and nineteenth-century Sikh cultural formations. However Fox focuses solely on the recruitment of *Khalsa* Sikhs to the British army and the subsequent privileging of the *Khalsa* by the colonial authorities, drawing a conclusion that Sikh identity was a product of colonialism. Fox ignores the heterogeneity present in Sikh history or the impact of Sikh and Muslim empires in the Punjab but more problematically overlooks the religious origins of the *Khalsa*. To argue that the *Khalsa* is a product of British colonialism is a glorious reductionism and takes us back to an old debate over the situational and functional definitions of religion. The reduction of religion to cultural formation leaves out the 'transcendent' framework of religion as a cultural phenomenon and will lead to limited analytical framework to explore the ongoing transformation of a religious tradition. Finnström notes that Ranger (1996) had emphasized the importance of not over-stressing the contrast between the colonial and the postcolonial political agencies and offers a similar note of warning when we are comparing elements of tradition in precolonial and colonial times, and make the mistake of limiting our understanding of local history and tradition to that of Western presence and Western hegemony.

ISLAM IN THE CONTEMPORARY WORLD

Arguably it is the academic study of Islam which has felt the full impact of colonial and postcolonial theory. Muslim migration to the West has created a significant area of study within the study of religion drawing upon many disciplines including sociology, international relations, politics, cultural anthropology, history, human geography and cultural studies, to name only a handful of disciplines involved. This interest in Islam in the West has focused on the study of Muslim community formation and the causes of radicalization, and is to a large degree concerned with implicit or explicit interests in integration. However, it is also true to note that Islam and the West has generated its own sizable literature since the history-changing events of 9/11 and their aftermath. Both the relations of Muslims with the West and Muslims in the West are to a considerable degree the consequences of colonial and postcolonial relationships. Much of the Muslims world was either directly colonized or under the influence of powerful European empires throughout the nineteenth century until the middle of the twentieth century. Indeed it can be argued that much of the present-day existence of Muslim states owes its existence to the creation of nation states as part of the European project to recreate the world in its own image. Egypt was colonized by the French under Napoleon, the Mughal Empire in India fell to the British and the Ottoman Empire collapsed under the pressure of siding with the Axis in World War I and the consequent nation-state building in Turkey and the Middle East. An unintended consequence of European dominance of the Muslim world has been the reverse migration of millions of Muslims from various parts of the colonized world to Britain, France and Holland.

Muslims who live in the West are faced with a dilemma. On the one hand, they want to live out their Islamic life incorporating Islamic values in a total way including involvement in the civil society of their new locations, but they may have to face the reality that the democratic institutions that they inherit in the West arose outside of the framework of Islam and may even embrace a secular mentality that has no place for religion in public life. Even worse secularism may be celebrated in the West as the means through which the people discovered individual freedom and liberated themselves from the restraints imposed by organized religious life. This is not a position that is likely to find much sympathy from the religiously orientated Muslim who sees citizenship as more to do with divinely given responsibilities conferring certain rights that are to be enjoyed by the faithful than a human rights paradigm based on individual liberty. Rippin argues that in the face of such difference Muslims will divide into three basic typologies; isolationary traditionalists, radical rejectionists and involved reformists (Rippin, 2005).

All these positions are amenable to postcolonial theorizing to discover causes for the various positions held. The problem here is that Islam in the West gets caught up in the politics of Islam and the West. To complicate matters it will depend on where the Muslims living in the West originated and the history of the relations between religion and politics in the respective nation in the West where Muslims have settled. The relations between Islam and democratic processes vary in different regional locations and according to the way in which Western modes of government integrated with Muslim governance at the end of the colonial era. Sometimes the process of integration was more complimentary but in other places it was contrary. A number of scholars have analysed the processes whereby democratic institutions have appeared in Muslim nations and divided them into instances where Western modes have been imposed upon a Muslim location and those where Islam has been used as a resource to commit Muslim countries to the values of democracy (Esposito, 1991 and 1987; Eickelman and Piscatori, 1996; Esposito and Voll, 1996; Hefner, 2005; Makris, 2007).

The process has been nowhere easy. Islamic religious revival has complicated the process even further. Democracy may be perceived as the rejection of Islamic legal systems in favour of aping the West. This may be seen as secularization and the continuation of colonial relations in a postcolonial setting. On the other hand, Islamic movements may challenge undemocratic institutions in their respective political systems and seek to develop and protest for the implementation of Islamic democratic models such as shura (Esposito and Voll, 1996, p. 3).

The phrase 'Islam and the West' needs to be taken with care by students of the subject area. At its worst it can be seen to represent a polarization of two irreconcilable and immutable entities which regard each other with hostility and suspicion as repositories of 'uncivilized' values. In such a scenario Muslims would typically regard the West as a moral desert which had moved away from the God-given laws of Christianity to post-Enlightenment man-made legal systems which replaced divine revelation with human-centred secularism. In such an analysis of Western society secularism is often equated with atheism. There is no doubt that certain elements among conservative and radical religionists perceive the West in these terms and brand it a new 'jahiliya' (age of ignorance). From the other side, since the 'war on terror' was announced by the neo-conservative government of US President George Bush, there have been a number of academics and journalists who have posited the idea of a clash of civilizations in which Islam is perceived as the barbarous 'other', outdated and outmoded in the face of democratic liberal values which are implicitly heralded as the pinnacle of human social, moral and political achievement (Huntingdon, 2002; Pipes, 2003a and 2003b; Lewis, 2010). In reality the positions taken from both sides is far more nuanced.

Clarke, writing in 1997, believed that the 'master-myths of polarity and complementarity between East and West may be at last in the process of out-running their usefulness'. He considers that both terms, 'East' and 'West', have lost whatever coherent meaning they may once have had (225). Promoting an optimistic version of globalization, Clarke argues that, worldwide, ideas and institutions are being transformed by 'cultural and political energy' whose origins lie in the West. In this respect, he agrees with Francis Fukuyama's position that in the post-communist era, Western institutions and political ideals will spread throughout the world.

This optimism of Clarke and Fukuyama is sometimes contrasted with Huntingdon's 'clash of civilizations' thesis. However, Fukuyama's optimism originates in the economic boom of South-East Asia, now joined by China. So far there is little evidence of Muslim nations benefiting in the same way. Bedevilled by corrupt regimes, they remain among the world's poorest communities, thus providing ammunition for those who would seek solutions in conspiracy theories and external threats of a war on Islam. Huntingdon's thesis is located in tensions between the Muslim world and the West and thus contributes to the body of Orientalist literature that has historically promoted divisions. What is certainly significant; is that even when one removes the politicization of Islam, Muslims are returning to their religion and its traditions around the globe. They may well form the strongest resistance to the globalization features proclaimed by Fukuyama, and do not tend to see them in the same optimistic light. It is not necessarily because they oppose the economic benefits of Western consumer society, but because they see in it deficiencies that all the world's great religious founders warned against.

A closer examination of 'Islam and the West' would reveal that the phrase contains a number of distinct categories that require unpacking. The first category would indeed include an understanding of the constructed realities of 'Islam' and 'the West', historically competing with each culturally, politically and religiously. The second category is 'Islam in the West'. This category can be subdivided into a) the historic contribution of Islamic civilization to European cultures, b) the colonization of European territory by the Ottomans and Moors which has resulted in large territories in Eastern Europe maintaining large Muslim populations to the present day, c) the influx of significant Muslim populations into Western Europe and North America through the movements of people from Muslim majority nations as a consequence of economic migration or fleeing wars, disasters or political regimes. The latter has resulted in Islam becoming the second largest religious grouping after Christianity in most European and North American nations.

Reading

Clarke, J. (1997), *Oriental Enlightenment: The Encounter between Asian and Western Thought*. London: Routledge.

Eickelman, D. and Piscatori, J. (1996), *Muslim Politics*. Princeton: Princeton University Press.

Esposito, J. (1987), *Islam in Asia: Religion, Politics and Society*. New York: Oxford University Press.

— (1991), *Islam and Politics*. Syracuse: Syracuse University Press.

Esposito, J. and Voll, J. (1996), *Islam and Democracy*. New York: Oxford University Press.

Fukuyama, F. (1992), *The End of History and the Last Man*. London: Free Press.

Geaves, R. A. (2010), *Islam Today*. London: Continuum.

Hefner, R. (ed.) (2005), *Remaking Muslim Politics: Pluralism, Contestation, Democratization*. Princeton: Princeton University Press.

Huntingdon, S. (2002), *The Clash of Civilisations and the Remaking of World Order*. London: Free Press.

Lewis, B. (2010), *Faith and Power: Religion and Politics in the Middle East*. Oxford: Oxford University Press.

Makris, G. P. (2007), *Islam in the Middle East: A Living Tradition*. Oxford: Blackwell.

Pipes, D. (2003a), *Militant Islam Reaches America*. New York: W.W. Norton.

— (2003b), *Miniatures: Views of Islamic and Middle Eastern Politics*. Transaction Publishers.

Rippin, A. (2005), *Muslims: Their Religious Beliefs and Practices* 3rd edn. London: Routledge, pp. 181–8.

Conclusion

In this chapter we have discussed the impact of colonialism on the study of religion and also the theorization of religion made possible by colonial and postcolonial studies. A number of theorists in postcolonial theory have been introduced and their impact on the study of religion assessed. In our discussion of World Religions we demonstrated that the category World Religion cannot be taken as an a priori fact but has to be understood as a construct within the study of religions. This is also true of hierarchical notions within the study of religion that privilege text over the vernacular and the historical processes by which a variety of Indian religious traditions have been labelled as discrete and separate, with clearly demarcated borders between them. Our discussion of the world's religions has assumed that there are fairly clear demarcations between religions. How true is this? What, if anything, prevents us from treating Sikhism as a form of Hinduism, for example? Might there be other examples of categories that are blurred? We can see that the nineteenth century was key in understanding the reification of religion as a generic category when eastern traditions were first classified by Westerners as 'isms'. However, we can see that new constructions of religions pay far more attention to the cultural context or to cultural conditioning and open the doors for religion to be studied in the field in addition to textual and hermeneutical study. Yet a warning is issued that too much emphasis on the cultural context can lead to crude reductionism. It is right to argue that Muslims create Islam, for example, but Islam also creates Muslims. It is necessary in the view of the author to strike a balance between cultural studies and social science theorization of religion as an aspect of society/culture and religions as systems to discover a world beyond the social and the cultural.

DISCUSSION POINTS

1 To what degree can the classification of religions as commonly used in the Western academic study of religion be considered a product of colonial and postcolonial structures in European societies?

2 Can the emphasis on colonial and postcolonial history as a factor in the creation of various religious phenomena (the *Khalsa* code or Islamic fundamentalism, for example) lead to an underplaying of the significance of religions as systems to reach out for the Divine?

3 To what degree does the demarcation of religions into well-defined categories with discrete borders between them, overlook the way in which eastern religions have often existed historically with considerable overlap?

4 To what degree does postcolonial theorizing help scholars of religion to understand various crucial areas of conflict between religion and society, for example fundamentalisms, terrorism, ethno/religious wars, debates concerning religion and secularization, religious pluralism?

8

Authenticity and diversity

Ron Geaves

Chapter Outline

Ways of authenticating religions 212
Sacred texts 213
Religious experts 217
Religious iconoclasm 224
Religious experience 229
Contemporary spirituality and new religions 230
Conclusion 238
Discussion points 240

Things break apart: the centre cannot hold.

YEATS (1921) 1965, p. 99

How to be considered authentic has always been a challenge for new religions, yet over time these same religions have developed ways of demonstrating authenticity that can become virtually unchallengeable, a part of time-honoured tradition and an obstacle to transformation. Such time-honoured traditions may not have the same claims to authenticity as those made by adherents in the early days of the religion's origin, and often established religions can find their traditional claims to authenticity under challenge from groups of followers who demand a return to the original past, who insist on shaking up the existing status quo. Thus sectarian divisions are formed, competing with each other, all claiming to be the authentic voice of the original truth. Such movements may challenge the parent tradition, even to the point of asserting that it no longer succeeds in delivering the 'truth'. Parent traditions, on the other hand, can accuse such new movements within their fold of not being a legitimate expression of the religion. Each can accuse the other of not reflecting the 'original' practice of the founders.

This chapter will explore a number of ways in which religions establish authenticity and will utilize *Khalsa* Sikhs as an example of orthodoxy and Sufis as an example of a marginalized voice within contemporary Islam, as case studies of the competing voices that offer discourses of authenticity which create diversity within religious traditions. However, the contemporary world is experiencing a plethora of new religions, and these present their own challenges to the creation of an authentic voice. In addition, the Western world is experiencing a disenchantment with traditional religion as seen in institutionalized Christianity, in spite of its long history of creating mechanisms for demonstrating authenticity. These no longer seem to be able to work on the hearts and minds of believers as in the past, and a crisis of 'credibility' has arisen. At the same time, the search for the 'authentic' or 'how to be authentic' has become an essential discourse of the twenty-first-century postmodern condition. In the world of religion, this has manifested itself as a distinct division between religiosity and spirituality, with the latter being perceived by increasing numbers of individuals as an authentic way to achieve personal self-fulfilment. These current developments in the transformation of religious belief and practice also need to be taken into account in any exploration of authenticity.

Ways of authenticating religions

Foremost among authenticity strategies must be the claim to a higher authority, the intense conviction that God, or gods, or some other-worldly entity, has intervened in human life, providing instruction or intimacy, a way to acknowledge the existence of the divine in the everyday affairs of human beings. Hebrew prophets characteristically claimed an inaugural vision as evidence of their mission to warn the people of their parting from the ways of God. Such inaugural visions remain a feature of some new religious movements today. These interventions of the divine into the ordinary realm of human affairs, sanctifying the everyday, can be categorized as revelation and inspiration. In simple terms, the first refers to a move by the divine into human existence, a move initiated by the divine being itself. The god(ess) reveals itself to a chosen person, usually a righteous human being. The second can be described as an experience of the divine or a supra-normal state of consciousness that comes about through the efforts of an individual to live a special lifestyle in which something beyond everyday existence can be experienced. Both revelation and inspiration provide their own authoritative expressions of authenticity which can either complement or compete with each other, as we will observe in the example of Sufism.

In the monotheistic religions, Judaism, Christianity and Islam, revelation is seen as primary authentication of their respective truth-claims, although all three provide a considerable history of inspiration, but such experiences are seen as secondary support for the original revelation. Thus inspiration comes to function as an authentication of revelation, either somehow throwing further light on its content or demonstrating that the revelation continues to hold true over the passing of time and changing circumstances. Sometimes it is argued that the experiences of inspiration can only be apprehended because the original revelation opened up a conduit between the divine world and the human world. However, inspiration can also create tensions with those who hold fast to the contents of the original revelation. Sometimes this can be framed within doctrinal divisions concerning the primacy of immanence over transcendence, as we will see.

In the eastern religious traditions, inspiration tends to be the main means to apprehend the divine or experience a higher reality. Although revelatory discourses exist in Hinduism and Sikhism, they are an unfamiliar terrain and probably influenced by the impact of Islam and Christianity in South Asia, both of which primarily arrived as powerful discourses linked to conquest and colonization. More familiar patterns in eastern traditions are the accounts of enlightened or liberated human beings who freed themselves from the wheel of samsara by their own efforts. Even the Vedic texts, the primary source of authentication for orthodox Hindus and often described in revelatory terms, are perceived as having been discovered deep within the consciousness of sages or seers through their unbroken meditations and austerities.

Sacred texts

Having introduced the *Vedas*, we can add that one of the most common means of religious authentication is a sacred text or texts. This can be the result of either revelation or inspiration, or a combination of the two. In Islam for example, the Qur'an is believed to be the unadulterated Word of God, existing for all eternity but revealed in its final form to Muhammad, who is thus chosen as Allah's final prophet. However, very few Muslims would deny that Muhammad was in a state of wahy (inspiration) when the revelation from God arrived, and thus his heart was able to receive the transmission. Sacred texts believed to contain a revelation can become very powerful sources of authentication built on the conviction that the original message of God is contained within them. For millions of Jews, Christians and Muslims, the text of their various scriptures can form the foundation for how they carry out their lives, relate to others, and view themselves and the world around them.

Some sacred texts are regarded as being the origin of a tradition, the revelation of the divine itself, and are therefore written down and maintained with great care to ensure that their contents remain unaltered. This is certainly true of Judaism and Islam. In such cases, both tradition and special practices ensure that believers do not waver in their faith concerning the inviolability of the text. In Islam, it is a very important doctrine that the Qur'an has never been altered since its origin and throughout its history Muslims have gone to great lengths to ensure that the contents are learned by memory, and even today it remains prestigious to be able to memorize and recite the complete contents.

Other sacred texts such as the Sikh Guru Granth Sahib came into existence gradually: it did not achieve its final form until the eighteenth century. The Guru Granth Sahib, however, maintains a unique place among sacred books in that it is considered to be the living Guru and is treated as though it were a human being: it is fed and placed in its room at night to take rest. The Guru Granth Sahib's authority lies in the orthodox belief that the last human Guru of the Sikhs, Guru Gobind Singh, asserted that there would be no more human gurus after his death, and that the Guru Granth Sahib would be the Sikhs' final guide. The contents are not regarded as revelation, but are the inspired poetic utterances of the Sikh Gurus and other saintly figures from Hinduism and Islam whose teachings held similarities. The authenticity of the text is derived from the experiences of those regarded as being in direct communion with God, transformed into poetry. Other forms of sacred text can function as spiritual manuals for practitioners, so that through imitation they can achieve the same transforming experience of the founder.

Where there is a time lag between the life and death of the founder(s) and the creation of sacred text, it is imperative that the authenticity of the contents is assured for future generations. Several religions including Buddhism and Jainism had high-level conferences or councils where gatherings of prominent leaders, those trusted by the

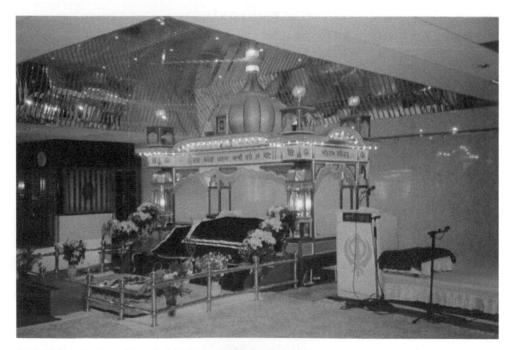

FIGURE 8.1 *Guru Nanak Sikh Temple, Wolverhampton.*

various religious communities on the basis of piety and scholarship, determined a canon of text that was deemed official and orthodox. Other texts such as the Christian Apocrypha may be excluded from the canon but still retain some prestige, though not the same level of authenticity as the canon. This can vary from sect to sect within a religion. Protestantism excludes the Apocrypha completely, whereas Roman Catholicism ascribes it authenticity but still distinguishes it from the books that make up the New Testament.

Religions that have an 'historic' revelation given by God at a particular moment in time and revealed in a particular cultural milieu (e.g. the Israelite tribes in Sinai or the sixth-century Arab populations of Makkah and Medina), but believed to contain all that the deity required human beings to know until the last days, have a particular challenge of maintaining the integrity of the revelation while shifting its message from the particular to the universal. Put in simple terms, if all that human beings are required to know about God and his will is contained within the revelation, how can it be kept authentic as society changes, or that the religion moves to new locations where the same cultural or social conditions no longer exist? The Qur'an, for example, is believed to be the final revelation, but it does not contain any information about contemporary life. There is no mention of modern technology, advances in medicine or ethical dilemmas that may arise from such developments. However, for believers the answer must be contained in the text of the revelation somewhere, otherwise it would neither be complete nor final.

The challenge is to be able to interpret the revelation over time for succeeding generations, without losing any of its authenticity or by departing from the original spirit and letter. In order to achieve this religions have provided for trained specialists to follow a due process of interpretation that is believed to maintain the authenticity of the revelation. In the case of Islam and Judaism, where the revelations of the Qur'an and Torah contain prescriptions for human behaviour and the formulation of a legal system based on a law of God, the interpretation over time by experts leads to secondary texts that can be investigated for precedent. Religious specialists skilled in seeking precedent and interpreting it for new situations take on more of a legal character than a priestly function.

THE STUDY OF THE QUR'AN

The traditional Muslim account of the Qur'an allows for no authorship by Muhammad. He was the recipient of God's message, usually through the vehicle of the Angel Jibreel, which was then dictated and recited until committed to memory. To support this religious narrative it is usually asserted that Muhammad was illiterate. Since the Qur'an is believed to be the literal speech of God, coexistent with him for eternity, it is absolutely essential in the narrative of Islam's arrival and raison d'être that the Qur'an remains uncorrupted and unchanged in its entirety from the version revealed to Muhammad.

Muslim history of its compilation suggests that it was recited by the Prophet every Ramadan before the Angel, and twice before his death. The location of the verses and surahs was identified by him. They were then written down by scribes who were selected by Muhammad. In addition his companions wrote down the Qur'an for their own use, and several hundred were believed to have memorized it. After Muhammad's death, Abu Bakr (632–634), the first caliph, was urged by Umar Ibn al-Khattab to preserve the Qur'an after the Battle of Yamamah, where many of the Qur'an's reciters lost their lives. Zayedibn Thabit was entrusted with the task, and with the help of surviving companions he succeeded in handing Abu Bakr the first authenticated copy which was kept in the home of Hafsah, one of Muhammad's wives and the daughter of Umar. The third Caliph Uthman ordered perfect copies to be made, as the Arab empire was expanding rapidly. Copies were sent throughout the Muslim world. The original was returned to Hafsah and kept in Medina. Some Western scholars have challenged this compilation narrative and argued that several versions of the text existed when Abu Bakr initiated the task of preserving an authentic version. However, the Muslim world has not challenged the standard version. Described by Schuon as the 'great theophany of Islam', the contents of the book can be categorized as 'doctrinal', 'historical' and 'magical'. It contains moral and judicial instructions, passages on the nature of God, and the creation and role of human beings, and records history as the rise and fall of the human soul; but the Qur'an is more than its contents. Muslims believe that because the book contains the literal words of God, there is a power that comes from reciting it that transcends meaning. For millions of Muslims the book is a sacred object endowed with blessings and power, and its physical presence is a manifestation of divine existence in the world. Those who are able to recite it from beginning to end hold a religious position (hafiz), and Qur'an recitations are a sacred performance throughout the Muslim world. They not only take place on religious occasions such as Ramadan, but also form part of popular culture. Recitations can be heard on TV and radio, purchased as audio tapes or DVDs, are played in taxis, on public transport, in private cars, in the workplace and at home. Skilled reciters are household names, and often double as singers of popular music. In addition, Qur'an verses are used in popular religion to heal, protect and bless. They are worn in small silk envelopes sewn to a thread, often around the neck or close to the heart.

The ubiquity of the Qur'an recital in Muslim culture throws up some contradictions in our understanding of Islam as a religion of the book. Such a description does not necessarily mean a focus on literacy and hermeneutics, as in Protestant Christianity or Judaism. The Qur'an was an oral revelation and is maintained through the generations as much through its oral transmission as through its interpretation. Often when interpretation does take place, it occurs through the intermediary of a teacher who explains orally the truths contained in the text. Even when the Qur'an was written down, orality was not neglected. The significance of the Qur'an being in Arabic is often explained to be because the original Arabic was how the revelation was received, or alternatively because translation loses meaning. However, the oral character of the Qur'an and its recitation are also significant in understanding the need for the Arabic to be paramount. Finally, the Qur'an is regarded as a miracle. Muslims often state that no human being can reproduce the beauty of its language and the richness of its content. The Qur'an's oral quality, its use in popular practices, and the sacredness of the book itself, lend it to anthropological study as well as to literary or textual examination.

Yet interpretation does take place. Some Muslims are wary of too much scrutiny of the text, as it may lead to questioning of God's veracity; others feel that scrutiny is unnecessary in that God provided his revelation in a form that was clear for all to comprehend and follow. Up to the present time, there has been little study of the Qur'an similar to what has taken place in biblical criticism. But some textual criticism has been undertaken by Muslim scholars. This has been carried out to determine which suras were written in Mecca or Medina, and the chronological order of the revelations. In addition, Muslim scholars have been concerned to make a distinction between text (the revelation or speech of God) and context (the historical setting in which the revelations were framed). The Qur'an is also full of allusions to particular people and events that would have been clear to the followers of Muhammad but are quite mysterious to subsequent generations. Muslim scholars have been highly skilled in elucidating and clarifying the circumstances of the revelation and writing *tafsir* (commentaries) that are usually included along with the text of the Qur'an. The earliest Muslim commentary which remains available is that of Muhammad ibn al-Tabari (d. 923). It contains not only his interpretation but that of well-known earlier commentators, and provides a chain of transmission. However, interpretation is a conservative art and so far Muslims have not developed a science of reinterpretation of the message that relates to the rapid transformation of modern societies or the requirements of non-Arab local cultures. A class of religious specialists has come into being whose task is to be the guardians and interpreters of sacred text in Islam. Known as the *ulema*, they are not priests but are responsible for collecting, systematizing and interpreting the Qur'an, and for constructing the epistemological frameworks upon which Islamic law (*shari'a*) is interpreted and applied in new contexts. Yet the *ulema* consider themselves to be conservers of the Qur'an's truths and on the whole their new understandings only modify or reformulate orthodoxy. Generally the *ulema* are perceived to be a conservative body with a lead role in maintaining orthodoxies. This canonical body of knowledge, deduced from sacred text, formally constructed and organized over the generations by the *ulema*, remains deeply embedded in the everyday lives of millions of Muslims. However, there are alternatives. Throughout the centuries Muslim mystics have provided an esoteric understanding of the Qur'an. A more modern alternative is provided by the Islamists who bypass the centuries of jurisprudence and offer the possibility for Muslims to read the text for themselves, and apply it to the conditions of modern life directly and without intermediaries. If the mystics (Sufis) pay too much respect to the Qur'an as a sacred object, in many ways the Islamists neglect the Qur'an's orality and the part it plays in creating a Weberian enchanted landscape; in a thoroughly modern development they emphasize literacy, interpretation and hermeneutics, albeit of a literal kind.

Religious experts

Religious experts come in a variety of forms, each with their own level of authenticity to religious believers. The most authentic are the primary experts, the prophets who receive revelation, humans believed to be manifestations of the divine or those who have achieved special states of consciousness that mark them out from other beings. Very often these are the historic or legendary founders of religions, but very close in terms of special regard can come the authentic experiences believed to have been granted to first-generation disciples of the above group. Usually it is believed that such very early followers had an understanding and a commitment that transcended those of slightly later generations who tend to use them as exemplars. Both of these categories can be labelled primary specialists. Later, as the religion developed into an institutionalized form, marked especially by political or social structures, a vast array of secondary specialists came into existence. But these too must be able to claim authenticity. Each religion has its own unique forms of such specialists. Some are readers of sacred texts on special occasions; others are guardians of sacred spaces, some are skilled in interpretation of law or doctrine; others can perform specific functions such as carrying out rituals; some are regarded as priests, specialists in retaining communion with the divine for ordinary worshippers who require their intermediary function.

The relations that exist between primary and secondary specialists are not reified. There is considerable movement and overlap between the two categories; the early Church fathers were often bishops and theologians, but also mystics with deep formative spiritual experiences enabling them to be close to the primary specialists. In Islam, the first three generations of Muslims are regarded as having a special affinity with the revelation which marks them out as more closely bound to the Prophet and his companions than later generations. They are seen as more 'authentic' in their experience and practice by contemporary Muslims.

In the older established religions, tradition itself can be a form of authenticity linking primary and secondary specialists. The Roman Catholic and Anglican churches, for example, draw upon the apostolic succession to legitimize their priesthoods, claiming an unbroken succession back to St Peter and the apostles of Jesus. In traditional Islam, all religious functionaries draw upon successions that are believed to go back to the original companions of Muhammad. For example the muezzin, the traditional callers of the faithful to prayer five times a day, usually from the minaret of the mosque, see themselves as part of an unbroken tradition that goes back to Bilal, the black African slave appointed by Muhammad to be the first caller to prayer. In Sufism, in particular, spiritual masters who may have disciples running into the tens of thousands stretching across the globe, or merely a handful in a small rural location, are authenticated by a silsilah, a direct lineage of masters that always lead back to Muhammad through either Abu Bakr or Ali, two of his closest companions and original Muslims. In Hinduism and Buddhism, spiritual guides and teachers are also considered to be legitimate if they can demonstrate lineages that go back to key figures in the religion's spiritual history.

Tradition allows the secondary specialists to claim legitimacy through historic links to founders, and in the case of Islam and Judaism to provide a meta-narrative to ensure the validity of the corpus of knowledge built upon the original revelation by generations of *ulema* and rabbis. In Christianity the Roman Catholic Church regards tradition, the body of theological knowledge and time-honoured practice confirmed as orthodox, to be of equal authority to scripture. However, there may be tensions between tradition and the message of the early founders based on perceived differences of motivation.

As religions develop over time into institutional formations complete with secondary specialists, established doctrines and rituals, official interpretations of sacred text and formal structures of organization, each of these can be used as authentication, appealing to tradition and time-honoured custom, even legal codes. In most religions there have been those who have challenged the legitimacy of these formal structures and demanded a more spontaneous and direct experiential link to the divine, often calling for a return to the immediacy of the founders, the primary specialists. Very often, new charismatic leaders arise claiming an authority that bypasses history and tradition, even claiming that it has been corrupted or has deviated from the original teachings. In such cases schisms take place, and new sects and religions emerge which are initially authenticated only by experience. As time passes these movements too become institutionalized, developing their own traditions of legitimacy. The older the religion, the more likely that this process has occurred many times, creating considerable internal diversity with each strand claiming to be the authentic voice of the original founders or primary specialists.

The sociologist Thomas O'Dea looked at this process in greater detail and argued that the symbols of a faith, especially sacred objects like scriptures or liturgies and sacraments, are preserved and formalized in sacred rites and objects to meet the requirements of successive generations of followers. These symbols too need to be regarded as authentic. One of the most effective ways of ensuring this is to create a division between the sacred and non-sacred realms of existence, imbuing sacred objects, behaviour and space with a special sense of being different, marked out and separated from everyday life. Sometimes these symbols of the faith may become so sacred that they cannot even be touched or approached by the faithful unless in a state of ritual purity.

When a geographical location or physical space is held to be sacred by a religious community, it will often be insisted that it has a religious history associated with key events or primary specialists in the tradition. However, it is often demonstrable that such places are depositaries for myths and hagiographies rather than actual historical events: sacred stories that demonstrate divine intervention in some way, usually miraculous events or indications of a special relationship of the deity with the place, or the sanctity of the person who lived there. The historical veracity of such events and stories will be highly contested by believers when any doubt is cast upon them. Tensions can occur where sacred places are jointly revered by two or more religions, as with the Babri mosque in Ayodhya or the Temple Mount in Jerusalem.

The Babri mosque incident provides an example of how claims to authenticity have become a flashpoint for political and religious rivalries between Hindus and Muslims in the Indian subcontinent. Interestingly both sides of the dispute and the Indian government are trying to determine the history of the site itself in regard to how long it has been a mosque, and whether a temple to the Hindu god Rama occupied the site prior to the Muslim conquest. But the added dimension here is that the conflict is between two very different religions. Whereas Islam, like Christianity and Judaism, places its emphasis on linear time, and origins and development that can be demonstrated and validated by historians, Hinduism deals with vast sweeps of cyclical time populated by gods, demons, sages, *avatars*, other divine beings and sacred realms that are the subject of legend and myth. The Hindu claim that the temple stands on the sacred site of Rama's (an *avatar* of the god Vishnu) birthplace provides the site with a sacred history which authenticates its status, but would make no sense to Muslims or others with a more traditional sense of what is meant by history: they might argue that there is no evidence for Rama's actual existence. On the other hand, the mosque is an indisputable part of the historical heritage of India.

It is not uncommon for sacred spaces to have contested histories, each one reinforcing the sanctity and 'specialness' of the place, which is then claimed by different groups of believers. Sacred persons can also be contested. Both Islam and Christianity possess their own sacred narratives for the birth, life and death of Jesus authenticated by, in the case of traditional Christians, belief in eye-witness accounts, miracle stories and doctrines concerning his divinity. Islam, on the other hand, has no eye-witness accounts but resorts to belief in the absolute veracity of God's revelation of the Qur'an to provide an alternative view. Where such contested histories exist, questions of ownership arise both as a topic for religious scholars and as debates or disputes between the respective religions. Can Christians claim sole and exclusive ownership of Jesus, who is their historic founder, or does the global situation demand that they give weight, possibly equal weight, to other religious narratives concerning their founder?

It is difficult for a religious believer to see with the eye of a practitioner of an alternative tradition, as both views are steeped in authenticity devices that play on the affective domain of life, as well as the intellectual and physical. Religious practices which involve the physical domain through performance also need to be authenticated: rituals, in particular. To some degree, authentication comes from regular repetition in the prescribed manner. Controversial disputes can take place in religions which focus on correct practice (orthopraxy), and can be as heated as doctrinal disputes concerning orthodoxy. For Muslims the exact position of the hands against the body in the ritual prayer (*salat*) can indicate sectarian differences to the insider and the trained outsider. Ritual too is inextricably bound up with sacred history, repeating myths and other events deemed to be of primary importance, linking a sacred past to the present, and thereby sanctifying the present moment for each generation of believers. Mircea Eliade wrote that myths have their own time, a sacred time standing outside normal time and in ritual re-enactment the person is able to stand outside time, and enter the domain of sacred reality. Ninian Smart describes this as 'then becomes now' (Smart, 1995, p. 80). An example of this sacralizing of everyday time is found in the Christian liturgical calendar. When Muslims attend the annual pilgrimage, the *Hajj*, they perform a series of daily rituals that link them to the history of Allah's relationship with human beings. These go back far beyond the historical beginnings of the religion in the sixth and seventh centuries to sacred accounts of God's dealings with Adam and Eve, Abraham and his son Ishmael. Through ritual enactments performed in the geographical locations believed to be the sites of the original encounter with divine mercy and will, each performer of the pilgrimage is linked to history, prophecy, revelation and miracles of divine intervention, thus affirming faith and sharing also in an overwhelming experience of communitas (intense community spirit). Christians also ritually re-enact the events of the Last Supper, thus becoming not only linked to an important event in the life of their founder, but literally joined with him in a spiritual communion. Such myths, with their accompanying ancient sense of unquestionable truth linked with repetitive performative ritual action, combine to create powerful vehicles for establishing a religion as authentic. Sometimes the rituals themselves may be endowed with such a sense of the presence of the sacred, the 'numinous' as defined by Rudolf Otto, that it is not possible to perform them without secondary rituals of purification that allow the performer to enter a state of closeness to the divine. Thus Muslims, before the performance of prayer, carry out prescribed ritual washing in which they also announce their intent to pray. Christian participants in communion or mass first undergo prayers of confession and forgiveness.

Although Rudolf Otto considered that such religious devices as ritual or sacred space could provide feelings of awe or mystery, a perception or glimpse of the divine power which he called a 'numinous' feeling, some significant figures in the histories of religion have taken a more iconoclastic view of the externals of religion, considering them as distractions or even falsehoods on the path to spiritual truth or the discovery of a divine realm of existence. Any discourse about authenticity is a discourse about authority. Max Weber was the first figure to identify charismatic authority, defined as: 'a certain quality of an individual personality by virtue of which he is set apart from ordinary men and treated as endowed with supernatural, superhuman, or at least specifically exceptional qualities' (Eisenstadt, 1968, p. xviii).

For many new religions, or even offshoots from old ones, charismatic authority is all that is required to authenticate the message, even though such authority may be claimed as a result of a vision or communication with some divine agency. Those who choose to follow a guru, prophet or Sufi shaykh consider that the claimed connection to directly access the divine is the only authority that is required. The spiritual experience of the leader authenticates his/her utterances or actions. Obviously, in this case, a considerable degree of trust is required in the leader's experience of or connection to the divine. Some charismatic leaders may be self-proclaimed spokespersons for the deity, asserting their own authority; others may be more modest, but proclaimed by their followers to have a certain status.

Charismatic religious leaders may create new rituals or sacred texts which then come to have an authenticity because of the leader's status in the community of believers. On their death, when charismatic leadership may be replaced by more institutional forms of leadership, the rituals and sacred texts created by the deceased leader will come to have authority of their own. On the other hand, there are charismatic founders

FIGURE 8.2 *The Wudu tank where Muslim visitors to the shrine of Muinuddin Chishti in Ajmer perform the ritual washing of head, eyes, ears, nose, mouth, arms, lower legs and feet before participating in prayer.*

of religion who have not created any rituals, external practices or a body of sacred text. These have been developed at a later stage by successive generations of followers. In this case, authentication is often achieved by the consensus, usually, not of the whole community but of its acknowledged leadership. Thus Christianity, Jainism and Buddhism were developed in a series of councils consisting of religious leaders who determined a canon of sacred text decreed to be authentic and representative of the religion's doctrines. Not everyone will agree. In fact, it could be argued that the need to call a council of leaders to determine correct doctrine or practice only occurs in situations where divisions have already taken place. The councils function as a means to restore unity or, if unity cannot be achieved, to cast out those who disagree. Some of the first divisions in a tradition have occurred as a result of this process. Examples are Mahayana and Theravada Buddhism, or Svetambara and Digambara Jainism. Those excluded by the council are unlikely to admit their heresy, and themselves become a movement of the wider tradition that usually claims it is a more authentic version. Thus, for example, Shi'a Islam perceives itself as a more authentic version of the revelation than that of the Sunni majority, because its leadership was the one originally planned by the Prophet and because it retained the bloodline that was believed to have mystical properties.

BUDDHISM AND AUTHENTICITY

When the First Buddhist Council met three months after the Buddha's parinirvana (death after the attainment of enlightenment), at Rajagaha in India, 500 of his monks congregated to recite, classify and agree the teachings they had learned from him, and thus the agreed canon of scripture was formed. There is a postscript to the story, however. One monk is said to have arrived late and, having enquired what the Council had agreed, said, 'I prefer to follow the Buddha's teaching as I remember them.' It is usually assumed that the Theravada tradition, being more conservative than the Mahayana, is closer to the 'original Buddhism' as Siddhartha Gautama – the historical Buddha and founder of the Buddhist religion – taught it. However, this detail in the story introduces seeds of doubt. If it is true, the dissident monk was suggesting that the agreed version of the Buddha's teaching was not truly authentic, and that he possessed a primordial version.

'Authenticity' can be taken to mean the original form that a religion once took. But religions develop, and arguably there are quite legitimate forms of a religion that make no claims to replicate the teachings and practices of its founder-leader. They can certainly be regarded as legitimate if most other versions of the religion agree that they are acceptable expressions of that faith – although, obviously, those who follow a specific tradition will believe it to be the best expression of the religion, at least for them. One tradition that arose within the Mahayana schools was that the Buddha did not deliver the full truth during his lifetime, since humanity was not at a sufficiently advanced intellectual or spiritual stage to be ready for it. He therefore used 'skilful means' (upaya), delivering 'provisional truth' at a level which men and women were capable of absorbing.

Particularly in the Tibetan tradition (sometimes known as the Vajrayana), ancient texts are sometimes reported to have been found in caves, having been hidden from humankind for centuries. Such texts are known as terma. Western scholars tend to be sceptical of such claims, preferring to regard them as new texts, and contending that the stories of these remarkable discoveries are attempts to legitimate the new teachings by giving them a historical pedigree.

If the Buddha did teach a provisional message, Mahayana Buddhism does not regard his immediate disciples as having been 'sold short'. One important Mahayana scripture, the Lotus Sutra, relates a parable of some children in a burning house. Their father who is outside the building warns them of the danger, but they are too intent on their play to pay any heed. He therefore devises a ruse: he offers them expensive carts if only they will come out. (A cart was obviously a child's prized possession in those days.) The offer successfully appeals to them, and they escape from the building unharmed. The father, however, being an honest man, does not simply tell the children that they have been tricked: he gives them new carts, but of course these are not nearly as valuable as their lives, which he has saved by so doing. The parable makes the point that if the Buddha did not proclaim his full message, humanity received something that was at least more valuable than their previous state of ignorance, and certainly more worthwhile than the form of Indian brahminism which his doctrines superseded. The fact that humanity had still more to learn did not diminish the Buddha's contribution to the world: further learning could come later.

There is another aspect of authenticity. The textbook versions of Buddhism emphasize the historical, philosophical and scriptural aspects of Buddhism. Western converts are often attracted to Buddhist philosophy and take up spiritual practices such as meditation, which was the means by which the Buddha gained enlightenment. However, even in the professedly 'authentic' Theravada tradition only a minority of Buddhist monasteries practise meditation, and members of the laity will at best support the *Sangha* (the Buddhist monastic community) by providing them with food when they undertake their early-morning alms round, or they may participate in ceremonies to bring about good fortune or a long life.

The contrast between the serious Western uptake of Buddhism and the form in which the laity practise it was brought home some years ago at a local celebration of Wesak, the festival marking the Buddha's birth, enlightenment and parinirvana. The laity had provided tea and cakes and the children had practised songs and dances, which they performed as part of the festivities. The time came for speeches. One Western convert, who had taken the robe as a member of the *Sangha*, mounted the platform and rebuked them for these frivolities. Refreshments and entertainments were all very well, he said, but they will not help anyone to progress on the path to nirvana.

Enlightenment may indeed be the supreme goal towards which Buddhists can strive, but it is not what the majority of Buddhists realistically expect to attain. As we have argued in the main text, religions can exist at various levels and can be used by their followers for different goals, from pragmatic benefits to high spiritual aims such as salvation, liberation or enlightenment. Is any one level the 'authentic' version of a religion? One writer has stated that 'the only complete and logical Buddhist is the monk' (Masson, 1977, p. 17). Yet the monks only constitute a small proportion of the Buddhist population, and in any case much of their work tends to involve educating the young and maintaining their monastery, rather than pursuing the meditative life.

One of the difficulties of studying religion is to decide which strands we will study. Religions exist in various traditions and cultures, and are taken up differently by people from different strata of society, with different aims and purposes. It is difficult to see why one particular form of a religion should be privileged for academic study by being labelled as the 'authentic' version. Although clearly it is not possible to examine all versions of a religion, the study of religion needs to reflect the variety of levels and forms of the religions it addresses.

Reference

Masson, J. (1977), *The Noble Path of Buddhism*. Milton Keynes: Open University Press.

Religious iconoclasm

An iconoclast is a breaker of images. I am using the term more generally than its very specific use in Christianity, where it refers to those that took part in the eighth- and ninth-century movement against the use of images (icons) in worship within Eastern Orthodoxy; or sometimes to the Protestant Puritans of the sixteenth and seventeenth centuries. Most religions have had reform movements which have criticized over-elaborate rituals in favour of a simplicity usually regarded as a more authentic imitation of the teachings of the founder. In the world of Islam, the Wahhabi movement founded in Arabia in the eighteenth century, and similar manifestations in other parts of the Muslim world, criticized traditional Islam, highly influenced by Sufism, for introducing perceived innovations to the original faith such as a hierarchy of saints, intercession, worship at tombs, and a neo-platonic doctrine of Muhammad's pre-creation existence as the Light (Nur) of Allah. In Arabia, the first generation of Wahhabis destroyed countless shrines located at the remains of Muslim holy men, and asserted a much more scriptural version of Islam.

However, my focus here is on those who have founded religious traditions or new movements within traditions, who appeared to oppose the externals of religion in favour of internal transformation based on experience of an immanent divine. The Buddha, for example, criticized the Hindu caste-stratified society and asked whether a member of the Brahmin (the traditional priest-caste at the summit of Hindu social stratification) should be appointed by birth or conduct. Greg Bailey writes that at the time of the Buddha, 'the Brahmins' own perception of themselves is based to a large measure on social pretension deriving from status in a society rapidly becoming highly stratified' (Bailey, 1998, p. 16). For the Buddha the term 'Brahmin' signifies a role, not a birthright and is determined by individual inner qualities usually associated with self-restraint, desirelessness and absence of aggression. The Buddha's understanding of a Brahmin was much closer to that of a sage (muni), an individual who has achieved self-fulfilment and enlightenment associated with mastery of the mind and senses, rather than the traditional understanding of a ritual specialist. This contrast between priest and sage repeats itself throughout Indian religious history. Bailey states:

> A common thread running through all the instances of such argument is that social designations of class arise because people come to an agreement that such and such social category refers to an arbitrarily designated category, often transcending occupational specificity, that becomes connected with birth and over time is reified into hereditary descent. The Buddha, on the contrary, requires that a person prove himself anew each time according to a set of standard criteria determined by the conditions required to be met by the attainment of arahatship (one who has achieved the conditions for enlightenment). (1998, p. 19)

In the medieval period of India's history, a number of iconoclasts, jointly defined as *sants* by Western scholars, followed in the footsteps of the Buddha and others from the Indian sage traditions, and opposed blind adherence to the externals of religion, whether manifest in Hinduism or Islam. Here is the voice of Kabir, believed to have been a low-caste weaver from near Varanasi, claimed today by both Hindus and Muslims as their own, as he scorns the everyday religious conventions that he sees around him:

> I have seen the pious Hindus, rule followers, early morning bath-takers –
> killing souls; they worship rocks.
> They know nothing . . .

And posturing yogis, hypocrites, hearts crammed with pride,
Praying to brass, to stones, reeling with pride in their pilgrimage,
Fixing their caps and their prayer-beads,
Painting their brows-marks and arm marks, braying their hymns and their couplets, reeling.
They have never heard of the soul.
Kabir says, listen sants:
They are all deluded. (Embree, 1988, p. 375)

The same critique of the outer forms of religion can be heard in the poetry of Nanak (1469–1539) believed by the Sikhs to be their historic founder. Nanak goes one step further and states that all religious worldviews are mental shackles:

There are many dogmas, there are many systems,
There are many scriptural revelations,
Many modes to fetter the mind:
But the Sant seeks for release through Truth. (Singh et al., 1973, pp. 74–5)

Nanak's classic device in his poetry was to refer to the outer forms of religious adherence and compare them to inner qualities, which are then asserted as the authentic religious experience. Typical of these poems are the following:

Make your discipline the practice of Truth,
Make the square that you draw around your kitchen
The practice of virtue;
Make the ceremonial cleansing of your body
The meditation on the Holy Name
Let the heart first be cleansed
All other outward appearances of piety are worthless. (Singh et al., 1973, p. 12)

Here Nanak refers to the ritual practices of Brahmin Hindus, but he is no less scathing of the externals of Islam:

Let mercy be your Mecca:
Instead of fasts use humility:
Seek no other paradise than abiding by the Word of your teacher;
For houris, seek in your paradise
The fragrance of the light
That streams from the Lord;
Seek no other palace or pleasure than devotion to God.
To practice truth is to be a Qazi [Muslim judge],
To purify the heart is to be a Haji [a Muslim who has undertaken the pilgrimage],
To shame the devil is to be a Mullah [a Muslim cleric],

To praise God is to be a Dervish [a Sufi mystic known for ecstatic dancing].
Let your first prayer be God's praises,
Your second inner peace,
Your third humility, your fourth charity,
Your fifth subduing the five senses to God.
While you live, remember God.
Instead of washing your hands before prayer
Get rid of your evil deeds. (Singh et al., 1973, pp. 198–9)

Yet despite their virulent critique of both Islam and Hinduism, most of the *sants* accepted the worldview of Indian traditions in that they accepted the concepts of samsara, *karma* and final liberation, even though their own experience of salvation was both imminent and immanent, thus providing an eschatology that invariably ignored the afterlife in favour of a liberation found in the present.

The *sants'* overriding conviction that the divine resided within all beings, manifested as the name or word of God, led them to disregard social barriers in regard to the spiritual quest. All had access to the divine, regardless of caste, gender or religion. This was seen as the way to salvation for everyone, and has been called a 'universal path to sanctity' (Vaudeville, 1987) based on inner transformation rather than the outer manifestations of religion.

The Hindu sant and the Muslim Sufi share the pain of separation and the longing for union with the divine. Both can be absorbed into the divine, in a state where all awareness of individual self is lost, the bhakta in the condition of samādhi and the Sufi in the state of fanā Both accept the idea that God is one all-pervading reality, essentially without form. Both perceive the divine to be immanent in creation, and therefore capable of being experienced through indwelling the human heart/soul. They both practise contemplation or remembrance of the word or name(s) of God as the central discipline through which unity with God is achieved. The names are different according to language and culture, are remembered silently in the heart or chanted by the tongue, but essentially Sufi *dhikr* and the nāmasimarān of the *sants* perform the same function.

The goal of both Sufis and *sants* is continuous remembrance of the divine, and both speak of a state where the divine takes over and the devotee is lost to normal ego-perception, immersed in an experience of overwhelming recognition of the deity. The *sants* were iconoclasts; they criticized caste, sectarian differences and exterior forms of religion such as sacred languages, scriptures, image worship, fasting, ritual bathing, pilgrimages and asceticism. Sufis are more ambivalent about the external forms of worship, since the Islamic *shari'a* insists upon several of the above as essentials of revelation. However, they agree with the *sants* that the externals of religion are of no avail if the esoteric path of the heart has not been discovered.

We can see something of the *sants'* attitude to externals in the verses of Jalalu'd-din Rumi, the great Persian mystic of Islam, taken from his masterpiece, the *Mathnawi*. Rumi recounts the meeting of a Sufi sage with Bayazid, a future Sufi master, who is on route to the annual pilgrimage to Makkah, one of the five pillars or essential practices of Islam.

> The Sage said, 'Whither are you going, O Bayazid?
> Where will you bring your caravan to a halt?'
> Bayazid replied, 'At dawn I start for the Ka'ba.'
> Quoth the Sage, 'What provision for the way have you?'
> He answered, 'I have two hundred silver dirhams;
> See them tied up tightly in the corner of my cloak.'
> The Sage said, 'Circumambulate me seven times;
> Count this better than circumambulating the Ka'ba;
> And as for the dirhams, give them to me, O liberal one,
> And know that you have finished your course and obtained your wish,
> You have made the pilgrimage and gained the life to come,
> You have become pure, and that in a moment of time.
> Of a truth that is God which your soul sees in me,
> For God has chosen me to be His house.
> Though the Ka'ba is the house of His grace and favours,
> Yet my body too is the house of His secret.
> When He made that house (the Ka'ba) He has never entered it,
> But none but the Living One enters this house.

> When you have seen me you have seen God.' (Whinfield, 1979, p. 89)

I have quoted the passage at length because it provides an excellent example of the transferral of the sacred space from the paraphernalia of religion, rituals, pilgrimages and special places to the purified human heart where God is believed to reside. Note that Rumi does not deny the sanctity of the Ka'ba in Makkah, as Kabir and Nanak denied the validity of the externals of religion, but rather advocates the living presence of God in the human heart as opposed to his absence from geographical locations. Rumi further clarifies his position in another passage from the *Mathnawi:*

> The real Workman is hidden in His workshop,
> Go you into that workshop and see Him face to face. (Whinfield, 1979, p. 71)

The relocation of Allah's presence from a heavenly abode to the human heart causes more difficulties for the followers of Islam than it does for the *sants*, who are located within Hinduism which contains ancient and venerated texts teaching the unity of Brahmin and *Atman*, the omnipresent being and the human consciousness. The issue for Muslims was one of authority. For most Muslims the edicts of the Qur'an, supported by the Hadith, contain the authority required to legitimate human behaviour. An authentic Islam would be that which most fully appears to follow the revelation contained in the Qur'an. However, the mystic such as Rumi could claim that the authority of God as discovered within himself provided another source of authority to guide his actions. His behaviour is authenticated solely on the basis of his inner experience. No problem arises if both inner experience and outer revelation are in harmony, but considerable problems arise if they conflict. Muslim scholars and mystics had to resolve this apparent contradiction between revelation and inspiration, and the final consensus was that both the exoteric (outward) and the esoteric (inward) should be essential to the authentic experience of being a Muslim. However, there have always been those in both Hindu devotional traditions and Muslim mysticism who have argued that the knowledge of God's presence within overrides all other sources of authority, and who have felt that they are above the everyday outer activities of the religion which are undertaken by the masses.

Religious experience

I have been exploring a number of prominent figures drawn from Indian and Muslim traditions who have felt that the inner experience of the divine provides the ultimate authority. Such figures are collectively known as mystics, regardless of which religion they have originated within. In Chapter 11 we will look more closely at mysticism in regard to the topic of truth-claims. Ninian Smart defines mysticism as a purification of the mind to such a degree that all thoughts and images are left behind leaving an experience of inner bliss, complete peace, a non-dualistic sense of union where there is no longer any subject/object experience (Smart, 1995, p. 61). However, this tends to describe Indian religious experiences of unity belonging to non-dualistic traditions such as Buddhism, *Advaita Vedanta* or Yoga, rather than the mystical experiences of theists who feel a communion with a loving God, often brought about by their own feelings of intense devotion. In addition to these two kinds of mystical experience, Smart also mentions the experience of the shaman who is able by trance and by means of a special personality to enter the world of the god(dess) and to contact the spirits, thus providing a bridge between the natural and supernatural worlds (1995, p. 64).

Although there are considerable differences between these experiences, they are all likely to be claimed as authentic in the sense that they involve direct contact with or access to the world of divinity. There are those who claim that the experiential dimension is the kernel of religiosity, the heart or essence of religion. After all, even sacred texts generally tell the stories of those who have had extraordinary relationships of closeness with the divine. Original Buddhist texts tell the story of Buddha's enlightenment, the New Testament resounds with the experience of those who felt the impact of Jesus' presence, and the prophets of the Jewish scriptures had their own intimate relationship with their God. The key moments that bring a faith into existence are usually experiential, and founders relied on their experiences to authenticate their message, not on the externals of religion which existed, if at all, only as some vague, unformed prototype.

However, authenticity is also sought by those who utilize the externals of a religion as the means of approaching the divine. The performance of rituals, visiting sacred spaces or reading sacred texts, all inspire feeling. The everyday religious life of believers is maintained by the feelings that are inspired by cathedrals, temples, mosques, inner and outer architecture, artefacts, music, processions, special dress or religious language. Through these the human being is helped to feel that they are in the presence of something greater than themselves, a sense of majesty or awe. The authentic performance of ritual is one where the participant engages the emotions rather than mechanically going through the actions.

Contemporary spirituality and new religions

From the middle of the twentieth century Western societies have increasingly witnessed a search for authenticity, often expressed in the voices of counterculture or alternative discourses. In the 1960s, disillusioned with the apparent emptiness of modern life and material values, a number of young people sought more authentic experiences for expressing the meaning of human existence. This search for authenticity was echoed in the language of popular culture, in expressions like 'get real' or 'get a life'. Those who conformed were accused of living 'plastic' lives, and a well-known Beatles song describes 'nowhere man living his nowhere life in nowhere land'. Quests for authenticity need not be religious, on the contrary they might involve the rejection of religion as part of a conservative status quo. They may include radical political demonstrations or back-to-nature lifestyles. Yet the 1960s also saw an increase in new religious movements, recruiting primarily from the young. The most popular of these movements borrowed or adapted eastern spirituality, and were influenced by mysticism. The expressions 'you are in your ego' or 'in your mind' indicated the influence of eastern mysticism with its relegation of the ego-self to a more transitory or illusionary awareness, often identified as the source of negative emotions that disturb self-harmony, and harmony between human beings or with nature. The quest for the real self led some individuals to membership of new religious movements, to psychotherapy and the whole range of phenomena commonly known as the 'New Age'.

This quest for authenticity drew a line between religion and spirituality. Spirituality was perceived as living or participating in the life of God or other divine being, whereas religion was seen as the human product of the expression of such a life. However, it is believed that religion loses its authenticity when it becomes institutionalized and politicized. The traditional churches are associated with religion and a lack of spirituality, and perceived to be dull, conformist and doctrinally rigid. Spirituality is appropriated from traditional religions into the hands of authentic spiritual seekers, who are free from the constraints of religious organizations and hierarchies, and seek ways of achieving primal experiences of the divinity of the self and/or nature. In 'New Age' discourse, spirituality is perceived as the incoming individual experience of a new era which replaces the old organized religions. Stuart Sutcliffe writes:

> It should also be clear that 'spirituality' rather than 'religion' is now firmly on the public agenda, and in retrospect, making spirituality public – enabling an autonomous spirituality to 'come out', so to speak – can be seen to have been a major function of alternative spirituality in general and the networks associated with the incubation of the 'New Age' in particular. (Sutcliffe, 2003, p. 130)

Religion, then, is perceived to be not the repository of spirituality, but even the antithesis of the spiritual; it is shunned and even criticized as unimaginative, restricting human development and socially constricting, and at its worst pathological – creating sexual repression, exploiting nature and causing conflict. It is perceived as consisting of mundane rules, whereas spirituality is seen as alive and spontaneous.

Sutcliffe writes about the results of a questionnaire that he distributed to the occupants of Findhorn, a 'New Age' centre in Scotland. He notes the results:

> 'Spirituality' was overwhelmingly preferred by the respondents to 'religion'. The latter was associated with ideas like the 'system', 'dogma', 'organised belief', and 'narrow' outlooks, whereas spirituality was linked to 'living experience' and to 'open', 'inner', 'inclusive', and 'natural' discourse. (Sutcliffe, 2003, p. 215)

Thus some new forms of religion in the West have rejected the externals of the established religions, showing high regard for the founders of new religions who embody spirituality and spontaneity; criticizing existing religions; and wanting to avoid creating organizations or institutions. This separation of the authentic origins embodied in the founder from the inauthentic religious institution that follows allows for an appropriation of the founder to the cause of new spiritualities, which claim to possess an esoteric key to understanding his or her teachings. Thus mystics such as Kabir or Rumi put their emphasis on experience and inwardness, renewing their authority as authentic sources for the contemporary seeker, but with the focus on inclusiveness and on the universalism that sets them apart from the culture and tradition they occupied in their lifetimes. They reappear in alternative spirituality discourse as personifications of a claimed authentic religiosity that reflects the values of the new seeker.

Authenticity for new spirituality is found not among traditional authorities such as priests, theologians, churches or other places of worship, but rather among mystics, masters and teachers who may be drawn from the established religions. They may be reinvented or presented as spirits advising their chosen 'mediums' from astral or other 'spiritual' planes of existence where these advanced beings now exist after leaving their physical existence on the earth plane. The overriding ethos is universalist, 'picking' and 'mixing' from a range of religious ideas and techniques, under the commonly held meta-narrative that all the world's spiritual paths lead to the same goal of human potential and self-fulfilment. The overarching ethos of new spirituality is anti-belief, promoting personal experience as a 'science', empirically demonstrated by the achievement of inner transformation and well-being or contact with the supernatural by whatever means. Thus the focus is on technique and certainty rather than faith or dogma.

Any discourse about authenticity has to be about authority, and in the new spiritualities the 'heart' symbolizes both wholeness and the authentic, whereas the mind is regarded with suspicion. Too much use of the intellect and reason is seen as part of the current difficulties experienced by humankind. Thus politicians, business leaders, academics and the functionaries of established religion are viewed with the same suspicion, presumed to be contaminated by the Enlightenment and rationality, and therefore unable to enter the 'enchanted garden' of unity and interconnectedness. Sutcliffe states:

> With the dilution of traditional sources of corporate authority such as a master-narrative, a priesthood and the discipline of the congregation, religion has become by default a self-sited and personally negotiated practice of strategically-interacting individuals. (2003, p. 171)

The domain of the affective becomes the principal source of authenticity with terms such as peace, love, happiness, fulfilment dominating the spiritual discourse. How it is achieved becomes secondary to the claim of personal experience. Thus practitioners are authorized by their own claims rather than by the more formal training given to 'experts' in the established religions. Their authenticity is verified by the ability to gain similar experiences from the techniques taught, and passed on in workshops and seminars. The shift to experience as the marker of authenticity democratizes spirituality, as opposed to the hierarchies and spiritual elites of established religions. Anyone can be an expert. As stated by William Bloom, spiritual practice is something that you and you alone can put together for yourself (1993, p. 21). Spirituality is perceived as innate to everyone, and can be accessed by an unlocking of our truest feelings. The experiences of gnosis and charisma, seen as the province of a God-selected elite in the established theistic religions, or of arduous commitment in non-theistic traditions, both of which produce the mystics of history, can come within the range of everyone.

However, the absence of authoritative meta-narratives, although part of the *zeitgeist* of our age, at least in Anglo-American cultures, leads to further fragmentation and diversification of the religious terrain. Already facing the impact of migration and globalization, dominant religious worldviews associated with a particular culture or nation are under pressure to maintain their hegemony. In the age of the individual, with its emphasis on self-fulfilment, we can each choose our own paths, avoiding traditional religion or taking what we want to retain from them. On the other hand, we can borrow from several World Religions. But the aim of the individual increasingly becomes the pursuit of the authentic.

Not all new religions pursue spirituality in opposition to ritual, sacred sites and hierarchies. Some do not create an opposition between spirituality and religion, and fully intend to establish as quickly as possible the traditional routes to authenticity. However, their difficulty is the absence of time-honoured traditions. The new is regarded suspiciously and easily labelled negatively as 'cult' behaviour, with adherents accused of being brainwashed or manipulated. Like all new religions they will in turn become old, creating new avenues of authentic practices and beliefs. Even in the 'New Age' establishments discussed above, problems of continuity versus spontaneity will arise. In Sutcliffe's study of Findhorn, now one of the most established loci for 'New Age' practice, he notes that the original caravan in which the founders, Peter and Eileen Caddy, lived on the site has now been restored and placed in a garden dedicated to nature spirits. The restoration took place within a year of Peter Caddy's death, and was described in the opening ceremony as the 'site where spirit first became matter' (Sutcliffe, 2003, pp. 165, 166). Although it was opposed by some residents, Eileen Caddy approved it, and it may mark the beginning of a sacred space, a future location for authenticity, a sacred relic associated with beginnings.

The problem also exists for old religious traditions that move to a new location. Adaptations have to take place in the new environment that can disturb ancient practices. Heated discussions can arise between traditionalists and modernizers concerning whether the changes maintain authenticity. In Britain, Hindu and Jain temples are accommodated within existing buildings such as churches and schools. However, authentic architecture is maintained by shipping the internal housing of the deities from custom-approved craftsmen in India. Where temples are purpose-built, the land is blessed by Brahmin priests who perform elaborate ceremonies to sacralize the earth beneath the foundations.

Recently in Nuneaton near Coventry, in the heart of Britain's Midlands, four young Muslim Sufis created the first shrine to a Sufi master whose body was buried there in the grounds of a Muslim college. The *mazar* (tomb-shrine) is built to traditional subcontinent Sufi specifications and the veneration practices are maintained in the traditional manner. At the time of the Sufi's *urs* (day of death regarded as the deceased's birth into eternity), thousands of Muslims of subcontinent origin gather to perform time-honoured practices including intercessionary prayers and all-night chanting of the names of Allah. However, it is also traditional for older Muslims who comprise the first generation of migrants to attend religious lectures delivered by Islamic scholars in Urdu. The young successors to their father felt that a college teaching British-born Muslims needed to develop new educational methods more in keeping with the expectations of the younger generation. They have stopped the old-style lectures and replaced them with educational summer camps on Islamic themes. There was some resistance from the older generation. However, old religions adapting to new surroundings, or facing rapidly changing societies, have to continuously negotiate what is essential and what can be abandoned or transformed. In doing so, careful decisions have to be made about authenticity.

FIGURE 8.3 *The tomb and shrine of Pir Wahhab Siddiqi, a British Muslim leader and Sufi who is buried in the grounds of Hijaz College, Nuneaton, England. His tomb is the first Sufi shrine located in Britain.*

Case study: Sikhism and religious diversity

The problem of authenticity and religious diversity exists within every religion but I have chosen to examine Sikhism as it is relatively small and historically young, and yet generally regarded as one of the major world traditions. We have already seen that the founding figure, Guru Nanak, was an iconoclast espousing inner experience of God and personal transformation over and above religious externals. Although the nine human teachers (Gurus) who followed Nanak introduced various externals of religion such as sacred sites, texts, pilgrimages and bathing tanks, their poetry reflects the continuation of Nanak's essential teachings. However, the last human Guru, Gobind Singh, lived a radically different lifestyle from Guru Nanak, who was cast in the traditional form of an Indian holy man and depicted as such in Sikh iconography. Guru Gobind Singh was a warrior prince who ruled over the hearts of his disciples and functioned as the temporal ruler of the Sikh people. On his death Guru Gobind Singh declared that there would be no more human gurus in Sikhism, but that the community would be guided henceforth by the collection of sacred writing containing the poems of the gurus and various *sants* and Sufis whose teachings reflected the Sikh masters. This collection, known as the Guru Granth Sahib, remains the focal point of Sikh veneration and ritual practice to this day. Its authenticity is established through the line of succession from the human gurus declared by their last representative, and its contents contain the 'authentic' words of the God-inspired.

In addition to ending the lineage of human gurus, Gobind Singh changed the face of Sikhism in one more dramatic way. According to traditional Sikh sources, the tenth Guru initiated the *Khalsa* brotherhood on the first day of Vaisakhi at Anandpur in 1699. On the festival of Vaisakhi it was usual for Sikhs to gather together with their Guru and celebrate. On this occasion, tradition states that Guru Gobind Singh stood before his followers with a drawn sword in his hand and announced, 'I want a Sikh who can offer his head to me, here and now. My sword is thirsting for the head of one who had learnt the lesson of surrender to me.' It is stated that the Guru repeated this three times until a Sikh named Daya Ram of the Khatri caste came forward and offered his head in sacrifice to the Guru. The *Khalsa* myth affirms that Guru Gobind Singh took Daya Ram into a tent or enclosure where a goat was beheaded. The Guru then returned to the crowd with his sword covered in blood and demanded another human sacrifice. Many of the participants fled in terror believing the Guru to have gone mad, but four more Sikhs of different castes obeyed their Guru's request. Each time a goat was slaughtered and the procedure repeated.

Finally, the Guru introduced to the crowd the five obedient Sikhs armed with swords, dressed in long loose yellow shirts and blue turbans. He named them the panjpyares (five dear ones). These five were initiated into the new order known as *Khalsa* by the Guru and his wife. The initiation took place by creating *amrit* (nectar) by stirring water and sugar with a double-edged steel dagger. The *amrit* was given to the five disciples, who in turn were requested to initiate the Guru himself. Guru Gobind Singh then introduced the crowd to the *Khalsa* and explained the requirement to wear five outer symbols of Sikh identity, popularly known as the five Ks. He also renamed male initiates Singh (lion) and female initiates Kaur (princess). Gopal Singh cites traditional Sikh sources that claim that 80,000 Sikhs joined the new order within two weeks of its foundation.

The *Khalsa* movement came to embody obedience to the instructions of the Guru, and therefore the ultimate and only form of Sikh orthodoxy. During the 1980s, for various political, religious and social reasons, some Sikhs became involved in a struggle to create their own independent state of Khalistan, culminating in a bloody massacre at the most sacred site of Sikhism in Amritsar and a virtual state of civil war with the Indian government. The creation of the *Khalsa* was therefore a unique way to provide a formal structure in order to unite the community both religiously and socially, and create this Sikh corporate identity. There are two important reasons for the creation of the *Khalsa*, which both relate to the idea of a separate Sikh state. According to McLeod these are:

1 Guru Gobind Singh provided his followers with a militant and highly visible identity, essential if they were to withstand imminent trials arising from the conflict with the Mughals.
2 The Guru was determined to have a united following, therefore the control of the masands needed to be dismantled, restoring political, financial and religious commitment to the Guru himself. (McLeod, 1995)

After examining the reasons given for the birth of *Khalsa*, it is clear that the most important aim of Guru Gobind Singh was to create a single community undivided by caste prejudices. It took the form of a community of saint-soldiers who were devout in their religious commitment but also able to defend their faith. Their primary obedience and loyalty was to their Guru.

The use of the word *Khalsa* is also very significant. McLeod explains that 'Khalsa derives from the Arabic/Persian Khalisa ("pure"). However, a secondary meaning was applicable to the organization of the Mughal empire and indicated "lands under the Emperor's direct control"' (McLeod, 1995, p. 122). It is difficult to decide either way whether the use of the word 'Khalsa' was an intended ploy by Guru Gobind Singh, because if the word is used in its Arabic context Guru Gobind Singh was declaring the Sikhs to be an independent people under the direct leadership of his Guruship, and therefore engaged in a liberation struggle against a powerful Mughal empire. If this is true then it could be construed by Sikhs as an early indication of the formation of a state ruled by the Sikhs themselves.

Finally, although tracing the origin of the creation of *Khalsa* does not give firm support to the view that Guru Gobind Singh created the *Khalsa* with Khalistan as his ultimate intention, there are inclinations in his use of language (i.e. Khalisa/*Khalsa*), the imagery borrowed from the Mughal courts, and the use of their royal terms that does suggest the concept of an independent territory with a temporal and spiritual ruler at its head.

Although the creation of the *Khalsa* did not create the notion of Khalistan in Guru Gobind Singh's own time, the use of the scripture and the way in which the *Khalsa* was established (saint-soldiers/*miri-piri*) can be used to support the ideas of Khalistan. It is possible for Sikhs who desire an independent Sikh state of Khalistan to use Guru Gobind Singh's period as an ideal foundation and legitimation for its creation, and utilize the slogan 'the Khalsa shall rule' to influence and unite public opinion to their cause. The problem here is one of insiders' conceptions of a religious event loaded with significance and capable of generating several overlapping meta-narratives. There is considerable distance between the contemporary notion of Khalistan and the formation of the *Khalsa* by Guru Gobind Singh. However, there are enough powerful symbols that can be drawn upon, especially surrounding Guru Gobind Singh's relationship between statecraft and spiritual authority, to leave the Guru's conception vulnerable to new forms of political demands against perceived injustice.

Although there were certainly unitive motives in Gobind Singh's formation of the *Khalsa*, for example the attempt to break down caste distinctions in the Sikh community and the quest to bring all followers under his sole authority, there were also inherent problems with the *Khalsa* inception that would tend to move Sikhism in a completely different direction from that envisaged by the founder Gurus. The *Khalsa* initiation and outer forms of identity marking would have changed the meaning of the term 'Sikh'. Originally defined as 'learner' or 'student' and denoting discipleship, it was surely not meant to be conceived by the founder Guru as a separate religious identity. Guru Nanak attracted disciples from both Muslim and Hindu backgrounds, and there is little evidence to suggest that they did not remain in their faiths while living as his disciples. The focus was a mystical and universal experience arising out of namsimaran (remembrance of the name of God) and faith in the teaching of the Guru rather than any outer marker of religious identity. The provision of the *Khalsa* identity would surely have pushed Sikhs not only to an awareness of their own religious identity as distinct from Hindus and Muslims, but also to an exclusive sense of identity rather than the inclusive understanding associated with the sant tradition in which the early Gurus can be grouped on the basis of their teachings.

Paradoxically, the creation of the *Khalsa* threw into relief other ways of being Sikh, and all those who followed the teachings of the Gurus but did not observe the *Khalsa* code of discipline became known as Sahajdharis. *Khalsa* Sikhs tend to see Sahajdharis as either doctrinally incorrect or in a process of gradual development towards full *Khalsa* initiation and observance. However, Sahajdhari Sikhs are unlikely to agree with the *Khalsa* analysis of their religious beliefs and practices, and are far more likely to authenticate their own traditions by associating themselves with the Hindu idea of an eternal religion that is continuously renewed (*sanatan dharma*). Thus the creation of the Khalsa not only divided Sikhs into those who join and those who do not, but provided the possibility of a number of contesting voices to appear in each category.

We have already seen that *Khalsa* discourse opened the way for a separatist religio-political movement rallying around the idea of a Sikh state. Thus a fundamentalist tendency was initiated within the already orthodox *Khalsa*. On the other hand, various reform movements who regarded the *Khalsa* as creating a variant of the religion which was too caught up in ritual practices sought their authority in the teachings of Guru Nanak, attempting to refocus on a spiritual or mystical return to an emphasis on namsimaran. Some of these movements even challenged the doctrine that living gurus were no longer a possibility within Sikhism. In the villages and towns of the Punjab, tens of thousands of Sikhs practised a religion that did not subscribe to the *Khalsa* orthodox view that Sikhism was an independent religion. They merged into the wider world of Hinduism while continuing to uphold a Sikh ethnic identity and maintaining Sikh religious practices.

Anyone who has spent any time travelling in the Punjab will know that there is no shortage of Sikh sadhus and ascetics. Many wear their hair long and unmatted, carry rosaries in cotton bags, smear their bodies in ashes and sit on a deer-skin when practising their yogic sadhana. The Udasis (detached ones) are typical of this phenomenon. They claim that Shri Chand, the son of Guru Nanak, was the true successor to the Sikh Guruship, rather than Guru Angad Dev. Sahajdharis on the other hand cut their hair, have no initiation rites, sometimes believe in different versions of the line of succession from Guru Nanak and often do not accept that the Guru Granth Sahib is the present Guru of the Sikhs.

Following Oberoi, I have used the term Sanatan Sikhs to describe the countless numbers of the Punjabi rural population who do not make a distinction between the Sikh tradition and the preceding Hindu *dharma*. Sanatan Sikhs consider the *Vedas*, *Puranas* and Hindu epics to be authoritative; they associate Guru Nanak and Gobind

Singh with Hindu *avatars* and worship Hindu images along with living gurus. They perceive the Sikh tradition as a continuation of Krishna's eternal promise to humankind enshrined in the *Bhagavad Gita*:

> I manifest myself in a finite form.
> Whenever dharma declines and the purpose of life is forgotten,
> I manifest myself on earth.
> I am born in every age to protect the good,
> To destroy evil and to re-establish dharma. (Easwaren) (trans. 1986, pp. 85–6)

The prevalence of the worship of Baba Balaknath in the Punjab demonstrates the continued strength of popular religion in the region. Oberoi refers to this as the existence of 'an enchanted universe' (Oberoi, 1994, pp. 140–203). The province of Punjab is still primarily village culture. In the village of Danda I observed the activities of the Baba Balaknath priest every evening after *arti*. Villagers, mostly women, would queue to seek solutions to the everyday problems of village life. The stories of the annual pilgrimage to Baba Balaknath's main shrine in Himachal Pradesh indicate the prevalence of this enchanted universe. Although there is now a road to the pilgrimage centre, traditionally devotees began their pilgrimage through the jungled hills by releasing a consecrated goat and following it wherever it led. The popular pilgrimage itself is an indication of the eclecticism of Punjabi religious life. It takes place during the month of March and lasts for a period of three weeks. On the way to the temple complex thousands of Punjabi pilgrims, including hundreds from Britain, visit Shiva and Durga temples and the tomb of a Sufi. Alongside the gurdwaras and the temples of Baba Balaknath, the villages of the Punjab also contain many small shrines. Some of these are specifically Sikh shrines, but others are not associated with any one religious tradition. Even at Sikh shrines the custodians may be contemptuous of the *Khalsa*, claiming a direct possession by the resident deity of the location. One such figure accused the *Khalsa* functionaries of reading the Guru Granth Sahib 'like parrots' and having no inner awareness of the truth revealed by Guru Nanak.

Conclusion

The example of Sikhism provides an opportunity to observe the degree of diversity even in this relatively young religion, and to realize that each variation is hotly contested by its adherents. They will all argue that theirs is the authentic version, even though the justifications for authenticity will vary from group to group. Students should also beware authenticity that is provided by being described in an academic text. Scholars may lend authenticity to a tradition through the reputation of the academy. This is particularly true in the case of religions such as Islam or Sikhism, where definitive versions are presented that express the discourses of prominent orthodoxies. We need to ask ourselves who is being omitted and why. Most textbooks on Sikhism, for example, do not describe the complexity and variety of forms of Sikh identity, but rather present the *Khalsa* as the definitive and discrete Sikh World Religion. This is particularly true in Western Sikh diasporas, where the *Khalsa* is rapidly manifesting itself as the dominant form of Sikh identity and orthodoxy. It is also true of books on contemporary Islam that rarely indicate the prevalence of popular or folk traditions or the continued resilience of Sufism in many parts of the Muslim world. As scholars of religion, one common stance is that we are not in a position to judge truth-claims or suggest that one is more authentic than another, although we may well want to assess claims to authenticity in order to understand how they are utilized by insiders. All religions are true in their own fashion and it cannot be our decision to distinguish between the *Khalsa* and other forms of Sikh identity, or in the diversity in any other religious tradition with regard to claims of authenticity. If we do so, we are open to the accusation that we are assisting one element of a religion to claim itself as the definitive version over all others. The point to realize here is that most religious followers will claim that their particular tradition is authentic, although not necessarily exclusive. Religion exists on two spheres: in the physical, and in the domain of meaning. Maria Leppokari states that 'religion stands, in general, for a meaning – creating orientation in life' (Leppokari, 2002, p. 11). Many of the phenomena of religion are meaningless except that human beings bring to them symbolic meanings or functions that move them out of the realm of the purely physical and into the realm of the sacred. When this is achieved, authenticity is required. What now makes this object, ritual or space authentically sacred? To achieve this, the devices and processes explored above come into play. But levels of meaning and interpretation are manifold, and this leads to fragmentation and diversity.

Because religion deals with the sacred, for millions of believers it is non-negotiable; but scholars are more likely to explore religion as culture rather than as 'truth', and some may even see religion as resistance to truth which can be found elsewhere in the scientific paradigm. However, a view is emerging as an alternative to that of neutrality to authenticity. Since the events of 11 September 2001, many non-Muslims and Muslims have engaged in a discourse that argues that the religion of the 'terrorist' organizations in the Muslim world is not 'authentic' Islam. The question is then raised concerning what is authentic when there are so many movements and expressions within the overarching tradition. If it is admitted that we cannot decide which is 'true' since all are interpretations of a particular historical moment, then is not Osama Bin Laden's version also equally authentic? In the contemporary world, religion is undergoing a revival in which many of the new forms are associated deeply with politics. The question needs to be asked by all who study religion: isn't the neutral stance to authenticity one of cowardice, standing back from crucial issues that will determine the kind of world we live in? Shouldn't we be more engaged? After all, religion can be used as a tool for tyranny, complicit with models of power that humankind needs to liberate itself from. Some forms of religion can also be used as a tool for emancipation in opposition to extreme worldviews, a force to represent the marginalized. It can represent the poor, the oppressed, non-white populations of the majority world and women who have been victims of patriarchy. Armin Geertz stated at the 2001 inaugural conference of the European Association for the Study of Religion in Cambridge that scholarship should be resistance: emancipatory and reflective (published 2002). If so, then scholars of religion may have to make their own choices concerning the authentic and inauthentic voices that defend various narratives.

DISCUSSION POINTS

1 Identify the reasons why some religious communities feel a need to return to their roots, and the reasons why other communities prefer development and progression. Consider whether some religious groups attempt to do both simultaneously, and how they reconcile the tensions this creates.

2 'Mircea Eliade wrote that myths have their own time, a sacred time standing outside normal time, and in ritual re-enactment the person is able to stand outside time and enter the domain of sacred reality'. Explain this statement. Suggest examples of the ways in which myths and rituals achieve this.

3 Consider examples of specific versions of a religion that have come to be equated with the 'true' or 'authentic' version. (For instance, Sikhs are popularly identified with those who wear the *khalsa* symbols, even though they are a minority.) What causes such identifications to occur? Why is it important to avoid such stereotyping?

4 What makes religions so diverse? Why are there seldom, if ever, religions that are monolithic?

9

Fieldwork in the study of religion

Ron Geaves

Chapter Outline

Introduction	241
Religious diversity and complexity	246
Doing fieldwork	250
Access to religious communities	257
Gaining entry	263
Relations between observer and observed	268
Conclusion	272
Discussion points	274

Introduction

Fieldwork in the study of religion provides an exciting dimension in addition to textual study. It offers an approach to the study that focuses on a horizontal as opposed to a vertical analysis of faith tradition, and indeed can be used to complement vertical approaches. Above all, fieldwork acknowledges that religions are lived traditions, central to the lives of millions of believers around the world and providing a major motivation for action and life choices. It is essential to know how a believer understands the world and operates in society. Thus it is important for study to focus on living religious communities, in order to know their worldviews and how they determine their motivation for action. In addition, many religions are far more diverse and heterodox than both insider and outsider accounts convey through written texts. Studies in the field provide the opportunity to engage with this diversity without making value judgements concerning the truth-claims of self-proclaimed 'orthodoxies' or movements, or of individuals accused of being heretical or unorthodox.

FIGURE 9.1 *South Indian and Sri Lankan devotees of Murugan gather in the temple in Ealing, London before participating in the Kavali street processions in which the god is paraded in a chariot pulled by devotees.*

Most modern societies, including Britain and the United States, are increasingly multicultural. Large urban centres provide a plethora of religious communities that include not only the major faiths such as Hinduism, Islam, Buddhism, Sikhism and various Chinese religions, which have all arrived through economic or political migration, but also a host of small religions which have developed in the last 50 or 100 years. These are either sectarian formations of existing traditions, or cultic forms with the potential to develop as new religious traditions.

Even the countryside is not without signs of this increased diversity, as various religious movements take the opportunity to buy or build retreat centres, headquarters or bases for committed followers either to live completely according to the religion's beliefs and practices, or to promote the religion's teachings to others. Country houses in Britain now function as Buddhist monasteries, filled with saffron-robed monks; and a castle has been constructed as the headquarters for Scientology in the United Kingdom. In the United States, where space is less at a premium, large areas of land function as visionary utopias for an alternative lifestyle based upon a new 'revelation' or teaching that encourages followers to remove themselves from mainstream society in pursuit of their ultimate spiritual goal. Thus a new landscape of religious possibilities is beginning to emerge as part of the religious map of pluralist societies. In addition, there is the existing patchwork of sacred spaces represented by the rich variety of Christian tradition. In proximity to every university campus is a rich vein for research, inviting students and staff to engage in fieldwork and discover communities that may not have been studied in great detail, and to add to the existing knowledge of contemporary religious landscapes. This type of ethnographical study is challenging, and requires the student to develop skills that are not discovered in textual study. First and foremost, it needs 'people skills' that are very different from those found in the library. In fieldwork, we are meeting with fellow human beings who usually hold very different understandings of reality from our own. Whether we are atheists, agnostics or committed believers in a faith tradition different from that of our informants, we are likely to be intellectually and emotionally confronted by unfamiliar worldviews. Some of them may repel, affront our sense of what is reasonable, believable or rational, and others may attract us both intellectually and emotionally, modifying or transforming our own worldview.

Stereotypes of particular communities or individuals can be shattered, thus awakening and developing our perceptions. One of the authors remembers the first time that he was invited to attend a *dhikr* gathering held late on a Saturday night in an inner-city mosque frequented by Pakistani-origin Muslims who were members of a Naqshbandi Sufi *tariqa*. The lights were dimmed so that the participants could not observe each other's ecstasies, and to avoid pride arising from spiritual achievement or frustration at one's inability to enter into loss of self. The environment had been created to allow uninhibited communion with Allah through chanting his names, and by moving the body rhythmically in time with the repetition. First, the observer was struck with awe as he realized that he was witnessing a scene that had been carried out thousands of times throughout the Muslim world, sometimes by some of the greatest exponents of mysticism that the world has known; he then experienced a sense of displacement as he comprehended that this was taking place in a British city. When the lights came up, he realized that he would never perceive the elderly Muslim man sitting next to him on the bus, or the Muslim shopkeepers from whom he purchased his spices and Oriental vegetables, through the same lens; for he had been permitted an insight into a dimension of their lives he had not formerly been aware of. A full account of this ethnographical study of the Ghamkolvia Naqshbandi Sufi *tariqa* can be found in Geaves (1995).

Fieldwork also offers the opportunity to enhance our understanding of a faith tradition by observing what it means to living practitioners, and how they negotiate official doctrine or practices as part of a living and dynamic process. Religions do not stay the same; if they remained static, they would be unlikely to survive, and there is a continuing process of differentiating the essential from the peripheral; the negotiable from the non-negotiable. This process may lead to splintering and diversity as various groups disagree with decisions bringing change; such groups feel that something which has been deemed negotiable is part of the core message, revelation or hallowed tradition.

Fieldwork provides the opportunity to explore this process as it happens, and to observe at first hand the relationship between heterodoxy, orthodoxy, elites, organizational structures, and the views and practices of the 'grassroots' believers. This process challenges our perceptions concerning who owns a faith tradition and its sacred texts, hallowed doctrines and special people. In the above context, fieldwork provides the chance to study a religion from the bottom upwards, acknowledging the significance of the mass of believers as well as the leaders. In so doing it transforms the study of religion, which has traditionally focused on sacred texts and sanctified elites or scholars within the faith tradition.

Finally, fieldwork challenges us and our perceptions of others as our own sense of identity encounters the equally precious and deeply held convictions that help form the identity of others. Much has been written in both sociology and anthropology on the subject of neutrality or 'value-free' research, the impact of the researcher on the community studied, the power relations between observer and the observed; and Religious Studies has its own contribution to make to this debate. We need to ask ourselves as scholars of religion whether we are merely a multidisciplinary subject, made of several subjects such as the two above-mentioned, and also politics, philosophy, psychology, history and other disciplines that also consider religion to be of interest; or whether there is something unique in a 'study of religion' approach that offers a methodology and consequent insights independent of those reached by the above subject areas. The fieldworker in Religious Studies needs to consider what they hope to achieve by this type of research, and what kind of questions should be asked.

This chapter will develop all of the above in some detail, and will also present a number of case studies and events drawn from the experience of the authors in a number of religious traditions. The chapter will thus provide a helpful and practical series of insights into both the pitfalls that can face the researcher, and the extraordinary benefits of this approach to the study of religion. It is not intended to be a definitive guide, listing the right ways and the wrong ways of doing fieldwork, because in the authors' experience one key to being successful is remaining open, flexible and ready for the unexpected. In this realm of study it is always good to remember that living religions are not the coherent, ordered packages found in theological or philosophical understandings of the sacred, or even the accounts found in academic texts that introduce us to various religious worldviews. In the field, religions are messy, paradoxical and chaotic, and they feed on the irrational. Indeed it could be argued that fieldwork is diametrically opposite to the scholar's rational process of ordering a faith tradition into neat packages of history, doctrine and practices. Always remember that what may appear problematic to the researcher is not a problem at all for the believer. A difficulty often arises from translating the distinct worldview of the observed into the alternative view of the scholar.

In Britain, the increasing religious plurality and the focus on promoting multicultural values has led to many religious education teachers taking their pupils to visit places of worship, although it is unlikely that this approach can be found in continental

Europe. In Britain, most teacher-training programmes in higher education, and Study of Religion departments in colleges whose historical focus has been teacher training, have provided fieldwork activities on their degree courses.

Along with social sciences, religious education has introduced the possibility of fieldwork into the discipline of studying religion. However, neither approach has spent much effort on developing a methodology of fieldwork that enters the world of the believer and provides a more informed understanding and analysis of religious behaviour that acknowledges the believer's worldview. The social sciences have been able to provide the methodology of ethnography and participant observation, but their results are more concerned with a religion's function than with eliciting a deeper understanding of the beliefs and practices taking cognizance of the sacred dimension: quite correctly they have been accused of reductionism in their undoubtedly invaluable insights into the motives of believers. However, there have been signs of new approaches to the sociology of religion among some sociologists. Pals has pointed out that sociologists such as Robert Bellah and Peter Berger see the best way to enter the world of the religious phenomena as accepting the idea of the 'irreducible sacred' (Pals, 1999, p. 180). Pals quotes Berger as stating: 'I would recommend that the scientific study of religion returns to the perspective on the phenomenon from "within", that is, to viewing it in terms of the meanings intended by the religious consciousness' (1999, p. 180).

The training of teachers increasingly involves visits to places of worship and religious events, as schoolteachers enable children to observe other religions. Multiculturalism, with its ethos of respect for all faiths, has informed Britain's creation of an integrated society, and has demanded a method of study that will observe with neutrality and empathy. Teachers of teachers have begun to draw upon the phenomenological method, being heavily influenced by the essential contribution of Ninian Smart. However, this method of study has sometimes suffered from an overly descriptive approach which noted what people did and believed, but rarely entered controversy or probed deeper into contradictions, issues of religious diversity or the analysis of motivation. This is not the case with the excellent body of research created by the Institute of Education at the University of Warwick: there, Robert Jackson and Eleanor Nesbitt have pioneered an ethnographic approach to religious education that utilizes over 30 years of fieldwork among children from Sikh, Hindu, Muslim and Christian backgrounds (Jackson, 1997; Nesbitt, 2004). In addition, the work of phenomenologists like Ninian Smart has been crucial in reclaiming phenomena for the study of religion, embodying the well-known words of Rudolf Otto: 'for if there be any single domain of human experience that presents us with something unmistakably specific and unique, peculiar to itself, assuredly it is that of religious life' (Otto, 1958, p. 4).

Several British departments of Theology and Religious Studies offer fieldwork opportunities of various kinds, ranging from site visits placed within a course to full courses based on placements in religious communities. There are signs that fieldwork is being taken more seriously by Religious Studies departments in US universities and the journal *Religious Studies News*, published by the American Academy of Religion in 2004, included a section in its 'Spotlight on Teaching' on site visits; the Academy's prestigious conference at Atlanta in the same year provided a panel on fieldwork pedagogy.

Religious diversity and complexity

Participation in field research often leads the researcher in the discipline of Religious Studies to ask whether the religion discussed in academic textbooks bears any resemblance to the tradition as expressed in actual practices and beliefs within concrete social contexts. This is particularly pronounced in the case of Indian religious traditions, including the varieties of Islam found in the Indian subcontinent. In this context, Harjot Oberoi has commented that:

> . . . it is all very well for historians of religion to think, speak and write about Islam, Hinduism and Sikhism, but they rarely pause to consider if such clear-cut categories actually found expression in the consciousness, actions and cultural performances of the human actors that they describe. (Oberoi, 1994, p. 1)

Robert Jackson (1995) has quoted Feuerbach's (1841) claim that each religion contained an essence, and that early phenomenologists provided a methodology for identifying and classifying essences in particular religions. Field research reveals the problems of this essentialist approach. For example, A. Embree has argued that Jainism is distinguished by its atheism, which clearly separates it from Hinduism. He went on to state that the role of a pantheon of deities in Hinduism is replaced by legends of the *tirthankaras* in Jainism (Embree, 1988, p. 57). Yet a visit to a Jain ashram in Birmingham highlighted the problems of interpreting a tradition from a canon of scripture, without observing the reality through fieldwork. At the ashram two visiting *samanis* representing the Terapanthi Jains, on a preaching tour of Britain, were perfectly at ease with the Hindu theistic view of the world. They spoke of *bhagwan* (personal god or Lord) and interwove incidents from the life of Mahavir with traditional legends of Hindu deities such as Lakshmi, Vishnu and Krishna. One nun referred to Mahavir as following on from Rama and Krishna, the two human *avatars* of Vishnu, rather than the succession of previous *tirthankaras*. In the same way, the Jain religious practices at the ashram demonstrated no clear demarcation from Hinduism. The nuns preached, sang traditional *bhajans* and finally performed *arti* along to the image of Mahavir with the congregation. This particular religious ritual was even more problematic, as anyone reading about Terapanthi Jains would have found out that they do not venerate any images. Participation in the ritual was probably undertaken as a concession to the British Jain populations who are predominantly *murtipujakis* (venerators of images). This particular instance is a very good example of how religious practitioners make compromises, or adapt to new or changing situations, from pragmatic motives.

In the context of religions that have arrived in a new location through migration, fieldwork is essential in order to discover more about their development, and in particular any transformations that might have taken place to accommodate the new location. One of the key areas of study in this regard is the relationship between religion and ethnicity. Typically, social scientists have seen religion as a function of ethnicity. Kim Knott has stated that 'the predominant view in Britain and the USA is that religion is the passive instrument of ethnic identity' (Knott, 1992, p. 12). This perspective is exemplified in E. K. Francis' statement that 'it is the ethnic group which sanctions a particular church affiliation, and which supports a religious congregation and its institutions as an effective means for its own maintenance and the preservation of its cultural traditions' (Francis, 1976, p. 157). This viewpoint is helpful to analyse the religious symbols and organizations developed by first-generation migrants, but the relationship between ethnicity and religion is complex. Muhammad Anwar sees both ethnicity and religion as variables of identity, independent but interrelated (Anwar, 1980). But there are certainly occasions when religion plays a central role in forming ethnic group identity. South Asian ethnic communities are actually identified by their religious affiliation. We generally refer to Hindus, Muslims and Sikhs rather than Punjabis, Gujaratis, Bangladeshis or Mirpuris.

Conversations with British Sikhs and Muslims indicate that religion and culture are inextricably woven together in their experience and very rarely do they grasp my own position, which clearly demarcates my path to spiritual salvation from my awareness of Englishness. In modern European or North American societies, religion is regarded as a matter of faith commitment and not usually as a marker of community identity. This is important to understand when undertaking fieldwork in South Asian communities, as it helps to explain apparent contradictions such as Sikh Buddhists, for example. The individual may be Sikh by birth but he/she decided to adopt Buddhism as their religion.

Edward Said has drawn attention to the conflicts that exist within cultures that generate a negotiated and continuous process of self-definition (Said, 1981). This process of identity formation is an important aspect of understanding migrant communities, and fieldwork can help us to develop a body of knowledge that contributes to our understanding of ethnicity and religion, and their relationship to each other. It should be remembered that both are also very difficult to define and their relationship is constantly undergoing transformation, especially in the context of migration processes.

Field studies which take place within either the British context among South Asian communities, or the villages of the Indian subcontinent, demonstrate the prevalence of eclecticism which blurs the religious boundaries. L. Fruzzetti has demonstrated that Hindus and Muslims often share rites of passage derived from Hindu practices in the villages of some regions of India. The distinction between the two traditions comes into play at the level of public festivals, but not in the performance of household rites (Fruzzetti, 1985). Various studies on the cult of Baba Balaknath show that many of the worshippers defined themselves as Sikh, even though their primary loyalty is to a Hindu folk deity whose devotees offered their allegiance either because of historical *biraderi* (extended family) networks or because of the deity's reputation for healing (Geaves, 1997). Both of these motivations for allegiance cut across the borders between Sikhism and Hinduism, and interweave the two religions. This research raised the question whether Sikh identity was primarily ethnic or religious. Such eclecticism, in which ethnic and religious identity are blurred, is also discovered in Eleanor Nesbitt's work on the Valmikis (Nesbitt, 1991).

The research on Baba Balaknath also demonstrated that the process of transmigration from the villages of the Punjab to urban Britain introduced changes of identity and religious 'history' concerned with authenticating the cult so that it linked with the 'greater tradition' in Hinduism (Geaves, 1998). An example of this change of identity was demonstrated by the priest of the Baba Balaknath Mandir in Walsall, England. Three years ago he defined himself as a Jat Sikh, but on a recent visit with students he had changed his self-identity to Rajput Hindu. Such changes can be confusing, but need to be investigated. In this case, the priest may have felt that less identification with Sikhism was a safer option due to *Khalsa* Sikh criticism originating in the nearby gurdwaras, and protests against another neighbouring Baba Balaknath Temple in Wolverhampton. The eclectic mixing of traditions, although normative in the Punjab, is not always greeted warmly in the British diaspora communities where identity issues have a different context. As the above examples indicate, any curriculum which is concerned with the formation of religious identity among faith communities originating in the Indian subcontinent needs to deal with the processes of community formation as a shifting and complex interrelationship between religious and ethnic identity.

Jackson argues that the tradition may be a reference point but the individual, although influenced through membership of the group, is nevertheless unique (Jackson, 1997). Some years ago one of the authors interviewed a devout Palestinian Muslim belonging to a branch of the Naqshbandi Sufi order, who had recently returned from teaching the Buddhist monks at Kagyu Samye Ling Tibetan Centre in Scotland how to construct traditional Mongolian nomad tents. This scenario challenged simplistic views of identity formation, and required an intimate biographical knowledge of the individual concerned in order to understand how a Muslim from the Middle East knew how to construct Mongolian tents. He recounted an intense personal religious experience which had happened to him. He had been appointed by his *Shaikh* (religious teacher) to be the caretaker of the *dargah* (Sufi centre and hospice) at St Mary's Islamic Priory in London. The name of the centre indicates its previous use as a Catholic convent and suggests a more encompassing perspective of Muslim tolerance towards other faiths than is usually depicted, especially in the media. In this particular Muslim religious community the statue of the Virgin Mary remained over the door of the mosque, and the remaining elderly nuns were permitted to remain on the top floor of the *dargah* until their demise. Many of the *murids* (followers) recounted tales of nuns who came to join them in *dhikr* (remembrance or chanting of the names of Allah), and prayer. One evening, while praying in the gardens, my informant was reflecting on the performance of his duties as a caretaker which he felt he had neglected during the course of the day. Looking up he observed a vision of a nun, surrounded by light, standing in the midst of the garden. Her finger appeared to be admonishing him. My informant took the vision to be a judgement on his performance by the previous owners of the building, and passed the remainder of the night cleaning.

FIGURE 9.2 *An image of Baba Balaknath, the Punjabi deity believed to be Kartak, the second son of Shiva, but more likely to be a medieval Nath yogi whose cult has been assimilated into older Shaivite traditions.*

Such personal accounts indicate the importance of acknowledging the experiential in the study of religion, and taking into account the often eclectic nature of mystical or contemplative spirituality. The multicultural dimension of contemporary British society is also offering choices in religious experience that need to be explored more fully. In spite of the exclusive truth-claims of Christianity and Islam, very few religious traditions are homogeneous, self-contained communities of belief and practice, and fieldwork provides us with evidence of this.

In reference to this, Jackson has argued for the introduction of an interpretive approach to religious education which acknowledges the gap between textbook representation of discrete traditions on the one hand, and the findings of ethnographic studies in the field and individual believers' accounts of their faith commitment on the other (Jackson, 1997, p. 3).

Doing fieldwork

The subject area of the study of religion needs to adopt its own approach to fieldwork which acknowledges the beliefs, practices and development of living traditions in the contemporary world. If you want to know what is going on, get out there and find out! Of course, students of religion need to test their discoveries in the field against the literature, particularly where theories and hypotheses concerning the study of religion rather than individual religions are involved. This is the gold dust of the scholar. A visit to a religious location can be a healthy corrective to generalizations and stereotypes about a religious tradition, but for students to recognize that, they need to be prepared. It is particularly important for a course that includes field trips to devise strategies for relating discussion and readings to the site visits. For this reason disconnected field visits are not recommended, as they tend to become religious sightseeing. It is important that the experiential dimension of the visit is brought into explicit relationship both with classroom experience and student reading. Jeffrey Carlson advises that 'disconnected field trips can become moments of hiatus from the course, rather than an expression of it' (Carlson, 2004, p. iv), and that would certainly echo the experience of both authors. He advises that specific texts are read prior to the field visit, and that digital photographs of the sites are used to revisit and 'reread' the course texts.

Once you decide to embark on fieldwork you enter the realm of ethnography, and your challenges will begin. Ethnography is sometimes used as an alternative term for fieldwork. 'Ethno' means 'people' and 'graphy' means 'writing', thus Harry Wolcott describes it as research where the researcher is present in person to gather the data and thus provide a 'people picture' (Wolcott, 1999, p. 43). Ethnography is defined by M. Hammersley and P. Atkinson as a social research method in which the ethnographer participates, overtly or covertly, in people's daily lives for an extended period of time, watching what happens, listening to what is said, asking questions – in fact collecting whatever data are available to throw light on the issues (Hammersley and Atkinson, 1983, p. 2). However, it is likely that students will experience contact with a religious location through a short site visit, as opposed to prolonged contact.

In this section we do not intend to provide a manual for ethnographical study as there are several excellent books on this topic, but to develop some ideas and practical guidance for students of religion embarking on fieldwork, some of which may borrow from the experience of skilled ethnographers in anthropology, and others learned through trial and error by the authors. We are therefore using ethnography to refer to the process of fieldwork rather than to the final product, which has a more specialized meaning for the ethnographer since data is interpreted in a way that is different from the questions and answers sought by the scholar of religion. Wolcott, for example, makes the distinction between doing ethnography and borrowing ethnographic techniques (Wolcott, 1999, pp. 41–2).

In the field of the study of religion rather than religious anthropology, field researchers are still a minority. Although many religious traditions are now transplanting themselves from their place of origin to new locations, and new religions are forming around the world, these have all generated interest from sociologists seeking to comprehend both their relationship to society, and the organization of the movements. However, the scholar of religion needs to know what is happening both at the source of the tradition and in its adaptations to a new home. The necessity to learn what and why people of other religions and cultures do what they do is imperative to this kind of research, but one needs to understand how religious belief and practice can determine human action.

Wolcott argues that we are limited in how much we can learn about undertaking fieldwork from reading, and states that sometimes advice to the prospective fieldworker seems like a set of clichés – act natural, remain sceptical but open, develop a tolerance for contradiction, and so on (Wolcott, 1999, p. 15). Practice is essential, but it is unlikely that the undergraduate student in the study of religion will be able to develop fieldwork skills over three years. There may be opportunities for site visits to be undertaken – individually or guided – and perhaps placements for one or two weeks. However, some students may choose to write dissertations based on fieldwork. The advice in this chapter will try to cater specifically to these typical undergraduate learning situations.

The researcher is in the position of a stranger who gradually acquires the knowledge of the insider, but in the process achieves an 'objectivity' not always available to the true insider (Schutz, 1964). However, the encounter between 'insider' and 'outsider' is one of relationship and reflexivity rather than simple observation. Patrice Brodeur notes that 'within the academic study of religion, insider/outsider questions are literally embodied, rather then simply intellectualised', when conducting fieldwork of any kind (Brodeur, 2004, p. x). Site visits can embolden some students to express negative stereotypes of the community that they visit, especially if they have a bad experience on the visit. Students who previously felt that they did not know enough about a religion to articulate negative opinions may feel that a 'bad' site visit provides them with the credentials to voice stereotypes. It is therefore important for both students and tutors to develop learning strategies in which they choose the degree to which they are to disclose subjectivities, either prior to or on return from a field trip.

Students will be interested in the direct experience of the world visited, especially when it is an unfamiliar one, and some ethnographers even argue that you should try to surrender yourself to the culture you wish to study (Jules-Rosette, 1978). This might be a successful strategy to utilize for prolonged contact with a religious community but it is unlikely that the site visit will provide such opportunities. On some occasions, one of the authors has only been allowed to enter a community if prepared to participate fully in the lifestyle, and there have been cases of students who have stayed in a religious community for a prolonged period of time becoming so enamoured of the beliefs and practices that they have joined the religion under investigation. These instances are few, at the other extreme to researchers who develop a strong antipathy. Sometimes our own religious convictions may prevent us from participation, and usually that is understood. However, misunderstandings can arise. Such occasions usually develop because of lack of cultural literacy on the part of both observers and observed. Joyce Flueckiger provides an example of a field visit to a Hindu temple in the United States in which she advised students that they did not have to partake of *prasad* (the food offerings made to the deity). She taught the students the polite way to refuse, advising them to retreat to the back of the temple or group and make the appropriate gestures of refusal. However, some students returned saying that it did not work and that they were 'forced' to partake. The Telugu priests had learned some English and called 'Come, eat!' The imperative had been mistaken by the students as a command, whereas in Telugu it was a request (Flueckiger, 2004, p. iii). The best advice is not to be too concerned by these cultural miscommunications. All fieldworkers will have their own favourite stories of embarrassment.

Ethnography can sometimes involve no more than attending regular meetings of the group being studied. Some ethnographers have gone further than this, however, and have committed themselves to 'living in' and 'going native'. These phrases are fairly self-explanatory: studying a religious group that lives as a community can usefully involve living residentially within that community for a limited period of time. One of the present authors undertook 'living in' for brief periods in the 1980s when undertaking research on the Unification Church (popularly known as the 'Moonies'). This enabled him to experience the overall lifestyle of the group, the demands made on members (early rising, and late prayer and study), how they ate, how they relaxed, what was permitted and what was discouraged. 'Going native' involves adopting the lifestyle and practices of the members – a step beyond simply being there and in effect shadowing the rest of the group.

Participant-observation, living in and 'going native' all have their limits, and it is often important to stipulate in advance what these are. At times there may be issues of conscience: at times we have taught evangelical Christian students who were unhappy about receiving *prasad* at Hindu temples, their reasoning being that since Hindu temples have images to which food is offered, the *prasad* is 'food sacrificed to idols', which the early Church forbade (Acts 15.29). It would be inappropriate to insist that accepting *prasad* was expected in Hindu temples as a respectful custom. Just as worshippers in Hindu temples want the environment to be respected by visitors, equally students of religion have their own integrity to maintain, and sometimes compromise is needed. In researching the Unification Church, one of the authors identified a number of activities which were beyond the limits of his participant-observer's comfort zone; these included street-preaching, fund-raising and bowing in front of the image of founder-leader Sun Myung Moon.

At other times, attempts at 'going native' can be thwarted by issues of prudence rather than conscience. In researching Jehovah's Witnesses, for example, would it be appropriate for the ethnographer to follow their example of carrying a 'No Blood' card? (Practising Jehovah's Witnesses carry 'No Blood' cards instead of donor cards, so that in a medical emergency doctors will know not to give them a blood transfusion.) One author still has some scarring on his left arm, where he allowed a Buddhist priest to burn joss-sticks at a nun's ordination. At other times, the constraint may simply be time: is it really feasible for a researcher to commit himself or herself to attending five weekly meetings, as is expected of the Jehovah's Witness? One has to find the time to write as well as to undertake fieldwork, and although it is sometimes tempting to attend increasing numbers of events, one has to strike a balance between collecting even more data, and writing it up.

Doubtless, fieldwork will challenge conceptions that can arise from too much reliance on textual research. Ethnography is fluid and does not involve extensive pre-fieldwork design. You can change in mid-flow and follow leads that arise in the field, but you need to be flexible and observant. Religions are not static: institutions, communities and individuals who participate in such communities change. Single site visits may be problematic in this context. They can produce generalizations that may not be exactly accurate, or maybe idiosyncrasies of the particular place of worship. In this respect, comparative visits to other sites in the same tradition are to be advised. For example, there are three Baba Balaknath temples in the West Midlands region of England, but each has a remarkably different set of practices and beliefs concerning the deity. The absence of women in public ritual within a mosque can lead to a generalized stereotype about the lack of female participation in the religion, which would fail to acknowledge the role of women in domestic ritual life. The same is true of Hindu women.

Fieldwork involves little investment in terms of equipment, but we would suggest that a small tape recorder, a notepad and pencil, and a camera are essentials. Malinowski, one of the founding fathers of anthropology, as long ago as 1922 suggested that fieldworkers should sometimes put aside the tools of their trade and join in with whatever is going on, and certainly that has been the view of one of the authors when multiple visits or prolonged stays have been available (Malinowski, 1922, p. 21). Malinowski considered that this approach might be difficult for reserved Western Europeans, but it is more problematic than that for scholars of religion undertaking fieldwork. Researchers who are adherents of a particular monotheistic tradition with exclusive truth-claims may feel uneasy about joining in with the religious activities of other faiths, especially those with a non-monotheistic worldview, and atheist researchers may feel queasy about engaging in religious activity of any description, under any pretext. Some researchers have never had any problems with joining in but you have to find your own limits, and maintain both your own integrity as you observe the beliefs and practices of the community under observation. Sometimes it is simply not possible to join in, as the practices are not permitted to outsiders. Sometimes we may misunderstand certain situations. Few Hindu priests would be aware that refusal to take *prasad*, for example, might arise because of theological difficulties, and would be more likely to view taking *prasad* as an acceptance of hospitality.

FIGURE 9.3 *Ek Niwas, Wolverhampton. The guffa (literally 'cave') is on a raised platform, only accessible to men, out of respect for Balak Nath, who was a celibate ascetic. 'Ek Niwas' means 'one truth', and the temple seeks to bring various faiths together.*

CUSTOMS TO OBSERVE

When undertaking fieldwork it is important to know and observe the practices of the communities one is visiting – at least, as far as possible. There are several reasons why this is important. One should avoid causing offence, out of respect for one's hosts. On religious premises, there is much that is sacred, and religious communities typically believe that it is important for everyone to show respect, not simply the adherents. Tourists in the Far East frequently cause offence when they sit on the floor in a Buddhist temple, and inadvertently point their feet towards the Buddha *rupa*. The benefit to students of religion is that they are more likely to be better received by the community, and to inspire confidence that they have undertaken at least enough background work to know how to conduct themselves. Communities in turn are likely to be more willing to spend time with them, and to communicate good information.

Observing customs is not something that can be done 'on the hoof'. Certain factors need careful advance preparation, for example conforming to dress codes. Some Sikh temples keep a supply of headscarves for those who come unprepared; but one should not rely on this, and one's own headgear normally looks better than something that is simply provided as a contingency measure.

There are times when religious communities do not appear to be altogether happy with the way students or staff have dressed. The reasons are not always obvious, but it is best to conform. Head and feet are specific parts of the body to be aware of: some communities want heads to be covered, while others want head coverings removed, and the requirement can vary according to one's gender. To confuse matters further, some communities like shoes to be removed in certain parts of the premises, but not throughout. If in doubt, it is always best to ask: religious communities are usually pleased that visitors are attempting to be respectful; they do not usually insist that one gets everything right first time.

Apart from head coverings and shoes, there are some generic matters that apply practically everywhere. Men should wear long trousers rather than shorts on most religious premises. On one occasion, on a study tour of Israel, some students were refused entry to one of the principal churches in Nazareth; they were wearing shorts because of the heat, but unfortunately the church officials did not accept any extenuating circumstances, and that part of their journey was in vain. Generally, women should dress modestly – which usually means wearing a dress or skirt that comes below the knees, and not showing cleavage or flesh around one's waist. Many students wear T-shirts and sweaters bearing slogans: consider carefully what they say! Any sexual innuendo could be offensive, and clothes that refer to alcohol or bear the logo of breweries could prove unacceptable in certain places. Sometimes deliberate efforts to please can cause offence. Someone recently bought one of the authors a T-shirt with a picture of the Buddha printed on it. One might suppose that this was ideal for visiting Buddhist temples: what could be better? Actually, the reverse is true: an image of the Buddha is something that should be bowed to, and respected. If I wore the garment, any Buddhist who bowed to the image would be bowing to me!

Behaviour as well as dress needs consideration. Chewing gum and mobile phones should be regarded as totally out of place. I have occasionally seen worshippers in Taoist temples continue to wave incense at the images while conducting a conversation on their mobiles, but in most communities the ring of a mobile phone is disruptive. If a service or ceremony is in progress, then unnecessary talking should be avoided. How much one participates in the ritual activities of a faith other than one's own is a matter for individual decision. I have known Christian students who feel that they cannot bow to the Guru Granth Sahib in a gurdwara, and Muslim students who do not want to sing Christian hymns. It is quite legitimate for students to assert their own religious identity, just as the community being visited asserts theirs, and I would never encourage students to do anything that violated their own consciences. If one cannot bow before the Guru Granth, clasping one's hands towards it is a sufficient gesture – or, if a student feels that even that is going too far, then quietly adopting a seated position on the floor is sufficient.

The expected behaviour may relate to gender. In some places, such as Orthodox Jewish synagogues, Hindu and Sikh temples, mosques, and some Buddhist places of worship, men and women are expected to sit separately, or enter through separate doors. There may be some parts of a building where one gender is not permitted. In a temple in Wolverhampton, women are not allowed to mount the platform (*guffa*) where the image of Balaknath is housed. This should not be construed as sex discrimination: it is a matter of realizing that the medieval Indian saint Balaknath was a world-renouncer and a celibate. Since murtis in Indian temples are regarded as being alive, the presence of a female close at hand would be tantamount to a provocative gesture. Religions do not offer the kind of equal opportunities that are required by law in the secular world, but it is not the scholar's role to try to change these.

Although it is generally a good rule to copy the behaviour of one's hosts, there are times when this is inappropriate. Certain forms of participation are only for those who are suitably initiated. The Christian Eucharist (Holy Communion) is a case in point. The sacrament can only be received by members of the community who are deemed eligible to partake: criteria of eligibility vary according to the denomination, but it does not include those who do not belong to the Christian faith. In this example, the rules are normally made clear to the congregation: those who cannot receive the sacrament can simply remain in their seats, or possibly go forward to receive a priest's blessing if they so desire.

It is worth remembering, too, that requirements may vary according to the tradition. One of the authors was taken to a Greek Orthodox service many years ago. When the procession came round, the priest stopped near him, and said something in Greek that did not sound particularly welcoming. It was later explained what my offence was: his hands were behind his back instead of in front of him! (Participants in Orthodox worship should not cross their legs when seated, either.) Such behaviour would not normally be demanded in other Christian traditions.

What follows is a brief summary of customs to be observed. Religions are complex, however: students should take account of the diversity of traditions, and seek appropriate guidance.

Community customs

Bahá'í	No particular requirements.
Buddhist	Remove shoes before entering the shrine room. Do not point feet towards the Buddha *rupa*.
Christian	In many traditions Christian worship is very formal. Unnecessary talking is inappropriate. Men should remove headgear; a few strict communities prefer women to wear hats.
Hindu	Remove shoes before entering temple area; some temples prohibit leather altogether. *Prasad* is often given to visitors on departure. As in Buddhist temples, do not point feet towards the *murtis* (images).
Jain	Remove shoes before entering temple area; women may not enter this area during menstruation.
Jewish	Men need a head covering; long dresses are preferred for women. Married women should also wear a head covering in Orthodox communities.
Muslim	Women must dress modestly (cover head, shoulders and legs; avoid tight jeans/trousers). All visitors should remove shoes before entering the mosque area. When sitting, do not point your feet towards the qiblah.
New religious movements	Various expectations exist, depending on the community. Please seek prior advice as appropriate.
Sikh	Head covering needed for men and women; do not bring tobacco or alcohol into the gurdwara. Remove shoes before entering the temple area. When sitting, do not point your feet towards the Guru Granth Sahib.

Access to religious communities

Access to religious communities is not simply a matter of gaining initial entry, but also achieving a condition of empathy or trust in which the world that you have entered remains as unrippled as possible. Remember that the researcher is a stone thrown into the pool. The aim is to enter as softly as possible. You will become a part of the religious/cultural world that you enter, and therefore influence its behaviour. Covert entry to a religious community is difficult, unless it is your own, as insiders have their own worldview which it is difficult for the outsider to emulate, and if you are studying religions where there is an ethnic element it is impossible unless you are actually a member of that community. In addition, there are difficult ethical considerations that need to be taken into account with regard to covert entry.

In my experience, entry to a religious community offers two categories of challenge to the observer. The first category arises from visiting a religious tradition with which one is overfamiliar, for example, a practising Christian student studying a local church or a Muslim visiting a mosque. Today, of course, it cannot be assumed that students are familiar with Christian institutions or practices, but where they are, the challenge is to discover a way of making the familiar appear strange, to somehow come inside the phenomenon under observation yet taking the stance of an outsider.

Although familiarity with one's own tradition may seem an obvious benefit, overfamiliarity can at times create its own problems. Insiders may be tempted to give privileged status to their own tradition (e.g. the Church of England at the expense of Roman Catholicism or Eastern Orthodoxy), and may ignore the need to explain phenomena that are puzzling to the outsider. Someone once said that ethnography should seek to make the strange familiar, and the familiar strange. In looking at other people's customs and practices, there is much that is difficult to comprehend and in need of explanation: the ethnographer endeavours to make strange practices more familiar to us. Reciprocally, however, if we are thoroughly familiar with a practice, we need to distance ourselves from it, realizing that it may be incomprehensible to those outside the tradition. A Christian who receives the sacrament of Holy Communion regularly may well regard this as 'normal', but an outsider who is unfamiliar with the rite may well find it puzzling that participants queue up at an altar to take a sip of wine and a piece of bread, and to be told that this is Christ's body and blood.

Training the mind and senses to make the familiar become strange can be achieved in planning the visit with a reminder that we are looking for patterns of behaviour, descriptions of ritual, doctrines, organizational forms, architecture and interior landscapes. Where students are given a choice to visit a site as individuals or groups, the tutor may make it a condition that the community selected cannot be one's own. Previously one of the authors taught a 'Fieldwork in Religious Studies' course, where there was a residential stay in an unfamiliar community, which was not the participant's own allegiance, there was a guided group visit to the local cathedral, which was familiar to most of the students as the university had close links and holds several annual functions there. The tour utilized Peter Pawlowsky's elements when taking students on site visits to Christian places of worship. Pawlowsky lists five elements of Christian worship: 1) confession and prayer for forgiveness; 2) reading from the Bible; 3) the confession of faith; 4) the Lord's Supper; and 5) praise, thanksgiving and intercession (Pawlowsky, 1994, pp. 92–3). Observation of the emphasis placed upon particular elements within certain denominations can be linked to doctrinal differences. Such tasks help to maintain focus on a visit, and also provide distance that helps to develop the sense of unfamiliarity in familiar places. It also helps beginners in the art of fieldwork to develop observational skills that are not engaged when students merely visit a place of worship without being task-orientated.

However, it is more likely that students will be attracted to fieldwork because of the possibility of meeting the unfamiliar. Many texts on ethnography speak of the attraction of the exotic, and the sense of adventure arising from travelling to unknown places and cultures. Although anthropologists these days carry out studies of the familiar in their own villages and towns, there is no doubt that the study of religions will bring students into contact with practices and beliefs that are unfamiliar and seemingly exotic. Today in pluralist Britain it is not necessary to visit India to meet many forms of Indian religion, or the Muslim world to find the varieties of belief and practice that coexist in Islam. A fascination with the Orient can be fulfilled by visiting Southall in London, Leicester, parts of the West Midlands, or Yorkshire – all in England. However, this produces a different kind of problem for the observer. Visits to unfamiliar worlds in which we as observers feel completely lost, bewildered and nervous can lead to a condition where we are overawed to the degree that at first we cannot make sense of anything.

To add to your problems, the world that you enter changes as its members transform their behaviour in order to present their world conforming to the image that they want the stranger in their midst to embrace. For example, it is highly unlikely that a visit to a mosque in Britain or any other non-Muslim country will elicit the information that the community of users belong to a particular school of thought within Islam, or even come from a particular ethnic group. However, this is likely to be the case, as in general the mosques are established by particular ethnic communities or members of discrete movements within Islam. Yet if you as a student are a non-Muslim and a stranger, your informants will want to present to you the unity of Islam: the ideal of a community that transcends race, culture and sectarian divisions. The official representatives of a Hindu temple – a priest or member of the committee – are unlikely to respond to questions concerning the maintenance of caste in diaspora communities. They know that there is a negative image in the dominant community around them concerning caste divisions, and they will not want to provide you with material that they feel will portray a negative image of their religion or community to outsiders. Official spokespersons for religions, both established and minority faiths, are engaged in promoting their community, defending its beliefs and practices from suspicious outsiders, and are motivated by maintaining public relations rather than the interests of the researcher. Where possible it is good practice to interview individuals or groups that do not represent the official view of the community. One of the difficulties of individual site visits is that they are usually organized through, and conducted by, official representatives. Remember that they represent the institutional form of the religion, and our knowledge of the domestic or private spaces for worship may be limited. Karen McCarthy has argued that visits to institutional spaces of religion limit the study of religion generally, and particular religious traditions specifically (McCarthy, 2003).

One area of transformation that takes place within migrant religions adapting to a new location concerns religious language. All religious traditions have a specialized language, and as a student of a particular religion you will have already been bewildered by the array of terminology to be learned. If you are a student of religion you will find yourself learning key terms for several religions. If you are a specialist in one religion, for example Islam, you will have a wider command of religious language. Either way, fieldwork can present a challenge. Religious language presents its special problems. The word 'God' for example is highly problematic, and will rarely mean the same thing to more than one individual. It becomes even more of a problem when you are faced with informants who are bilingual and can switch codes. Eleanor Nesbitt has pointed out how Sikh children commonly use 'gods' or 'God' to describe their gurus. It is also common parlance among Sikhs who take parties around gurdwaras to describe the ten gurus as 'prophets'. The fieldworker with a knowledge of Sikhism might easily dismiss such terminology as 'wrong' displaying insufficient knowledge of doctrine concerning the institution of Guruship. However, Nesbitt has demonstrated that the use of such terminology can provide fresh insights into the ever-fluid landscape of religion and identity in diaspora communities. She points out that when Sikh children use the word 'God' they are not only translating concepts that they have learned through English, but also using their mother tongue learned at home and in the gurdwara. They are also influenced by a Hindu milieu in which the oneness of God, the plurality of gods, and fluid borders between the guru and divinity are all taken for granted (Nesbitt, 2004, pp. 72, 73). If the student is writing an essay on Sikhism in which Sikh doctrines of Guruship and the relationship of gurus to God is the topic, it would be sloppy to describe the ten gurus as 'gods' or 'prophets'; but in fieldwork the language used may not be defined as wrong, but may rather yield significant analysis of the community under observation. The language used is part of the emic (insider) narrative and needs to be interpreted in order to further our understanding of hybrid identity formation, always shifting and ongoing. Remember that informants in a religious institution may deal with many types of field visit, from researchers to school children, and these successive encounters with the ethnographer (both junior and senior) create, develop and facilitate such narratives. Nesbitt points out that the responses to a question should not be viewed as definitive, permanent and exclusive, but rather as a 'clue to one version of the narrative' which has 'situationally determined variations' (Nesbitt, 2004, p. 123).

The example of a religious community's attitudes towards women is particularly relevant with regard to the problem of meeting institutional responses. Very few religious traditions would openly admit to discriminating against women. Islam and Sikhism, in particular, regard themselves as religions that have paid special heed to gender equality. It is certainly true that historically they can boast of proud records in liberating women from the inequalities of the prevailing social systems: in Islam's case, at its origins in seventh-century Arabia; and in the teachings of the Sikh Gurus from Nanak to Gobind Singh. In both cases the rights of women are enshrined in their sacred texts, the Qur'an and the Guru Granth Sahib. One would expect most informants representing their respective faiths to cite these historical and scriptural sources to demonstrate that their faiths hold women in high regard. There will be in both cases an official line in response to questions about women that is difficult to surmount.

On one visit with students to a large gurdwara in the Midlands, some of the female students began to ask the male informant questions about gender equality in Sikhism. He cited the examples of history and the teachings of the sacred text, and also volunteered the information that women are allowed to become granthis and publicly read the Guru Granth Sahib at festivals and religious ritual occasions. One of the students asked him if there was any female officiating as a *granthi* in Britain. The informant answered that there was not, and was then asked if he could explain the reason for the absence of women in this capacity. (There is a woman *granthi* at the Ramgarhia Sikh Temple in Wolverhampton, and another in Southall – informants often overgeneralize, believing that what they experience is to be found everywhere else.) The informant responded that since there was no accurate way for a woman to determine when she would begin to menstruate, it was not considered advisable for them to be granthis even though it was permitted. What would happen to the sanctity of the sacred text if a woman who was reciting began to bleed, thus rendering the Guru Granth Sahib impure?

FIGURE 9.4 *Narasimha Temple, Pushkar.*

Unknowingly the informant had been led by the student's persistence to offer an insight into traditional Sikh views on menstruation, as opposed to the ideal encompassed in scriptural teachings where there is nothing mentioned about female impurity on such occasions (on the contrary, Sikhism differs from Islam and Hinduism in this regard). The gap between the living reality and the scriptural ideal can often be found in many faith traditions, and in this case demonstrated how difficult it is to overcome traditional prejudices, taboos or social practices which are given substance and authority by custom – even when the founders of the religion have opposed such an outlook and attempted to reform such practices.

Sometimes this kind of discrepancy between ideal and reality can be discovered by the aid of chance or serendipity, something that will be discussed in more detail later. Once during a visit to a mosque, one of the author's students was being addressed by the imam with practised competence on the issue of female equality in Islam. The talk was taking place in a meeting hall near the mosque itself. The author was familiar with the mosque, having visited on several occasions, and the imam requested him to take the students around the mosque itself, as the imam had to make an urgent telephone call. On the author's entering the mosque, an elderly Muslim man arrived to make his prayers, saw a number of our female students correctly dressed in long skirts and headscarves, and mistook our party for Bosnian Muslims. It was explained to him that we were a party of students visiting from the local university. The man's facial expression changed to one of displeasure, and he turned to the female students and asked whether they were clean. The students were highly embarrassed and very unsure how to respond, and the tutor felt that he had to intervene to defuse the situation. The man was asked politely why he had not enquired if the male students in our group were clean. After all, ritual purity applies to both genders in Islam when entering a mosque to pray. Once again, a discrepancy had been found between the official talk of the imam and the chance encounter with the views of the elderly Muslim, who placed the onus for purity on women. Of course, such encounters should be followed up as they provide questions that need to be pursued by further research.

It is not easy for inexperienced researchers to overcome the problem of being presented with the official view or making sense of data that arrives through serendipitous encounters, but one of the ways that I have found very helpful is to demonstrate one's knowledge of the community to informants so that they recognize that you already have insights into their insider world. This will require as much pre-knowledge gleaned from studying the existing scholarship as you can find. This includes knowledge of how the world that you are entering works: its values, behaviour patterns, dietary prohibitions, dress codes and so on. Your informants will be placed more at ease when you know their world and can act accordingly. Remember that you are trying to solve a problem or resolve a question, so remain problem-driven and keep to your task rather than taking the line of least resistance, which will always be the one that your informants want to take you along (Warren, 1974). However, refusing to take the line of least resistance does not mean getting involved in arguments with informants. We are there to ask questions of informants that elicit information, and it is the spirit of enquiry that must be paramount, not the spirit of hostility.

Remember that representatives of religious communities also welcome school parties. If you are going to elicit degree-level answers from informants, you have to show your level of knowledge. This can only be done by preparation. Questions need to be prepared in advance. Most representatives of a religious community will provide the time for questions. The opportunity should not be wasted by long silences. In addition, lack of preparation will elicit low-level responses from informants. It is better for a teacher to provide a site visit with specific pedagogical goals, so that students can prepare within a particular context. Before a site visit it is better to discuss with students one or two problems, specific topics of interest or questions to focus on. Collecting data during the visit is crucial, but students are helped if some discussion takes place beforehand on the kind of useful data pertinent to the place being visited. After the field visit, there should be a chance for topic-focused feedback concerning the data collected. One of the authors always sets a formal assignment on site visits, but at least there should be an opportunity for discussion at the next taught session. Wherever possible a guide or informant should take the students through the field visit, even when it falls into the tutor's area of expertise and he may know it much better.

As a final note of caution, be ready to give attention to the time factor. Many undergraduate projects are completed within a limited and tight time framework, and fieldwork always takes longer than you think. Many students come to see the author for advice on their final-year dissertations because they want to include a small piece of fieldwork and are disappointed when advised against it if it is not essential to the project's aims. Sometimes informants do not show up, access is difficult to obtain or all the other vagaries of human interaction appear as obstacles to completing it on time.

Gaining entry

Often the first contact that you have with a religious community will be a letter of introduction requesting permission to visit. This is usually recommended as the correct approach, but sometimes it might be a better strategy to arrive at the place of worship without a prior announcement. The best mode of entry is an insider contact who can open doors to you. The term 'gatekeepers' was first used by J. E. Hoffman (1980) to describe such contacts, and is now common parlance. The world that you enter will probably have invisible or visible boundaries, which may be policed by gatekeepers. Visible boundaries may consist of various forms of restricted entry. The Baba Balaknath Temple in Coventry has security volunteers who check and question all strangers before entry to community worship. Certain mosques do not allow non-Muslims to enter. Negotiating entry to Mormon temples is impossible unless you are a Mormon. Some places of worship do not allow access to certain parts of the premises that are considered to be very sacred. For the stranger these rules may not be known, and it is easy to break them unwittingly unless accompanied by a guide. Invisible boundaries are more difficult to negotiate without a gatekeeper. These may consist of suspicious attitudes that are not formalized towards strangers or doctrines concerning pollution and purity. One of the authors has often attended domestic worship and eaten with Brahmin families in India, only to discover later that all the utensils were ritually washed after his departure to remove the pollution caused by his lack of 'caste'.

Gatekeepers may be official and need to be approached formally, for example presidents and secretaries of formal religious organizations, priests, imams, rabbis and other religious functionaries, or guest officers. Sometimes there may be unofficial gatekeepers who operate as boundary mechanisms for the protection of the group from unfriendly observers, or to maintain the sanctity of the religious domain. Gatekeepers are important because they have the power to block your access and finish your research before it has even begun. In the case of Indian subcontinental religious groups, the letter of introduction rarely works, particularly in the subcontinent itself. Letters may fail because the gatekeepers may not have access to your language, or because they do not know you or your motivation. Insider contacts that you might have made unofficially are themselves gatekeepers in their role as gate openers. Often they will only function as a gate opener if you have already created a relationship of trust and empathy with them. Our advice would be, if you are not bold enough to visit without an invitation, at least make telephone contact which can be followed up by a letter or an email to confirm the appointment. Gatekeepers have been known to forget that you are coming. A telephone call has the advantage of allowing you to state your case, introduce yourself and ease any qualms that the gatekeeper may have about opening the doors to you.

It has been mentioned that chance is a factor in fieldwork. One of the authors prefers to borrow from the sacred language of several religions and call it the 'grace factor'. However much preparation you may have undertaken, sometimes you need good fortune and synchronicity to bring about a successful outcome to your research. Several years ago, the author was in the Indian subcontinent investigating a number of movements that have been influential in the development of contemporary Islam, not only in that region but throughout the Muslim world. He had crossed the border by road from Pakistan and travelled by train from Amritsar to the small Muslim-populated town of Deoband, famous for its nineteenth-century college which had initiated one of the most influential reform movements in South Asia. No one had been informed of his arrival as he had feared that a refusal of entry in response to a letter from a stranger in Britain was highly likely, and his project would have to be abandoned before it had begun.

The coach attendant on the train directed him to get off at a small station so totally devoid of lighting that he had mistakenly thought the train had stopped at a signal. In the midst of the darkness, a cycle rickshaw appeared and offered to transport him, without mentioning a destination. After several miles of travelling through narrow alleyways, pitch-black and filled with packs of stray dogs, he had the nervous thought that no one in the world knew where he was or would know where to look for him if anything happened. Eventually he arrived at two large closed gates which were opened by an irritable-looking night watchman after heavy knocking from the rickshaw driver. A lengthy discussion took place and he was beckoned inside the building. He had no idea where he had been taken, but on being shown a room with a bed he was too tired to enquire. After a short sleep he was woken at around 4:00 a.m. by the Muslim prayer call, and took a shower. At around 5:30 a.m. two young Muslims knocked at his door, fully bearded and dressed in white *shalwar kameez*. To his surprise, they spoke in broad Bradford accents (at the time he lived in Leeds) and informed him that he was staying in the guesthouse of the *dar al-ulum* (Muslim college) of Deoband. They were British Muslims who were studying at the college, hoping to qualify as imams and to be employed in Bradford mosques.

After hearing that the researcher hoped to stay in the college and complete his study, they suggested that they would arrange an interview with the *Shaikh al-Hadith* (the teacher in charge of teaching Hadith) who they felt would be sympathetic to his cause, and recommend to the Principal that he be allowed to stay. He agreed with the proposal, the interview was arranged, and he found himself being gently interrogated by an elderly Muslim who had spent his whole life, both as student and teacher, at Deoband. After assuring himself that the researcher's intentions were sincere and that he was not intending to write something harmful to the reputation of the college, he took him to the roof to meet the Principal and recommended that he should be allowed to stay. Permission was given and he remained in Deoband for ten days. The *Shaikh al-Hadith* and the two students from Bradford helped him to find interviewees. The *Shaikh al-Hadith* was particularly loved by his students, and his endorsement opened most doors and helped to secure the trust that was essential to success.

On another occasion, the same author was staying at the Golden Temple in Amritsar (Harmandir), the most sacred site for Sikhs, with a party of undergraduates. The students had told him of a very spiritual old Sikh who had spoken to some of them and impressed them with his gravitas and charisma. The man was a retired civil servant who had purchased a small house near the Golden Temple so that he could spend his nights praying and cleaning the precincts. He had no official status in the temple administration but lived a life of complete devotion to his faith.

One evening the researcher and his wife left a restaurant early, saying goodnight to all the students, as they wished to get back to the temple and observe the ceremonial procession that takes place when the Guru Granth Sahib (the sacred text of the Sikhs) is transferred from the Golden Temple across a narrow causeway over the lake to its night-time abode in the Akhal Takht. They sat inside the Golden Temple and participated in the evening singing of *kirtan* and the placing of the Guru Granth Sahib into a large and ornate silver sedan chair. The chair was then carried by 20 male *Khalsa* Sikhs, several to each pole. They followed in the procession's crush across the causeway. Suddenly, an old Sikh appeared and asked the researcher an enigmatic question: 'Would you like the opportunity?' He knew immediately that this was the man spoken about by his students, and answered in the affirmative. The old man took the researcher by the hand, parting the crowd right up to the sedan chair, where he removed the last of the Sikhs on one of the rear poles and placed the researcher in his position. He nearly dropped it as his legs buckled under the weight, but he managed to carry the most sacred object in Sikhism to its night-time abode. He was thrilled with the incident, a piece of participant-observation, probably never experienced by most Sikhs, let alone a non-Sikh. Afterwards, he passed several hours interviewing the old Sikh when he found him sitting by the side of the lake, enjoying his experience and observing the Golden Temple's reflection under the moonlight. The point of these two stories is that not everything can be planned for when doing fieldwork: things happen which are not expected, and which provide not only fascinating insights into the religions but personal life-experiences that can be transforming.

Fieldwork can provide such events that will be treasured memories for all one's life, and provide very good anecdotes, but it would not be a good idea to expect all field experiences to be like this. These are highlights in the life of a scholar who spends several weeks or months a year studying religions in situ. The same scholar would also be able to speak of hours passed in meetings where he did not understand a word that was being spoken because of language differences, walking around streets lost, the failure of informants to turn up for interviews, or religious buildings that were locked and empty after several hours were wasted in travel. In addition, religious occasions sometimes take place when all your colleagues or friends are enjoying leisure time. For example, key events take place at Christmas or Easter in Christian churches. Mosques, gurdwaras and Hindu temples may not have much going on in them until evening when worshippers gather after the daily work. All of this takes commitment, and the ability to deal with prolonged periods of boredom on occasion; in addition, fieldwork requires preparation, reflection and analysis. Students may often feel that fieldwork is an exciting option but it should be remembered that interviewing, visiting and processing the information are time-consuming and may use up more resources than projects that can be undertaken in the library. Also, it is important to bear in mind that the disciplines of checking facts and sources, assessing logic, asking critical questions and analysing various perspectives are no less rigorous than reading a book or a journal article, but in addition the powers of perception and visual intelligence need to be developed.

The two anecdotes described above from fieldwork experiences also make us aware that serendipity plays an important part, even in single site visits. This element of unpredictability may well excite students and indeed, it could be argued, provides a pedagogical rationale for doing them (Burford, 2004, p. xiv), but we need to be cautious when we stumble across the unexpected. It may reveal features of the religious community that are little known, and open up possibilities for further research. On the other hand, it may lead to us to generalize inappropriately about the particular or specific event that does not happen routinely. In this context, the more preparation that has been done beforehand, the more likely it is that we will be able to contextualize the unusual or unplanned. A visit to the relevant website, if one exists, should always be a part of preparation.

The two anecdotes also provide examples of meetings with two very different categories of gatekeepers: official and unofficial.

Official gatekeepers

Offical gatekeepers are likely to be the first contact with a religious community or place of worship. Without their permission and approval it will be extremely difficult to gain entry and ensure the co-operation of the members in your enquiries. For example, our stay in the Golden Temple would not have been possible without prior consent from senior officials in the temple administration. It is such people that one needs to write to or telephone in order to gain access. They might be members of a committee, or religious specialists such as priests, imams, granthis, *pandits*, abbots or abbesses who have a different kind of authority from administrators. However, although such gatekeepers will open gates they will always be concerned with their own reputations and the reputation of the world that they protect. How will you represent it? The research will be affected by the co-operation of your gatekeeper, as he or she will introduce you to the people and the events that they want you to see in order to provide the best picture of their world according to their perceptions, not yours.

Unofficial gate openers

Correctly speaking such people are not gatekeepers but they are important gate openers, and you cannot plan to meet them. They are an essential part of good field research. They might be attracted to you because you are a stranger in their midst and they are curious. On the other hand, they might represent a faction within the religious movement and wish to provide an alternative viewpoint. They probably will not have an official position, but they might have spiritual authority based on their experience or piety which is respected by grass-roots believers, such as the elderly Sikh at the Golden Temple. On the other hand, there may be circumstances that attract them to assist you, such as the two students from Bradford who, although Muslim and of Pakistani origin, were British, and wished to meet a fellow countryman in a strange land. There are all sorts of reasons why contacts with unofficial gate openers take place, but in my experience the more effectively you can become a part of the world under study, the more likely you are to make such invaluable contacts.

Another category of valuable informants can come from opponents of the community. Most religions are not homogeneous, and they include factions that are sometimes rivals to each other. Some will be disaffected ex-members. Such opponents will usually be very happy to provide you with information. Their testimonies have to be treated with extreme caution, but will offer a counterbalance to the bias of official gatekeepers. Sometimes this kind of material can be achieved by searching for opposition websites.

Even after gaining their trust, gatekeepers can be playful as they know their world far better than you, however well you achieve the ability to transform yourself into a part of their environment. Pnina Werbner, in her account of spending time with the followers of Zindapir (now deceased), a Naqshbandi Sufi who lived in permanent retreat in the mountains of Pakistan at a place named Ghamkol Sharif, tells of how the high-caste sayyid women who came to the *urs* (an annual celebration of a Sufi master's death) and performed all the menial tasks at the festival would gather around their Sufi master at night enjoying his company. She tells us that the women would provide Zindapir with amusing anecdotes and pieces of gossip, especially those concerning 'the ridiculous behaviour of the anthropologist, which he found particularly amusing' (Werbner, 1998, p. 112). One of the authors has his own experience of playful informants: while staying at Deoband, one of his key student informants invited him to attend the student cafeteria in the evening between the final *salat* (prayer) and the late-night Qur'an memorization that took place in the mosque until after midnight. This was one of the few moments of relaxation in a very full curriculum which combined learning with religious piety and devotion. The informant had noticed with approval that the author wore traditional subcontinental Muslim dress while on campus, and had asked to see his collection of *shalwar kameez*. He was impressed that the author owned a black outfit and pleaded with him to wear it to the student cafeteria for the evening leisure period. On the author's entrance to the cafeteria all the students went absolutely silent. The author sat at a table and ordered some samosas and tea, feeling very self-conscious in an ocean of white *shalwar kameez*, the customary dress of dar al-ulum students. Slowly conversation resumed, but the stares of outraged students continued until he finally left. His student friend and informant was highly amused and informed him that black *shalwar kameez* was considered to be Shi'a dress, and also the traditional costume of the prophet when he rode into battle. The author's chosen attire had become the highlight of the students' evening. Whether it is true that black *shalwar kameez* were associated with the prophet on *jihad* or with Shi'a Muslims is irrelevant in this context. The association existed among the students, they were all Sunni Muslims, and the author had been conned into wearing the outfit to provide amusement in the midst of demanding and repetitive schedules.

Relations between observer and observed

The above examples bring us onto the important issue of power relations between the field researcher and informants, especially where a traditional imbalance of power has existed, such as historic colonial relationships, or where the field researcher represents a university in a white, wealthy and powerful capitalist society among rural, poor or indigenous peoples. One of the authors used to utilize an Indiana Jones analogy to describe his approach to fieldwork, in which he attempted to become part of the religious environment that he was entering. However, one day he realized that the analogy with Indiana Jones has a darker aspect. In fact, Indiana Jones does not become a part of his environment. He is backed by influential sponsors to bring valuable items from other less powerful and less wealthy cultures, back to where they will be displayed in museums and lose their cultic or cultural use in religious or social rituals. The whip he carries is a symbol of this cultural appropriation, rather than him blending into and respecting the environment. We need to be on guard in our reflexive observations, to be observing our attitudes and values as researchers. In the study of religion we are not involved in the appropriation of material objects, but nevertheless there are a number of pitfalls of which we should be aware.

One such problem is that of the superiority or power advantage of the researcher over the researched, mentioned above. One form of superiority can arise from the researcher's own worldview, in which one may feel more rational, objective, knowledgeable or educated than the individual under investigation. The issue of who has a better claim to 'know' the religion, the insider or the outsider observer, has been dealt with in a previous chapter, but in regard to other forms of feeling superior, the researcher needs to keep a close awareness of their own thought processes and utilize the described methods in their research and their reporting of it. In this respect, it is important to remember that we are not in the field to dispute with informants over what we regard as true or accurate. We are in their domain, receiving their hospitality, and taking up their time for our purposes. Politeness and respect are requirements of successful fieldwork, and both authors have long-term relations with some of their respective gatekeepers.

With regard to other institutionalized or cultural forms of superiority, these are balanced or even outweighed by the relations between the researcher and the researched. It is, after all, the researcher who is in a strange world, unanchored from familiar cultural moorings and possibly ill at ease with unknown surroundings, practices and beliefs; whereas the researched are in their own territory where everything is familiar, among people with whom they feel close affinity, possibly even against the rest of the world. Outside of their realm there is a world that consists of unbelievers who are not under a deity's protection, guidance or grace, including the researcher who is to be pitied for his or her inability to experience the truth, and their feeble attempts to apply intellect to something that transcends such limited knowledge. It is not the researcher who is in a position of authority or power being the only representative of a particular culture, even if it is a powerful or elite one. You may be a BA student for the first time entering a mosque full of worshippers at Friday prayers (*juma*), or a postgraduate involved in fieldwork that takes you for an extended stay to a shrine or pilgrimage where large numbers of devotees are gathered, but you will probably be more nervous of the occasion than those participating in the event. One of the authors personally remembers feeling distinctly ill at ease taking photographs of large numbers of Murugan pilgrims at a temple in Tamil Nadu, who were participating in ecstatic healing trances under the guidance and exhortations of their priests. His instincts were found to be correct when a large party aggressively refused permission for photography, even though others had allowed his activities. He was alone, several thousand miles from home, and also experiencing communication difficulties as he did not speak Tamil. It is in these situations that 'native wit', knowledge of how the world works, its values, behaviour patterns, dietary prohibitions, dress codes, manners and courtesy and, if possible, some language skills will aid you far more than the fact that in another world you belong to an intellectual elite. This is also where you rely upon your gatekeepers.

At the very least the individuals under investigation, especially gatekeepers, can refuse you entry and prevent any successful completion of your research. The author remembers well an incident of spectacular failure to achieve his goals when completing the fieldwork for his PhD thesis. He had successfully researched a Muslim movement in India and Pakistan, and wished to compare his findings with a transplant of the movement which had its headquarters in an old mill town in West Yorkshire. He arrived at the mosque during a time of great activity and was asked to sit outside the prayer hall while permission was obtained for him to attend the function. While waiting, someone mistakenly thought that he was already invited, and ushered him into a meeting of Muslim missionaries planning their campaign. He was only in the gathering for two minutes before he was angrily ushered out, not only from the prayer hall but the building itself. Two young Muslims escorted him up the street and told him never to return. He asked whether it would be possible to return if he was genuinely interested in converting to Islam, and was told to contact the local mosque in such an eventuality.

Experiences of this kind are a shock to the system of experienced researchers, let alone the novice. However, in this case he was able to rescue his final chapter by focusing on why the British variety of the movement had emphasized the isolationist stance and the historical roots for maintaining such a position originating in nineteenth-century British India, and its applicability to some Muslims dealing with life in contemporary Britain.

Sophie Gilliat-Ray has also written on the difficulties of being refused entry, and the alternative strategies for success on such occasions (Gilliat-Ray, 2005). Carol Bailey notes that Murphy's Law (if something can go wrong it will) operates in fieldwork, so be ready to be flexible and adaptable, and even to change plans in mid-project. She notes that German fieldworkers use the term *Glück im Unglück* (fortune in misfortune) (Bailey, 1996, p. 45). The above example of being refused access is a case where an unfortunate event had to be turned to the author's advantage.

In the social sciences, much debate has taken place concerning a value-free stance, and how to eliminate one's own biases from the research. Religion is a topic that carries a very high value-laden burden which needs to be acknowledged, especially in fieldwork encounters. It is almost impossible not to carry preconceptions arising out of our own attitudes towards religion in general, or particular manifestations of faith and practice. These may arise because we follow a different faith to the one we are studying, or do not have a faith position at all. On the other hand, we may find that the beliefs and practices of the group under investigation outrage our own deeply held sense of rational or acceptable behaviour. It may be hard to treat seriously claims by informants to have been abducted by aliens, or to have sympathy with forms of religion that engage members in violent activities against others or themselves.

As an extreme case, cannibalism would probably create feelings of antipathy in most of us, but it is possible to recognize that for the people concerned there are reasons for their behaviour which make sense in their worldview. You can recognize and be aware of your own inbuilt bias against cannibalism, but also perceive that the cannibal may wish to consume the body of the dead enemy in order to assimilate his or her power. The student of religion must always try to appreciate and understand what a given manifestation of religion might mean to those directly and personally involved in it.

As discussed in previous chapters, recent developments in methodology acknowledge that what we describe in our research does not exist apart from our relationship to it. In other words, we cannot reveal the world to be known independently of our involvement in it. Such an approach to research is known as social constructionist theory, and argues that research socially constructs a world that includes the researcher within it. This advances Ninian Smart's ideas of moccasin-walking and introduces the concept of reflexivity. The point is still to see through the eye of the other, but reflexivity suggests that it is possible to reverse roles and ask the question: 'What would the researched say about our process of researching them?' Eleanor Nesbitt states that 'reflexive awareness requires probing reflection on the extent to which one is an insider or an outsider to the community which one is observing' (Nesbitt, 2004, p. 6).

Research tells a story not only of the researched, but also about yourself. Social constructionist theories challenge the traditional view of enquiry which attempts to keep the world under investigation at a distance, and argue that it is naïve to keep oneself out of one's constructions. Such approaches will lead to a different type of writing, in which the researcher tells of his or her own involvement with the world under investigation, which can include both negative and positive emotions. Students may be surprised to find themselves being asked to engage reflectively upon their own experiences in the fieldwork encounter, alongside the more conventional approaches of objective knowledge gathering and analysis.

My final advice concerning problems of access is to cultivate and look after your gatekeepers. In order to facilitate this it is helpful to maintain communication, visit them or contact them sometimes when you do not want anything from them. Also remember that your relationship may be viewed as one-sided if you always contact them for your benefit. This can lead to resentment, and the author has found that the best way to deal with this is reciprocal exchange of favours. We have to ask ourselves what we give back to the religious communities and individuals that we research. We need to be aware of empowering certain communities that are marginalized or badly represented elsewhere. At the very least we need to give religious groups a fair hearing, and a chance to be represented in a world to which they may not normally have access.

Conclusion

Both positivism and naturalism are methodologies that attempt to remove the impact of the researcher on the data, but whereas the former standardizes research procedures in an attempt to discover universal laws, the latter strives for direct experience of the world entered. Positivism is the usual model that comes from science, and it begins by creating a hypothesis and then testing it in the field to find out whether it is true. For example, that ethnic minorities from India and Pakistan do not join the police force because they believe the police to be institutionally racist is a hypothesis. In order to test the hypothesis, the researcher will be engaged in number-crunching, statistical analysis, questionnaires and surveys. In other words, a quantitative methodology as opposed to a qualitative method of discovery is used to test the hypothesis. On the other hand, Eleanor Nesbitt states that ethnography is an 'approach to understanding others which relies on a discipline of deep listening and close, reflective observation' (Nesbitt, 2004, p. 5). One's assumptions need to be challenged continuously, and the end result is to communicate sensitively a deeper knowledge to others.

Intentionally there has been no discussion of various methods of undertaking fieldwork including participant observation, which is variously defined in texts as any kind of fieldwork whatsoever, through to burrowing covertly into a sub-culture. Although the authors would generally distinguish between observation and participant observation, the latter involving a degree of involvement and participation in the events taking place; they are aware that all fieldwork involves participation to the degree that as soon as one enters a religious rite one is involved in the action at some level, and the rules of the community apply. You will have to decide the level of your participation according to your comfort zones and the expectations of the community under observation.

One of the best models for categorizing fieldwork is provided by Harry Wolcott, who lists three types of activity that are engaged in by fieldworkers. First, there is experiencing, where the participant observes and experiences information through the filter of all the senses including his own reactions such as bewilderment, fear, pleasure, disdain and the like. Second there is enquiry, where active observation takes place through the medium of interviewing. This may range from casual conversation, asking informants to explain what is going on, collecting life histories, formally interviewing key informants with either structured (every interviewee is asked the same question) or semi-structured (the interview takes shape as it progresses) interviews or getting informants to complete questionnaires. Third and finally there is examining, which involves searching through what has already been produced by others: this will include studies by other scholars, archival material and insider materials such as personal accounts by devotees, biographies, devotional tracts, and other religious materials which these days might consist of video, film or website material (Wolcott, 1999, pp. 44 ff.). You will need to choose from these possibilities of experiencing, enquiring and examining how you are going to carry out your fieldwork according to the individual circumstances and aims of your project.

Throughout this chapter, the authors have used ethnography to refer to the process of research rather than how the data is processed and interpreted. This has been intentional because they are not anthropologists, sociologists or cultural studies scholars. They are happy to acknowledge and refer to such findings in their work, but they are primarily concerned with a study of religion's approach that provides a window into the world of the believer and furthers our knowledge of the religions themselves, rather than interpretations of social or cultural behaviour. Their main concern has been to develop the use of fieldwork to elicit knowledge of the world of the religious believer rather than the social or cultural questions that reduce that world to economic, political or social underlying causes. To remain a scholar of religion engaged in fieldwork you will need to understand the various religious worldviews from the bottom upwards, taking into account the grassroots believer as well as institutional structures: but remember to remain problem-driven rather than descriptive in your approach. In our experience it is essential when visiting religious places to take with you a question for exploration that throws light on religious belief and practice in the particular tradition. For example, rather than merely sitting in the Sikh gurdwara, a question can be provided such as 'In what way does the gurdwara reflect the Sikh doctrine of the Guru?' You are now engaged in exploration of behaviour, practice, architecture, ritual, dress and, inevitably, a process of triangulation in which you can begin to collect testimony and check it with both academic texts and Sikh texts. Thus your eye is being trained to observe and analyse by making comparisons and noting contrasts.

Be aware that there are many religious questions that have not been answered. The religions themselves may have conflicts as various groups struggle to claim orthodoxy through claiming their doctrine and praxis as authoritative. Texts written from the top downwards may represent only the viewpoint of a particular historical period or the views of the powerful. There may well be discrepancies in the worldview of the practitioners from those proposed by scholars, theologians and religious experts. For example, Christianity does not accept reincarnation, which was defined as a heresy in 533 CE at the Council of Florence, but today it is common to find Western Christians who believe in it. However, such fieldwork is rarely carried out in the study of Christianity. I hope that these examples clarify what I mean by religious questions rather than the questions of the social sciences, although these may also be useful to provide insights into understanding motivations and causes for behaviour.

We hope that in Chapter 9 we have been able to convey some of the possibilities opened up to the student of religion by fieldwork. Above all, to follow such an approach you need to enjoy it, especially the challenge of observing your own inner processes as well as meeting with people whose worldview may be very different from your own; and also comprehending their beliefs and practices in their own terms, as well as interpreting them to provide greater insights into understanding religion generally or one religion in particular. We have not provided a detailed account of ethnographical methodology, as there are many textbooks that do that task very well. Instead we have attempted to show how fieldwork can contribute to our understanding of religion as we meet it in lived realities rather than textual study, and to give some practical advice that might provide some guidance to the novice fieldworker daunted by the prospect. We have also attempted to give some advice to both teachers and students whose only encounter with living religions may consist of a field visit to a local place of worship, so that it can become more than simply an afternoon or day out from the classroom or lecture theatre. We would hope to inspire you to engage with this fascinating and rewarding approach to the study of religions. With all its frustrations, it will teach you a lot about yourself and your relations to other human beings, as well as providing insights into the world of religion.

DISCUSSION POINTS

1 Discuss the ways in which ethics is important in fieldwork. What considerations would you wish to be addressed in a professional code of practice relating to fieldwork? Attempt to locate some relevant codes of practice.

2 How would you account for differences between 'textbook' versions of a religion and what is discovered through fieldwork?

3 Much of a student's fieldwork is likely to involve 'diaspora religion'. What are the likely consequences of this? What differences might one expect between a diaspora form of religion and its indigenous expression?

4 Consider the limitations that exist in student fieldwork. How might one compensate for these?

10

Religion and gender

Ron Geaves

Chapter Outline

The struggle within Christianity	277
Biblical Studies	278
Church history	281
Strategies of resistance and transformation	283
The Goddess and healing	286
Islam and other religions	290
Islam	292
Methodology	299
Discussion points	301

From the perspective of reflexivity it is interesting to note the apprehension felt by me as a male academic writing this chapter. Not only am I not an expert on gender and religion but there are emic/etic issues involved in writing about the feminist contribution to the study of religion. By definition, a female academic presents an emic view to which she is unashamedly committed. As a male academic, however sympathetic, my position is etic, as an outsider looking in. In my defence I would argue that the term 'feminist' need not necessarily be confined to women and I hope that my own sympathies lie in that direction. I am aware in writing this section that women's religious experience has usually been described and categorized until fairly recently by male academics or male religious professionals within the religious traditions. I do not wish to further marginalize women's voices, so at best I am a voice from offstage saying, 'Listen to the voices from centre stage – women themselves.' In short, women's writing on religion and gender is confessional, engaged and transformative. There is no intention to create a neutral distanced perspective, but rather to utilize knowledge in order to create change.

This chapter will begin by examining the struggle for equality within Western Christianity, and will explore the variety of strategies developed by Christian feminists to reassert themselves and overthrow a historical legacy of discrimination and neglect. However, some women have struggled with their Christianity and gender issues and come to the conclusion that the former is irrevocably permeated by patriarchal attitudes and structures, and therefore irredeemable. These women have chosen to place their loyalty to their gender over and above belief in a particular version of the Christian narrative and have sought new avenues for liberation, maintaining a religious worldview but constructing fresh meta-narratives of 'she-ness' – a 'her story' rather than history. For those who have committed themselves to the transformation of Christianity from within, a threefold attack has been made on language, theology and hierarchical structures. Loosely speaking, these correspond approximately to the three main disciplines that have traditionally been used for studying the faith tradition, that is Biblical Studies, theology and church history.

The struggle by women in the West with their respective religious traditions has led to a criticism of Eurocentrism in religious feminism – a focus on white, middle-class, educated Christian or Jewish women that ignores the plight of millions of women in other religions or, worse, tries to impose upon them solutions that were developed for the above elite as a 'universal truth' – a way of liberation for all women. Many women who struggle for their rights in other religious traditions would resent the label 'feminist', and reject the freedoms achieved by Western women as unsuitable for their own cultural or religious circumstances. This is particularly true of Muslim women, whose agenda is remarkably different from that stereotypically placed upon them by outsider observers. An essentialist view of Muslim women superimposes a 'gaze' that sees passivity and focuses on gender separation, clothing restrictions and marriage customs as the primary loci for discrimination. On the other hand, Muslim women themselves rarely see these as the main areas of concern, especially the issues of *hijab* and veiling or gender separation, and prefer to demand the rights given to them by revelation and taken away from them by patriarchal cultures. Most Muslim women would not agree with the statement made by Daphne Hampson in conversation with Rosemary Radford Ruether:

> Religion is potent. It is the most potent ideology the world has known for undermining the integrity of women as first-class members of humanity. (Hampson, 1987, p. 6)

On the contrary, most Muslim women would regard the revelation given to human beings and contained in the Qur'an, exemplified in the life of Muhammad, as liberating – a potent message of equality that restored women to dignity and fulfilment in the eyes of God.

Finally, the challenge made by women in the academic realm has contributed to the methodological debates in the study of religions, subverting the borders between the etic and emic voices and challenging the edifice borrowed from the social sciences of a neutral, value-free pursuit of knowledge, and reasserting the place of subjectivity and reflexivity – listening to women's narratives or 'hearing voices'. Most women writing on religion do not consider themselves to be free of bias, but endeavour to enable the biases to be just what allows women's religious experiences to be penetrated and made transparent, to be tested in the mirror of our own experience.

The struggle within Christianity

For those countless women who have decided to remain within the Church and struggle to eradicate a deep-seated historical misogyny and structural patriarchy, their journey has not been without pain. Women who seek to transform the Church see within its structures and history a deep-rooted illness that emerges from a theological position which divides body and spirit and can lead to hatred of the body. Susan Dowell and Linda Hurcombe claim that the question of women's roles has changed from 'What work can a woman do, suiting their own special talents and training to a male-orchestrated Church?' to 'What can women do to cure the deep-rooted illness from which Christianity is suffering?' (Dowell and Hurcombe, 1981, p. 62).

Away from religion in the secular sphere, women in Anglo-American culture have made spectacular gains, picking up momentum in the last hundred years. It was not until the late Victorian period that married women were given rights over their own property and earnings or the right to sue for maintenance in cases of desertion, but since then there have been considerable victories including the right to vote, the right to participate in the political process (in the case of Britain, producing a formidable prime minister), and the right to higher education from which they have carved out successful career opportunities in education, law, medicine, banking and financial institutions. Divorce laws have been changed in their favour, and new systems of contraception have provided the freedom for them to pursue their own sexual fulfilment. More controversially contraception has provided women with the freedom to choose family or economic opportunities and resulting independence from patriarchal family structures often endorsed by religions. Perhaps the most dramatic breakthrough has been in social attitudes, where it is no longer assumed that women are the property of their fathers, husbands or brothers, relying for their well-being on the goodwill of such male authority figures.

The premise of Christian feminism is that the Church has ignored these social changes and failed to incorporate them into its own liturgical and hierarchical structures. Neither has it reflected upon the fact that Christian women have experienced dramatic transformation in all areas of life, and could rightly expect similar changes to take place in the realm of their religious and spiritual existence. Although Western feminism has been predominantly secular, often seeing religion itself as deeply suspect and therefore absent from feminist discourse, Christian women began to suspect the contemporary and historical narratives of their faith in regard to gender. Dowell and Hurcombe, both practising Christians of diverse traditions and upbringing, express this suspicion succinctly:

> Our two very different childhood traditions have taught us that the Church holds and guards some special truths about women's nature and their place in God's creation. We have put this claim to the test and have been compelled in all honesty to shed the 'special truths' argument as the Church presently interprets it. We remain nevertheless committed to the Church and maintain a conviction that Christian feminism has something important to teach the community whose name is 'Church'. (1981, p. 111)

Biblical Studies

A woman's viewpoint of the canon of Christian scripture cannot help but be alarming. First it notes the lack of female consciousness: that even when woman is present, she is often unnamed or merely exists to illustrate or highlight an event in the life of a significant male. However, it is the myth of creation and the fall from grace of the first human pair, Adam and Eve, that has most significantly damaged the place of the female in both Judaism and Christianity. From her very origin, Eve, although bestowed with the gift of creation, is not created in her own right but from the ribs of the man, the firstborn of God. However, worse is to come: it is her temptation and disobedience to God's command that leads to their expulsion from the Garden of Eden and the presence of God. Adam himself is beguiled by her to eat the fruit of the tree of knowledge of good and evil. To this day the orthodox Jew thanks God in his prayers that he was not born a woman. Thus Monica Furlong can write: '. . . the most fundamental of Christian stereotypes is the stereotype of Eve – woman as incurably treacherous' (Furlong, 1991, p. 16). She goes on to say:

> if we interpret this magnificent story mythically rather than literally, it claims that the ills of humankind derive from women's power to tempt, that is the downfall of men, who, were it not for women, would live in bliss. (1991, p. 17)

If the first woman of the Old Testament provides the endemic image of women as temptresses (no less found in other faiths), the first woman of the new dispensation, the Christian era, is no less problematic. Mary, although regarded as the mother of God, is lauded and even venerated as a chaste virgin. If the domestic realm, especially motherhood, is perceived as the primary sacred realm for women, then the idea of a perfect mother who is also a 'pure' and 'chaste' virgin places women in a double bind. If they remain celibate, they have become in a sense male – renouncing their unique function to create. On the other hand, if they become mothers they have, by definition, lost their purity.

The Jewish scriptures provide a legal framework derived from God's revelation on Sinai, still the mainstay of the orthodox Jew's existence. Dowell and Hurcombe note that the focus of most biblical legal injunctions is to protect male authority, honour and property. Along with his slaves and herds, his wife and children were his property. Her position demanded that she provide offspring, especially the male heir, and barrenness was the chief grounds for divorce. Widows had no legal or economic security, and a wife's adultery was punishable by death. In the realm of the religion she was denied participation in the public cultic life, and there were no women priests in the Old Testament. Virginity was highly prized, and a bride who was proven to have already had sexual intercourse was likely to be stoned to death. Above all a woman was a bearer of children, and barrenness was regarded as a sign of God's disapproval and displeasure (Dowell and Hurcombe, 1981, pp. 25–31).

However, women were granted equal authority as parents, still claimed by Jewish religious scholarship as of ultimate spiritual significance, and there are significant women in the Jewish scriptures. Esther and Ruth have their own books, but Dowell and Hurcombe point out that:

. . . the vast majority of female characters are portrayed as types of womanhood. They are either idealised as super-mums, super-wives, super-queens – or vilified as temptresses, seductresses, deceivers, stupifiers, betrayers, sorcerers, in a plot whose story revolves around the deeds of men. (1981, p. 31)

Perhaps in the Christian era, the ultimate super-mum is the Virgin Mary, who is impossible to emulate.

If the Old Testament provides us with the image of a woman who is always dependent on the goodwill of the men who own her, first her father and to a lesser extent her brothers who protect the family's honour, and then her husband, the New Testament provides a challenge to the dominant patriarchal worldview of Jewish society. Jesus emerges as a figure with very different attitudes from those of the traditional Jewish male: critical of blind adherence to the law and the practices of religious ritual devoid of the inner life, he also appears to offer a challenge to the contemporary view of women in Jewish society. His radical treatment of women was sufficiently different to be noticed by his biographers, and a female presence among his close followers is noticeable even if they do not make the ranks of the twelve apostles. At least three are significant: Jesus' conversation with the Samaritan woman at the well-challenged rigid codes of social behaviour (Jn 4.7–26); the Martha and Mary story demonstrated that he did not perceive women's ministry as confined to the domestic sphere (Lk. 10.38–42); but perhaps most significant of all, female disciples were the first witnesses of the resurrection, demonstrating a victory of feeling over rationality and making a point about the validity of women's testimony (Lk. 24.1ff.).

FIGURE 10.1 *A street shrine to the Virgin Mary located in the Algarve region of Portugal.*

The post-resurrection period seems to provide evidence of growing egalitarianism which included gender. Women are mentioned by name in Acts and in the greetings of Paul to the early Christian communities, and women appear to have had leadership roles in ministry and missionary activity. The famous statement that 'there is neither Jew nor Greek, slave nor free, male nor female, for you are all one in Jesus Christ' (Gal. 3.28) seemed to herald a new dispensation that proclaimed a spiritual unity transcending social boundaries, even those that were prescribed in the law of Moses.

However, in spite of this revolutionary and transcendent proclamation of unity through baptism apparently manifest in the structures and hierarchies of the early

Christian communities, not all was well in the Pauline and Deutero-Pauline letters to the fledgling churches. Perhaps written in order to contain the impact of Gnosticism, a number of controversial statements, especially those in 1 Timothy and 1 Corinthians, were to have a disastrous impact on the position of women in Christian history, and still provide powerful and emotive scriptural authority to maintain patriarchy and misogyny in contemporary Christianity.

In Eph. 5.22–23 an ancient hierarchical divine order is reasserted in which wives are asked to 'submit to your husbands as to the Lord. For the husband is the head of the wife as Christ is head of the Church'. This is repeated in the letter to the Corinthians (1 Cor. 11.3–16), along with an injunction to remain silent in church (1 Cor. 14.34–35). It is in the letter to Timothy that the harshest words are reserved for women, reinforcing the ancient world's insistence that the female realm is the domestic one. 'Women will be saved through childbearing – if they continue in faith, love and holiness with propriety' (1 Tim. 2.15). It is tempting to ask whether the characteristics and qualities listed would be sufficient in the realm of religion without the requirement to bear children. The refrain to remain silent is repeated with more force:

> A woman should learn in quietness and full submission. I do not permit a woman to teach or to have authority over a man; she must be silent. For Adam was formed first, then Eve. And Adam was not the one deceived; it was the woman who was deceived and became a sinner. (1 Tim. 2.11–14)

The reference to Adam and Eve brings us back full circle to where women were perceived as weak, deceitful and even dangerous to righteous men. The view of women's different nature, less able to reason and discern, is seen in the warning to avoid the 'false' doctrines of Gnostic preachers: '. . . those who make their way into households and capture weak women . . . who will listen to anybody and never arrive at the knowledge of the truth' (2 Tim. 3.6ff.). However, Gnosticism was not confined to women and it is interesting to ask what kind of explanations would be sought for male attraction to Gnostic Christianity. In a world where the young churches were reaching out to convert Gentiles, it must have been reassuring for the men of the ancient Mediterranean cultures to know that the status quo in regard to gender roles would not be challenged by the new path to salvation. Men would still be the repositories of wisdom, reason, prudence and common sense, maintaining order in their households with authority over their wives who were subject to uncontrolled emotions, irrationality and weakness.

Church history

The history of the church from the immediate post-resurrection period to the present does not reveal significant gains for women until the present time. The scriptural passages cited above have been continuously used by male theologians and church leaders to reinforce their own entrenched positions. If scripture provided legitimization for misogyny and patriarchy, tradition was no less problematic. The patristic period reveals the deep influence of neo-platonic attitudes which further polarize matter and spirit, body and soul. The cult of celibacy already advocated in the Pauline period, linked to the high status given to virginity, would have further eroded the domain of female spirituality in the domestic sphere.

In the patristic period, we observe the development of an orthodoxy, winning over both the Gnostic and Jewish influences that had provided more syncretistic versions of Christianity in the first and second centuries. In spite of this considerable diversity remained; however, it cannot be within the scope of this chapter to deal with the rich variety of attitudes towards women, or the number of prominent women who arose in various movements such as the Marcionite or Valentinian constructions of Christianity. These movements were eventually marginalized and disappeared into the backwaters of history. The lesser objective is simply to demonstrate a number of opinions of women expressed by prominent men who have contributed to the construction of mainstream Christian theology.

As theology focused on the role of Jesus in God's plan for salvation, so it also attempted to understand the nature of the Fall. Consequently Eve's role was highlighted and she was made representative of all women. Although salvation remained open to all Christians, nearly all the church fathers condemned women, leading to a view that echoes Clement of Alexandria's (150–215 CE) statement that 'the very awareness of her own nature must arouse a sense of shame in women' (Furlong, 1991, p. 20). In addition the widely acknowledged view that there was something innately deficient in women that went beyond the male/intellect and female/emotion divide remained prevalent. Some perceived her as not made in the image of God as men were, and this has continued down to the opinion of St Thomas Aquinas, who regarded women as 'biologically monstrous' (1991, p. 27), caused by the implantation of a weak male seed in procreation.

Virginity was associated with purity, an overcoming of the flesh, and some men even went as far as castration to overcome the possibility of subjection to the temptress with her powerful sexual appeal. Furlong cites the case of St Augustine who wondered why God had created women at all, even though he acknowledged that both sexes would remain at the resurrection. So entrenched was the body/spirit division that church fathers and councils advocated celibacy even in marriage, and Furlong again informs us that by the Middle Ages virtue was equated not only with sexual abstention as personified in the monastic orders or the priesthood, but with 'despising and rejecting women' (1991, p. 22). Furlong cites St Bonaventure (thirteenth century) describing St Francis' attitudes to women, in which he forbade all conversations or meetings with them as running the risk of corruption, an 'occasion for falling' (1991, p. 23).

Perhaps the culmination of these attitudes towards women in Christianity was the witch hunts of the Middle Ages, which are described with some justification as pogroms against women. The vision of women as a source of temptation has persisted to the present day, keeping them out of high visibility until relatively recently; and throughout the twentieth century the story of Eve has continued as a justification for keeping women in their place within Christian institutions.

In recent years there has been a struggle to enter the priesthood by Anglican women in Britain which has refocused many of the opinions historically related to the female gender in Christianity. Although the Church of England remains a relatively small denomination compared to Roman Catholicism or Eastern Orthodoxy, the debate not only focused on whether women could represent Christ at the altar as a priest, but even raised the ancient spectre of impurity through menstruation. Some of the statements made by male clergy showed clearly how negatively women were regarded, and the attitudes presented were intended to continue to deny women access to power or authority within church structures. Furlong writes:

> The Church of England, Roman Catholicism and Orthodoxy which place major emphasis on sacraments are the ones which demonstrate most clearly how deep the prejudices against women are. They focused on the issue of priesthood, this is representing Christ at the altar, holding the sacred objects of bread and wine. (1991, p. xi)

Somehow there was something not quite 'Christlike' about women, barred from the maleness of the incarnation, somehow unclean because of menstruation, and thus they could not be part of the apostolic succession which was seen to incorporate the maleness of Christ and to be continued through the male disciples. Yet Furlong concludes that in her opinion a wider change than merely ordination is required: changes in Christian attitudes to women (1988, p. 11).

Strategies of resistance and transformation

Perhaps most importantly we will learn from the silences not to absent ourselves from history.

DOWELL AND HURCOMBE, 1981, p. 37

For us the stories are so overwhelmingly emptied of female insight that we are left with little other than an impression of our own invisibility.

1981, p. 56

It is not so much that women are absent from the biblical stories, but rather that the accounts are rarely written from their perspective. One strategy for women is to go back and reclaim their story, to render women visible by switching the perspective. One shocking example of this would be the story of the Levite's concubine told in Judges 19–21. The story of her rape and murder and subsequent mutilation, cut into

FIGURE 10.2 *Women's ordination. Two women celebrate their ordination as deacons in the Church of England. In one year's time they will become eligible for full ordination as priests.*

12 pieces for distribution to the tribes of Israel, is harrowing enough; but it becomes even more disturbing when one realizes that she is not even the central character in her own tragedy. Thus Majella Franzmann writes:

> When a woman appears in a story only as a secondary figure or as one who does not speak, imagine that she moves to centre stage, and see the story unfold again from her point of view. (Franzmann, 2000, p. 2)

She advocates the same strategy for dealing with the alignment of women's spirituality to the domestic realm.

> Where women's religious practice is relegated by the dominant group to the domestic sphere, place the woman and her domestic setting in the centre of the social and religious network and imagine how she might speak of the value of her religious practice in this space that is hers above all. (2000, p. 2)

Thus marginalization of women can be offset by placing them at centre stage. In addition women have historically existed as one half of Christian conviction and faith, perhaps proportionately more at the grass-roots. Thus feminist historians can seek her out and re-evaluate her contribution, trying to discover her authentic voice under the imposition of misogyny and patriarchy. A number of women existed throughout church history as significant figures, especially among the mystics. Others have founded monastic orders or lived as abbesses of institutions. The numbers are many but, as stated by Furlong, the process of adjustment is at best sketchy and although there is now a considerable body of feminist biblical scholarship and church history, the overwhelming impression is invisibility; the countless women whose voices are not heard can only be mourned (Furlong, 1988, p. 3).

Language, too has become a problem. Some Christian feminists have criticized the language of both scripture and liturgy as male-biased, reinforcing a view of the deity itself as masculine. Already presented with two aspects of the Trinity as God the Father and God the Son, some – such as the male theologian Yves Congar – have attempted to discover femininity in the Holy Spirit (Coakley, 1988, p. 125). However, Sarah Coakley is concerned that the designation of feminine qualities to the third aspect of the Trinity stereotypes masculinity and femininity, thus further reinforcing the duality rather than emphasizing Christian wholeness (1988, p. 126). Dowell and Hurcombe state:

> Study in the language of sexism is another exciting area for Christian feminists. We are beginning to recognise the inescapable link between the use of words and the reality that use reflects in society. (1981, p. 66)

As a result some Christian feminists are insisting that God be described as S(he) or Father/Mother God, so that the focus on fatherhood is redressed. Female theology is beginning to focus on the feminine qualities of the divine, such as nurture or creativity. Furlong states that 'the language of the prayer, with the emphasis on the male God and His male Son, the use of "man" (apparently meaning both men and women) and on "he" (apparently meaning both he and she) declared women's invisibility' (1991, p. 74). Thus there is a plea for inclusive language, recognizing that any description of God, whether male or female, can only be a metaphor. In addition, women have rewritten Christian liturgy to include women, and even written new, distinctly female forms of liturgy to be used where Christian women gather together for worship. The use of male-dominated language is believed to promote male superiority by association. Mary Daly writes: 'since God is Male, the male is God' (Daly, 1973). The final word on language will be given to Monica Furlong:

> Follow this with the exclusion of references to women, female pronouns, female imagery, even female vocatives in church, and the woman is reduced to a religious nonentity. (1991, p. 79)

The General Synod of the Church of England in 1985 set up a commission on inclusive language but the conclusions were not optimistic about transformation to any great extent, although some minor changes were made. Overall the Commission declared that it did not consider male pronouns and possessive adjectives in relation to God as inappropriate and that the issue should simply conform to scriptural and traditional usage (1991, p. 81). Yet women have continued to write books of feminist prayers utilizing female imagery of pregnancy, labour, nurture, feeding, tenderness and intimacy (1991, p. 84). One difficulty that arises for Christian women rewriting sacred language rests in the treasured familiarity of certain prayers and liturgies that have become hallowed by time and usage. To the familiar ear of the worshipper changes can sound stilted, and lose their power of repeated use so essential to the successful ritual.

For many Christian feminists the most intractable problem remains the dualism at the heart of most mainstream Christian theology. The body/spirit dichotomy that has caused so many problems concerning sexuality throughout history becomes even more significant with the environmental crisis of our time. Many see the stewardship of the earth and its creatures advocated in Genesis as maintaining the male or patriarchal relationship with creation based upon dominion. Furlong, although numbering herself among those who wish to reform the Church while affirming their faith, does not perceive Christianity as irredeemably sexist; but she does reserve strong language for its lack of a holistic theology:

> It is a twisted sexuality out of a desperate dualism, a dualism in which woman is defined as flesh, body, nature, matter which must be overcome, controlled, subdued. Man, on the other hand, is identified with intellect and spirit. (1988, p. 5)

While some have attempted to heal the divide, reasserting a holistic theology that provides a feminist Christian critique of exploitation of the planet and its resources, others are not so convinced and argue that the body/spirit divide is embedded in Christian theological thought and practice. The question is a larger one in the study of religions: namely, how far can one go in transforming a religious tradition before something integral or essential to the fundamental existence is removed? In short, to what degree does Christianity remain Christianity? What is considered essential differs from person to person, but certainly some Christian feminists have perceived Christianity as having sexism built into its very dualistic fabric, and have therefore chosen to leave the tradition and seek new avenues to express female spirituality.

The Goddess and healing

Earth traditions

Daphne Hampson, for example, feels that Christianity is by its nature sexist and therefore women should remove themselves from the churches and look elsewhere.

She states: 'I hold that it be the case that in feminism Christianity has met a challenge to which it cannot accommodate itself' (Hampson, 1987, p. 6). However, there are many women who have never entertained the possibility of finding their fulfilment in Christianity. Thousands have come to the Goddess in earth-bound spiritualities direct from the women's movement, influenced by consciousness-raising and suspicious of all institutionalized religion. In opposition to religion they prefer to assert feminist spirituality: polyglot and diverse, celebrating its own diversity, acknowledging a world imbued with sacredness that permeates animate and inanimate forms, populated by spirits and other supernatural beings, but above all the realm and being of the Goddess.

To outsiders these new female spiritualities beg a number of questions. Is she one Goddess or many? Is her worship monotheism, monism, pantheism or polytheism? Is she a real Goddess who exists objectively or a symbol for women's self-discovery? However, it should be noted that these questions rarely disturb the emic consciousness. Goddess theology, to the degree that it exists, is essentially experiential rather than a worked-out intellectual position, instead focusing on the reality of women's contact with the sacred, around her and within her, and rejecting the idea of belief. Above all, the Goddess is seen as healing the duality created by patriarchy, reaffirming a unity in which life, nature and sexuality are celebrated. Cynthia Eller quotes Marguerite Keane in her book *Living in the Lap of the Goddess*:

> I don't make these kinds of distinctions that you hear about, they don't make any sense to me. You can say it's the Great Goddess, and that's the One Goddess, but she's also all of the many goddesses and that's true. And She's everywhere. She's immanent in everything, in the sparkle of the sun on the sea, and even in the animistic concept. I think certain objects can embody that force and power. So I worship the Great Goddess, and I'm polytheistic and pantheistic and monotheistic too. And I also have a feeling for nature spirits and what we call the realm of faerie. And the earth elements, and the guardian spirits of the home. I feel all of those, and I feel in contact with all these different realms. (Eller, 1993, p. 133)

Therefore the outsider looking in discovers women who worship individual goddesses drawn from all the ancient traditions and cultures of the world wherever they are discovered. Some have particular form(s) which suit the requirements of the individual seeker. Others see these forms as manifestations or qualities of the Great Goddess, above all regarded as the Mother Goddess. Although the full diversity of humankind's understanding of the forms of the Goddess is revealed in the litany of names that often accompanies the liturgies of female spirituality, others regard the 'triple goddess' of paganism: the maiden, mother and crone, whose existence draws upon and connects the phases of a woman's life, the phases of the moon and the eternal cycles of nature.

Above all else, the Goddess is not transcendental in the sense of requiring from her children some kind of renunciation of the body in celebration of the incorruptible. As stated by Eller, '"the sacred game" for feminist spirituality is immersion in the material world rather than escape from it' (1993, p. 136).

For those like Karen Whiting, who states 'my personal experience and belief is that there's one Goddess who manifests in different forms' (1993, p. 133), but who may choose to focus on a particular form, theirs is a kind of henotheism, more familiar to the Hindu worldview than the monotheistic religions of Judaism, Christianity and Islam. For many others, the Goddess is not within and without nature, or a symbol for nature, but nature itself. Certainly all forms of female spirituality are overwhelmingly aware of immanence. This focus on the individual seeker experiencing her unity with interwoven natural and supernatural forces denies external religious authority and hierarchies, and attempts to discover identification with the Goddess herself. Each individual woman is not only part of the living earth, the corporeal form of the Goddess, but is herself a manifestation. This can become for some the overriding focus in which the actual existence of the Goddess is seen as secondary or, even worse, creating once again a creator/creation divide. Sonia Johnson expresses this succinctly:

> Goddess worship is not really about worshipping the Goddess, it is really worshipping women and ourselves, and saying we are peers, we are what creates everything, we are the created and the creator. (1993, p. 142)

Others may even perceive the Goddess as fiction invented by feminists as a tool for challenging patriarchy, providing a unique female perception of the world.

Although some women may adhere to one understanding of the Goddess, rejecting others, it would be wise for the student to recognize that several or all perspectives may be held simultaneously and paradoxically. Goddess worship provides women with a means to celebrate their own bodies and their own sexuality, heterosexual or otherwise. Starhawk speaks expressively of her experience of sharing imprisonment after the Diablo Canyon nuclear power plant blockade. She describes the women dancing naked and sunbathing with each other under the scrutiny of the guards. She states:

> We are all the Goddess in her multitude of forms: an Aphrodite, an Artemis, a Maiden, a Mother, a Crone. We are all Persephone dragged into the underworld by the authorities of patriarchy. But our living bodies transform hell. The situation is pornography brought to life, a constant humiliation that enacts a classic sadomasochistic guard/prisoner fantasy. Yet we are transformed by the presence of the erotic. We are connected with each other, and in our love for each other there is no footing for shame. (Starhawk, 1987, p. 15)

The women in their solidarity achieve victory, celebrating their own bodies.

> Yet we dance, because this is after all, what we are fighting for: this life, these bodies, breasts, wombs, this smell of flesh, this joy; this freedom – that it continue, that it prevail. (1987, p. 16)

The pantheistic dimension of female spirituality, perceiving the Goddess as both within nature and inseparable from it, and the emphasis on experience especially among those who identify the earth as the centre of their nature worship, led to identification with both indigenous cultures and ecological concerns. For many the pillage of the earth through exploitation of its resources is synonymous with the domination of women. This has given rise to eco-feminist movements.

However, some caution is required when approaching the identification of northern hemisphere women with indigenous cultures of their southern hemisphere sisters. Like many religious traditions, feminist spirituality looks back to an ideal past to be recaptured in a utopian future through struggle in an imperfect present. In this case, the ideal past consists of a prehistoric period in which a matristic civilization existed worldwide, to be destroyed by the conquering male-dominated central Asian warrior cultures somewhere between 4500 and 2500 BCE. The hordes promoted values of domination over both women and nature, replacing the Goddess with male divinity figures, and replacing matriarchy with patriarchy (Eller, 1993, p. 150).

For many northern eco-feminists, these male-dominated religions have reinforced the domination of women and nature, especially in their monotheistic manifestations. Thus indigenous nature religions remain as outposts, survivors of an earlier era, often remaining in an unequal struggle with colonial and postcolonial powers that still seek to destroy their holistic relationship with nature, replacing it with one of exploitation and dominion.

In the southern hemisphere many female voices are joining in the protest too, discovering their own voice of protest, developing an eco-feminism that also attempts to demonstrate how religion either reinforces exploitation or alternatively can be utilized as a resource for liberation of both women and nature. Very often, these marginalized voices of women are 'crossing worlds' within themselves (Ruether, 1996, p. 2). The product of both indigenous cultures in Asia, Africa or Latin America and colonization by Western cultures and religion, they seek to restore their indigenous roots to reframe their worldview. However, the view of northern hemisphere spiritual feminists, discussed previously, especially in regard to Goddess meta-narratives, can be viewed as a 'recreational self-indulgence' (1996, p. 5) belonging to a privileged counterculture elite. Ruether argues that northern hemisphere privileged narratives need to go further than 'psycho-spiritual' understandings of the feminine and 'make real connections between their own reality as privileged women and racism, classism and impoverishment of nature' (1996, p. 5).

In the United States in particular, successful middle-class women are open to the damning criticism that their freedom to operate in both the domestic sphere and pursue self-fulfilment in the public arena, while at the same time enjoying leisure activities, was achieved through the exploitation of their southern hemisphere sisters who are employed as nannies or domestic servants.

Although southern hemisphere women may also see the need for a return to a special relationship with nature and to reclaim a more positive period in which the immanence of the feminine divinity allowed for the experience of the sacrality of nature, their story differs radically from the feminist spirituality of the northern hemisphere in regard to impoverishment. In this respect, their northern sisters may also be part of the very exploitation protested against – the exploitation of the poor nations by the wealthy consumers of the north. Thus southern hemisphere women can utilize living indigenous traditions that exist as authentic voices of their own cultures, still thriving in spite of religious and cultural colonization. This is more difficult for northern hemisphere women, who may draw upon indigenous cultures of the south as a utopian ideal but can never achieve the same level of belonging.

In this regard, Ruether suggests that northern hemisphere spiritual feminists need to draw upon resources in their own indigenous roots, for example Celtic, Nordic or Slavic Europe (1996, p. 7). However, two problems exist in retrieving these roots: first, they have already been appropriated by various manifestations of fascism or extreme nationalism; second, there is the argument that revivals of these ancient traditions are actually new narratives created by a number of twentieth-century movements whose claims to unbroken connections to ancient religions are highly disputed. For example, Celtic Christianity, Wiccan witchcraft and revivals of Druid traditions have all been criticized by academics on these grounds. Even Eller admits that feminist spirituality in the northern hemisphere has more in common with the 'New Age', neo-paganism and post-Jungian psychotherapy, appropriating selectively from eastern religions and indigenous traditions, and can thus be defined more accurately as a new religion rather than a revival of an ancient one (Eller, 1993, pp. 62f). On the other hand, their southern hemisphere sisters can much more easily reclaim living traditions that remain part of their present heritage, and reach back into a precolonial past.

Islam and other religions

Other major World Religions also exhibit the exclusion of women from official positions, especially those positions concerned with the performance of ritual or as custodians of sacred space; in addition they also tend to argue that the place of women is in the domestic sphere. Generally, more women are denied access to priesthood, or in cases where priesthood does not exist, to the roles of rabbi, imam or to certain monastic orders. There are exceptions: thus in various reform movements or in 'folk' or 'popular' religions women can still find specialist roles. This section of the chapter cannot engage fully with all the major traditions and the variety of divisions within them, which vary in their attitudes to women, but will demonstrate particular examples, with a focus on Islam, that illustrate both the gender imbalance and the attempts by some women to resolve them.

Southern hemisphere eco-feminists are not the only women to criticize the attempts by northern hemisphere feminists to include them within their own experience and to search for identical solutions that encompass all women. Sheila Greeve Daveney, for example, argues that it created a 'flattening out of differences' among women in an attempt to create a homogenized group that provided self-identity for women (Davaney, 1987). She argues that this position is too heavily based upon the experiences of a 'white bourgeois-feminist stance' (1987). The first critique of white feminists from among the ranks of women came from African-Americans who argued that the elitist experience of white middle-class feminists did not in any way reflect the experience of oppression by black women. They preferred the term 'womanist' to 'feminist' to describe their own struggles for liberation.

Hindu, Sikh and Muslim women also see their struggles as unique and different from those of Western feminists. One stance from outside Western feminist positions has been to argue that religion in itself is not oppressive, providing rights to women that have not been implemented by male-dominated cultural formations. Thus religion and culture have been juxtaposed in those very societies that, it is often argued, do not distinguish between those two categories. Two examples from Sikhism serve to illustrate the strategies of women to offset patriarchy, and also to highlight the differences in approach from those of Western feminists.

Sikhism differs sharply from other religions of the subcontinent in that there is no ambiguity in its sacred text or the teachings of its founders with regard to the equality of men and women. Guru Nanak, the primary founder, was explicit in his strong advocacy of all forms of equality, condemning caste and gender differentiations, especially in regard to access to the divine. His successors appointed female missionaries, and the meta-narratives of Sikhism provide a strong discourse of gender equality. When Guru Gobind Singh originated the *Khalsa* movement at the end of the seventeenth century it was open to all, with the same conditions for both men and women. In addition, Sikhism, unlike Hinduism, Jainism or Islam, has no teaching regarding the exclusion of women from the public arena of worship during either menstruation or childbirth, and it has no purity/impurity focus as in Hinduism. Both men and women are permitted to read the sacred text publicly in the gurdwara and there is no official teaching that debars women from becoming granthis, the religious functionaries of Sikhism who are custodians of the gurdwara.

However, in spite of this, visits to Sikh gurdwaras rarely provide evidence of female granthis, and at one prominent gurdwara in Britain I was informed that, although it was permitted, in practice it was difficult to implement as there was no way to accurately determine when menstruation would begin. The sacred text, the Guru Granth Sahib, would be defiled if a woman reader should begin to menstruate while in the act of reading, so to prevent this happening women were discouraged or even prevented from taking such roles, even though the teachings of the religion permitted it. A kind of catch-22 position functioned in practice. The taboo on menstruation, although not taught in Sikh sacred texts, remains in place as part of the overriding Hindu cultural heritage, as does caste differentiation which is also discouraged in Sikh sacred teachings. The contrast between the ideal of the religion as expressed in sacred texts and taught by the founders, and the cultural reality, provides a means for Sikh women to develop strategies of resistance, asserting their religious rights over cultural baggage which their very founders had criticized.

The second illustration arises from a story contained in the Sikh sacred texts that recount biographical material of Guru Nanak, called the Janam Sakhis. Although it is disputed whether the texts are actually historical or hagiographical, that is not relevant in this example. In the story Guru Nanak visits the palace of an Indian ruler who hates religious preachers, believing them to be hypocrites and impostors. In order to test their authenticity, he orders his concubines and dancing girls, kept in his harem, to seduce the visiting itinerant 'holy men'. Up until Guru Nanak's visit all succumb to the spell of female seduction, and are consequently exposed and disgraced.

Guru Nanak not only resists the temptation but gathers the women together and begins to teach them. In addition he initiates them into discipleship. I utilized the story as a case study with a mixed group of students from white and South Asian backgrounds. The responses of both ethnic groups were radically different in regard to the attitudes to women shown in the story. The white middle-class females, especially those that considered themselves feminists, were outraged by the stereotyping of women as seductresses challenging male virtue, and by the ownership of the women by the Rajah who could order them to fulfil his whims. One or two noted that the women's voice was absent and that at no point was it considered necessary to tell the reader how they felt in the role of seductresses. The South Asian students, although acknowledging these criticisms, preferred to place the story in an historical context, focusing upon the fact that Guru Nanak both taught the women and initiated them – something not permitted to Hindu women in that period, and certainly not given to women who would have been considered defiled or of low status. For them the story indicated Guru Nanak's equal treatment of women, and his iconoclastic approach to status.

For the female Sikh students, the story reinforced their conviction that the founders of their religion supported female equality even in the fifteenth century. The problem for them did not lie in the religious teachings but in the erosion of those equalities from that period of the religion's inception to the present day. Thus the strategy for achieving equality is not to condemn religion as irredeemably sexist and therefore to be perceived as the enemy, but rather to see religion as a tool for liberation from the inbuilt inequalities of South Asian culture. The project for resistance is one of reclamation of the ideal from the reality. Nowhere has this strategy been more articulated than among Muslim women.

Islam

It is reasonably safe to assert that Islam receives more negative criticism concerning the role of women than any other religious tradition. The Western media have focused on *hijab* (veiling), *purdah* (female segregation) and non-Islamic cultural practices such as 'honour killings', often isolating individual movements such as the Taliban in Afghanistan as typical of Muslim female experience. On the other hand, many Muslim women argue that their religion safeguards women and that the Qur'an provided rights to seventh-century Arabian women that were not given to British women until the nineteenth century. The debate both within and without the Muslim communities is intense. Western feminists tend to regard Islam as hopelessly misogynist and Muslim women as being dominated by surviving patriarchal cultures from another period of time which need to be overhauled and brought in line with modern or postmodern Western cultures. Many Muslim women would regard their Western 'sisters' as corrupted by secular materialism, unprotected by the laws of God, seeking freedoms that are not permitted by God's revelation, and horribly exploited by sex industries and consumer advertising that use women to sell products.

However, that is not to say that large numbers of Muslim women are satisfied with the current or historical place of women in Muslim societies. A number of women from within Islam are challenging the overwhelmingly male voice of religious authority and reassessing the roles of prominent women in early Muslim development, most notably the women of the Prophet's household. Both the Qur'an and the Hadith are put under close scrutiny in order to discover what they say about women.

Before embarking on a condensed overview of these challenges to male interpretation of the final revelation, believed by Muslims to have been given by Allah for the benefit of all humanity, it is important to post a warning to anyone interested in the position of Muslim women. The traveller in their domain, whether intellectually or emotionally stimulated, needs to beware the errors of essentializing the Muslim female. We are infiltrated by media stereotypes of Muslim women that need to be recognized, confronted and expunged from our consciousness. For not only is 'woman' problematic, but so is the label 'Muslim' itself. Khan argues that the term 'Muslim' needs to be problematized, in that we need to remind ourselves of 'the power that the term "Muslim" holds in our imaginations', and that we need to recognize both the wide variety that is contained in the term 'Muslim women' and the increasing fluidity of cultural expressions of Muslim belonging (Khan, 1998, p. 465). Fauzia Ahmad argues that:

> Historical and contemporary encounters continue to embody Muslim Women through cultural and religious frameworks as essentialised oppressed figures of victimhood and despair. (Ahmad, 2003, p. 43)

The danger of essentializing will remain as long as the Western 'gaze' continues to focus on *hijab* and 'arranged marriages', projecting on to Muslim women an image of passivity and powerlessness, thus severely limiting the scope of debate. It may surprise many students interested in the subject that neither of these two issues are high on the agenda of Muslim female liberation discourse. The reasons for a Muslim female to wear a head covering are varied. It may be tradition, simply the way that it is done and therefore unquestioned; it may be practicality; it may be for religious or cultural reasons; or it may be because her family insists upon it. On the other hand, she may have decided to cover herself by her own conscious decision, independent of her family's views, who may even disapprove of her actions. If so, she may intensely defend her reasons for doing so as liberating, not binding. She may argue that the *hijab* protects her from unwanted male attention. These arguments need to be seriously assessed as they constitute the attitudes of millions of young Muslim women around the world who are voluntarily taking up Muslim dress codes and contributing in their own unique way to the phenomenon known as 'Islamicization'.

The other minefield to be avoided is setting ourselves up as an elite voice, somehow more knowledgeable or enlightened than Muslim women who are assumed to need our assistance to liberate themselves from the innate patriarchal structures of their religion and culture. This raises wider questions, already discussed, concerning who claims ownership of feminism itself. Western feminists need to be careful that they do not place themselves in the position of protectors and liberators of silent but suffering Muslim sisters. In this regard, the Algerian-born sociologist Marnia Lazreg argues that the Western feminist emancipatory project has failed as it continues to impose one social standard on another (Lazreg, 1988, p. 96). She powerfully asserts that it is essential to respect the rights of women to express their lives through their own constructs.

These two cautionary notes are particularly important in Western Europe and North America, where migration has created significant Muslim communities contributing to an official ethos of multiculturalism. The term 'Muslim women' is itself a problematic label because of the dangers of essentializing, but the reality of having living Muslim women appear under our gaze can lead to them being categorized as familiar strangers. Familiarity is created by their everyday presence, but it then becomes very easy to create categories from the immediate impact of their appearance. What is she wearing? What is her skin colour? What language is she speaking? And after 9/11, is she dangerous? These superficial identity markers can easily lead us towards an essentialized view. It is far more likely, with some rare exceptions, that Muslim women will remain strangers to us. For me this is certainly true for, although I have extensive contacts with Muslims as valued friends and colleagues, as a man I am segregated from most Muslim women. However, segregation does not equate to discrimination, although it could contribute to it.

Although the experience of a Muslim woman will be influenced by class and family background, age, rural or urban locality, national identity, and her place within the wide variety of religious understandings of Islam, it is from the revelation of the Qur'an and its subsequent rendering into everyday life through the example of Muhammad and his companions that her understanding of her place in society is finally made authoritative. Unlike her Christian feminist compatriots, who have recognized serious imperfections in the way women are treated in the religion itself, even in sacred histories and texts, many Muslim women who seek to change their position in society perceive Islam as the ideal which their menfolk, both historically and today, have failed to attain.

It is common to find the emic voice of young activist Muslim women arguing that the Qur'an not only has a complete chapter devoted to women, but that it also asserts her complete equality with men. This is although she operates in a complementary but different arena of life with her own qualities suited to that sphere, whereas men are suited to operate in the public realm. However, the Qur'an's proclamation of equality is in regard to her individual capacity to attain God's rewards and punishments, to follow the revelation of Allah's will. In this respect, the text makes it clear that men and women are equal:

> Lo! Men who surrender unto Allah, and women who surrender, and men who believe and women who believe, and men who obey and women who obey, and men who speak the truth and women who speak the truth, and men who persevere (in righteousness) and women who persevere, and men who are humble and women who are humble, and men who give alms and women who give alms, and men who fast and women who fast, and men who guard their modesty and women who guard (their modesty), and men who remember Allah much and women who remember – Allah hath prepared for them forgiveness and a vast reward. (Holy Qur'an, Sura 33.35)

However, in other areas equality is not so assured. For example, the testimony of a man is equivalent to that of two women, suggesting that women are less trustworthy. But the Qur'an does provide assertive statements concerning her rights in marriage and divorce, the status of her property and the maintenance of her dignity. She also has a number of Qur'anic models for both right and wrong behaviour. Four women – Asiyah the wife of Pharoah, Mary the mother of Jesus, Khadijah the first wife of Muhammad and Fatimah his daughter – are regarded as perfect role models. The wives of Lot and Noah provide a warning against wrongdoing.

These women of the Qur'an are archetypes of virtue or vice but they are, at least in this respect, free agents, able to choose to obey both God and God-fearing husbands. On the other hand, they can oppose unrighteousness in their menfolk, striving to bring their men to the right path. Barbara Stowasser writes:

> Many of the Qur'an's women's stories bear the lesson that a woman's faith and righteousness depend on her will and decision, and that neither association with a godly man nor a sinner decides a woman's commitment to God. (Stowasser, 1994, p. 21)

In addition, Muslim women do not have to deal with the stigma placed upon their Christian and Jewish counterparts, who are blamed for the fall of 'mankind' through the actions of their primal ancestor. Both Adam and Eve share the guilt of disobedience equally, but their weakness did not result in a permanent rift between God and humanity. Human nature remains intact with no lasting defect. Both Adam and Eve are restored to Allah's mercy and forgiveness, and this is celebrated by all Muslims who attend the annual *Hajj* in Makkah. Human beings, regardless of gender, are weak and forgetful but remain always in the vicinity of God's forgiveness. In addition, Islam rejects celibacy and monasticism in favour of married life. Sexuality is celebrated within the confines of marriage, and there are Hadiths which proclaim the importance of foreplay and sexual fulfilment for both men and women.

Stowasser, however, notes transformations in attitudes to women in various historical periods. She argues that medieval Muslim society was far more patriarchal than the early communities established in Makkah and Madinah, those who first received the Qur'an's revelation and followed the Prophet of God. Stowasser appears to agree with the assertions of many Muslims, both male and female, that the original equality was lost as Muslims conquered territories inhabited by earlier religions such as Zoroastrianism or Orthodox Christianity, and consequently came under their more sophisticated cultural influence. Stowasser states:

> Mediaeval Islamic exegesis, however, viewing women's innate nature as weak but also dangerous to the established moral order, largely excluded the Qur'anic theme of female spiritual freedom and moral responsibility in favour of the exegetic maxim that woman is (i.e. should be) man's follower in all things. (1994, p. 21)

Thus the theme of women's weakness, or woman as a threat to men and society, began to dominate scripture-based arguments on gender. These attitudes continue to prevail in traditional Muslim societies which remain highly influenced by medieval interpretation of the Qur'an and Hadith. Thus today, it is common for Muslim men to place the onus in maintaining the virtue and honour of the family and wider society on their womenfolk, punishing them sometimes for lapses that bring shame and dishonour.

However, since the nineteenth century, Muslims have had to deal with the reality of their political decline and the prevailing threat of Western culture and secular consumer values that focus on the material acquisition of possessions as the means to human fulfilment. The more that Muslims have felt their own cultural and religious way of life threatened, the more the onus has been on women to protect and nurture 'authentic' Islamic values and behaviour. Stowasser writes in this context:

> As the images of female spiritual, mental and physical defectiveness were being replaced by those of female nurturing strength and the female's importance for the struggle for cultural survival, old Bible legends ceased to be meaningful. (1994, pp. 23–4)

Although the modern era has resulted in a male-led discourse on the importance of women in maintaining Islamic values, women too have embraced the role, defending it staunchly as their own special domain, but this has led to considerable self-reflection on the rights of women within Islam, and the search for truly Muslim role models of womanhood rather than the isra'iliyyat (the Jewish women of the biblical period mentioned in the Qur'an).

The formative years of Islam's beginnings provide a number of high-profile women from among Muhammad's wives and descendants. Young Muslim women looking for female role models are likely to cite Khadijah, the Prophet's first wife, or A'isha, his youngest wife. As economic change in the Muslim world brings more women into full-time paid employment, it challenges the prominent discourse that limits women to the domestic sphere. Increasing employment opportunities bring women into the public domain, and some will achieve leadership roles in professions and government. The Qur'an has little to say on women in such roles, and the Hadith are ambiguous and contradictory. For every individual Hadith that positively endorses female equality, including even their rights to sexual satisfaction, there will be another that denigrates women as weak and foolish.

Fatima Mernissi, in her important and controversial book, *Women and Islam* (1991), looks at the most authoritative Hadith on women included in both al-Bukhari's and al-Muslim's collections, which states: 'those who entrust their affairs to a woman will never know prosperity'. The Hadith appears to be a damning indictment of women operating in public life and leadership roles traditionally assigned to men. Mernissi does not challenge the content, but uses the traditional Muslim science of contesting Hadith by analysing its *isnad* (chain of transmission). She successfully rediscovers the cultural and political context of the chain's main contributors, and seeks out their hidden motivations for taking up a misogynist position.

Certainly the Hadith could be accused of appearing to be critical of the Prophet himself who entrusted his affairs to Khadijah, the older widow with children from two previous marriages, when he was appointed her caravan manager. Khadijah traded in her own right and even asked Muhammad to become her husband. Yet there is a problem with pushing Khadijah forward as an example of female independence and leadership. Muslims like to believe that the position of women in pre-Islamic Arabia was one of atrocious exploitation and lack of rights, only corrected by the implementation of the revelation of Allah. Although Khadijah was the first to embrace Islam, her independence and assertiveness were achieved in the pre-Islamic period, suggesting that women were not as badly treated in pagan Arab society as Muslims would ideally like to believe.

After Khadijah's death the Prophet married several women, and certainly the young A'isha and Umm Salama were not passive women restricting themselves to the domestic sphere and blindly obedient to their husbands and menfolk. Mernissi points out that the Qur'an's revelation concerning women's equality with men, cited above, came about after Umm Salama asked the Prophet why the Qur'an did not speak about women as it did about men (Mernissi, 1991, pp. 118–19). Certainly this early period of Muslim history provides a number of examples of powerful women, some of whom opposed the Prophet from among his enemies in Makkah.

After the Prophet's death, the young A'isha became a public figure of some authority. Known as Muhammad's favourite wife and called the 'Mother of believers', she was immensely respected and even led Muslim armies into battle during the first civil war, when she challenged the fourth Caliph, Ali, over his failure to bring the murderers of the third Caliph to justice. Yet once again, A'isha is a double-edged sword as a role model. On the one hand she provides an example of a woman leading the community, but on the other hand she could be accused of causing the first division in the Muslim community and thus providing men with a justification to cite the Hadith's message.

Mernissi like Stowasser agrees that the independent, assertive desert Arab woman of the early period gradually disappears as patriarchy reasserts itself in the expanding Muslim world. Mernissi believes that the turning point arrived with the dynastic absolutism of the Ummayyad dynasty founded by Mu'awiyya, which finally ended the Prophet's experiment in equality and destroyed the democratic tendencies of the desert Arabs. She shows that the women of Makkah who opposed the new religion offered their own oaths of allegiance to Muhammad and the new religion, taking part in the negotiations for the city's future (1991, p. 191). She states:

> They were not going to accept the new religion without knowing exactly how it would improve their situation. The critical spirit on the part of these women towards the political leader remained alive and well during the first decades of Islam. (1991, p. 191)

Thus for many Muslim women it is not rejection of Islam that leads to their liberation, but rather an attempt to restore the rights given to them at Islam's inception, affirmed by the revelation and lived out in practice by the early generation of Muslim women. However, although Muslim women may assert that the Qur'an provided rights for women that were not achieved by Western women until many centuries later, the newly achieved rights and freedoms of the twentieth century have far surpassed anything that the original Muslims could have conceived. Many women may not be satisfied merely with a return to the rights of the Makkan and Madinan period.

There is also an ironic contradiction in the attempt to reclaim the rights and freedoms of first-generation Muslim women. In doing so, women who choose to follow their religion seriously and make the distinction between the Islam practised by the first generation, believed to be unsullied and true to the revelation, and that of those who came after, corrupted by innovation created by contact with other cultures, find themselves allied by this discourse to various revivalist and reform movements. This allegiance is likely to involve Islamic feminists with other aspects of revivalist political and religious arenas that extend far wider than the field of women's rights. Often these are the very same movements which seek to create Islamic states based on complete application of Muslim religious law, or even wage *jihad* against the West. Thus these women find their natural allies among the men of the twentieth-century fundamentalist movements who may well champion their right to wear the *hijab*, but not necessarily their right to leadership and independence. In Fatima Mernissi's terms, 'the security will never return to the city'. The veil, she asserts, intended to protect women from violence in the street, would need to be displayed everywhere (1991, p. 191).

Methodology

In this chapter we have tried to introduce the reader to a number of views put forward concerning the position of women within religious traditions, or alternatively to consider how various religious traditions regard the women within their ranks. This account cannot attempt to be comprehensive but for those whose appetites have been whetted, the field of study now provides a comprehensive literature. The most fascinating challenge for the student of religion in the area of women's studies is in the arena of methodology. The literature is often written by activists, not necessarily members of academia, and even where a contribution is from a female scholar of religion it is likely to be impassioned, engaged, polemic, written to transform the open-minded and to enrage the entrenched positions of patriarchy. It is rarely the voice of the social sciences seeking neutrality, or even that of phenomenology looking for empathetic understanding of 'the other'. Women's voices in religion are the material in which religious experience is expressed, and they have to be listened to attentively. Sometimes we will disagree with their voices; sometimes they will infuriate; on other occasions we will weep with them; and on others we will feel their anger as our own. The voice of women in religion has created a liberation narrative that requires the student to develop a means of listening and understanding.

In listening to women's voices we need to be aware that a number of problems occur in the emic realm. The question arises of who decides which of the countless and contradictory voices are authentic. Not all women agree with each other. We have seen the differences that exist between southern and northern hemispheres, and it is highly unlikely that the Western spiritual feminist from North America would find much in common with the Muslim women who belong to the Islamic Brotherhood and seek their liberation in a return to the principles of the Qur'an and exemplified in seventh-century Arabia. The peasant woman speaking from a poverty-stricken area of the majority world may not have much in common with the highly erudite theologian (a female theologian) trained in a Western university. Women too have to learn to listen to each other, recognizing a range of conflicting authentic voices, as much as men have to listen to women's demands for justice and equality. Majella Franzmann writes:

> Although the process of understanding is an academic exercise when one carries out studies in religion, this should not be taken to imply that it is a clear, objective, rational process, or that the understanding process should exclude a strong emotional and psychological aspect when a person studies by participating. (2000, p. 19)

Although studying women's experience of religion and women's religious experience can be achieved by reading secondary sources, it is better to have first-hand experience of primary sources. The student is likely to find herself examining women's testimony, poetry, films, artefacts, dialogues with each other, drama, dress, architecture, paintings, rituals, dances, liturgies and so on. All of these are texts to be interpreted in order to go deeper in understanding the religious experience of women.

Franzmann suggests both an objective and subjective approach. The student needs to assess both the text and her own reaction to it. She posits the following questions as a guide to exploring the phenomenon:

- What is the story of the phenomenon? (What has happened to it through history, and how has it developed?)

- What does it tell of the religious experience of those who cherish it or who are informed by it?

- Who has spoken of this text and attempted to really hear it and understand what it says (both believers and academics)?

In addition she suggests questions to develop reflexivity:

- Where am I standing in order to listen to the material with both my head and my heart?

- Am I listening as an outsider or as an insider, as one opposed or as one who is sympathetic?

- What kind of study has already 'tuned' my ear to hear, or has dulled my sense of hearing?

- In what ways does this phenomenon move me personally? (2000, pp. 18–19).

Armed with these few questions, the student should find herself ready to engage with the many ways in which women choose to interact with religion.

We have introduced some of the options. Women may choose to reform or transform the religion they have given their personal allegiance to, or they may develop independent religious lives of their own. Some may work within institutions, while others may prefer to ditch religion in favour of spirituality; some may attempt to reclaim women's voices from the margins, to hear their voice more distinctly, while others may change the language of sacred text and liturgy. Some may assert that they desire only the same opportunities to express their religious lives as men, while others may feel that women's spirituality is a unique experience different from men's experience even in ideal conditions without patriarchy. As we have seen, some women look back to a golden age when women were equal partners in their respective traditions before second-generation institutionalization processes set in and changed the vision of the founder(s). Their strategies involve trying to reclaim the purity of the 'original core'. Others have given up on the major World Religions and attempted to rediscover the feminine in the Goddess, while similarly, others have gone back to reclaim the body and the Earth as sacred, declaring nothing to be profane. All are involved in the process of moving women's voices from the margins to the centre. Franzmann warns us that if we are 'approaching the study of women's religious experience from a place within the academic community, we cannot presume to stand outside either the centre or the margins in order to do that' (2000, p. 135).

DISCUSSION POINTS

1 How does one distinguish between gender issues in religion or the study of religion, and women's issues? Consider examples.

2 Has gender equality been attained in the study of religion? If not, what still needs to be done, and how might it be accomplished?

3 Conferences in the study of religion sometimes have women's panels to discuss feminist or women's issues in the subject. Do you think this is appropriate, or does an all-female panel create a form of ghettoization in academia?

4 Must feminists be female? What contributions can men make in debates about women in religion, or women in the study of religion? Should men be allowed a greater voice in this area?

11

The question of truth

Ron Geaves

Chapter Outline

Religious pluralism   306
Religious pluralism and Christianity   311
Christian exclusivism   313
Christian inclusivism   314
Christian pluralism   316
Mysticism   318
Summary   323
Philosophical comments on the issue of religious truth   325
Truth and knowledge   326
Fundamentalisms   328
Syncretism   332
The rational/secular view   333
Postmodernism   334
Religious Studies   334
Conclusion   336
Discussion points   337

Alex believed in the God Chip in the brain, something created to process and trigger wonderment. It allows you to see beauty, to uncover beauty in the world. But it is not so well designed. It's a chip that has its problems.

ZADIE SMITH, 2002

The Truth has to be experienced, like the fragrance of a flower.

PREM RAWAT, 2002

As we have already seen in Chapter 6, religions are concerned with the domain of the sacred, a meeting of external and internal spaces set aside, imbued with special meaning and characteristics, to deal with ultimate concerns. Because religions have traditionally had a monopoly on the realm of the sacred, they have also provided meta-narratives, overarching ways of understanding creation and the purpose of human life that are regarded as truth. For thousands of years, the essential pursuit of knowledge was sought through the prism of religion. The earliest subjects of academia in the Western world were theology and philosophy, and their equivalents can be found in other civilizations. Religion was the repository of truth, originally embodied in revelation or inspiration and then developed through doctrine and practice sometimes to become transglobal worldviews in which, for most adherents, the truths were non-negotiable.

However, since the Enlightenment and increasingly throughout the nineteenth and twentieth centuries, religion in the West found itself under attack from those who perceived it as hampering the development of free and just human societies, repressing the freedom and growth of the individual, and suppressing other forms of knowledge – most notably science – that provided alternative ways of seeing the world. The view of the Christian theologian Farmer (1892–1981) that religion arises in human experience 'at the point where ultimate reality impinges on the human spirit' was challenged by very different interpretations from Karl Marx, Emile Durkheim and Sigmund Freud, who all basically argued in different ways that religion is the product of economic, political, social or psychological factors.

Throughout the twentieth century, the study of philosophy parted company from religion in the Western world, although they remain hand in hand as complementary pursuits of truth in the eastern worldviews. Theology remained in the secular universities, as part of the Christian heritage, continuing its attempt to make sense of the message of the gospels within the framework of a constantly changing world, convinced that the illuminating moment of encounter with God through incarnation can be renegotiated and understood. Where philosophy still dealt with religious issues, it was taught as philosophy of religion, more often in theology departments than philosophy departments, and overwhelmingly dealing with the Western philosophical tradition where it has been used primarily to continue the work of natural theology by attempting to rationally prove the existence of God, his attributes or the immortality of the soul. It has also developed a second-order activity which is to think about religion itself. John Hick makes the point that philosophical thinking about religion should not be a branch of theology but a branch of philosophy (Hick, 1990, p. 1). Revealed theology continued to apply human reason to further understanding of revelation, those truths which are ultimately considered not to be accessible to reason but primarily understood only if revealed by God.

Thus in simple terms theology remained as the insiders' attempt to grapple with one's own faith and the world perceived through the eyes of the narratives of that faith. Theology usually accepts the essential truth-claims of the religious tradition, most commonly Christianity (in the Western academic world, theology is still taken to mean Christian theology), and seeks further understanding of these claims. Certainly, the study of theology acknowledges religious definitions of reality, attempting to clarify and expand those understandings. However, increasingly the study of religion has moved into the arena of social sciences and the humanities, where it is studied as the human construction of reality rather than divinely revealed; and perceived as cultural construction rather than the domain of truth. Certainly in secular universities, the overriding search for truth defined as the pursuit for knowledge will be influenced almost completely by the scientific paradigm of discovery, and it is highly unlikely that anyone in the contemporary world of academia would expect 'cutting-edge' discoveries to come out of either the theology or religious studies departments.

On the other hand, in the last two decades we have experienced the revival of religion, manifested in new spiritualities in the West and a global resurgence where some religious believers are insisting upon the role of faith in public life. Religion is back under the spotlight as a result of high-profile events, personified by the destruction of the twin towers on 11 September 2001. The politicization of religion has brought with it conflict and violence, and various truth-claims both across and within religions are being highly contested. In the contemporary climate of identity politics and struggles for equality, religion is playing a prominent role, as it is in various rational arguments concerning the ethics crisis produced by advances in science. Nevertheless, in spite of all this, epistemologically science continues to be regarded as the best route to truth.

However, the truth-claims of both science and religion have been challenged by postmodernism and the hermeneutics of suspicion. In the postmodern situation there are so many possibilities of religious experience that the external authority of tradition breaks down. Postmodern ideas provide a self-proclaimed commitment to heterogeneity, fragmentation and difference and a deconstruction of narratives, including the overarching meta-narratives of worldviews. Peter Berger has argued that in the conditions of postmodern societies with their dramatic possibilities for choice, direct experience becomes the most compelling evidence of reality in any realm of life (Berger, 1980). This is also true of religion, where the emergence of new 'spiritualities' focuses on experience rather than traditional sources of authority. On the other hand, the existential dilemmas of an increasingly relativized society can lead to a search for certainty which favours a resurgence of religion, and a search for identity in which foundational claims for truth dominate.

Christianity, as the most exclusive of all the major religions, has had to face the crisis of religious pluralism and the tendency of the social sciences to bracket it with all the other religions, to be studied as cultural formations. Thus a prominent development in both theology and philosophy has been the degree of critical thought focused on the relationship of the Christian revelation to other world faiths. This has led, at one end of the spectrum, to some writers asserting that Christianity is not a religion. Brunner states categorically that 'Christianity is not one of the religions of the world' (Brunner, 1980, p. 258). Karl Barth explains why this is so. He argues that:

Religion is the attempted replacement of the divine work by a human manufacture. The divine reality offered and manifested to us in revelation is replaced by a concept of God arbitrarily and wilfully evolved by man. (Barth, 1956, p. 136)

Farmer, however, argues that it is possible Christianity may be in a category of its own but also included in the generic category of religions. Wilfred Cantwell Smith draws our attention to insiders and outsiders as a distinction when assessing truth-claims. He states:

> Outsider scholars have avoided the issue of sacredness by focussing upon studying or analysing scripture as if it was any other piece of literature – historical documents that can be used to reconstruct the conditions of life in a particular culture or period.
>
> Religious followers duck the issue of pluralism by asserting that there is only one scripture and that it has only one meaning – usually orthodoxy – there is a particular version of understanding that is the 'true one'. (Cantwell-Smith, 1993)

However, no insider would accept the conclusions of a scholar unless it verified his or her own truth-claims, thus insiders are privileged by religious traditions as the final authority in deciding what is or is not true.

Thus it would seem that in order to assess the issue of truth-claims, this chapter needs to at least assess the impact of modernism and postmodernism, the role of religious experience exemplified by mysticism, foundationalism and fundamentalism, insiders' and outsiders' claims of privileged access to the 'real' understanding of the religion, and finally the reaction of theology and philosophy to religious pluralism. We will begin with the latter.

Religious pluralism

The increasing contact between the world's largest religions as a result of colonization and more advanced communications has resulted in the problem of how to deal with competing truth-claims, apparently expressed in overriding meta-narratives that explain creation and the purpose of humanity within it. I stress 'apparently' because we shall see that the idea of an overriding meta-narrative that somehow defines the essence of a unique, homogeneous religious faith is itself extremely problematic. Religions do not only compete with each other in regard to truth-claims, but they also have significant divisions within each one. However, each religion can be approximately described as either inclusivist or exclusivist in regard to its attitudes towards other religions, allowing for the diversity of views that can exist within each one.

An inclusivist view generally asserts that truth exists in an independent, autonomous, self-existing, transcendental realm where it is not the property of any one culture or religion, but each has access to it either through revelation coming down from the realm of truth, or the inspiration of unique individuals who have succeeded in achieving access to it. The differences between the world's various religions is perceived as cultural or as mental interpretations arising out of human limitations in dealing with the absolute or the inexpressible. As a broad division, the eastern traditions of Hinduism, Buddhism, Jainism and Sikhism, arising out of the Indian subcontinent, and Confucianism, Taoism and Shinto, originating in China and Japan, are inclusive in their approach to each other, despite intensive historical debate concerning various doctrines whenever they have interacted through missionary activity or colonization.

As an example of inclusivism, the Jain doctrine of *anekant*, one of its three central teachings, upholds the view of many-sidedness, or manifold aspects, which asserts that the objects of knowledge are seen from many changing modes of perception. It is only in the state of omniscience that the human being can see things as they truly are. Everyone else possesses only partial knowledge of reality. This doctrine is best expressed in the famous story of the elephant and the seven blind men who can only sense parts of the animal by touch and are not able to describe the totality of the elephant. The Jains regard their notion of 'many-sidedness' as a unique contribution to Indian thought that provided the only pragmatic and realistic solution to the infinite complexity of the universe, which the Jain *tirthankaras* regarded as constituted of innumerable material and spiritual substances, each the locus of innumerable qualities, each subject to infinite variations. To the Jain philosophers, such a complexity could not possibly be grasped by either sense perception or intellectual reasoning. Any apprehension of reality by the means of sense experience and reason had to be limited to the perspective from which it is known. All knowledge claims, unless viewed from the perspective of omniscience, must be tentative, thus it is not possible to say that x is y, but rather that x may be y.

Exclusivism, on the other hand, is the assertion by believers, often based on scriptural authority, that their own religion contains the truth and all others are false or partial understandings created by human inability to know the truth unless it is revealed to them by one God or higher reality, knowledge of whom is the possession of that one religion alone. Often exclusivism is associated with the monotheistic religions, but it should be noted that although Islam and Judaism both believe that they have special relationships with an omnipresent and personal deity, neither is totally exclusive. Most Jews do not deny the possibility of human beings gaining access to righteous living by other paths, but perceive their special role, defined as 'chosen', as exemplary. Muslims on the other hand, although believing that they possess the final revelation by Allah to humanity, consider that they are part of an unfolding of one truth or one religion that belongs to God but is continuously corrupted by human beings and therefore requires renewal. Islam is exclusive in that it is believed to be the final renewal, but inclusive in that it accepts that other religions contain earlier revelations, especially those given to Jews and Christians.

However, as religions have come into contact with one another each has developed discourses or strategies that neutralize the implicit threat of another to its truth-claims. This process is known technically as 'nihilation' – the attempt to overcome or overpower one version of 'truth' with another. In practice, the less a religion has had contact with other traditions, the less developed will be its doctrines of nihilation. However, since most religions developed in historical contexts where they competed for supremacy with existing traditions, most contain such doctrines in their advent and further developed or modified them as cultures mixed and merged with each other. Even the tolerant Jains, for example, would regard their practice of *ahimsa*, or non-violence to all creatures, as being closer to the 'truth' of the omniscient than the non-vegetarian eating practices of Muslims and Jews, which are equally scripturally authorized. Arguably the most exclusive of all the major religions is Christianity and it is not surprising to find therein not only the most developed doctrines of nihilation, but also the most intense debates concerning exclusivity. These may be best expressed by the words of Alan Race:

> Is the presence of God to be found only within one community of faith? Or is he more chameleon-like than that, dancing through history, enticing men and women into faith irrespective of the cultural shape of their response? (Race, 1983, p. 1)

THE APPROPRIATION OF JESUS

Most people around the world would probably not have a problem identifying Jesus of Nazareth as the founder of Christianity, yet they might have more difficulty identifying the orthodox doctrines concerning his role in human salvation, particularly the teaching that identifies him as both fully human and fully divine. Christianity struggled in its early centuries before arriving at a developed Christology which expresses this position, and there were groups within Christianity that believed Jesus was fully human, along with those that took an opposite position and believed him to be fully divine.

However, we are not writing about the conflicting voices in the development of Christian theology with regard to the nature of Christ, but rather the difficulties incurred when a number of religions provide competing narratives that appear to be problematic for the religion that claims ownership of a particular personality. There are other religious figures that create this problem. For example, the Muslim Sufi Jalalud'din Rumi has become famed in Europe and North America as a type of universal mystic who transcends any one religious allegiance. Such depictions focus on passages in his poems where he speaks of divine love or transcending religious differences but avoids any reference to the Qur'an or Rumi's love for Muhammad. These representations appropriate Rumi for the New Age, but Muslims feel offended by them, claiming that they lose sight of the devout Muslim who is immensely respected in the world of Islam and whose writings in some parts of the Muslim world are regarded as second only to the Qur'an. However, the difficulties of appropriation experienced by Muslims are slight compared with those felt by Christians. Jesus is acknowledged by many World Religions, and rarely do their narratives conform to the Christian story. In part, the appropriation of Jesus owes much to the success of Christianity as it spread across the globe. But that is not the full story. Some followers of other religions were able to recognize in Jesus aspects of their leaders, founders or divinities and felt that he belonged to their pantheons. Others felt that Christians had come to the wrong conclusions concerning the life, death and nature of Jesus, perhaps influenced by unorthodox movements in their vicinity, and wrote conflicting narratives. It is not surprising to find that Jews are in conflict with traditional Christian narratives, but other than the firm conviction that Jesus was not divine, there is no agreement among Jews about his status. They acknowledge him as a Jew who may have been a failed messiah figure, one of many who have claimed to be the expected Jewish messiah. Others see him as a devout Jew who did not reject the law of Moses, as claimed by early Christian writings. In various theories he is said to be a Pharisee or an Essene, and the conservative orthodox Jewish scholar Jacob Emden (d. 1776) regarded Jesus as a heroic figure who brought the teachings of Judaism to a gentile world in need of civilization. Others consider Jesus (Yeshua) to be a Jew of his time, caught up in nationalist struggles against Roman imperialism and expectant of the imminent arrival of the Messianic era. He was faithful to the law of Moses, learned in Jewish scriptures and oral law and steeped in the teachings of the Pharisees (ironically dealt with harshly in the gospels). Not surprisingly he provoked the anger of the Roman authorities who were anxious to avoid Jewish insurrections and rebellions, and was crucified. Many Jews are negative concerning Jesus, but this reflects the very poor relationships between the Christian world and Jews in Europe, especially in the medieval period, rather than any deep knowledge of Jesus' life and teachings.

Surprisingly perhaps for many, Jesus (Isa) is highly regarded in Islam. Visitors to the ruined city of Fatehpur Sikri in Rajasthan, North India, built by the sixteenth-century Mughal emperor Akbar to celebrate his victories, will find the inscription: 'Jesus (peace be upon him) said "This world is a bridge. Pass over it, but build not your dwelling there."' Additional non-biblical statements of Jesus can be found in the works of the great Muslim scholar Al-Ghazali (1058–1111) and in writings of Al-Muhasibi, a ninth-century Muslim moralist. Some of these sayings are attributable to the Hadith, the collections of writings that contain Muhammad's words and deeds, the most authoritative sacred text after the Qur'an.

The Qur'an has little to say on the teachings of Jesus but it regards him highly as the prophet who preceded Muhammad. It insists upon his mortality and humanity and confirms the virgin birth and the miracles, but denies the crucifixion. He is usually referred to as the 'Son of Mary' but he is also called the messiah and the 'word of God'. He is brought into existence through God's verbal command and is described as a 'spirit from God', but remains a messenger. The idea of sonship is rigorously opposed. The description of the crucifixion follows the Gnostic line that a substitute was killed in his place and that Jesus was then taken up by God without experiencing death. In popular tradition, his lack of a physical death will bring him back to the earth again, when he will triumphantly herald the last days. In this respect it is important to bear in mind that Islamic theology tends towards 'manifest success'. God cannot be associated with failure, and nor would he allow his messenger and beloved to die an ignominious death. Manifest success is vindicated by the role of Jesus in the last days. Although Christians might consider that Jesus is demoted to a prophet in Islam, it is important to bear in mind that the position of *rasul* (a messenger who brings a revelation) is the most elevated possible for a human being, and is considered to be a position of deepest intimacy and favour with God. There is no one higher in creation than a prophet, and it is arguable that among the prophets the position of Jesus, for pious Muslims, is second only to Muhammad.

In Islam Jesus remains human, but interestingly many Hindus agree with Christians that Jesus was an incarnation of God. The *Bhagavad Gita*, perhaps the most influential of all Hinduism's countless sacred texts, teaches that whenever evil is in the ascendancy, and righteousness forgotten, God incarnates to save his devotees and restore the truth. Such manifestations are known as *avatars* and it is among the Vaishnavites, devotees of Vishnu, that one finds the most developed articulation of the idea that God (Vishnu) incarnates in various manifestations. It is a common occurrence to find statues of Jesus in Vishnu temples, where it is claimed that he was an incarnation of Vishnu. In addition, many Hindus claim that Jesus spent the missing years of his life in Kashmir. The Hindu text, *Bhavishya Mahapurana*, contains ten verses that indicate that Jesus was in Kashmir during the reign of King Shalivahan, around 39–50 CE. The king is claimed to have met Jesus near Srinagar. Upon being asked to identify himself, he claimed to be Isa Masih (Jesus the Messiah). Certainly throughout Central Asia, Kashmir, Ladakh and Tibet, there are oral traditions that Jesus visited these areas, including India, and in some accounts he survived the crucifixion and is buried in Kashmir.

Some Buddhists also believe in the narratives of a visit by Jesus to Northern India and the Himalayan region. Tibetan Buddhists claim that he was taught Samatha meditation and gained supernatural powers before going back to Palestine to teach. Buddhists focus upon Jesus' teaching concerning patience, non-violence and compassion, and argue that it was in contradiction to the dominant themes in Jewish law. In addition they argue that the Book of Seven Seals mentioned in Revelations bears remarkable similarities to the Mahayana text The Perfection of Wisdom, which is sealed with seven seals. In Mahayana Buddhist narratives Jesus is a *bodhisattva*, a buddha who delays final release into nirvana out of compassion for all suffering beings. The narrative of his second coming to the world supports the view that he is a *bodhisattva*, for such rebirths are common belief in Buddhism.

The narrative of Jesus' connection with India is also picked up by a number of Western esoteric movements and has become prevalent among New Age practitioners. The most influential work that has influenced New Age belief concerning Jesus is *The Aquarian Gospel of Jesus the Christ*. Believed to have been channelled through Levi Dowling (1844–1911), a Protestant minister, soldier and medical practitioner who claims that he had a vision in his childhood to 'build a white city'. The book was eventually transcribed to him through Visel, the Goddess of Wisdom or the Holy Breath, who also gave Levi access to the Akashic Records, the imperishable records of all life. Here he was provided with the details of the life of Jesus, including the years not covered by the gospels. The book contains details of the journeys and deeds of Jesus in Northern India, Tibet, Egypt, Assyria and Greece before his return to teach in Samaria and Judea. The book asserts that Jesus was the master of the astrological Piscean age, and that now the world has entered the spiritual sign of Aquarius and is ready to receive the true teachings of the Christ. It is this claim that makes it one of the early texts of the New Age movement, coming out in its eighteenth edition in 1964. Little is known of Levi's life, but the stories of the journeys to India conform closely to those in the *Bhavishya Mahapurana* and more research needs to be done on the influence of the Theosophists with regard to bringing these narratives into circulation in Europe and North America.

Not surprisingly it is Christians who feel most aggrieved by the alternative versions of the life and role of Jesus, and there are a number of sites on the internet written by Christians which deconstruct the various narratives recounted by other religions. It is these attempts by Christians to defend their narrative as the 'truth' which should interest scholars of religion. It is not the task of the study of religion to ascertain the 'facts' of the various versions, but there are issues here of ownership, appropriation and the reasons for such narrative constructions. No other religious figure seems to have gripped the religious imagination across the world to the same degree as Jesus, and the reasons for this are surely worth exploring by the scholar.

Further Reading

Cragg, Kenneth (1999), *Jesus and the Muslim.* Oxford: Oneworld.
Barker, Gregory (ed.) (2005), *Jesus in the World's Faiths: Leading Thinkers from Five Religions Reflect on His Meaning.* Orbis Books.
Dowling, L. (1977), *The Aquarian Gospel of Jesus the Christ,* 24th edn. London: L. N. Fowler.

Religious pluralism and Christianity

It is assumed that only in recent history did each of the different religions of the world develop the capability of substantial knowledge of the others unless competing in the same geographical locality. It remains true even today, when many of us have access to the teachings of the major world faiths, that if I had been born in India, I would probably be a Hindu; if in Saudi Arabia, probably a Muslim; if in Tibet, probably a Buddhist; but as I was born in England I am more likely to be a Christian. But knowledge of other religions and cultures is likely to lead to the question: does my religiosity depend upon the religion that I was born into? In other words, would the practising Christian be a practising Muslim if born elsewhere in the Muslim world, or vice versa?

However, in today's world global communications and the subsequent democratization of knowledge provide millions of Western Christians with access to the teachings of other faiths. For scholars like John Hick, the most important factor influencing the development of a theology of other faiths in Christianity has been the recent 'explosion of knowledge among Christians in the West' concerning the other great religious traditions of the world (Hick, 1987, p. 17). Alan Race comments on how movement of people and information has 'shattered older conceptions of the religious history of the world which viewed the faiths as confined, culturally and geographically, within particular boundaries' (Race, 1983, p. 1). In multicultural nations such as those of Western Europe or Northern America, traditionally associated with Christianity, there is more opportunity for meetings at work or as neighbours between men and women from different cultures and faiths. In addition Race comments on the work of academia, filtering down into the school systems, providing many Christians with at least a working knowledge of other faith traditions (Race, 1983, p. 2).

In addition, many Western Christians have become far more knowledgeable concerning the relations between missionary activity and European colonialism, and therefore more sensitive to the intellectual domination of other peoples through the doctrines of religious exclusivism. As expressed by Hick:

> . . . the realization that Christian absolutism, in collaboration with acquisitive and violent human nature, has done much to poison the relationships between the Christian minority and the non-Christian majority of the world's population by sanctifying exploitation and oppression on a gigantic scale. (Hick, 1987, p. 17)

It is also a factor that Christianity has had to face up to the realization that it is unlikely that the world will embrace it as the one true religion and will continue to remain religiously diverse as in the past, if not more so. In addition to acknowledging the persistence of other religions as viable spiritual alternatives, those who have studied other faiths have accepted that they possess moral and ethical truths of great integrity, writings that contain poetic beauty and wisdom, and figures of spiritual statue that rival those of Christianity itself.

As a result of the above factors, a number of challenges to Christian exclusivity have arisen, not least because any interfaith encounter has to deal with a critical position maintained by other faith representatives that the normative Christian position is one of superiority. As expressed by Paul Knitter:

> The uniqueness of Christianity has taken on a larger mythological meaning. It has come to signify the unique definitiveness, absoluteness, normativeness, superiority of Christianity in comparison with other religions of the world. (Knitter, 1987, p. vii)

The same author has identified three bridges to other faith traditions as Christian theologians have attempted to build a theology of other faiths that is able to acknowledge the authenticity of other faith commitment, while maintaining their position within a Christian framework that acknowledges the central truths of the gospels. These are as follows:

> The ethico-practical bridge that pragmatically looks to the suffering of humanity and practical solutions to alleviate it;
>
> the theologico-mystical bridge, best articulated in the writings of Wilfred Cantwell Smith, that seeks to discover a common essence, a transcendental reality that lies behind the historical forms of the major world faiths;
>
> the historico-cultural bridge, best articulated by John Hick, and the position that attempts to address the criticism that it is necessary to go outside the traditional Christian framework as it is impossible to judge the truth claims of another religion or culture from the insider position of one's own. (Knitter, 1987, pp. ix–xi)

The above positions tend to be formulated by those who have attempted to move Christian theology from an exclusivist stance to a greater awareness of plurality and a more inclusivist position. The tension between exclusive truth-claims and acknowledgement of the truths of other faiths is built into the paradox of Christianity's claim to be simultaneously universal and exclusive. The message of the gospels and the act of God incarnating in the world is of salvation for all humanity, but this is usually interpreted as requiring a conscious act of acceptance of Jesus Christ as saviour. Thus Donald Dawe correctly identifies the problem of developing a theology of other faiths: 'spiritually and intellectually the root problem is one of finding new ways for the Christian community to relate the particularity and universality of its faith' (Dawe, 1980, p. 14). In their attempts to do so, Christian theologians can be broadly categorized into three positions – exclusivism, inclusivism and pluralism – but all three arise primarily from the question whether adherents of other religions can obtain salvation.

Christian exclusivism

The exclusivist position adopts the belief that all other religions are superseded by Christianity and, at best, contain only partial truths in comparison with the fullness of truth manifest in God's incarnation and expressed within the Christian community. Although Christians can engage in dialogue with the members of other religious communities, their primary aim should be to proclaim the Gospel to the members of other religious communities. Those Christians who maintain this position are unlikely to admit a problem in acknowledging the truth-claims of other religions, simply asserting that the Christian faith demands exclusive loyalty to Christ. The revelation in Jesus Christ is the sole criterion by which all religions, including Christianity, can be understood and evaluated (Race, 1983, p. 11). Other religions are perceived as the various attempts of human beings to understand their existence. The exclusivist stance is best expressed in its purest form by the Protestant theologian Karl Barth, who argued that the revelation of God as understood by Christianity 'abolishes religion' and thereby the practice of all other religions is considered to be 'unbelief', error and 'sinful blindness' (Barth, 1956).

In Barth's view, the revelation documented in the gospels and epistles of the New Testament is a declaration of a truth concerning humanity's salvation and the nature of God that is completely new, and the moment that it is received it provides the impetus for a relationship with other religions that perceives them as only human inventions to be judged solely as limited attempts by human beings to know the divine, and thus to be the ground for missionary activity: the preaching of the gospel. Revelation rather than dialogue is the means of reconciliation for all humanity, thus Christianity is not to be included in the realm of comparative religion since it belongs in the realm of revelation, whereas other religions are sincere but misguided untruths. Race points out a vital distinction in this perspective, that it is not the historical Christianity as a developed religion replete with tradition, institutions and hierarchical structures that is being compared with other religions, but rather the message of Jesus Christ; and thus Christianity alone has a divine mandate to be a missionary faith (Race, 1983, p. 13).

The exclusivist position, expressing traditional Christian doctrines, emphasizes the particularistic claims to universalism and is critiqued by Dinoia, who argues that although it might recognize parallels with other religions these are merely cognates, parallel understandings which arise out of human reason; but this fails to resolve the problem of alternative revelations with their own particularistic claims to universality that seem to be embedded in the doctrinal schemes of major religious communities (Dinoia, 1992, p. 164). The other monotheisms of Judaism and Islam spring to mind immediately. Although Judaism could be seen as a special case, preceding Christianity as a partial revelation of God's truth, Islam remains problematic.

Thus the main criticism of the exclusivist position is that it reduces any discussion between rival truth-claims to respective assertions of 'we are right, you are wrong' but with no means of verification. Any dialogue would be fraught with overcoming the difficulty of pre-judgement and could not provide a theology of religions that in any way acknowledged the position that adherents of other religions had towards their own doctrines and practices. Thus Dawe is able to say that the dilemma of loyalty to the truth as perceived through one's own tradition, and sensitivity to the truth in the lives of people of faith in other traditions, is not resolved (Dawe, 1980, p. 3). It is also problematic that the Barthian position makes a comparison with the message of the gospels, perceived to be unproblematic in interpretation and distinct from the institutions of Christianity. In this respect, he petrifies the Christian religion and then compares it with reified versions of other religions. In this sense there is no acknowledgement of recent scholarship in the study of religion that recognizes that religions survive by being continuously in process, adapting and changing in the light of new circumstances and new knowledge, even as early as the writings of their primary sacred texts. As stated by Race, 'a reified faith is much less likely to be open to other forms of faith than one which has learnt adaptation in the field of serious intellectual debate' (Race, 1983, p. 6).

Christian inclusivism

Dinoia outlines some of the positions taken up by Christian inclusivists as follows:

1   Other religions could play some role in the divine plan of salvation;

2   Members of other religious communities could be in fellowship with God and thus in some hidden way be members of the Christian community;

3   Members of other religious communities could possess an implicit faith, which could become explicit in Christianity;

4   Members of other religious communities could perform good actions, having a salvific value for them;

5 Christians could engage in dialogue with the members of other religious communities;

6 Christians should collaborate with the members of other religious communities in projects of common human concern. (Dinoia, 1992, pp. 15–19)

Christian inclusivism can work when it is understood that certain other religions contain moral or spiritual truths which are compatible with Christian doctrines or, even if perceived to be erroneous compared with the Christian revelation, can still function as mechanisms for progress along a path regarded as godly or as benefiting human moral and ethical behaviour.

However, inclusivists both accept and reject the teachings of other religions. They accept the above areas of comparability or agreement but still have serious reservations as to whether salvation is achievable outside Christianity. Thus Christianity is still regarded as the final revelation but other faiths can be perceived as part of God's plan for humanity to attain salvation. Herein an essential distinction is made between the man Jesus and the cosmic Christ. Jesus' life and death remain unique to the final bridging of God and humanity, but it is Christ who has been working in a hidden fashion in all that is best in other religious traditions.

Although for Christians there are certain benefits derived from this position, not least in dialogue, but also in the non-requirement for missionary activity which is often greeted negatively by other world faiths and has certain historical links with colonialism, theories of inclusivism are still imposed on other religious communities and remain open to accusations of arrogance. Thus the inclusivist theologian is not only vulnerable to 'objections by members of that community (and others) to the effect that he had misstated or misconstrued its doctrines or that he had mistaken merely permitted opinions for doctrines in that community' (Dinoia, 1992, p. 157); but also the criticism that the unique worldview of the insider is being distorted to fit a Christian framework.

Race makes the point that 'if several ways of salvation really exist, parallel in some manner, then we are faced with a great dispersal, not a spiritual convergence' (Race, 1983, p. 53), which creates problems for the Christian belief in a final rapprochement for all humanity. Inclusivism also raises significant questions concerning the knowledge of insiders and outsiders about a particular faith. Dialogue might well entail the necessity to be 'truthful' in what is perceived to be erroneous in the other's patterns of action and belief. Even the theologian well-versed in knowledge of another faith is likely to be selective in interpretation and in which aspects of the religion he investigates. They are also likely to find their expertise challenged from within the other religious tradition. Placed into the reverse situations, Christians may have to resolve issues of ownership where other religions, for example Hinduism and Islam, maintain their own inclusivist views regarding Jesus but with very different narratives concerning his role. One of the main criticisms of Christian interaction with other faiths from within is that Christianity has a poor record in listening to the viewpoint of others, and in this respect inclusivism still does not take the other religion as seriously as it does Christianity (Driver, 1987, p. 208). Mark Heim makes the point that two assumptions need to be upheld in the inclusivist position, first that Christ is central in the world's salvation, and second that this is the authentic salvation offered to all humanity (Heim, 1998, p. 13). However, not only may other religions have an alternative view, they may not view salvation as even being the essential goal of human life. As pointed out by Dinoia: 'religious communities actually propose distinctive aims for human life, in which soteriological doctrines have varying degrees of significance and varying sorts of affinities with Christian doctrines about salvation' (Dinoia, 1992, p. 165).

Christian pluralism

John Carmen makes the point that if God is able to grant salvation to those outside of the Church, or at least take human beings a substantial part of the way, 'it is only one step further to affirm that the divine grace making possible the salvation of non-Christians normally comes through the rituals of their own religious communities' (Carmen, 1980, p. 88). However, pluralism still tends to focus also on the soteriocentric principle, but differs from inclusivism in that it embraces the view that salvation can be achieved in various ways, rather than viewing it in a Christocentric fashion. In many ways, pluralism can be seen as a recent phenomenon arising out of a contemporary reaction to exclusivism and the erosion of traditional authority in Western societies. Once unquestioned authority is challenged, along with the view of there only being one truth, there arises the problem of how to assimilate or deal with the vast range of other worldviews. Race expresses the pluralist position very succinctly:

> . . . what they wish to establish is that the divergences between beliefs are comprehended least by the model which views the truth of one expression as automatically entailing the falsity of another which is at odds with it. Truth, especially in religious matters, belongs within a whole context of life and culture. To say that the divine is manifest in different ways in different cultures is not to sidestep the issue of truth in a religiously diverse world, but is to pave the way for a dialogue in which the cognitive discrepancies can be better evaluated in a wider setting. (Race, 1983, p. 144)

The leading proponents of pluralism are John Hick, Wilfred Cantwell Smith, Ernst Troelsch, W. E. Hocking, Fritjof Schuon, Ninian Smart and Arnold Toynbee, but whereas both exclusivism and inclusivism can find their roots in interpretations of the gospels, pluralism has little pedigree within Christian theology, although its origins can be found in liberal Protestant thinkers such as Paul Tillich and Friedrich Schleiermacher, and also among Roman Catholic monks who lived and worked in India such as Bede Griffiths and Abhedshiktananda. Schleiermacher accepted the fact of a universal religious consciousness in human beings and perceived Christian piety as one particular form of human religion, recognizing other religions as positive expressions of the same common religious feeling. The emphasis on feeling as opposed to ritual practice is common among most liberal Protestants, whereas Roman Catholics are more inclined to acknowledge the validity of other religious practices. Very often, however, as noted by Race, pluralist views begin with the validity of the idea of common religious experience which is regarded as an authentic but indescribable encounter with the divine but characterized differently within the traditions (Race, 1983, p. 139). In this respect such thinking builds upon the ideas of the numinous first expressed by Rudolf Otto. In the realm of religious experience, Christians belong in the world's religious life as one strand of faith alongside others, as equals with a partial understanding of the divine shared with others. There may be an underlying assumption that humanity's knowledge of the divine can be pooled collectively from all the major religions in order to arrive at a fuller understanding.

Most pluralists see the differences between religions as arising from the historical development of religions as institutions, where both practices and doctrines are perceived as human constructions, influenced by culture and power relations. Even sacred texts are regarded as the work of human inspiration, although this flies in the face of many core beliefs within individual religions. Wilfred Cantwell Smith, for example, distinguished between faith and religion, where the former is perceived as an ongoing continuum of relations between the human being and the divine, an innate aspect of human spiritual life in which major occurrences have from time to time established new concentrations and understandings, but the latter is perceived as a human construction, partly originating in the Western world's rational need to classify through identifying difference (Cantwell-Smith, 1967, p. 73). Thus he questions whether 'religion' is a reality at all, and suggests that it distorts human spirituality more than it understands it. He prefers to talk about 'cumulative tradition' and 'faith' as more accurately describing human religiousness than 'religions'.

John Hick, primarily as a result of his pastoral experiences with other faith traditions in Birmingham, England, asked the question of himself primarily, and then publicly: 'Do we regard the Christian way as the only way, so that salvation is not to be found outside it; or do we regard the other great religions of mankind as other ways of life and salvation?' (Hick, 1973, p. 120). His now famous solution was to offer up the idea of a 'Copernican revolution' in which Christ was replaced by God at the centre of various orbiting religions including Christianity (1973, p. 131). Thus the World Religions become religio-cultural manifestations to various peoples of the same underlying reality. Their differences can be put down to different mentalities of the nations or tribes that received revelation or inspiration, and then developed further sophistication and diversity as a result of cultural expressions in history (1973, p. 139).

These various understandings of the different religions as rivers of spiritual experiences, containing a common core at their experiential roots where contact is made with an ultimate divine reality at some point in history but then transforms into established traditions through complex cultural interaction, are not without their critics both from within the religions and from secular atheists. First of all, the underlying premise that there is a single essence that links all religions has been criticized by many, perhaps most notably by Katz in his writings on mysticism. John Cobb also notes that true dialogue can only begin with the recognition that each religion is unique with different end goals, and that any idea of a common essence should be abandoned (Cobb, 1990, pp. 81–96).

We have already commented that most pluralists still work with the paradigm of salvation, usually conceived in terms of a move from self-centredness to reality-centredness, thus positing mystical experience as the ultimate or authentic religious experience. However, it is here that a basic contradiction is discovered. It may be true as claimed by the pluralists that there is no way to ascertain if the factual claims that arise as part of tradition are no more than the cultural expressions of one way of faith, therefore equally limited departures from the 'essence', but it is not on the basis of these aspects that major differences between religions are asserted. As noted by Race, very often the major conflicting truth-claims arise primarily in connection with the revelatory aspects of a religion which lie at its core and in its origins (Race, 1983, p. 146).

In addition, most inclusivists are highly selective as to which religious expressions are permitted entry into their framework of universality. Hick and Cantwell Smith operate within a World Religions paradigm that acknowledges the truths of traditions that had their origin in what is known as the post-Axial period. Neither is able to handle with equal weight indigenous traditions or new religions.

Dewi Hughes argues that there is no evidence for the pluralist view expressed by Hick and others. He is particularly alarmed that the pluralists define themselves as Christians, and sees the cause as lying in liberal Protestant theology which he blames for 'moving the focus of theology from the objective to the subjective', thus playing into the hands of scientific rationalism and placing human beings and their needs at the heart of religion rather than God (Hughes, 1996, p. 232). He also argues that the spirit of pluralism is closer to certain kinds of Hinduism than it is to Christianity (Hughes, 1996, p. 232).

However, perhaps more damning than all the critiques that have to be faced by the pluralists is the one that those who teach religions from such a perspective are also guilty of dogmatizing and proselytizing. This is particularly pertinent in the light of the pluralist's antipathy to exclusivism. Peter Clarke and Peter Byrne, for example, argue that 'the pluralist hypothesis itself becomes an exclusivist religious truth to which all other religions are a preparation' (Clarke and Byrne, 1993, p. 93).

Mysticism

Once John Hick acknowledges that all the main traditions contest that God is infinite beyond description, transcending the grasp of the human mind (Hick, 1973, p. 139), he shows himself to be influenced by a group of thinkers who perceive the mystical experience as the underlying and authentic experience of the divine reality. This is succinctly expressed by Frithjof Schuon in his *The Transcendent Unity of Religions* where he asserts that all the major religions contain 'an esoteric core that affords mystical participation in the form of transcendence usually called the divine'. Schuon acknowledges that most followers of a religion never penetrate to this unifying core, but those who do so arrive at something known also to the spiritual elite of other religions (Schuon, 1975).

Stace (1960), Parrinder (1976) and Smart (1978) also argue that the mystical experience has enough common features, in spite of the obvious differences arising from a multiplicity of religious traditions in which they occur, to be defined as universal. Stace provides a seven-point categorization to assert the universalism of the mystical experience: 1) a unifying vision in which the One is perceived by the senses in and through many objects; 2) the One is apprehended as the inner life, or presence in all things, so that 'nothing is really dead'; 3) the experience brings a sense of reality; 4) there is a feeling of joy and peace resulting in fulfilment; 5) there is a feeling of the presence of the sacred; 6) there is a feeling of paradoxicality; and 7) the experience is ineffable or beyond description (Stace, 1960, pp. 131–2).

This belief in the universal characteristics of mysticism has often been labelled as the 'perennial philosophy', a term first used by Aldous Huxley, an ardent perennialist himself. Recently the debate has been reopened by a series of articles and books, not yet translated into English, by Leonardo Boff, the eminent Brazilian liberation theologian. However in Katz's seminal chapter of his edited work *Language, Epistemology and Mysticism*, he argues that mystical experience itself is shaped by the doctrines and practices which the practitioner brings to the experience, as well as by differences of interpretation arising from cultural and religious differences. This seriously challenges the idea of a universal mystical experience that underlies the various religious expressions (Katz, 1978).

Katz correctly identifies three positions used by universalists:

1 All mystical experiences are identical, and even their descriptions demonstrate enough similarity to prove that the experiences transcend cultural or religious diversity.

2 All mystical experiences are identical but the accounts presented by mystics of their experiences are varied according to the symbolic languages that arise out of the diversity of religious/cultural systems in which the mystics lived and practised their spiritual life.

3 Mystical experiences can be divided into a number of 'types' which cut across religious/cultural borders. Once again the language used to describe the experiences is bound by religion and culture, but the experiences are not. (1978, pp. 23–4)

Katz argues that his entire paper is a 'plea for the recognition of differences' (Katz, 1978, p. 25) in the study of mysticism, and disagrees with all the above positions in that he asserts that the 'experience itself as well as the form in which it is reported is shaped by concepts which the mystic brings to, and which shape, his experience' (Katz, 1978, p. 26).

Hick disagrees and makes the point that within the mystical strands of the major theistic World Religions the distinction is made between 'the Real or the Ultimate or Divine in sich (in him/her/itself) and the Real as conceptualised and experienced by human beings' (Hick, 1990, p. 117). He acknowledges that the mystical experience is apprehended by human consciousness and thus influenced by the categorizing processes of the 'cognizing mind' which will be influenced in its interpretive frameworks by the religion and culture of the mystic (Hick, 1990, p. 119). Katz's oppositional position to the universalists argues that it is more probable that they undergo different experiences (even if sharing some common characteristics) due to the diverse conceptual frameworks and religious disciplines in which they participate. The author of this chapter takes a different tack and suggests that the commonality of the experience arises out of the similarities shared by contemplative or spiritual disciplines. These are listed as follows:

1 The narrowing of the field of consciousness so as to direct all the faculties to one centre;

2 The process of mental purification with the ideal of eliminating negative thoughts and emotions;

3 A conscious or contemplative attentiveness during the performance of daily or mundane activities;

4 Restraint on physical and sense activity, often resulting in dietary restrictions, fasting, celibacy and restrictions upon unnecessary speech;

5 Attempts to achieve inner stillness through meditation, contemplation or prayer;

6 Non-possessiveness which results in either the restriction of material possessions or the renunciation of the idea of ownership;

7 Ethical and moral behaviour embracing the ideal of amity which restricts reactive or retaliatory behaviour;

8 Daily mental disciplines that attempt to maintain the focus of the practitioner in the 'here and now';

9 Meditations or reflections upon the 'reality' of existence;

10 A common life – living within like-minded communities of practitioners;

11 Negation of the ego. (Geaves, 2003, p. 30)

However, it is not so much the contested argument over the universalism of the mystical experience that interests us here but the questions raised by the possibility of such an experience on the issue of truth-claims. As pointed out by Hick, the mystical experience appears to be an unmediated or direct apprehension of the divine that in itself is not 'distorted by the mechanisms of the human mind' (Hick, 1990, p. 119). Mysticism takes us beyond the usual position of most religions, where the intention is the experienced doctrine. Where the doctrine becomes a truth to be personally experienced it leads to the subjective position of 'I believe it because it is true – It is true because I believe it' (Vroom, 1989, p. 308). Truth is being defined as the experience of a life which conforms to the rules of the religion, interiorized by a process offering an alternative reality perceived in opposition to 'normal reality', which is categorized as ignorance or imperfection. When the doctrine is understood and lived through religious practices, moral behaviour and ethical codes, one is able to perceive a deeper truth. In this sense, truth is regarded as a state of being. The mystical path offers a way of training that leads to progressive insight in which the person is sanctified, and the condition of ignorance or imperfection reversed.

MYSTICISM

The study of mysticism is a contentious and theoretically complex issue broadly divided into two camps: the perennialists and the constructivists. The perennialists argue that mystical experience is a common dimension that extends across most major World Religions, providing an essence or core that transcends external differences. The idea is that mystical experiences transcend other religious phenomena because they provide a universal state of consciousness or emotional condition, based upon an attempt by exceptional human beings to transcend ordinary existence in the pursuit of an immediate experience of the divine reality. This idea is attractive to many, and methodologically provides the basis for a comparative approach to the study of mysticism. In addition, such an approach was able to critique the late-nineteenth-century evolutionary view of religion in which Christianity represented the pinnacle of human religious endeavours.

The constructivists, on the other hand, have observed that the category of 'mysticism' has been informed by Western cultural presuppositions of universality, and by the objectivity of analytical language. In other words, 'mysticism' is as much a construction of specific cultural locations as it is a part of human religious experience. Recent studies have tended to focus on the concerns and assumptions of the creators of the category 'mysticism', as well as on the experiences of elite religious individuals regarded as being in touch with divine being.

As with the term 'religion', the term 'mysticism' is rooted in European intellectual history. The process whereby 'mysticism' has come to represent an authentic experience of the divine, to be contrasted with an inauthentic or lesser involvement with religious affiliation (e.g. ritual practice, allegiance to institutions or adherence to doctrine) is part of twentieth-century Western processes of secularization, and the separation of religion and 'the spiritual' into two separate and conflicting domains. Mysticism has not always been viewed in such a light, and such categories that we may now perceive as distinct were not always so, and remain inseparable in many non-Western cultures.

Even in a Western context, mysticism has changed its meaning over the centuries. The basic etymology of the word is probably derived from the Greek root mūo (to close), and the adjective mūstikos was used to refer to ancient Mediterranean mystery religions which were secretive and exclusive with regard to their rites. The idea of being secretive and mysterious remains with us in common usage, for example 'Mystic Meg' as a title for a well-known psychic and astrologer.

In medieval Christianity mysticism was used to describe allegorical interpretations of sacred texts, especially where such interpretations were seen to suggest an esoteric insight into the reality of God. Similar developments can be observed in Judaism and Islam in the same period. From this arose the connection to the idea of a universal experiential dimension of religion in which mystics were somehow perceived to transcend their individual religious traditions. The phenomenology of religion completed the transformation, turning 'mysticism' into a pan-religious label for certain types of experience that could be compared with each other. Ninian Smart completes the process by perceiving 'mysticism' as the 'ideal type' for the experiential dimension of religion.

Postcolonial studies have challenged the knowledge hierarchies and categories established in the colonial era concerning European constructions of the Orient. In this process, the idea of an objective category of experience, to be labelled 'mysticism', has come under scrutiny. 'Mystical' traditions and experiences remain a category of study to be investigated, but to be explored within specific cultural and historic contexts. It is no longer possible to identify mysticism as a universal experience independent of linguistic construction, power dynamics, social function and other cultural forces. It may well be time to reconsider the category 'mysticism' and speak of 'mysticisms' instead, in order to avoid essentializing a category which itself has served as the ultimate symbol of a religious essence that transcends culture.

Bibliography

De Certeau, M. (1992), *The Mystic Fable*. Chicago: University of Chicago.

Katz, S. (1978), 'Language, epistemology and mysticism', in Steven Katz (ed.), *Mysticism and Philosophical Analysis*. London: Sheldon Press.

King, R. (1999), *Orientalism and Religion*. London: Routledge.

Sharf, R. (1998), 'Experience', in M. C. Taylor (ed.), *Critical Terms for Religious Studies*. Chicago: Chicago University Press.

Yet there is an even higher truth which is the absolute being or God as perfect and eternal being, which remains transcendent and self-existing. Vroom points out that if God, some other perfect entity or state of consciousness alone is the absolute truth, then that implies that human knowledge is never completely true, but rather partial and infallible (Vroom, 1989, p. 317). God as perfect knowledge is claimed to be accessed by the mystical experience, but now truth is understood in the sense of experiencing the absolute. Even within a single religious tradition there may be those who stress the acceptance of doctrine as truth, and others who place good conduct in the foreground, but those who pursue contemplative or meditational paths have focused primarily on the inward experience.

The mystical claim to a higher knowledge of reality through unmediated experience challenges the idea of truth as a result of discursive reasoning, and lays claim to a higher-order apprehension of reality. Thus in some religious traditions, notably those originating in the East, those who pursue paths to mystical union not only assert a higher truth than that of 'normal' sense perception, but also claim a more rarified vision of the truth-claims of the tradition they originate within. In order to apprehend the ultimate it is necessary to transcend the dualism present in thought and in everyday reality. Thus to attain awareness of transcendent unity, it is necessary to pass beyond beliefs, even those of religious traditions. Many of the exercises of mystical paths attempt to empty the practitioner of thought. In Zen Buddhism, the koan (short epigrammatic and paradoxical statement) functions as a contradictory riddle unsolvable by the discursive reason but capable of transferring a different kind of knowledge.

In addition to the critique of Katz, which calls into question the idea of a unitive experiential knowledge at the heart of the major world faiths, others have commented that an immediate experience of God, even if it is assumed to be possible, is a rare occurrence even among those who pursue the means to its attainment. Vroom notes that it is unlikely to be the achievement of scholars within the tradition, or common to the majority of believers (Vroom, 1989, p. 317). So even though many traditions relate such experiences to the truth, its attainment is restricted to a small elite and it may generate conflict within religious traditions whose revelation or doctrines claim that salvation or liberation is available to all through some kind of divine dispensation. However, Race comments that the assertion of the mystical experience as the meeting place between religions is not meant to affirm that all faiths have at their heart the same truth, but that God has been revealing himself to all peoples throughout time (Race, 1983, p. 60).

Summary

Even though Christianity is the ideal case study as an example of a religion with exclusive truth-claims, Christians in the Western world have had to wrestle with the demands of a changing world and consider the competing truth-claims of other world faiths. Race makes the point that 'Christianity has never been understood merely as an abstract faith or an esoteric theory in a sense which implies a disjunction between divine revelation and historical happenings' (Race, 1983, p. 138). Thus actual events and cultural transformations impact on theology, and it is inevitable that a theology of other faiths would have to be worked out in the twentieth and twenty-first centuries. The choices were presented by Farmer earlier in the twentieth century as between exclusivism and some kind of inclusivism. Farmer stated that either Christians should perceive the other world faiths as 'totalities' in error, despite occasional 'rightnesses', because Christ is absent (Farmer, 1939, p. 206); or, as stated by Partridge, summarizing Farmer's work:

> More accurately, 'living religion' is the result of, on the one hand, the initiative of divine revelation, and, on the other, humanity's self-conscious apprehension of, and response to, that approach. That is to say, revelation is, to a large extent, defined in terms of religious experience: 'all religious experience, if it is living and formative, has the quality of revelation in it, has within it the sense that the divine Thou makes himself known to man in his personal situation'. (Partridge, 1998, p. 5)

Truth-claims lie at the heart of religion, and any attempt to make such a radical choice, as presented by Farmer, will involve the believer in a cognitive decision that entails a risk of being mistaken if there is an objective truth standard that belongs to the transcendent.

Farmer appears to belong to the school of thought that looks for rightnesses in experience, and this way forward is regarded by the sociologist of religion Peter Berger as the most profitable for religious adherents in view of the secularization and pluralization premises. Berger argues that heresy (literally derived from the word for 'choice' in Greek) has been transformed from a dissident to a normative position in modern societies which celebrate diversity (Berger, 1980). However, experience is not the only way to regard religious truth-claims as doctrines; moral codes and ritual also have to be taken into account, and can be significant stumbling blocks for inclusive theories. Revelationary religions such as Islam regard their practices as God-given and therefore to be maintained and promoted as the correct way to worship, with other religions seen as in error. For many Christians, the focus will be on doctrine as derived from sacred scripture interpreted in a literalist manner.

A number of positions become available to us in assessing the truth-claims of various religions. We may decide that our commitment to a particular religion as true negates the possibility for believing any other religion to be true. Alternatively we may believe that all or some of the religions contain an inner core that is universal, the differences being due to historical development in diverse cultures, possibly where intercultural communication was undeveloped. On the other hand, we may decide that the truth-claims of religions are unverifiable as they consist of the personal beliefs of the adherent which can only be shared by other like-minded human beings. However, such subjectivity could lead to the position that since different religions cannot all be true, even though each one claims to be the definitive statement on the human condition, probably none of them are true. If we position ourselves with the latter, then religions cannot be judged as systems of truth and falsehood, although we may still consider them in terms of better or worse. Hick makes the point that we can no more judge the truth-claims of a religion than we can a culture or civilization. He goes on to state that 'the religions, in the sense of distinguishable religio-cultural streams within human history, are expressions of the diversities of human types and temperaments and thought forms' (Hick, 1990, p. 112).

Philosophical comments on the issue of religious truth

So far we have concentrated on the case study of a religion associated with exclusive truth-claims, and explored attempts by theologians to resolve the paradox of Christianity's simultaneous universalism and particularity in a world where meeting with other faith communities is more common, and need of dialogue is urgent. However, theologians are constrained to some degree by their position as faith insiders while philosophers of religion have no such limitations placed upon them. They are free to explore the topic of religious truth-claims without privileging any one discourse, as the philosophy of religion cannot be confined within the context of a specific religion.

There are a number of philosophical themes that are relevant to religious truths. The first is the exploration of knowledge and how human beings come to know what they know about the world. The second is the nature of language. The third is the context in which knowledge comes to be formulated or possessed. Before going on to look at these three themes, we will overview some of the reflections of philosophers of religion on religious truth, especially touching upon the themes that have already been explored in this chapter.

In regard to the possession of truth by one religion, we have already seen that all religions consider their own beliefs better than those of alternative views, but Vroom assesses the two conflicting positions of exclusivity and inclusivity and comes to the following conclusions. He considers that exclusivity is untenable because it absolutizes the differences between religions, but the pluralist position does the same for similarities (Vroom, 1989, p. 379). Vroom considers that there are too many similarities between the religions to dismiss the pluralists, even though the question of truth is at stake since individuals in each religion claim that they know reality as it really is. However, he argues for a multi-centred view of a religion which does not characterize the tradition from the perspective of one central conviction, but rather as a series of insights which they may or may not share with others. Thus Vroom advocates the idea of family resemblances which show both similarities and differences (Vroom, 1989, p. 383).

However, Vroom makes the point that we must be careful not to regard religions as the unified entities suggested by labels like Islam, Hinduism or Buddhism (Vroom, 1989, p. 379). He states: 'Notions such as a worldview, view of reality and belief system suggest more unity and coherence in a religious tradition and a worldview than is actually present' (Vroom, 1989, p. 323). There are a number of ways in which the view of each religion as a monolithic whole can be disputed. The question of what is truth arises in the first place because people do not always agree with one another. This disagreement is as much within a religion as it is between religions. First there is a personal element in the interpretation of religious truth-claims that is part of an individual's faith commitment, and second there is a collective renewed interpretation located in new knowledge of the world. Vroom makes the point that not everything is held to be true, and that significant figures within a religion have reflected thoroughly on their faith (Vroom, 1989, p. 372). Since religions deal with the imperfections of human beings and ways of transformation, sincere followers can be very critical of themselves and even the condition of the religion they practise, demanding reflexivity and reform.

Even within a religious tradition, the word 'truth' is used in more than one way and moreover does not mean the same thing to people in other religious traditions. Thus not only are religions associated with multiplicity, but the term 'truth' is as well. It could refer to the public teaching, the original revelation, insight or wisdom, the sacred text, the faith in practice, the ideal that should be lived, an elite understanding, religious experience or even, as already mentioned, to the higher power itself. Since most religions declare humanity to be incapable of discerning the deeper truth as it is in a state of unknowing, this becomes problematic because truth may then be perceived as belonging to some type of enlightened elite. Thus it is possible that similarities and differences may not always apply to each discrete religion, but to particular trends and groups of individuals within a tradition who more closely resemble those with similar understandings of truth in other religions than with others in their own. For example, there is commonality found among mystics or fellow contemplatives across traditions.

Truth and knowledge

Philosophy is concerned with the production of knowledge, and has long been asking the question 'how can real knowledge be known?' How can we be sure that we know what we know is true? As far back as the Upanishadic period, Indian philosophers were questioning whether the data assembled by our senses was a reliable or purely neutral account of reality. However, in Western philosophy the Aristotelian notion of 'correspondence' was borrowed in which there is a one-to-one relationship between the thing observed (the form of the thing) and the thought about it. In simple terms, the thing and the thought were expected to correspond. Since the nineteenth century we have depended on a common-sense theory which demands that knowledge should conform either with scientific investigation, or with the proven experience of everyday practical life. John Hick states:

> Philosophy recognizes the two ways in which human beings may come to know whatever there is to be known. One way (stressed by empiricism) is through experience, and the other (stressed by rationalism) is through reasoning. We cannot by logic and reason alone demonstrate any matters of fact and existence; these must be known through experience. (Hick, 1990, p. 68)

The emphasis on 'fact', due in large part to contemporary emphasis on systematically acquired scientific knowledge, however, is problematic. If knowledge cannot be explained without referring to its factuality, then it is necessary to acknowledge the developments in nineteenth- and twentieth-century thought which argue that knowledge of factuality is itself temporally and culturally determined.

Most religions assert that their historical origins and their core doctrines are 'fact', but increasingly throughout the twentieth century religious believers were asked to submit their narratives to logical analysis and even scientific scrutiny, somehow assumed to be higher-order facts to which religious truths should conform. However, as Vroom points out, whether we believe that true knowledge is in some way awareness of a greater or deeper reality or rather a construct of the human mind, neither 'uninterpreted experience nor neutral, culturally independent articulation of experience' can exist (Vroom, 1989, p. 40). He goes on to state that this is why agreement between people is the touchstone of a statement's truth (Vroom, 1989, p. 41). Religious traditions, as we will see, are not satisfied by language conventions and common sense. However, religious traditions can be highly suspicious of general consensus being defined as common sense. After all, most religions assert that human beings, unless having access to enlightenment or awakening, are inauthentic, and that the truth is concealed from 'normal' understanding or consciousness.

Hick points out that the philosophical developments in the theory of language, highly influenced by the work of Ludwig Wittgenstein (1889–1951), are relevant to any discussion of religious truth-claims. He states that according to 'language games' theory, 'religion is an autonomous form of life with its own language which neither requires support, nor is required to fend off objections, from outside itself' (Hick, 1990, p. 97).

Thus different kinds of language pertain to various aspects of life, such as science or religion, and each language has its own criteria, internal to itself, to assess what is true or false. In 'language games' theories, what the believer learns is a shared religious language, and to know how to use this language skilfully is to know God. However, Hick points out that 'religious beliefs do not constitute an autonomous language-game but ramify out to connect with the whole of reality' (Hick, 1973, p. 36). Such a position also overemphasizes the role of doctrine. As stated by Vroom: 'objectification of doctrine vis à vis experience takes place because one thus starts at the wrong end, i.e. with doctrine and not with experience' (Vroom, 1989, p. 322). Although it is true that the nature of experience may be influenced by religious language discrete to a particular tradition, one can also make a common-sense assumption that the religious language itself was derived from experience. If language is mediated from an experience of the transcendent in some way, then it remains at best qualified, not able to express the unutterable, and therefore containing a high symbolic and metaphorical content. Experience is always interpreted, and religious traditions decide to nurture certain interpretations as truth. Another kind of 'truth' would be to discover the historical reasons why certain kinds of interpretations were chosen over and above others.

Knowledge always has a power element. When one person can claim to possess knowledge, it presupposes that someone else has less understanding or is in a condition of ignorance. In the case of religions, an assertion of knowledge proclaims an understanding of an absolute entity which is also lived in daily life as a personal commitment. The combination of such elements make the transferral of religious knowledge a highly affective as well as rational process.

In addition, the special cognizance of the divine as comprehended by the individual believer within a particular tradition renders normal comprehension of a factual statement redundant. If I say as a Christian to a Hindu that 'God exists', the Hindu may agree but there can be no way of knowing whether the framework in which the term 'God' is understood is identical to both of us. I would argue that this holds true even in conversation between two believers of the same religion. As stated by Vroom, the normal shared experience breaks down because:

1 The context plays a constitutive role in determining the meaning of statements. They have meaning only within a certain frame of reference, a certain horizon of understanding, a 'language-game', a worldview, or whatever one may call it;

2 The relationship between knowledge and action implies that there are interests at stake. Religions usually regard people's erroneous interests as obstacles which prevent them facing the truth. (Vroom, 1989, p. 38)

Thus, philosophically we can conclude in agreement with Vroom that 'the criteria for the assessment of religious truth claims are not of such a nature that what is true and what is untrue can be established intersubjectively' (Vroom, 1989, p. 384).

FUNDAMENTALISMS

Both inclusivity and cultural explanations for religious phenomena have found themselves under attack from a number of fundamentalisms that have appeared in most of the world's major faith traditions with growing popularity, throughout the latter half of the twentieth century in particular. Strongly critical of pluralism, each fundamentalism has developed an exclusive truth-claim which usually resurrects a particular version of religious 'facts' based either on a literalist interpretation of scripture or on a chain of events believed to have been inviolable at the religion's origin. The monotheistic religions of Judaism, Christianity and Islam, in particular, have developed fundamentalisms whose adherents insist upon scriptural truths being utilized as the foundation of society's moral and even legal life. The Indian religions tend to focus less on scripture, but more on a particular vision of history that provides religio-political arguments for nationalist sentiments and the strong assertion of outsiders as 'other'.

FUNDAMENTALISM

The term 'fundamentalism' presents a number of problems to the scholar of religion. We need to go beyond the popular use of the term by the public and the associated media depictions of certain typologies of religion that are perceived to be anti-modern, traditionalist, intolerant or reactionary. In addition, there are divisions among scholars as to whether it is more useful to speak of 'fundamentalism' or 'fundamentalisms'.

Underlying the difference of opinion are two quite different perspectives. In the first, perhaps most clearly represented by the ambitious 'Fundamentalism Project' edited by Marty and Appleby (1994–6), is an application of the term as an umbrella appellation describing a common phenomenon that is manifest in a number of different religious traditions. This approach leads to an analysis that seeks to uncover global causes that create the same religious reaction worldwide. This approach, unfortunately, also suffers from a Christocentric analysis that seeks to impose upon all religions a model for the development of 'fundamentalisms' and their causes that imitates certain developments in Protestant Christianity. Even as far back as 1987, Lionel Caplan was criticizing such an approach as 'glib use of concepts whose roots lie in western tradition' (Caplan, 1988).

Chris Partridge, on the other hand, takes the view that 'fundamentalism' does not do justice to the diversity of religious traditions and their own unique historical developments, practices and beliefs, and although he acknowledges enough common features to identify similar patterns, he prefers to speak of a family of correspondences in which each religion contains unique aspects, better understood by the term 'fundamentalisms' than the singular 'fundamentalism' (Partridge, 2001). This approach avoids the inherent dangers of simplification and of imposing upon other religions a term whose roots lie in a particular historical and theological development in contemporary North American Christianity.

Some scholars have attempted to define 'fundamentalism' more precisely than the popular usage of the term. These scholars tend to take two approaches. They either attempt to identify a more penetrating understanding of the phenomenon by seeking to define it or, alternatively, they provide a list of common features. Thus Hadden and Schupe, two sociologists of religion, in 1989 provided the following definition: 'a pattern of contemporary socio-political movements that share certain characteristics in their responses to a common globalisation process which can be described as secularisation' (Hadden and Schupe, 1989).

The two authors go on to list the common characteristics as:

1 Resistance to secularization;
2 Denial of religious forms which have developed by compromising with modernity;
3 A coherent ideology which seeks to bring religion back to the centre stage of public life as well as private life;
4 Fundamentalists claim authority over a scriptural tradition;
5 They accept the benefits of modernity, particularly technology, while rejecting modernism as an ideological framework;

6   Fundamentalism is a modern phenomenon which attacks the ideology of modernism and very often traditional religious forms. (Hadden and Schupe, 1989)

A more recent 'list' approach to fundamentalism is found in Harriet Harris's 2001 article. There are some parallels with Hadden and Schupe:

1   Reactive to marginalization of religion – especially secularization;
2   Selectivity – selecting particular aspects of a religion to emphasize their opposition to modernity;
3   Moral dualism – the world divided into good and evil, light and dark;
4   Absolutism and inerrancy – absolute validity of the fundamentals of the faith – sacred texts are inerrant;
5   Millenialism and messianism – victory to the believer at the end of history;
6   Elect membership – the faithful remnant;
7   Sharp boundaries – the saved from the unsaved;
8   Authoritarian organization – charismatic leadership with no possibility of dissent;
9   Behavioural requirements – members expected to participate fully. (Harris, 2001)

Both sets of characteristics are open to critique. Some of the characteristics listed by Harris seem to be more attributable to the kind of sectarian organization more often described as 'cult' than 'fundamentalist'. On the other hand, Hadden and Schupe provide us with the useful analytical boundary of 'political' to describe fundamentalism. Therefore no religious movement can be described as fundamentalist unless there is a 'coherent ideology which seeks to bring religion back to the centre stage of public life as well as private life'. However, this may or may not be in response to secularization. Neither Harris nor Hadden and Schupe mention the link between certain fundamentalisms, nationalism and the tensions that can exist between loyalty to the nation and loyalty to God. Also implicit in both attempts to identify 'fundamentalism' is a horizontal approach to the investigation of religious phenomena that looks for common elements across the globe but ignores a vertical investigation that looks back into the history of a particular religious tradition, to acknowledge unique features that would predispose it to take particular forms and patterns of development. Both the historical context and contemporary social and cultural forces need to be explored.

Further reading

Caplan, L. (ed.) (1988), *Studies in Religious Fundamentalism*. New York: State University of New York Press.

Hadden, J. K. and Schupe, A. D. (1989), *Secularization and Fundamentalism Reconsidered*. New York: New Era Books.

Harris, H. (2001), 'How helpful is the term fundamentalist?' in Christopher Partridge (ed.), *Fundamentalisms*. Carlisle: Paternoster Press.

Kaplan, L. (ed.) (1992), *Fundamentalism in a Comparative Perspective*. Amherst: University of Massachusetts Press.

Marty, M. and Appleby, S. (eds) (1994), *Accounting for Fundamentalisms*. Chicago: Chicago University Press.

— (eds) (1995), *Fundamentalisms Comprehended*. Chicago: Chicago University Press.

Partridge, C. (ed.) (2001), *Fundamentalisms*. Carlisle: Paternoster.

Besides a strong resistance to secularism and an insistence on their own version of religious truths being utilized to bring religion back into the centre of public life, each of the fundamentalisms has little in common with each other, and they all promote exclusive visions of identity which provide sometimes deeply antagonistic attitudes towards each other. Philosophically, each fundamentalism is foundationalist. In other words, they each proclaim certain truths or doctrines which are accepted as inviolable, very often the product of revelation. It is possible to build on these truth foundations to create new visions of society or ways of life, but the truths themselves cannot be challenged. Gilles Kepel summarizes the above in the following words:

> Each of these religious cultures had developed specific truths which, insofar as they provide the basis for a strong reassertion of identity, are mutually exclusive. All they have in common is a rejection of secularism; beyond that point their plans for society diverge and then become deeply antagonistic, with the potential for bitter conflict in which none of these doctrines of truth can afford to compromise, on pain of losing followers. (Kepel, 1994, p. 192)

In keeping with this view of religious truth, there is a strict separation of insiders and outsiders, true believers and unbelievers, but this is directed not only to other religious adherents and the secular world, but also to those within the same religious affiliation who do not accept the fundamentalist version of history or interpretation of scripture. Often the first generation of believers are regarded as the most 'true' to the scriptural revelation or the teachings of the founder, and subsequent generations, with the exception of rare individuals and their close followers, are treated as suspect, as watering down or corrupting the original vision. Tradition becomes suspect as a vehicle for embodying the original truths, and fundamentalist believers seek to return to some kind of pristine past and re-embody it in the present with the hope of transforming the future. That their pattern of events or interpretation of sacred text could be mistaken is unthinkable.

Niels Nielsen considers that fundamentalist versions of religious truth-claims are 'first and foremost a negative response to what is seen as the spectre of modernity' (Nielsen, 1993, p. 3). Bitterly opposed to the relativity and pluralism that is usually found in secular societies, they consider the desertion of a particular religious narrative as the foundation for society to be a betrayal of a sacred power, where human beings have taken charge of their own history. They may also consider that the 'true version of the religion' is under threat unless reclaimed by a spiritual vanguard. Such vanguards are often led by self-selected charismatic authority figures who consider themselves the chosen vehicle to renew the original truth. Such figures gather around themselves loyal followers wherein personal identity is discovered through belonging to the movement or group. For such fundamentalists, religious truth is not only paramount and literal but it is resorted to as a template to discover all truths. Any new discovery is taken back and compared with the truth-narrative: if it can be seen to conform then it may be embraced, otherwise it is a falsehood to be rejected.

Syncretism

Although Wilfred Cantwell Smith claims religious beliefs and practices are not as limited to a particular geographical setting as they once were (Cantwell-Smith, 1962, pp. 148–9), religions, contrary to the fundamentalist view, have rarely been completely new, but rather build on existing foundations, mixing and merging with new streams as they develop, coming into contact with other religious narratives and converting their symbols into new patterns. Such processes are not viewed favourably by insiders, especially when a notionally 'pure' religion such as Islam or Christianity comes into contact with indigenous traditions and absorbs their practices and beliefs. Fundamentalists are especially critical as this appears to point towards invention of tradition as a human process. Syncretic processes are certainly common to all religions, and offer an overt criticism to ideas of either religious or cultural purity. Charles Stewart and Rosalind Shaw point out that even scholars of religion and anthropologists are guilty of comparing syncretic phenomena with some kind of 'authentic' tradition (Stewart and Shaw, 1994, p. 2). However, they argue that syncretism 'has presumably always been part of the negotiation of identities and hegemonies in situations such as conquest, trade, migration, religious dissemination and intermarriage' (Stewart and Shaw, 1994, pp. 19–20).

Both culture and religion have always engaged in creative borrowing, but Cantwell Smith was correct to identify the possibility of this process accelerating through increased cultural contact as a result of global communications and mass movements of people. Fundamentalisms are likely to claim purity and authenticity based on direct contact with divinity, but Stewart and Shaw point out that claims to religious purity and syncretic traditions can both be regarded as 'authentic' if people claim that these traditions are unique, and uniquely their (historical) possession (Stewart and Shaw, 1994, p. 7). However, the claim that 'pure' equals 'authentic' is equally disputable on the grounds that 'pure' traditions rarely exist, and that some kind of syncreticity exists in most religions.

What is beyond dispute is that in the twentieth century, discourses of 'purity' or 'authenticity' were usually associated with nationalist or ethnic struggles where religion is regarded as a significant marker of identity. Syncretic features are not only a challenge to truth-claims of discrete religions but also indicate contact with alien cultures deemed to be 'other'. In both Hindu and Muslim fundamentalisms, for example, struggles are taking place to eradicate or diminish religious syntheses branded as 'foreign'. The growth of a Western-dominated world cultural system may bring about both 'pure' forms of religion in order to assert regional and national identities; but equally, depending on the local context, new syncretisms may arise as strategies of resistance, for example the rise of New Age religions in American and North European cultures.

The rational/secular view

The modernist period, dated by Stephen Toulmin as arising from a 'complex inter-weave' where it emerges from sixteenth-century humanism and the development of science in the seventeenth (Toulmin, 1990, p. 43), introduced the idea of progress to replace providence. No longer could history be assumed to have a beginning, end and purpose based on biblical understandings of the world, but rather the discoveries of both natural and physical sciences emerged as the dominant discourse to understand the universe and all that exists within it. Religion had found a major competitor for both explaining the world and promoting human well-being. As a result of new knowledge the world became a place of human discovery, and that included the realm of religion. Even sacred text came under scrutiny.

Nineteenth-century philosophers such as Nietzsche paved the way for distrust in religious narratives: he stated that they 'after long usage seem to a nation fixed, canonic, binding: truths are illusions of which one has forgotten that they are illusions' (Nietzsche, 1911, p. 180). Nietzsche also challenged the idea of an independently existing truth. The human will becomes the sole arbiter of truths, ephemeral and contingent. He stated facts and actions are precisely what there is not; only interpretations (Nietzsche, 1968, p. 481). There is no foundation, no ground, no origin that ultimately is not governed by a perspective.

Beginning in the nineteenth century and remaining a significant factor in understanding religion to the present time, the social sciences appropriated knowledge of religious phenomena, providing an alternative series of truth-claims to those put forward by the religions in their various narratives that explained the world and human existence. Numerous theories explained religion in economic, sociological and psychological frameworks. However, not only had Nietzsche's ideas challenged the foundationalist thinking of religious believers, but they had also paved the way for cultural and linguistic relativism. Even scientific theories can be regarded as truth-claims which come into existence within a culturally specific location, to be replaced at a later date. Rapid change becomes the only certainty of human existence. Truth itself is relativized to become meaningful only in the sense of being useful or helpful to human development. Christopher Norris explains:

> In vulgar-deconstructionist fashion – treat all concepts as metaphors, all truth-claims as so many operative fictions, and all 'discourse' (scientific discourse included) as merely the product of this or that optional interpretative paradigm. (Norris, 1994, p. 8)

Richard Rorty declares himself to be 'ethnocentric', meaning that he has no choice but to speak from a particular standpoint (Rorty, 1991, p. 13). In this respect knowledge is localized. Truth-claims do not exist out there as objective realities, but rather if 'truth' exists merely as whatever we create to fit with our interests, then it is local interests that must decide what is of worth. Norris states:

> On this account 'local knowledge' is the most that we can ever hope for, since theoretical truth-claims amount to nothing more than the expression of in-place consensus beliefs on the part of some existing cultural enterprise, professional interest group, 'interpretative community', or whatever. (Norris, 1994, p. 5)

Thus scientific objectivity in the study of religion is also challenged not only by cultural relativity thinkers, but also by those who are attempting to re-impose religious truth-claims such as Dewi Hughes, who is dismayed by the variety of contradictory theories presented in the name of science. He argues persuasively that 'if "facts" are supposed to be transparent, they have failed to be so in the case of religion. This myth of "scientific objectivity" therefore needs to be laid to rest' (Hughes, 1996, p. 233).

Postmodernism

If the world is not out there as an independent entity but rather is only our perspective on it, continuously constructing and reconstructing it, then there can be no essence or essential nature of anything. Our culture is only one among many. Words themselves, rather than being depositories of ancient truths, are always filled with context and meaning drawn from behaviour or ideology. There is nothing to prevent us from retelling the old stories in new ways, creating constantly shifting meaning.

In the above description of cultural relativity we have already entered the realm of postmodernism, first defined by the historian Arnold Toynbee in the 1930s. Postmodernism defines itself in opposition not only to religious certainties, already under fire from modernism, but also to the certainties of modernism itself such as progress. Jean-François Lyotard has famously defined 'postmodern' as 'incredulity towards meta-narratives' where knowledge is marked by a hermeneutics of suspicion. But Graham Ward points out that when suspicion of meta-narratives becomes a condition of pervasive scepticism that challenges the worldview of modernity, then 'postmodern characterizes a sociohistorical and economic period which we can call "postmodernity"' (Ward, 1997, p. xxv).

Religious Studies

All of the above have repercussions for the academic study of religion, which can be simply summed up as who is best able to access religious truths, the insider or the outsider, known respectively as the emic or etic positions. It is not only a straightforward debate concerning the respective merits of Hindus studying Hinduism or Christians studying theology; but also a question whether the Religious Studies scholar should adopt a position of methodological atheism or agnosticism, or acknowledge the existence of the sacred as a *sui generis* reality, independent of any other realm of existence.

Certainly most scholars would agree that Religious Studies departments cannot become arbitrators between various truth-claims. John Hick notes that although it is not obvious to everyone that the sacred exists, most would acknowledge that religion exists (Hick, 1973, p. 19). Although theology remains in the domain of truth-discourse, dealing with the reality of the divine, the study of religion is moving rapidly towards seeing its object of study not as God but as human-constructed cultures. Although God cannot be accessed by scientific study, the phenomena of religion are available to historical, psychological, sociological, anthropological and comparative disciplines adopting the stance of methodological atheism. Thus categories of truth and falsehood are not an issue. However, those who adopt methodological agnosticism are more likely to acknowledge that the truths held by others, their responses to a supernatural being, are a valid line of enquiry and essential for exploring motivation for action either as individuals or as group behaviour. Either way, both categories would start from the premise that knowledge of 'God' is a human construction. Dewi Hughes, making a distinction between 'idealists' and 'positivists', sums up the position by stating:

> The idealists began from the presupposition that religion has been too pervasive a fact of human experience to be empty of any reality. The positivists began from those inexorable laws and attempted to explain religion from within nature. (Hughes, 1996, p. 237)

Max Muller stated early in the twentieth century that knowledge of only one religion was knowledge of none. Certainly the study of religion ranges further than one tradition and in doing so owes something to the pluralists of liberal Protestantism, but Hughes is critical of the pluralist stance, arguing that more often than not the 'essence' at the heart of religion is no more than the scholar's 'own religious belief or belief about religion' (Hughes, 1996, p. 238). The debates between these various positions rage on and remain unresolved. Religious Studies is at present entering a period of self-analysis and reflection, but in essence these remain the old battle lines drawn up by the early sociologists such as Durkheim, or those who acknowledged the existence of the sacred such as Eliade. Today, instead of sociology, the new positivists emerge from the ranks of cultural studies. Dewi Hughes makes an impassioned plea which, in an age where all meta-narratives are equally suspect, requires some reflection.

What is being objected to is the impression that the so-called modern scientific approach to religion is fair, tolerant and objective, while viewing religion as a whole from the perspective of a faith commitment is bigotry (Hughes, 1996, p. 234).

Conclusion

Kenneth Surin argues that the pluralism of Hick and Cantwell Smith itself represents a mode of cultural production which is historically, socially and politically constituted (Surin, 1998, p. 192). He points out that the pluralists depend upon an unspoken religious position which relies on a Kantian-type distinction between a 'noumenaltranscendent focus common to all the religions and the culturally-conditioned and hence "culturally-specific" phenomenal images which are a schematization or concretization of the Real' (Surin, 1998, p. 199). In doing so they fail to acknowledge specific localities, with their own narratives in favour of a global 'regime of the universal' (Surin, 1998, p. 196). Thus the various World Religions are presented as texts, beliefs and practices existing within a cultural vacuum. The difference between the religions, including their various truth-claims, can be perceived for the first time in history as cultural diversity.

Not everyone agrees that all our speech and behaviour are culturally moulded. The Protestant theologian Paul Tillich argued that it is not religious beliefs that have been relativized, but rather that religious conviction has become pluralized. In this position, the history of religions is not one aspect of the history of culture, but rather the sacred exists in the depths of culture arising from the depths of being (Tillich, 1966, pp. 82–3). Don Cupitt seems to foresee the end of exclusivism, positing that the new globalized culture removes the requirement of exclusive national and religious allegiances (Cupitt, 1997, p. 100). Noting that people have been able to find peace among themselves by uniting their aggression against a perceived other, he pleads that in a postmodern age we may be able to do without such loyalties and their respective truth-claims, to belong to no ethnic group, and to have no Other (Cupitt, 1997, p. 99). However, the opposite appears to be true: the breakdown of confidence in meta-narratives appears to result in increasing fragmentation and more diversity. However, numerous truth-claims can be celebrated. I complete this chapter with a long quote from Don Cupitt that seems to summarize the debate:

> If indeed there is no One Great Truth out there to serve as the basis for a future worldwide common human religious consciousness, and indeed there is no One True Morality out there either . . . there may be a number of subjective truths. In which case, surely one can be happy to see the three thousand or so NRMs, the thousand or so New Age groups, and the hundreds of sects of the various major faiths that are all flourishing, teeming, in Western countries today. If their beliefs work out well for them, then their beliefs are true for them; and since there is no independent Truth out there, and all of us are entirely free to build our worlds in the ways that seem best to us, we have no basis for calling other people's worlds irrational. Let a hundred flowers bloom! (Cupitt, 1997, p. 123)

DISCUSSION POINTS

1 'One can ascend the top of a house by means of a ladder or a bamboo or a staircase or a rope; so too, diverse are the ways of approaching God, and each religion in the world shows one of the ways' (Ramakrishna). Critically discuss this statement. Are all religions aiming at the same goal? What about the more controversial new religious movements? Does Ramakrishna's assertion equally apply to Satanism, the Church of Scientology, the International Society for Krishna Consciousness (the 'Hare Krishna' movement), and the UFO religions? Identify the specific goals of different religions: are they the same or different?

2 John Hick claims that one is saved, not by a religion, but by God; hence God is the centre of all religion (or at least all the major ones), not Jesus Christ, who belongs to a single religion. Do you agree? Suggest reasons for and against.

3 To what extent are the world's religions saying the same thing in different words? Is it possible to identify genuine differences between different religions? If so, does this mean that some religions must be wrong, while others may be right?

4 The interfaith movement is sometimes criticized for putting all religions on an equal footing. Is this a fair comment? If members of one religion feel constrained to criticize the beliefs or practices of another, is this necessarily bad?

12

The internet as a resource in the study of religion

George Chryssides

Chapter Outline

Using the internet   339
Evaluating web sources   342
Journals, reference works and e-books   343
The internet and ethics   348
ISPs, IDs, aliases and screen names   350
The effect on religion   351
Conclusion   359
Discussion points   360

Using the internet

The internet has had a profound impact both on the study of religion and on religions themselves. It is typically identified as one of the major factors in globalization, enabling academic collaboration across the world, and serving as a global resource for each religious organization. Its advent has caused students of religion and religious organizations alike to update themselves on Information Technology (IT), and it has been said that religion is the second most popular topic to feature in the World Wide Web. (Unfortunately the most popular is reckoned to be pornography.) There are now only a very few Western religious groups that have no presence on the Web. Understandably, the Amish are one, since they have largely rejected all technological innovations since their establishment in the seventeenth century; however, several 'outsiders' have been obliging enough to upload information about them. Where forms of Hinduism and Buddhism have been brought to the West by well-known teachers, their relevant organizations will typically have their official websites. In India major temples and pilgrimage sites have a presence – India is at the forefront of the ICT (Information and Communications Technology) revolution. Smaller temples, and temples in other countries are less likely to feature on the internet, through lack of resources: this is part of the phenomenon that has come to be known as the 'digital divide'.

The internet thus provides a great deal of primary source material on religions. However, there also exist research tools, as well as secondary electronic source material. At a mundane level, the internet provides the key research tools for literature searching. Until very recently, tracking down sources and devising bibliographies was a laborious task of scouring library shelves, delving through card indexes, and following up cross-references in textbooks. Such activities still have their place, albeit a limited one, but most undergraduates learn within their first week of study the methods of keyword searching. For more specialist work, anyone can readily access the Library of Congress in the United States, the British Library, several specialist libraries, and various electronic catalogues, such as Copac, which scour numerous library catalogues simultaneously, and can locate the places at which the sought book is available. Many educational institutions now subscribe to electronic versions of journals and past copies of quality newspapers, which can be accessed through the internet.

The advent of the internet was almost unheralded. Its beginnings can be traced back to 1973, when a military project was set up to minimize the risk of losing important information and documentation in event of a major world disaster in a single location, such as nuclear war, natural disaster or terrorist attack. What this project achieved was the ability to send information from one computer to another at a different location, by means of a cable link. Such information is transmitted 'digitally', by means of a binomial system. A binomial system is one which uses only two digits (such as 0 and 1), instead of our conventional 10-digit counting system, and can be signalled by an electrical current being on or off at a particular location, to correspond with the two digits.

The inventor of the World Wide Web, Tim Berners-Lee (b. 1955) combined this system of transmitting digital information with another invention in information technology: hypertext. Hypertext became popular in computer software packages like hypercard, which was a kind of electronic card filing system, affording cross-links to other cards by means of hidden commands placed invisibly beneath the visible text (hence the term 'hypertext'). As Berners-Lee (1999) points out, this system enabled computers to perform more 'intuitive' tasks than their previous functions of calculating data with ruthless logic. Just as humans can say, 'That reminds me of something else' (which need not be a strictly logical association), so a designer of computer software can insert hyperlinks to remind users of some useful associated piece of information. The internet thus combines the transmission of material on a computer, by means of a 'web' of international connections, with a system of associating one piece of information with others within this World Wide Web – hence the name 'WWW'. The internet encompasses the World Wide Web, which is the network of computers holding, among them, the enormous totality of information, most of which is publicly accessible, together with the email system, where subscribers send information that is targeted to specific recipients.

When devising the World Wide Web, Berners-Lee could have made himself a vast fortune by designing it to be compatible solely with certain designated software, and accessible only by payment of a substantial subscription fee. Berners-Lee, however, decided against making himself a personal fortune in this way, in order to make the Web as democratic as possible. It is not even necessary to own computer facilities to use the Web. In Britain, most public libraries offer free access, and it is easy to set oneself up with a free Hotmail, Yahoo or gmail address. The disadvantage of using such addresses, however, is that some recipients of emails – including the present writers – are wary of responding to unexpected messages from free email accounts. There is no guarantee that the sender is who he or she purports to be, and one cannot always be sure of the motives of a correspondent in attempting to elicit information. The student who pays a subscription to an Internet Service Provider (ISP) has a more definite identity. Better still, most universities and colleges now have their own server, and provide all students with their personal email address. Writing from an address with the suffix 'ac.uk' (in Britain) or 'edu' (in the United States) signals that it comes from an academic institution and thus establishes the sender's credentials.

One major problem facing the researcher is the sheer volume of information that resides on the Web. Unlike traditional publishing, much web publishing is not subject to any kind of quality assurance. A conventional book normally comes into existence by an author submitting a proposal (sometimes an entire manuscript) to a publisher, explaining what the potential book's merits are, what is novel about it, what gap in the market it will fill, what categories of reader are likely to buy it and so on. More often than not, a proposal is sent to a number of referees, who are themselves experts in the field, and who will report back on its suitability for publication. Similarly, journal articles have to be approved by an editor or editorial panel; if the journal is a prestigious 'refereed journal', copies of submitted articles are sent, usually 'double blind' – that is to say, neither the author nor the referee is given the other's identity, so that the referees are not swayed by any preconceptions about the writer, and can give a candid appraisal of the piece of writing, enabling the editor to come to a final decision.

This is generally not the case with the internet. Because of its 'democratic' nature, anyone who has the technical expertise can put any material on the Web. The basic skill involved is not great, and there are numerous websites that enable users to create their own web pages free of charge. Universities and colleges typically provide students with web space at no charge, with the proviso that it must conform to its acceptable use policy. Since anyone with access to the internet can contribute material, regardless of their expertise in a topic, the quality of information varies enormously, and while there is some excellent material on religion on the internet, there is much that is very poor, and in some cases even of negative value because of serious factual errors.

Because of the modest outlay and expertise that are needed, the Web tends to be swamped with material on almost any subject, thus posing a problem to the researcher who wants authoritative information on his or her chosen topic. Ten years ago one student who was researching the Salvation Army found that there were over 12,500 sites that purported to offer information, and she wondered how she would manage to access them all; there are now 43.7 million addresses that purport to have relevant data.

Evaluating web sources

In order to use internet material intelligently, critical evaluation is needed. It is not only students who can be insufficiently critical, but religious believers themselves, who can readily assume that material placed on an official (or seemingly official) website must be reliable. Since access to such sources of information is free, one must ask why the authors are offering it without payment, if they could sell it, for example in book form. Broadly speaking, there appear to be three different categories of authors who put their material on the Web: first, there are those whose material is of such poor quality that it cannot gain recognition in any other way; second, those who have a mission to perform or a campaign to carry out; and, third, those who are genuinely magnanimous and want to encourage the spread of good information. These categories are not mutually exclusive, of course: some campaigning material, for example, can be of very poor quality – ill informed and poorly expressed – for example, some of the more hysterical critics of controversial new religious groups.

It cannot be safely assumed that the first few sites listed by a search engine are the best. Webmasters can resort to a number of techniques to promote their sites. For example, a criterion that some search engines use for ranking sites is the number of hyperlinks from other websites. The present author has received frequent messages from one particular religious organization, drawing attention to its multiplicity of websites, and requesting that he inserts hyperlinks from his own. He has even been asked to contact Google to complain about Google's criteria for ranking websites, since their critics' sites had secured prominence over theirs. Another related technique for pushing one's websites up the ladder is to create multiple sites, hyperlinking each other, thus increasing the number of hyperlinks to each.

One great virtue of the internet is that it can provide excellent primary source material. Where a religious organization publishes its own self-description on the internet, we are hearing it speak with its own voice, unfiltered from detractors, commentators or even academics (although one should bear in mind that some of the material may be for public relations purposes). The Web has therefore been of particular benefit to new religious movements (popularly known as 'cults'), who have typically been subjected to hostile criticism by the media, the anti-cult movement and even mainstream religions, and who are now able to put their own case directly to the reader. This does not mean, of course, that we should suspend our critical faculties when perusing such material: obviously a religious group will want to present itself in the most favourable light, perhaps even in the hope of attracting more followers. Researchers must therefore consider a website's bias, and how this affects the information it presents.

Journals, reference works and e-books

The internet has expanded greatly since it began to be used in the latter half of the 1990s. Most university libraries provide a wide variety of electronic resources, including electronic databases, electronically available journals and e-books. These are generally only accessible to staff and students, but there are other valuable publicly available online resources. Some of these require subscription, such as the British Library Newspaper Archive, and electronic reference works from the major publishing houses. Others are freely available, and increasingly classical texts that are now out of print or appearing on websites such as www.archive.org and the linked Gutenberg Project. Free reference works include the *Catholic Encyclopedia Online*, James Hastings, *Encyclopedia of Religion and Ethics* (1926), the Stanford *Encyclopedia of Philosophy*, and the *Encyclopedia of Mormonism*, to name but a few. Because copyright law prevents the dissemination of copyright material without its owner's permission, websites like archive.org and the Gutenberg Project confine themselves to providing out-of-copyright material – that is, publications that are over 70 years old. This enables the dissemination of classical texts, such as the Bible, the Qur'an, and the major Hindu and Buddhist scriptures, as well as writings of scholars such as Augustine, Thomas Aquinas and many more. Project Muse and JSTOR offer limited access to certain books and journals; some may be accessible through institutional subscription, while a certain amount of older material is freely available. Because of copyright law, translations found online may frequently be old ones, and reference works such as the *Catholic Encyclopedia* and the *Encyclopedia of Religion and Ethics* are now around a century old. These works still have their uses, of course, but students of religion should bear in mind that they are not state-of-the-art material.

Other websites do more than simply present text. BibleGateway.com allows the reader to access a wide variety of translations of the Bible, with the facility of searching the text, and – for students studying the synoptic problem – the University of Toronto hosts John W. Marshall's 'The Five Gospels Parallels', enabling comparison of the text of the four canonical gospels and the Gospel of Thomas. A further facility afforded by the internet is the availability of facsimiles of ancient manuscripts. One such example is the Codex Sinaticus Project (located at www.codexsinaiticus.org), on which an international team of scholars at several academic institutions worldwide collaborated, and which would not have been possible before the advent of the internet. Another online facility with which the student of religion should be familiar is Google Scholar. This not only enables the researcher to locate a scholarly article using the title or author's name, but indicates where it has been discussed elsewhere in academic literature. The researcher then has the information to follow up discussion of the topic.

Probably the best-known reference work, and possibly the one most used by students is Wikipedia. Jimmy Wales and Larry Sanger, its inventors, had the innovative idea of creating an encyclopaedia that resulted from the collaborative efforts of its readers, and it was launched in 2001. Wikipedia is often disparaged by academics, who point out that the material is not peer-reviewed, and therefore lacks the guarantee of quality that one would expect of academic writing. In its own article entitled 'Wikipedia', the authors reveal that only a minority of contributors have a higher degree, and that the typical contributor is male, under 30, single and without a family. Inevitably, this raises questions about bias as well as overall quality, and its democratic nature enables readers to alter, and even vandalize its information. Wikipedia articles certainly vary considerably in standard, and students who use it are certainly advised to check any information with academic or relevant primary source material. As one colleague remarked to us, Wikipedia can be useful as 'pre-research': it can at least suggest useful ideas about a topic, and it often provides useful citations and good hyperlinks, some of which lead to important good-quality online resources. It also has the advantage of being constantly updated, unlike other reference works, where the revision process is markedly slower.

A number of e-journals and e-books are available on line for a subscription, and university and college libraries frequently subscribe to these at a cost to the institution, while making them available to their staff and students. In many cases, these are books and journals that already exist in hard copy and have therefore been subjected to the normal refereeing processes. Online versions of such journals are therefore no different from conventional journals when it comes to evaluating their content. There also exist some academic journals that appear only online: provided these are subjected to the same rigorous processes as traditional journals, their quality and authority can be presumed to be equally good.

It is important to use some definite criteria for evaluation, rather than just vague impression. The first and most obvious criterion relates to authorship. As with a book, the reader should ask who wrote it, what the author's credentials are and what reason he or she had for writing the material. In the case of internet sources, some are anonymous. Some time ago one of these anonymous web authors wrote to me, requesting that I insert a hyperlink from my own web pages to his Bible commentary. Unfortunately, I could not comply with the request, not simply on account of the quality of the material, but because the author's anonymity precluded any judgement about the point of view that the pages represented. Unless some very good reason can be seen to the contrary, anonymous material is usually worthless and should be discarded.

The domain name tells the reader something about the source of the information. The suffix 'ac.uk' is an abbreviation for 'academic, United Kingdom', and indicates that the material belongs to the website of a university or college. Thus, www.wlv. ac.uk is the domain name of the University of Wolverhampton. In the United States. the corresponding suffix is 'edu'. Suffixes '.gov', '.mil' and '.us' indicate government sources: for example www.statistics.gov.uk provides demographical information for Britain, including the 2001 census containing statistics on the population's religious affiliations. '.org' indicates a charity or non-profit organization, while '.co.uk', '.com', '.org', '.net' and '.biz' indicate domain names that can readily be bought, usually for a modest sum. Organizations tend to acquire domain names that are meaningful and memorable, although critics and detractors have sometimes purchased deliberately similar names, causing the unwary to encounter criticisms of a controversial religious group instead of the organization's own material. At the time of writing, the website www.watchtowerinformationservice.org bears a modified version of the Jehovah's Witnesses' logo, and bears no obvious indication of its authorship. Several of our students have mistaken this for the Jehovah's Witnesses' official pages, which are located at www.jw.org. Less disturbing, although still a matter for alertness, are religious groups or leaders with similar names: thus, someone who wanted information about Satya Sai Baba (the controversial Indian teacher, said to be God incarnate, who could allegedly produce objects such as rings and watches by miraculous powers) might plausibly try www.saibaba.org, without realizing that there was another earlier teacher, Sai Baba of Shirdi, who is the focus of another spiritual movement. At the time of writing, www. sai-baba.org (with a hyphen) is a critical site set up by British psychics, and seeks to evaluate the claims of Satya Sai Baba, among others who claim paranormal powers. The correct address for the Satya Sai Baba organization is in fact www.sathyasai.org. A web search on a topic by means of a search engine will frequently find hits on 'blogs' – electronic bulletin boards, on which anyone who has logged in to the facility's provider can write a comment on a topic. These are almost invariably worthless as sources of reliable information, being usually unsupported by evidence, with no reassurance that their authors are writing from knowledge rather than impression.

Even with academic sources, critical evaluation is still needed. Not only are academics themselves capable of error, and even prejudice, but students as well as staff can sometimes contribute material. One prominent website was The Religious Movements Homepage Project at the University of Virginia, an extensive and normally extremely valuable source of information on contemporary religious movements. Some of the material on these pages was compiled by students, some of whom, predictably, are better than others: while, arguably, Jeffrey Hadden (1937–2003), the project creator, could have exercised greater editorial control, he chose not to. David Bromley (Virginia Commonwealth University) has now taken over the editing of this material and has transformed it into the 'World Religions and Spirituality Project', having invited specialist scholars to rewrite a substantial amount of its content.

In addition to the domain name, the credentials of the author have obvious importance. The author is not necessarily the same as the webmaster, and a reliable website will clearly identify the author, with some brief biographical details that give some indication of his or her credentials for writing the material. Where a webmaster has appropriated material from an external source and made the full text available, care needs to be taken to ensure that the material has not been altered in the transition (either accidentally or intentionally): it is therefore best to locate the original material, rather to rely on someone else making it available. A good website will normally include some means of contacting the author or at least the webmaster, although some authors of cyber-material are wary of including an email address, for fear that it might be used by spammers.

Apart from the author's identity, it is worth considering the intended readership of any website. Why is it there? For whom is it intended? Religious organizations do not exist primarily for the benefit of researchers, and are probably there to promote their beliefs and practices and to provide a means of contact for seekers. In some cases, websites aim to sell merchandize, while others may want to promote discussion about spiritual matters. In other instances, a website is simply the author's hobby, and is amateur rather than professional. 'Amateur' websites should not be dismissed, however: there are some really good examples of individuals who have not gained professional qualifications, but who provide good information: one notable example is Bruce Robinson's 'Ontario Consultants on Religious Tolerance' (www.religioustolerance.org), which is superior to much professionally authored material.

This last example indicates the need to evaluate the web content itself, and not merely the credentials of those who put it there, and there is much internal evidence that signals the reliability or otherwise of web material. Several books have now been written on the evaluation of websites, and academics, as well as libraries, in a number of universities worldwide have now been obliging enough to create web pages with appropriate advice. The student would be well advised to consult these, as well as what follows. Much of the evaluation process is similar to evaluating conventional written material, the major difference being that there exists much more sub-standard and inappropriate material to consider than is normally found in the average university and college and library. Several authors of student support material now use the acronym 'CARS' as a mnemonic for four key features of good internet source material. 'CARS' stands for 'Credibility, Accuracy, Reasonableness, Support', which the McGraw-Hill (2005) e-book *Student Success* explains as follows.

Credibility means that the source must inspire confidence that its information is trustworthy and believable. A student who is new to a subject may find it initially difficult to determine what information is good and what is bad, but one remedy for this problem is not simply to assume that all information is good information, but to ask oneself whether the author has persuaded us of the credibility of his or her material. What positively *makes it* believable? Ask who is writing the web source. Is it a well-accredited academic? Does he or she already have peer-reviewed publications in the field? Is it an official body, such as a government department? (Know your suffixes – outlined above – to determine this.) A web source may be authoritative for one type of information, but not another. For example, the Jehovah's Witnesses' official website www.jw.org will give authoritative information about the beliefs, practices and publications of Jehovah's Witnesses, which would be useful for students of new religious movements, but it would be inappropriate to use this material for Biblical Studies, since the Witnesses' understanding of the Christian Bible is not one that would be accepted by the majority of mainstream biblical scholars. It is worth remembering, too, that any religious organization (not just the Witnesses) will want to present itself in the most favourable light, maybe suppressing negative and critical information. It would therefore be a mistake to suppose that primary source material is infallible material: one's critical faculties must never be left behind!

The authors of *Student Success* identify characteristics that undermine a source's credibility. We have already mentioned anonymity, which deprives the author of any credentials. Other web material has bad 'meta-information': that is to say, other web authors have commented unfavourably on it. Bad spelling, grammar and punctuation are also regarded as indicators of poor quality. Despite the liberal educators' view that only the ideas matter, it is reasonable to conclude that if an author cannot spell (particularly if the misspellings are of key technical terms), this does not inspire confidence that he or she has exercised better care over the subject-matter. Who would want to learn about Buddhism from someone who could not even spell the word? A site with inconsistent or inappropriate fonts and font sizes, which make it look scruffy, does not inspire confidence that the author has given more serious consideration to the content.

The second part of the 'CARS' acronym is *Accuracy*. It may be difficult for inexperienced students to evaluate the accuracy of information, particularly on topics that are new to them. Due caution is therefore appropriate before using web information on a topic, and traditional textbooks and reference works still remain the best way into a new subject. Accuracy also entails precision and appropriate detail. In this regard, one should consider the intended readership of the material. Sources aimed at schools may well be useful at their intended level, but will probably have insufficient detail and depth for undergraduate study. Imprecise or exaggerated statements like 'Thousands of Buddhists throng to celebrate Wesak' or 'When the word "Islam" is mentioned, everyone thinks of Osama bin Laden' are clear indicators that the author is not concerned with precision. Ascertaining the date of a web page is also important, just as it is important to note the date of a traditional book: this is particularly so if one is writing about information that is continually changing.

Reasonableness. One should expect good material to be written in a fair, objective way, with a good structure and convincing line of argument. At undergraduate level one should be able to distinguish between journalistic and academic styles of writing, for example. Journalism has its value in the study of religion, but journalists tend to paint in broad brushstrokes, and want to create 'a story', in contrast with academic writing, which tends to be unsensational, with more detail and precision. Journalists, too, protect their sources, whereas in academic study it is a cardinal rule that one cites sources of information. Students should, of course, be able to recognize rants and satirical material when they see them: the internal evidence often speaks for itself.

Support. Any author, whether publishing electronically or in conventional format, should back up his or her information, inspiring confidence that it is based on good research. Does it reference its sources of information? A good piece of academic writing always contains references and a bibliography, and scholarly footnotes are a reassuring indicator that research has been done thoroughly. Are there good hyperlinks, and are they up-to-date and well maintained? Reciprocally, are there hyperlinks elsewhere on the Web that direct users to this website? Keying the site's URL into a search engine can help to determine this. Ideally, one should be able to 'triangulate' information – that is to say, find at least two other independent sources that can corroborate a claim. Websites need to be maintained, and it is pertinent to ask how well web authors maintain their own material. Some provide support in the form of an email link, which is a definite bonus. How up-to-date is the website? A feature of good web design is an indication of the date on which the site was created, and when it was last updated. Broken hyperlinks are indicators that the site is not as well-maintained as one would hope.

One further comment may be appropriate on the use of the Web as a research tool. Internet material, like any other kind of material, needs to be acknowledged in one's writing, using an appropriate referencing system. As with traditional sources, there are various conventions for doing this, and most Higher Education institutions provide guidance on the fine detail. At the very least, one must include the URL, the date when the site was created and last updated, and when the researcher accessed it. Web material changes rapidly, and such details help to determine whether the material used by the researcher is the same as the material that is currently accessible. Publication details should also include the author, whether this is an individual writer or an institution. It is not sufficient to write, as some students have, unfortunately, been known to do, 'As on the internet'. As one colleague has remarked, this is like saying of a written source, 'As found in someone's garbage can'. The internet is vast, and there is a great deal of rubbish in it, so precision is needed, so that others can locate one's sources and evaluate them also.

The internet and ethics

The advent of internet was sudden and relatively unpredicted, and its rapid development left millions of users with a piece of technology whose implications were not immediately apparent. At the time of writing, not quite 20 years after the Web's inception, there still remain issues of spamming, pornography, controlling under-age access to 'adult' sites, copyright law, internet libel, to name but a few. The internet provides ample opportunity for users to invent bogus identities, to copy and paste material from web sources and pass them off as their own, to harvest users' email addresses for one's own purposes, to pass on viruses inadvertently or to decide how to deal with spam and chain mail. As is often the case, technological advance precedes reflection on legal and ethical issues, which require to be addressed with hindsight.

Several books have now emerged on the topic of internet ethics. Most of these are on generic issues such as software piracy, hacking, surveillance and invasions of computer privacy, and are therefore not of specific interest to students of religion. Those who are interested in such matters can browse the relevant sections in their libraries; what I shall attempt here is brief mention of some of the issues that have cropped up when students are studying religion.

As Robin Penslar (1995, p. 112) asserts, one paramount principle in research ethics – indeed in all ethical judgements – is Kant's principle of 'respect for persons'. The people one encounters, when in physical space or in cyberspace, are bearers of human rights, often defined as the right to life, liberty and property. Just as in physical space individual interests have often to be subjugated to the interests of society as a whole, there are times when individual users of the internet must curtail their own selfish pursuits in the interest of the majority of web users. For example, students have sometimes perceived the internet as affording an excellent opportunity to obtain large numbers of informants, to acquire potential respondents to questionnaires, or to put questions to published authors.

Students often distribute questionnaires online by emailing them as attachments, in the hope that recipients will fill them in electronically and return them. The internet now forwards more sophisticated methods of questionnaire administration with survey tools such as Survey-Monkey, which enable the entire questionnaire to be administered online, and results automatically processed for the researcher. Such methods of questionnaire distribution have the advantages of being inexpensive, allowing respondents to skip irrelevant questions easily, enabling swift data collection and immediate coding of data. While it may be tempting to use such easy methods of data collection, the response rate to such surveys is typically quite low, and invitations to participate restrict the range of respondents to those who use the internet, and whose email addresses are accessible to the researcher. Unless one wishes deliberately to restrict responses to a known category of people, such as a clearly defined class of students, it is doubtful whether the sample one uses is a useful one.

Opportunities for online survey work need to be handled with care. Unsolicited emails are often considered as spam, particularly if they are addressed to multiple recipients. It can be easy enough to email a questionnaire to an entire cohort of fellow-students, or even to the entire university or college staff, but does the majority of recipients really want to take the trouble to complete an undergraduate's questionnaire among their many other commitments? Ethics apart, there are methodological issues as well. Why should one want to define the entirety of a college's staff as one's target population? The fact that a sample is convenient to obtain does not mean that it is useful to do so, or that the results that one gets from any responses will be valid or representative.

ISPs, IDs, aliases and screen names

Because of the anonymity and pseudonymity afforded by internet, it is important that anyone with whom we correspond on the Web knows for certain who we are, and that we can be trusted as *bona fide* students of religion. Hotmail, Yahoo and other free email accounts enable anyone with access to an Internet Service Provider – in effect, anyone at all – to assume almost any user name, so long as it has not previously been acquired by someone else. This means that recipients of emails from these free addresses have no guarantee that the authors are who they say they are; someone claiming to be a student may really be a member of a religious group who is trying to assess the accuracy and bias of our portrayal of it, or they may belong to an interest group (maybe even a campaigning group) seeking some 'sound bytes' which might be quoted against us. It is preferable by far to use an email address provided by one's academic institution: this instantly gives the student status, as well as reassuring the recipient of his or her credentials.

A further note of caution should be given about choices of aliases. Light-hearted names are fine for contacting one's friends, but they may hinder the user from securing responses to serious enquiries. The present authors have at times found it difficult enough to secure responses from informants when using their (somewhat bland) university addresses. Serious students have to be serious! Some email addresses may even offend: references to 'piggy' or 'porky' are likely to be inimical to Muslims, for example, and the student who sent us a message from 'lady_of_the_night@hotmail.com' had to be reminded of the problems that this might cause. (The local vicar's wife might find it even less amusing than the local vicar, if she ever saw him open such a message!) In a chat room, some assumed screen names can even cause immediate exclusion. We mentioned the principle of 'respect for persons' earlier, and avoiding causing such offence is of paramount importance, both in everyday morality and in our professional ethics.

'Can we seek information in a chat room?' As the internet comes increasingly to replicate life in the physical world, students have sometimes asked whether they seek information from participants in chat rooms or use them as informants. Because of pseudonymous screen names, and the anonymity that the internet provides, the researcher is faced of the familiar problem of not knowing for sure who his or her informants are, and hence how any information is to be evaluated. Of course, if one were researching the internet's role in religion, then a chat-room might become a piece of primary source material. One problem about quoting from a chat-room conversation is that it is difficult to seek permission afterwards. Internet chat is ephemeral, leaving no trace, and with the participants difficult, often impossible, to find subsequently.

Apart from questions of obtaining and verifying chat-room information, there remain ethical questions about conducting one's research in chat-rooms. Although chat-room users may not be visible or identifiable to the researcher or to each other, they are nonetheless human subjects, and are individuals whose person is to be respected. Like any other human subject, they should give informed consent before being used as subjects for research, and, although there are chat-room and e-list users who choose to 'lurk' without contributing messages, it is deceptive to lurk with the sole intention of using chat-room discussion as research material without the participants' knowledge. Members engaging in free discussion probably do not want spontaneous remarks to end up in student dissertations or in textbooks. This is not to say that uses of chat-rooms and e-lists are excluded from being research material, but rather that one's research should not be covert.

Because of the interactive nature of the internet, it is possible for researchers to adopt a participatory role. As with field work that is carried out in the physical world, one's presence in a cyber-environment will necessarily change the phenomenon, however slightly. Consideration therefore needs to be given to the limits beyond which it is unacceptable for the researcher to go. Should one actively participate in a religious debate in a chat room, or does one remain – as far as is possible – the neutral observer? In a previous chapter we considered the respective roles of the observer, the participant-observer, and the action researcher. Similar researcher roles can be adopted in cyberspace: none are inherently unacceptable, but the researcher should bear in mind the principle of respect for persons, and the rights to free speech, privacy and informed consent.

The effect on religion

So much for the practicalities of using web resources and the ethical issues that arise from some of them. Not only has the advent of the internet greatly changed the face of the academic study of religion: the internet is having quite a profound effect on the nature of religion itself. The internet does more than offer religions a convenient public face: religions themselves can change by existing in a 'cyber' environment. Although some religious groups merely put information on the Web, to be accessed or downloaded by the surfer, many religious organizations have exploited the interactive character of the internet. The most obvious ways of doing this include setting up facilities for further questions and for dialogue with a designated office-bearer.

The sociologist Emile Durkheim is famous for his insight that religion is an inherently social phenomenon. Someone who simply reads a religious book, however inspiring it is, or who accesses information on spirituality from the internet is not, on Durkheim's definition, being religious. Most, if not all, internet users realize that the internet is more than a network of information, and parents who are sometimes worried that their children may become introverted by being constantly in front of a computer screen, rather than developing social skills overlook the fact that the internet is itself a social environment. Anyone who has participated in, or simply 'lurked' in an internet chat-room can recognize how human relationships can be developed, maintained and at times broken by a group of people who probably have never met in person, but who have come to know each other exclusively in cyberspace.

The Web has thus enabled the creation of 'cyber-communities', but to what extent is it possible for a cyber-community to function as a religious community, or vice versa? To what extent do religious activities still require a physical community and physical space, or can they exist exclusively online? As technology has developed, the nature of communities has changed radically. The contemporary Christian theologian Harvey Cox, in his famous work *The Secular City*, analysed the way in which advances in twentieth-century communication affected the nature of communities, with special reference to religious communities. The old-fashioned community, he points out, was geographically defined: few people stepped outside a five-mile radius of their home, and their friends were other people who inhabited this 5-mile circle. The parish church was the focus of activity, providing not only Sunday worship, but a centre for socialization and entertainment. From the late 1950s or early 1960s, things changed. Not only did high-rise buildings make the traditional church spire less visible; television provided a more constant and professional form of entertainment than the amateur dramatics club in the church hall, and – more significantly – the growth of car ownership not only afforded the possibility of a drive in the country instead of attending a church service, but enabled people to draw on a wider geographical community for their circle of friends and their chosen form of spirituality. We can choose our friends in a way that could not be accomplished in a by-gone era; we can travel to meet them, instead of confining ourselves to our physical neighbours, and, although the parish system still remains in Britain, some members will travel long distances – sometimes 20 miles or more – simply to attend the church that seems right for them. (Cox was writing in the United States in the 1960s, and therefore does not comment on the effect of British immigration during that period, or the availability of eastern forms of religion to Westerners. We can now choose our religion, not merely our church, if we so wish.) Similar comments can be made regarding affiliation to mosques, gurdwaras and Hindu temples, and of course the increased ability to travel usually entails a wide choice in forms of spirituality. In the first half of the twentieth century, being a Buddhist in Britain would have largely meant studying Buddhist texts; from the late 1960s, improved communications helped to provide a convert to Buddhism with a wide choice of Buddhist communities to belong to.

The possibility of cyber-community takes the redefinition of community, to which Cox drew attention, a stage further. The ability to travel physically to a community's meeting place has become no longer a constraint to becoming part of a wider community. Cyberspace transcends the traditional physical constraints, making it possible to set up a community drawn from all parts of the world, and being undisturbed by geographical movements of members. Physically, emigrants may leave behind their families and friends, but now, in cyberspace, one's community need not be affected by physical relocation.

Chat-rooms, forums and e-lists all offer opportunities for internet users to create their own virtual religious communities. Second to the acquisition of information, the online discussion is perhaps the most obvious online activity in which to engage. While this has obvious advantages for students of religion, religions themselves cannot exist by simply enabling members to discuss spiritual ideas; indeed, many religious tenets are not matters for discussion, but matters of spiritual practice and obedience. The question therefore arises about the extent to which religion can be practised, rather than simply discussed, on the internet. To what extent is it possible to engage in spiritual practice online? Indeed, could one have an entire religion that only existed in cyberspace, and whose members never required to meet physically?

On 22 February 1999, the Bishop of Southwark, the Rt Revd Dr Tom Butler, gave an address to the Weaver's Company, which attracted some publicity. In this address, he made some important contrasts between physical and online relationships, drawing attention to a range of problems about the web communities. In a conventional community, people meet physically and recognize each other by their physical features, and we trust our peers to be the people they say they are. Their body language, particularly facial expressions, serves as a guide to their emotions: we can tell when someone is happy, sad, amused or disapproving. In cyberspace, things are different: in a chat-room a man can pretend to be a woman, an old person can masquerade as a youth, a wheel-chair user can act as if he or she were able-bodied, and people who do not like their appearance can display a photograph of someone else, where such facilities exist. It can be argued that there is some merit in the internet's allowing ourselves to explore new identities, and the internet is a great leveller, offering the disabled – who can easily find themselves ignored or excluded – an equal voice with those who are able-bodied. The down side, of course, is that we do not know for sure the identities of the discussants in a chat room, an e-list or bulletin board. The recent publicity about paedophiles posing in chat-rooms as teenagers indicates the dangers that are at times inherent in cyber-relationships; more normally the problem is that chat-room participants are always going to be suspect, being inherently unknowable. There is no immediate solution to such problems, if indeed all of them are problems at all, and in the main most religious adherents have used the internet as back-up to their own, more conventional, spiritual practices; for example an individual Christian attending a local church, but participating in an international online prayer network.

In recent times, a number of new religions have grown up, which exist predominantly in cyberspace, and whose members do not normally 'eyeball' (meaning, meet physically). Such religions have sometimes been called 'invented religions' – a term devised by the Australian scholar Carole Cusack. Examples include the Church of the Flying Spaghetti Monster, Discordianism and the Church of the Jedi. The last of these grew out of an internet campaign in various countries around the year 2000, in which respondents to census questionnaires were encouraged to name their religion as 'Jedi'. While many no doubt did this as a joke or a protest, some decided that Star Wars offered a serious religious message, and the Church of the Jedi emerged.

There are three distinct but related questions pertaining to cyber-religion. What is it possible to do online? What is it desirable to accomplish? And, to what extent is it possible to research such groups? Many conventional religious activities are thoroughly possible in cyberspace. Sermons are among the most accessible items, being formal pieces of writing, in non-interactive form. One can access a wide variety of prayers and meditational exercises, as well as hymns and songs. The way in which the internet can incorporate sound-tracks, graphics and videos expands the possibilities for exploiting the medium. Several websites provide musical sound-tracks for hymns and songs, making it possible for religious communities who lack musical expertise to have good-quality accompaniments for sung items.

Somewhat more interactive is the 'cyber-*puja*' in the Indian tradition. In an attempt to replicate in cyberspace what devotees do in physical space, a shrine is depicted on screen, with appropriate cyber *murtis* (a *murti* is an image of a deity) and offerings such as flowers, fruit and incense. The user can perform *puja* by using the mouse or touchpad to drag the offerings on to the cyber-shrine. Other websites offer cyber-pilgrimage. This facility enables the seeker to visit places of pilgrimage online, view pictures of the principal sights and places of devotion. Appropriate devotions and instructions for online ritual action are provided. At the time of writing, internet users can 'visit' Jerusalem and Mecca, as well as shrines of saints and holy people from various religious traditions, without leaving their homes or offices. The obvious advantage of such possibilities is that the internet opens up worship and pilgrimage to those who lack the time or the ability to visit a Hindu temple or go to the *Hajj*, and they can serve as a useful educational tool to those who are not Hindus or Muslims, but who wish to gain some idea of what takes place.

It is pertinent to assess the functions that these facilities are intended to fulfil. Are they simply curiosities, created to see what can be done on the internet? Are they educational tools, either for followers of the religion, or for interested non-members, or perhaps both? Are they meant to be sources of inspiration to those who access them? It is unlikely that cyber-*puja* and cyber-pilgrimage legitimately have the efficacy and validity of their real-life counterparts. A Muslim could scarcely count a cyber-pilgrimage to Mecca as having performed the *Hajj*, affording the title '*hajji*' (one who has performed the pilgrimage) to the cyber-pilgrim. One of the key characteristics of pilgrimage is that it requires bodily effort, involving a degree of difficulty and personal inconvenience, and in many instance due spiritual preparation is needed.

In the case of *puja*, issues arise concerning sacred images and sacred space. As Jacobs points out, in many spiritual traditions sacred space has to be appropriately defined, and specially consecrated in a prescribed way. Rules for consecration apply to physical space, where one can readily define what spaces are sacred. It is not clear how any rules about 'holy ground' could be applied in sacred space. Can one consecrate and deconsecrate URLs, for example? Or is the floor on which the cyber-worshipper is accessing the material to be considered as temporarily sacred? The status of the cyber-*murti* raises other important issues. Traditionally, a *murti* (and also its Buddhist

FIGURE 12.1 *Fo Guan Shau Monastery, Taiwan.*

counterpart, the *rupa* – literally, physical form) is reckoned to be 'alive' in a very real sense. When the *murti* is in the final process of creation, an 'awakening' ceremony is performed, at which the artist paints in the eyes – the last part of the statue to be completed. It is appropriate to consider whether cyber-*murtis* are accorded the same 'living' status in cyberspace, and, if so, whether they are specially 'awakened'. Ultimately, the religious traditions themselves must decide what validity accrues to devotion in cyberspace, how and whether a sacred cyberspace can be defined, and whether or not icons in cyberspace can be considered to have a specially sacred status.

Questions also arise regarding communities in cyberspace. Hindu *puja*s are often solitary activities, and therefore do not require the simultaneous participation of others. Cyber-pilgrimage is often – although not always – different, and certainly the pilgrimage to Mecca gains much of its meaning to the Muslim through the fact that it is done by a 'brotherhood' of believers, rather than singly. Some attempts have been made to engage multiple internet users simultaneously in religious activity, and one notable example that comes from the Christian tradition is the Church of Fools. Christianity need not have problems with regard to the notion of sacred space for participation in worship. Although Christianity has specially consecrated buildings and grounds, there is no Christian rite that needs to be performed within sacred space. It is not a requirement that baptisms and Eucharists are conducted on church premises: any place in which good intention and sincerity can be maintained will suffice.

The Church of Fools was created as an experimental aspect of a broader website, The Ship of Fools (www.ship-of-fools.com), and emerged as a cyber-church in 2004. (The reference to 'fools' alludes to St Paul's assertion in 1 Cor. 4.10, that the Christian is a 'fool for Christ' – foolish by worldly standards, but wise according to Christ's.) This was more ambitious than a chat room, bulletin board and down-loadable worship facilities, but a cyber-church, affording a facility for Christian worship exclusively in cyberspace. The 'church' was a piece of cyberspace, set out visually in the form of a conventional church, with an entrance, pews and a chancel containing a communion table or altar at the front. On the left is a pulpit, and on the right the organ. To enter the church, the web user clicked an icon to indicate his or her gender, chose a name, and was provided with a cartoon icon, which he or she could customize by selecting from a small range of outfits. The cyber-visitor was now ready to enter the sanctuary, where he or she was greeted by one of the 'wardens': these were office-bearers in the Church of Fools, whose duty was to greet newcomers and to ensure that they behaved with suitable decorum in the 'building'. By clicking one's computer mouse appropriately users could make their customized cyber-selves move through the area, and simulate a number of religious activities. They could walk around the sanctuary, contemplating icons that enlarged at a mouse-click, sit in a pew, approach the altar, make various religious gestures such as kneeling, crossing oneself, raising one's arms in a 'hallelujah', and talk discretely in chat-room mode to the other visitors. There was a crypt that could be visited, which contained sacred relics as well as mock vending machines, which are becoming a feature of some avant-garde churches in physical space.

Services took place at regular intervals. These were live, complete with a service leader and a preacher. Services were conducted almost entirely by keying messages into text-boxes in chat-room style; at the service that the present writer 'attended', the only sound was a pre-recorded organ accompaniment to a hymn, which was 'sung' by members of the cyber-congregation keying in some of the words of the verse. (The hymn proceeded rather too fast for members to key in the entire text.) The Bible readings were texted, as was the sermon and the intercessory prayer. These were all slightly interactive: participants typically keyed in responses such as 'Amen' or 'Praise the Lord', somewhat in the style of a revivalist meeting. The congregation could add their own petitions during the prayer of intercession, and there was a point in the service in which the Peace was offered by means of text-messages. A monetary offering was solicited at one point: this done by requesting participants to use their mobiles to text the word 'Amen' to a designated telephone number: this would add three British pounds to the user's phone bill, with the proceeds being transferred to the Ship of Fools.

Just as a church can fill to capacity – although this is a rare phenomenon in physical space – the Church of Fools quickly became full. A maximum of 30 participants could enter simultaneously (this was because of bandwidth limitations), after which a would-be visitor could only gain admission as a 'ghost'. Ghosts did not have customized bodies, but were translucently white; they could drift around the sanctuary at will, but not participate by contributing texted messages, and could not be seen by other participants. One advantage of being a ghost was that one could not violate the house rules: despite being reduced to cartoon characters, participants were expected to behave with due decorum. Characters are technologically prevented from walking on to the chancel area or up into the pulpit, but other forms of irreverent behaviour, such as using profane language, or performing obeisance to the drinks machine, were censured by the wardens, who could 'smite' offenders. 'Smiting' entailed excluding from the sanctuary the offending participant, who could not subsequently return.

If all this sounds somewhat lacking in seriousness, it is worth noting that the project was sponsored by the Methodist Church, and that the opening sermon was 'preached' by the Bishop of London. Office-bearers and members took it seriously, being offended by inappropriate behaviour, and becoming upset if they believed that they had been unjustly excluded from the church, even though it would have been perfectly possible for them to return subsequently with a different alias. The project may have been prompted by the Christian notion of 'incarnation': the New Testament indicates that God's becoming human in the form of Jesus Christ, who is referred to as 'the Word' (Jn 1.1) entails that God descends to the level of those to whom he speaks, and communicates in a way in which they will understand. Thus, if a significant sector of humanity is to be found surfing the internet and 'texting', this is the language in which God will speak, through the Church. The project could claim practical benefits too: in a 24-hour period it could boast up to 41,000 visitors – far more than any physical congregation could expect! Through lack of funding, the Church of Fools held its last service in September 2004, reopening in December in a somewhat more limited form.

There are several important questions that arise concerning cyber-religion. First, could there be a cyber-religion that existed exclusively in cyberspace, without the need for any physical meeting of people? Cyber-*puja*, cyber-pilgrimage and a cyber-church like the Church of Fools seem simply to be mimicking traditional religious activities that are normally – and no doubt better – conducted in the real world of physical space. Typing the text of a hymn on to a computer seems a somewhat poor substitute for singing it with fervour and feeling in a real church, accompanied by a good choir and a powerful organ. While it is possible that those who cannot attend a conventional place of worship may feel that cyber-religion is a good enough substitute for real religion, other forms of media, such as television in particular, have already moved away from conceiving of religious broadcasting as the church for the house-bound, and have exploited their distinctive features, in order to present something distinctive rather than a second-best form of church service. While it may be advantageous for religious organizations to demonstrate their up-to-dateness in exploiting virtual reality, we have still to see the emergence of distinctive forms of cyber-religion that go beyond mimicry and the dissemination of information. What such forms will be will no doubt become obvious as the internet expands and develops. In the meantime, students of religion need to continue to monitor what cyberspace affords.

There also remains the question of what cannot be achieved in cyberspace. It seems self-evident that one could not conduct a baptism, a wedding or a funeral in cyberspace – although some web users have now created cyber-cemeteries in recognition of close friends, relatives and pets. But what about a Christian Eucharist? The elements in the Christian Eucharist cannot be consecrated at a distance, and it would not be sufficient simply to bring a piece of bread and a glass of wine in front of one's computer and watch an online service. However, one clergyman – Jonathan Blake – has set up a cyber-church called the Open Episcopal Church, and one of the facilities he offers is a 'Post the Host' ministry. To surmount the problem of consecrating bread and wine over the internet, intending participants can order communion wafers and wine which he has already consecrated, and they can then go online to view one of a variety of Eucharists, selecting the style that appeals to them most. Needless to say, this practice is controversial, and many mainstream clergy would contend that internet users who participate in such a service are not receiving a valid sacrament.

There exist some types of religious activity that could conceivably be enhanced by going 'cyber'. One example is the confession of sins. Traditionally the Roman Catholic Church (as well as some congregations in the Church of England) have used the 'confession box', which is a small dual-compartment booth, in which the priest and the penitent occupy each of the two compartments, separated by a grid. This practice, at least in theory, ensures anonymity, and of course the priest is duty-bound to ensure total confidentiality, however grave the offences that are divulged in the confession. Of course, in actual practice, the priest may recognize the penitent's voice, and the more recent post-Vatican Two innovations in the confessional system whereby the confession box is replaced by a face-to-face encounter between penitent and priest – a practice more akin to present-day secular counselling – militates against anonymity.

For those who want complete anonymity in confessing their sins, the medium of the internet may seem ideal. The confessional could be replaced by a one-to-one chat-room, in which the penitent can assume a screen name, achieving total anonymity, not even having to divulge his or her email address. Such a practice, although still uncommon, might have the advantages of encouraging the guilty to seek spiritual guidance for sins they might be reluctant to confess in person, and it is possible that religious organizations that seek to encourage confession and forgiveness might exploit the medium of the internet in this way. The use of the internet for confessions, however, has given rise to numerous problems. The most serious of these is that some sites that purportedly offer this service have aimed at providing entertainment, rather than having a genuine religious purpose. What priest would publish the confessions that he heard for everyone to see, invite comments on them, or ask other 'penitents' to rate them? Because of the internet's democratic character, there is no guarantee that anyone who 'hears' such confessions is a qualified priest or counsellor, capable of giving absolution or good advice. Seeking guidance for life on the internet is therefore probably less advisable than writing to an 'agony aunt' in a popular magazine, until such time as religious organizations can professionally offer such services on an official website, in which counsellors' credentials are assured, and where seekers can find advice that is consistent with the relevant tradition.

Whatever the pros and cons of online confession, however, the Roman Catholic Church makes it clear that sins can only be confessed in person: 'Individual, integral confession and absolution remain the only ordinary way for the faithful to reconcile themselves with God and the Church' (*Catechism*, 1497). In other words, confession must be done individually, face to face. The priest represents Christ, who during his life on Earth forgave sins by his physical presence. Thus confession and absolution cannot be given over the telephone, by letter, or by more technologically sophisticated methods such as Skype, email or posting one's sins on a website.

All these uses of the internet for religious or quasi-religious purposes provide much scope for innovative research in the study of religion. However, they have also given rise to problems for the researcher. Given the scope for internet users to remain anonymous, and to assume false or multiple identities, researching online groups cannot yield real certainty. How is it possible to be sure of the composition of an online group? How can one draw definite conclusions about its size, its gender balance, the age range of its members or any other details that one would normally want in connection with a conventional religious community? How can one be certain who is really answering an online survey or questions that are emailed to web users? While much useful research has been done on online religions, these are relevant questions that face any would-be researcher in the field.

Conclusion

In conclusion, we can certainly note the importance of the internet, both in religion itself and in the study of religion. As we have noted, because of the varying quality of internet resource, the student of religion needs to be able to assess critically and select ruthlessly the material that is likely to be of value. Because the internet is still in its very early stages, we are likely to see religion assume novel forms of expression as the Web grows and as followers of religions exercise their creativity. As the academic study of religion progresses, we can expect to find more material becoming available in electronic format, as well as new studies of online religion.

DISCUSSION POINTS

1 How feasible is it for a religious community simply to exist in cyberspace? How necessary is it to meet in physical space?

2 What religious services (facilities) are possible on the internet? Might there be some that actually work better in cyber form?

3 What advantages and disadvantages do electronic resources have in the study of religion?

4 What are the problems of conducting research on religion online? To what extent are such difficulties surmountable?

Bibliography

1 The tools of the trade

(1978), *Holy Bible: New International Version*. London: Hodder and Stoughton.

AOL News (2002), 'Indian woman marries statue' (AOL News, 29 June), URL: http://news/aol.co.uk

Alston, W. P. (1964), *Philosophy of Language*. Englewood Cliffs: Prentice Hall.

Chryssides, G. D. and Wilkins, M. Z. (2006), *A Reader in New Religious Movements*. London: Continuum.

Clark, F. (1977), *Seekers and Scholars*. Milton Keynes: Open University Press.

Connolly, P. (1999), *Approaches to the Study of Religion*. London: Continuum.

Dawood, N. J. (trans.) (1974), *The Koran*. Harmondsworth: Penguin.

Fowler, H. W. and Fowler, F. G. (1954), *The Concise Oxford Dictionary of Current English*. Oxford: Clarendon Press.

Frazer, J. G. (1911–15), *The Golden Bough: A Study in Comparative Religion,* 12 vols. London: Macmillan.

Gombrich, R. (1991), *Buddhist Precept and Practice: Traditional Buddhism in the Rural Highlands of Ceylon*. Delhi: Motilal Banarsidass.

Hoffman, S. J. (1992), *Sport and Religion*. Champaign, IL: Human Kinetics Books.

James, W. (1929), *The Varieties of Religious Experience*. London: Longman, Green.

Lao Tzu (trans.) and Lau, D. C. (1963/76), *Tao TeChing*. Harmondsworth: Penguin.

Marett, R. R. (1909), *The Threshold of Religion*. London: Methuen.

Mascaro, J. (trans.) (2003), *The Bhagavad Gita*. Harmondsworth: Penguin.

Otto, R. (1928), *The Idea of the Holy*. New York: Oxford University Press.

Robertson, R. (1970), *The Sociological Interpretation of Religion*. London: Oxford.

Smart, N. (1995), *Worldviews: Crosscultural Explorations of Human Beliefs*. Englewood Cliffs, NJ: Prentice Hall.

Thomas, T. (1999), *Paul Tillich and World Religions*. Cardiff: Cardiff Academic Press.

Tillich, P. (1948), *The Shaking of the Foundations*. New York: Scribners.

— (1964), *Systematic Theology*. Welwyn, Herts: James Nisbet.

— (1965), *Ultimate Concern*. London: S.C.M.

Turner, H. W. (1974/9), *Rudolf Otto – The Idea of the Holy: A Guide for Students*. Aberdeen: Aberdeen People's Press.

Tylor, E. B. (1871), *Primitive Culture*. London: John Murray.

Waddell, L. A. (1895/1972), *Tibetan Buddhism, with its Mystic Cults, Symbolism and Mythology, and in its Relation to Indian Buddhism*. New York: Dover.

Wallis, R. (1977), *The Road to Total Freedom*. New York: Columbia University Press.

Whaling, F. (1999), 'Theological approaches', in P. Connolly (1999), pp. 233–4.

Wittgenstein, L. (1953/97), *Philosophical Investigations*. Oxford: Blackwell.

Yinger, J. M. (1970), *The Scientific Study of Religion*. London: Collier-Macmillan.

2 Methodology in religious studies

Alper, M. (2001), *The God Part of the Brain: A Scientific Interpretation of Human Spirituality and God.* New York: Rogue Press.

Anttonen, V. (2002), 'Identifying the generative mechanisms of religion', in I. Pyysiräinen and V. Anttonen (eds), *Current Approaches in the Cognitive Science of Religion.* London: Continuum.

Arberry, A. J. (1987), *Muslim Saints and Mystics, Translations of Attar, Farid al-Din.* London: Routledge and Kegan Paul.

Ayer, A. J. (1946), *Language, Truth and Logic,* 2nd edn. London: Gollancz.

Beckford, J. (1975), *The Trumpet of Prophecy.* Oxford: Blackwell.

Berger, P. (1969), *The Sacred Canopy: Elements of a Sociological Theory.* Garden City, NY: Doubleday.

Bowie, F. (2000), *The Anthropology of Religion.* Oxford: Blackwell.

Chow, R. (1993), *Writing Diaspora.* Indianapolis: Indiana University Press.

Connolly, P. (ed.) (2001), 'Introduction', *Approaches to the Study of Religion,* 2nd edn. London: Continuum.

D'Aquili, E. and Newberry, A. (1999), *The Mystical Mind: Probing the Biology of Religious Experience.* Minneapolis: Fortress Press.

Flew, A. and MacIntyre, A. (1955/63), *New Essays in Philosophical Theology.* London: S.C.M.

Flood, G. (1999), *Beyond Phenomenology: Rethinking the Study of Religion.* London: Cassell.

Freud, S. (1907), 'Obsessive actions and religious practices', in S. Freud (1957), *Collected Papers,* vol. 2. London: Hogarth, pp. 25–35.

— (1962), *The Future of an Illusion.* London: Hogarth Press.

— (1983), *Totem and Taboo.* London: Ark Paperbacks.

Giovannoli, J. (2001), *The Biology of Belief.* New York: Rosetta Press.

Hardy, A. (1979), *The Spiritual Nature of Man.* Oxford: Clarendon Press.

Harvey, D. (1990), *The Condition of Postmodernity.* Oxford: Blackwell.

Hick, J. (1972), *God and the Universe of Faiths: Essays in the Philosophy of Religion.* London: Macmillan.

— (1988), 'Religious pluralism and salvation', *Faith and Philosophy* 5(4), October: 365–77.

Hirst, P. H. (1965), 'Liberal education and the nature of knowledge', in P. H. Hirst (1974), *Knowledge and the Curriculum: A Collection of Philosophical Papers.* London: Routledge and Kegan Paul.

— (1974a), *Knowledge and the Curriculum: A Collection of Philosophical Papers.* London: Routledge and Kegan Paul.

— (1974b), 'The forms of knowledge re-visited', in P. H. Hirst (1974), *Knowledge and the Curriculum: A Collection of Philosophical Papers.* London: Routledge and Kegan Paul.

Huxley, A. (1969), *The Perennial Philosophy.* London: Chatto and Windus.

James, W. (1902), *The Varieties of Religious Experience.* London: Longman, Green.

Joseph, R. et al. (2003), *Neuro-Theology: Brain, Science, Spirituality, Religious Experience.* California: California University Press.

Jung, C. G. and von Franz, M.-L. (eds) (1964), *Man and his Symbols.* London: Aldous Books.

Katz, S. (1978), 'Language, epistemology, and mysticism', in S. Katz (ed.), *Mysticism and Philosophical Analysis.* London: Sheldon Press.

Lawson, T. and McCauley, R. (1990), *Rethinking Religion: Connecting Cognition and Culture.* Cambridge: Cambridge University Press.

Lofland, J. (1966), *Doomsday Cult: A Study of Conversion, Proselytization, and Maintenance of Faith.* Englewood Cliffs, NJ: Prentice-Hall.

Lyon, D. (1999), *Postmodernity.* Minnesota: Minnesota University Press.

Lyotard, J.-F. (1984), *The Post-Modern Condition: A Report on Knowledge.* Minneapolis: University of Minnesota Press.

Mackie, J. L. (1985), *Selected Papers,* 2 vols. Oxford: Clarendon Press.

Moody, R. (1976/2001), *Life after Life: The Investigation of a Phenomenon – Survival of Bodily Death.* London: Rider.

Morgan, P. (2003), 'President's address to the BASR AGM 2003', *British Association for the Study of Religions Bulletin,* 100, November, pp. 25–30.

Newberg, A., D'Aquili, E. and Rause, V. (2001), *Why God Won't Go Away: Brain Science and the Biology of Belief.* New York: Ballantine Books.

Otto, R. (1958), *The Idea of the Holy,* trans. J. Harvey. New York: Galaxy Books.

Pals, D. (1999), 'Reductionism and belief', in R. McCutcheon (ed.), *The Insider/Outsider Problem in The Study of Religion.* London: Cassell.

Parrinder, G. (1976), *Mysticism in the World's Religions.* London: Sheldon Press.

Plato (1966), *The Republic,* trans. H. D. P. Lee. Harmondsworth: Penguin.

Poster, M. (1988), *Jean Baudrillard: Selected Writings.* Cambridge: Polity Press.

Puwar, N. (2003), 'Melodramic postures and constructions', in N. Puwar and P. Raghuram (eds), *South Asian Women in the Diaspora.* Oxford: Berg.

Smart, B. (1992), *Modern Conditions, Post Modern Controversies.* London: Routledge and Kegan Paul.

Smart, N. (1978), 'Understanding religious experience', in S. Katz (ed.), *Mysticism and Philosophical Analysis.* London: Sheldon Press.

— (1995), *Worldviews: Crosscultural Explorations of Human Beliefs,* 2nd edn. New Jersey: Prentice Hall.

— (2002), 'Foreword', in P. Connolly (ed.), *Approaches to the Study of Religion.* London: Continuum.

Stark, R. and Bainbridge, W. (1985), *The Future of Religion.* Berkeley: University of California Press.

Stevenson, I. (1974), *Twenty Cases Suggestive of Reincarnation,* 2nd edn. Charlottesville: University of Virginia Press.

Stoller, P. and Olkes, C. (1989), *In Sorcery's Shadow.* Chicago: University of Chicago Press.

Stringer, E. T. (1996), *Action Research: A Handbook for Practitioners.* London: Sage.

Sundkler, B. (1961), *Bantu Prophets in South Africa.* London: Oxford University Press.

Sutcliffe, S. (2003), *Children of the New Age : A History of Spiritual Practices.* London: Routledge and Kegan Paul.

Thomas, T. (1988), *The British: Their Religious Beliefs and Practices 1800–1986.* London: Allen Lane.

— (1995), 'Popular religion', in J. Hinnells (ed.), *A New Dictionary of Religions.* London: Routledge and Kegan Paul.

Troelsch, E. (1931), *The Social Teachings of the Christian Churches,* vol. 2, trans. Olive Wyong. New York: MacMillan.

Weber, M. (1988/04), 'Die "Objektivität" sozialwissenschaftlicher und sozialpolitischerErkenntnis', in Max Weber, *GesammelteAufsätzezurWissenschaftslehre,* ed. J. Winckelmann, 7th edn, pp. 146–214. Tübingen: Mohr, 1st edn, 1904, *ArchivfürSozialwissenschaft und Sozialpolitik,* vol. 19, pp. 22–87.

Weibe, D. (1999), 'Appropriating religion: understanding religion as an object of science', in *Approaching Religion,* Part I, ed. Ahlbach, T. ScriptaInstitutiDonneriani, 17:1. Abo: Donner Institute.

Zahir, S. (2003), '"Changing views": theory and practice in a participatory community arts project', in N. Puwar and P. Raghuram (eds), *South Asian Women in the Diaspora.* Oxford: Berg.

3 Insiders and outsiders

Arweck, E. and Stringer, M. D. (2002), *Theorizing Faith: The Insider/Outsider Problem in the Study of Ritual.* Birmingham, UK: University of Birmingham Press.

Augustine (1972), *The City of God,* trans. Henry Bettenson. Harmondsworth: Penguin.

Balch, R. W. and Taylor, D. (1977), 'Seekers and saucers: the role of the Cultic milieu in joining a UFO cult', *American Behavioral Scientist* 20(6), July/August: 839–60. Reprinted in Chryssides (2011): 37–52.

Brown, K. M. (1991, 2001), *Mama Lola: A Vodou Priestess in Brooklyn.* Berkeley, CA: University of California Press.

Chryssides, G. D. (ed.) (2011), *Heaven's Gate: Postmodernity and Popular Culture in a Suicide Group.* Farnham, England: Ashgate.

Dawkins, R. (2007), *The God Delusion.* London: Black Swan.

Dawson, A. (2010), 'Positionality and role-identity in a new religious context: participant observation at Céu do Mapià', *Religion* 40: 173–81.

Festinger, L., Riecken, H. W. and Schachter, S. (1956, 2008), *When Prophecy Fails.* London: Pinter and Martin.

Gordon, D. (1987), 'Getting close by staying distant: fieldwork with proselytizing groups', *Qualitative Sociology* 10(3): 267–87; cited in Waterhouse (2002): 65.

Got Questions Ministries (2013), 'What is a Christian?' URL: www.gotquestions.org/what-is-a-Christian.html. Accessed on 8 June 2013.

Lofland, J. (1966), *Doomsday Cult: A Study of Conversion, Proselytization, and Maintenance of Faith.* Englewood Cliffs, NJ: Prentice-Hall.

MacIntyre, A. (1964), 'Is understanding compatible with believing?', in R. McCutcheon (ed.), *The Insider/Outsider Problem in the Study of Religion: A Reader.* London: Continuum.

McCutcheon, R. T. (ed.) (1999), *The Insider/Outsider Problem in the Study of Religion.* London: Cassell.

Palmer, S. J. (2004), *Aliens Adored: Raël's UFO Religion.* New Brunswick, NJ: Rutgers University Press.

Phillips, D. Z. (1965), *The Concept of Prayer.* London: Routledge and Kegan Paul.

Prothero, S. (1996), *The White Buddhist: The Asian Odyssey of Henry Steel Olcott.* Bloomington and Indianapolis: Indiana University Press.

Sutcliffe, S. J. (2003), *Children of the New Age: A History of Spiritual Practices.* London: Routledge and Kegan Paul.

Waterhouse, H. (2002), 'Insider/Outsider perspectives on ritual in Sōka Gakkai International–UK'; in Arweck and Stringer, pp. 57–75.

Wittgenstein, L. (1963 [1953]), *Philosophical Investigations.* Oxford: Blackwell.

4 Does size matter?

Anon (2005), www.daisy.freeserve.co.uk/stolgy_3htm.

Balch, R. W. and Taylor, D. (1977), 'Seekers and saucers: the role of the cultic milieu in joining a UFO cult', *American Behavioral Scientist* 20(6), July/August: 839–60. Reprinted in Chryssides (2011): 37–52.

Barrett, D. V. (1996), *Sects, 'Cults' and Alternative Religions: A World Survey and Sourcebook.* London: Cassell.

Brierley, P. (1991), *'Christian' England.* London: MARC Europe.

— (1999), *UK Christian Handbook: Millennium Edition.* London: Christian Research.

Bruce, S. (1995), *Religion in Modern Britain.* Oxford: Oxford University Press.

— (2000), *God is Dead: Secularization in the West*. Oxford: Blackwell.

Central Statistical Office (2006), *Social Trends*. London: HMSO.

Christian Broadcasting Network (2007), 'Mormons are fastest growing religion'. URL: www.cbn.com/spirituallife/ChurchAndMinistry/Evangelism/Mormons_Are_Fastest_Growing_Religion.aspx. Accessed on 29 January 2007.

Clarke, J. F. (1879), *Ten Great Religions: An Essay in Comparative Theology*. Boston: Houghton, Osgood and Company.

Coakley, F. (2001), 'General background to the 1851 Religious Census'. URL: www.isle-of-man.com/manxnotebook/methdism/rc1851/rc_gb.htm. Accessed on 12 October 2006.

Cox, H. (1994), *Fire from Heaven: The Rise of Pentecostal Spirituality and the Reshaping of Religion in the Twenty-First Century*. New York: Addison-Wesley.

Crim, K. (ed.) (1989), *The Perennial Dictionary of World Religions*. San Francisco: HarperCollins. Originally published as *Abingdon Dictionary of Living Religions* (1981).

Family International, The (1998), *The Love Charter*. Zurich, Switzerland: The Family International.

Heald, G. (1999), 'Taking faith's temperature', *The Tablet*, vol. 253, no. 8,313, 18 December, p. 1729.

— (2001), 'The British Christmas', *The Tablet*, vol. 255, no. 8,415, 22–29 December, p. 1857.

Heathcote-James, E. (2002), *Seeing Angels: True Contemporary Accounts of Hundreds of Angelic Experiences*. London: John Blake.

Hubbard, L. R. (1950), *Dianetics: The Modern Science of Mental Health*. New York: Hermitage House.

Huff, D. (1954), *How to Lie with Statistics*. New York: Norton.

Hunter, P. D. (2006), 'adherents.com'. www.adherents.com. Accessed on17 November 2006.

National Statistics (2003), '390,000 Jedis there are. But did hoax campaign boost response in teens and 20s?', 13 February. URL: www.statistics.gov.uk/cci/nugget.asp?id=297. Accessed on 2 December 2006.

National Statistics Online (2006), URL: www.statistics.gov.uk. Accessed on 2 December 2006.

Nelson, D. (2006), 'Why is Buddhism the fastest-growing religion in Australia?', Buddhanet: Buddhist Dharma Educational Association. www.buddhanet.net/whybudoz.htm. Accessed on 23 June 2006.

Ontario Consultants on Religious Tolerance (2001), 'Growth rate of Christianity and Islam: which will be the dominant religion in the future?' *Religious Tolerance*.Org. URL: www.religioustolerance.org/growth_isl_chr.htm. Accessed on 2 December 2006.

Price, R. (1769), *Observations on Reversionary Payments*. London: T. Cadell.

Thomas, R. (2003), *Counting People In: Changing the Way We Think about Membership and the Church*. London: S.P.C.K.

Wah, C. R. (2001), 'An introduction to research and analysis of Jehovah's Witnesses: a view from the Watchtower', *Review of Religious Research* 43(2): 161–74.

Watch Tower Bible and Tract Society (2002), *Yearbook of Jehovah's Witnesses*. Brooklyn, NY: Watchtower Bible and Tract Society of New York, Inc. and International Bible Students Association.

5 Key figures in the study of religion

(1978) *Holy Bible: New International Version*. London: Hodder and Stoughton.

Bainbridge, W. S. (1997), *The Sociology of Religious Movements*. London: Routledge and Kegan Paul.

Becker, H. (1932), *Systematic Sociology on the Basis of the Beziehungslehre and Gebildelehre of Leopold von Wiese*. New York: Wiley.

Blavatsky, H. P. (1877/1976), *Isis Unveiled: A Master-Key to the Mysteries of Ancient and Modern Science and Theology*. Pasadena, CA: Theosophical University Press.

— (1888/1977), *The Secret Doctrine: The Synthesis of Science, Religion, and Philosophy*. Pasadena, CA: Theosophical University Press.

Burnouf, E. (1826), *Essai sur le Paliou langue sacrée de la presq'île au-dela du Gange*. Paris: Dondey-Duprépère et fils.

Carpenter, J. E. (1900), *A Century of Comparative Religion, 1800–1900* (Reprinted from The Inquirer). Oxford: Private publication.

Comte, A. (1830/1970), *Introduction to Positivist Philosophy,* trans. F. Ferré. Indianapolis: Bobbs-Merrill.

David-Néel, A. (1911/39), *Buddhism: Its Doctrines and Methods*. London: John Lane.

— (1927), *My Journey to Lhasa*. Harmondsworth: Allen Lane.

— (1931a), *Initiates and Initiations in Tibet*. London: Rider.

— (1931b), *Magic and Mystery in Tibet*. New York: C. Kendall.

— (1964), *The Secret Oral Teachings in Tibetan Buddhist Sects*. Calcutta: Maha Bodhi Society of India.

Durkheim, E. (1915/71), *The Elementary Forms of the Religious Life*. London: Allen & Unwin.

Evans-Wentz, W. Y. (1927), *The Tibetan Book of the Dead*. London: Oxford University Press.

— (1928), *Tibet's Great Yogi, Milarepa*. London: Oxford University Press.

— (1935), *Tibetan Yoga and Secret Doctrines*. London: Oxford University Press.

— (1954), *The Tibetan Book of the Great Liberation*. Oxford: Oxford University Press.

Farquhar, J. N. (1904), *The Age and Origin of the Gita*. n.p.

— (1906), *Gita and Gospel*. London: Christian Literature Society.

— (1913), *The Crown of Hinduism*. London: Oxford University Press.

— (1920a), *Hinduism: Its Content and Value*. London: Red Triangle Press.

— (1920b), *An Outline of the Religious Literature of India*. London: Oxford University Press.

Feuerbach, L. (1841), *The Essence of Christianity*. London: Trübner.

Frazer, J. G. (1911–15), *The Golden Bough: A Study in Comparative Religion,* 12 vols. London: Macmillan.

Freud, S. (1907), 'Obsessive actions and religious practices', in S. Freud (1957), *Collected Papers*, vol. 2. London: Hogarth, pp. 25–35.

— (1913/50), *Totem and Taboo: Resemblances between the Psychic Lives of Savages and Neurotics*. London: Routledge and Kegan Paul.

— (1927/62), *The Future of an Illusion*. London: Hogarth Press / Institute of Psycho-Analysis.

Graf, K. H. (1866), *Die geschichtlichen Bücher des Alten Testaments*. Leipzig: T. O. Weigel.

Heber, R., 'From Greenland's icy mountains', in *The English Hymnal* (1933), no. 547. Oxford: Oxford University Press.

Hegel, G. W. F. (1861), *Lectures on the Philosophy of History,* trans. from 3rd German edn by J. Sibree. London: Henry G. Bohn.

Humphreys, C. (1953), *Buddhism*. Harmondsworth: Penguin.

Jones, W. (1799), *The Works of Sir William Jones,* 6 vols. London: G. G. and J. Robinson.

Jowett, B. (1860), *Essays and Reviews*. London: Longman, Green, Longman and Roberts.

Lang, A. (1898/1989), *The Making of Religion*. London: Longman, Green.

Lopez, D. S. Jr. (1998), *Prisoners of Shangri-La*. Chicago: University of Chicago Press.

Malinowski, B. (1922), *Argonauts of the Western Pacific: An Account of Native Enterprise and Adventure in the Archipelagoes of Melanesian New Guinea*. London: Routledge and Kegan Paul.

Marett, R. R. (1909), *The Threshold of Religion*. London: Methuen.

Marx, K. (1843/1970), *Critique of Hegel's Philosophy of Right*. London: Routledge and Kegan Paul.

Marx, K. and Engels, F. (1848/1973), *Communist Manifesto*. Peking, China: Foreign Languages Press.

Monier-Williams, M. (1877), *Hinduism*. London: S.P.C.K.

Monier-Williams, M. (trans.) (1992), Shikshapatri. Accessible at URL: www.shikshapatri. org.uk/~imagedb/content.php/monier. Accessed on 30 November 2006.

Müller, F. M. (1879–1910), *Sacred Books of the East,* 50 vols. Oxford: Clarendon.

Office of National Statistics (2006), *Social Trends,* no. 36. Basingstoke: Macmillan.

O'Flaherty, W. D. (trans.) (1981), *The Rig Veda*. Harmondsworth: Penguin.

— (1991), *The Laws of Manu*. Harmondsworth: Penguin.

Osiander, A. (1545), *HarmoniaeEvangelicœlibri IIII* [Harmony of the Four Books of the Evangelists]. Lutetiae (Paris): Ex officina Rob. StephanitypographiRegii.

Rampa, T. L. (1959), *The Third Eye*. London: Transworld Publishers.

Rhys-Davids, T. W. (1921), *Dialogues of the Buddha*. Oxford: Clarendon.

Schmidt, W. (1912–55), *Der Ursprung der Gottesidee* ('The Origin of the Idea of God'), 12 vols. Münster: Aschendorff.

Smith, W. R. (1881), *The Old Testament in the Jewish Church: A Course of Lectures in Biblical Criticism*. Edinburgh: Adam and Charles Black.

— (1882), *The Prophets of Israel and their Place in History to the End of the 8th Century B.C.* Edinburgh: Adam and Charles Black.

— (1885), *Kinship and Marriage in Early Arabia*. Cambridge: University Press.

— (1889), *Lectures on the Religion of the Semites*. Edinburgh: Adam and Charles Black.

Spencer, H. (1858), *Essays: Scientific, Political and Speculative*. London: Longman, Brown, Green, Longman and Roberts.

Spiro, M. (1970), *Buddhism and Society: A Great Tradition and its Burmese Vicissitudes*. New York: Harper & Row.

Strauss, D. F. (1846/1973), *The Life of Jesus Critically Examined*. London: S.C.M.

Sugirtharajah, S. (2003), *Imagining Hinduism: A Post-Colonial Perspective*. London: Routledge and Kegan Paul.

Suzuki, D. T. (1927–34/70), *Essays in Zen Buddhism*. London: Rider.

Troeltsch, E. (1931), *The Social Teachings of the Christian Church*. London: Macmillan.

Tylor, E. B. (1861), *Anahuac; or Mexico and the Mexicans Ancient and Modern*. London: Longman, Green, Longman and Roberts.

— (1865), *Researches into the Early History of Mankind and the Development of Civilization*. London: John Murray.

— (1871), *Primitive Culture*. London: John Murray.

Waddell, L. A. (1895), *The Buddhism of Tibet, or Lamaism. Re-titled in 1972: Tibetan Buddhism: With its Mystic Cults, Symbolism and Mythology*. New York: Dover.

Ward, W. (1818), *A View of the History, Literature and Mythology of the Hindoos,* 4 vols. Serampore, India: Mission Press. (Originally published as *Account of the Writings, Religion and Manners of the Hindoos*, 1811.)

Weber, M. (1904–5/1930), *The Protestant Ethic and the Spirit of Capitalism*. New York: Scribner.

Wellhausen, J. (1889), *Die Composition des Hexateuchs und der historischenBücher des Alten Testaments*. Berlin: Georg Reimer.

Wilson, B. (1966), *Religion in Secular Society: A Sociological Comment*. Harmondsworth: Penguin.

Wilson, H. H. (1814), *The Meghaduta, or 'Cloud Messenger': A Poem in the Sanscrit Language*. London: Black, Parry.

—(1827), *Select Specimens of the Theatre of the Hindus*. Calcutta, India: V. Holcroft.

— (1828), *Mackenzie Collection*. Calcutta, India: Asiatic Publications.

Yinger, J. M. (1970), *The Scientific Study of Religion*. New York: Macmillan.

6 Phenomenology and its critics

(1978), *Holy Bible: New International Version*. London: Hodder and Stoughton.

Berkeley, G. (1962), *The Principles of Human Knowledge*. Glasgow: Collins.

Bettis, J. D. (ed.) (1969), *The Phenomenology of Religion*. London: S.C.M.

Buber, M. (1970), *I and Thou,* trans. W. Kaufmann. Edinburgh: T & T Clark.

Connolly, P. (1999), *Approaches to the Study of Religion*. London: Continuum.

Cox, J. L. (1996), *Expressing the Sacred: An Introduction to the Phenomenology of Religion*. Harare: University of Zimbabwe.

de la Saussaye, P. D. Chantepie (1887), *Lehrbuch der Religionsgeschichte* ('Handbook of the History of Religions'). Freiburg: J. C. B. Mohr.

Derrida, J. (1973), *Speech and Phenomenology*. Evanson, IL: Northwestern University Press.

Descartes, R. (1998), *Meditations and Other Metaphysical Writings*. Harmondsworth: Penguin.

Eliade, M. (1963), *Patterns in Comparative Religion*. Cleveland: Meridian.

Flew, A. G. N. (1971), *An Introduction to Western Philosophy: Ideas and Arguments from Plato to Sartre*. London: Thames and Hudson.

Flood, G. (1999), *Beyond Phenomenology: Rethinking the Study of Religion*. London: Cassell.

Husserl, E. (1913/82), *Ideas: General Introduction to Pure Phenomenology*. London: Allen & Unwin.

Kant, I. (1964), *Immanuel Kant's Critique of Pure Reason,* trans. N. K. Smith. London: Macmillan.

Locke, J. (1965), *An Essay Concerning Human Understanding*. London: Collier-Macmillan.

Lyotard, J.-F. (1991), *Phenomenology*. Albany: Suny Press.

Mascaro, J. (trans.) (1977), *The Dhammapada*. Harmondsworth: Penguin.

— (2003), *The Bhagavad Gita*. Harmondsworth: Penguin.

Open University, AD208 (1977), *Seekers and Scholars*. Milton Keynes: Open University Press.

Reachout Trust, 'A Christian witness to Islam', 1 August 2006. URL: www.reachouttrust. org/articles/world/islam.htm. Accessed on 1 August 2006.

Sharpe, E. J. (1977), 'Some modern approaches to the study of religion', in The Open University, AD208 (1977), *Seekers and Scholars*, pp. 48–83.

Smart, N. (1995), *Worldviews: Crosscultural Explorations of Human Beliefs*. Englewood Cliffs, NJ: Prentice Hall.

van der Leeuw, G. (1938), *Religion in Essence and Manifestation*, trans. J. E. Turner. London: Allen & Unwin.

Weightman, S. (1977), *Seekers and Scholars*. Bletchley: Open University Press.

7 Colonialism and postcolonialism in the study of religion

Akindele, S. T., Gidado, T. O. and Olaopo, O. R. (2002), *Globalisation, Its Implications and Consequences for Africa. Globalization.* 2.1 (Winter).

Anderson, B. (1991), *Imagined Communities: Reflections on the Origin and Spread of Nationalism.* London: Verso.

Appadurai, A. (1974), 'Right and left hand castes in South India', *Indian Economic and Social History Review* 11(2–3): 216–59.

— (1977), 'Kings, sects and temples in South India, 1350–1700 A.D', *Economic and Social History Review* 14(1): 47–73.

— (1981), *Worship and Conflict under Colonial Rule: A South Indian Case.* New York: Cambridge University Press.

— (1983), 'The puzzling status of Brahman temple priests in Hindu India', *South Asian Anthropologist* 4(1): 43–52.

— (with Halbfass, W.) (1986), 'History of the study of Indian religions', in M. Eliade (ed.), *Encyclopaedia of Religion.* New York: Macmillan.

— (1990), 'Disjuncture and difference in the global cultural economy', *Theory, Culture, and Society* 7(2–3): 295–310 (short version).

— (1995) 'The production of locality', in R. Fardon (ed.), *Counterwork.* London: Routledge and Kegan Paul.

— (1996) 'Sovereignty without territoriality: notes for a postnational geography', in P. Yaeger (ed.), *The Geography of Identity.* Ann Arbor, Michigan: University of Michigan Press, pp. 40–58.

Arberry, A. J. (1956), *Sufism,* 2nd edn. London: Allen & Unwin.

Asad, T. (1993), *Genealogies of Religion: Discipline and Reasons of Power in Christianity and Islam.* Baltimore and London: Johns Hopkins University Press.

— (2003), *Formations of the Secular: Christianity, Islam, Modernity.* Stanford, CA: Stanford University Press.

Ashcroft, B., Griffiths, G. and Tiffin, H. (1989), *The Empire Writes Back: Theory and Practice in Post-Colonial Literatures.* London: Routledge and Kegan Paul.

Ballard, R. (1996), 'Panth, Kismet, Dharm te Qaum: continuity and change in four dimensions of Punjabi religion', in P. and S. Thandi (eds), *Globalisation and the Region: Explorations of Punjabi Identity.* Coventry: Coventry University Press.

Berger, P. (1974), 'Some second thoughts on substantive versus functional definitions of religion', *Journal for the Scientific Study of Religion,* vol. 13, part 2.

Bhabha, H. (1990), 'Introduction: narrating the nation', in H. K. Bhabha (ed.), *Nation and Narration.* New York: Routledge and Kegan Paul.

— (1994), *The Location of Culture.* London: Routledge and Kegan Paul.

Bruce, S. (2002), *God is Dead: Secularization in the West.* Blackwell, Oxford. Unknown Publisher.

— (2003), 'The demise of Christianity in Britain', in G. Davie, P. Heelas and L. Woodhead (eds), *Predicting Religion: Christian, Secular and Alternative Futures. Religion & Theology in Interdisciplinary Perspective.* Ashgate: Aldershot, United Kingdom, pp. 53–63.

— (2011), *Secularization: In Defence of an Unfashionable Theory.* Oxford: Oxford University Press.

Césaire, A. (1955), *Discourse on Colonialism.* California: The University of California.

Chakrabarty, D. (2000), *Provincializing Europe: Postcolonial Thought and Historical Difference*. Princeton: Princeton University Press.

Chidester, D. (1996), *Savage Systems: Colonialism and Comparative Religion in Southern Africa*. Charlottesville: University Press of Virginia.

Durkheim, E. (1976), *The Elementary Forms of Religious Life,* 2nd edn, trans. J. Swain. London: Allen & Unwin.

Esposito, J. and Voll, J. O. (1996), *Islam and Democracy*. New York: Oxford University Press.

Fafowora, O. O. (1998), 'Management imperatives of globalisation', *Management in Nigeria: Journal of Nigerian Institute of Management* 34(2–4), April–December: 5–9.

Finnström, S., *Postcoloniality and the Postcolony: Theories of the Global and the Local,* www.postcolonialweb.org/poldiscourse/finnstrom/finnstrom1.html. Accessed on 1 May 2013. Previously published in the series Working Papers in Cultural Anthropology, No. 7, 1997. Department of Cultural Anthropology and Ethnology, Uppsala University.

Fitzgerald, T. (2000), *The Ideology of Religious Studies*. New York: Oxford University Press.

Fox, R. (1985), *Lions of the Punjab: Culture in the Making*. California: University of California Press.

Geaves, R. A. (2000), *The Sufis of Britain*. Cardiff: Cardiff Academic Press.

Gellner, E. (1968), 'The Pendulum Swing Theory of Islam', in R. Robertson (ed.), *Sociology of Religion*. Harmondworth: Penguin.

Knott, K. (2002), 'How to study religion in the modern world', *Religions in the Modern World: Traditions and Transformations*, ed. L. Woodhead et al. London: Routledge and Kegan Paul, pp. 13–36.

Kvaerne, P. (2002a), 'The religions of Tibet', in J. Kitagawa (ed.), *The Religious Traditions of Asia*. London: Routledge and Kegan Paul.

— (2002b), 'Bon', in J. Kitagawa (ed.), *The Religious Traditions of Asia*. London: Routledge and Kegan Paul.

Landow, G. (last modified 18 March 2002), *Political Discourse: Theories of Colonialism and Postcolonialism*, www.postcolonialweb.org/poldiscourse/said/orient14.html. Accessed on 1 May 2013.

Lehmann, D. (2002), 'Religion and globalization', in L. Woodhead et al. (eds), *Religions in the Modern World: Traditions and Transformations*. London: Routledge and Kegan Paul, pp. 407–28.

MacEwan, A. (1990), 'What's "new" about the "New International Economy"', mimeo, Boston: University of Massachussets.

Mandelbaum, D. G. (1966), 'Transcendental and pragmatic aspects of religion', *American Anthropologist* 68(5), October: 1174–91.

Nandy, A. (1983), *The Intimate Enemy: Loss and Recovery of Self Under Colonialism*. Oxford: Oxford University Press.

Ohiorhenuan, J. F. E. (1998), 'The South in an era of globalisation', in *Cooperation South*, no. 2, pp. 6–15.

Ohuabunwa, Mazi S. I. (1999), 'The challenges of globalisation to the Nigerian industrial sector', *Nigerian Tribune,* 14 December, pp. 20–1.

Overmyer, D. (2002), 'Chinese religion', in J. Kitagawa (ed.), *The Religious Traditions of Asia*. London: Routledge and Kegan Paul.

Parrinder, G. (1949), *West African Religion*. London: Epworth Press.

Roy, A. (1998), 'Islamicization in South Asia with special reference to the Bengali-speaking region: a conceptual and historic re-evaluation', in G. Oddie (ed.), *Religious Traditions in South Asia*. London: Curzon.

Said, E. (1977), *Orientalism*. New York: Pantheon; Harmondsworth: Penguin.

Sharma, U. (1970), 'The immortal cowherd and the saintly carrier: an essay in the study of cults', *Sociological Bulletin*, 19 September, pp. 137–52.

Singer, M. (1972), *When a Great Tradition Modernises: An Anthropological Approach to Indian Civilization*. New York: Praegar.

Spiro, M. (1970), *Buddhism and Society: A Great Tradition and its Burmese Vicissitudes*. Berkeley: University of California Press.

Spivak, G. (2001), Political discourse: theories of colonialism and postcolonialism (http://landow. stg.brown.edu/post/poldiscourse/spivak/spivak1.html). Accessed on 3 May 2013.

Srinivas, M. N. (1952), *Religion and Society among the Coorgs of South India*. Oxford: Clarendon Press.

— (1989), *The Cohesive Role of Sanskritisation*. Delhi: Oxford University Press.

Swearer, D. (2002), 'Buddhism in Southeast Asia', in J. Kitagawa (ed.), *The Religious Traditions of Asia*. London: Routledge and Kegan Paul.

Tarachand, S. (1963), *Influence of Islam on Indian Culture*. Allahabad: Indian Press.

Weightman, S. (1978), *Hinduism in the Village Setting*. Milton Keynes: Open University.

Werbner, P. (1998), *Embodying Charisma*. London: Routledge and Kegan Paul.

— (2002), *Imagined Diasporas among Manchester Muslims*. Oxford: James Currey.

8 Authenticity and diversity

Bailey, G. (1998), 'Problems of the interpretation of data pertaining to religious interaction in ancient India: the conversion stories in the Sutta Nipata', in G. Oddie (ed.), *Religious Traditions in South Asia*. London: Curzon.

Bloom, W. (1993), 'Practical spiritual practice', *One Earth* 12, pp. 18–21.

Easwaren, E. (trans.) (1985), *The Bhagavad Gita*. Harmondsworth: Penguin Arkana.

Eisenstadt, S. (1968), 'Charisma and institution building: Max Weber and modern sociology', in S. Eisenstadt (ed.), *Max Weber on Charisma and Institution Building*. Chicago: Chicago University Press.

Embree, A. (1988), *Sources of Indian Tradition*, vol. 1. Columbia: Columbia University Press.

Geaves, R. A. (1997), 'Baba Balaknath: an exploration of religious identity', *Diskus*, vol. 5.1.

— (1998), 'The worship of Baba Balaknath', *International Journal of Punjabi Studies* 5(1), January–July.

— (2002), 'The dynamics of Sikh fundamentalism', in C. Partridge (ed.), *Fundamentalisms*. Carlisle: Paternoster.

Geertz, A. (2002), 'Religion and community in indigenous contexts', *British Association for the Study of Religions Occasional Papers*, 23.

Leppokari, M. (2002), *The End is a Beginning*. Turku: Abo Akademi University.

McLeod, W. H. (1995), *The Historical Dictionary of Sikhism*. London: Scarecrow Press.

Oberoi, H. (1994), *The Reconstruction of Religious Boundaries*. Chicago: Chicago University Press.

Singh, T., Singh, J., Singh, K., Singh, B. H. and Singh, K. (trans.) (1973), *The Sacred Writings of the Sikhs*, 3rd edn. London: Allen & Unwin.

Smart, N. (1995), *Worldviews: Cross-Cultural Explorations of Human Behaviour*. New Jersey: Prentice Hall.

Sutcliffe, S. (2003), *Children of the New Age*. London: Routledge and Kegan Paul.

Vaudeville, C. (1987), 'Sant Mat: Santism as a universal path to sanctity', in *The Sants: Studies in a Devotional Tradition of India*. New Delhi: Motilal Banarsidass.

Whinfield, E. H. (trans.) (1979), *MasnaviiMa'navi: The Teachings of Rumi*. London: Octagon Press.
Yeats, W. B. (1965), 'The Second Coming' from *Selected Poetry*, ed. Norman Jefferies. London: MacMillan.

9 Fieldwork in the study of religion

Anwar, M. (1980), 'Religious identity in plural societies: the case of Britain', *The Journal of the Institute of Muslim Minority Affairs* 2.2/3.1: 110–21.
Bailey, C. (1996), *A Guide to Field Research*. Thousand Oaks: Pine Forge Press.
Brodeur, P. (2004), 'Integrating site visits in the pluralism project at Connecticut College', *Religious Studies News*, AAR Edition, October.
Burford, G. (2004), 'The nuts and bolts of site visits', *Religious Studies News*, AAR Edition, October, vol. 19:4, American Academy of Religions.
Carlson, J. (2004), 'Site visits and epistemological diversity in the study of religion', *Religious Studies News*, AAR Edition, October.
Embree, A. (1988), *Sources of Indian Tradition*, vol. 1. Columbia: Columbia University Press.
Flueckiger, J. (2004), 'Unexpected learning opportunities of the site visit', *Religious Studies News*, AAR Edition, October.
Francis, E. K. (1976), *Interethnic Relations*. New York: Elsevier.
Fruzzetti, L. (1985), 'Muslim rituals: household rites versus public festivals in rural India', in I. Ahmad (ed.), *Ritual and Religion among Muslims of the Subcontinent*. Lahore: Vanguard Books, pp. 91–112.
Geaves, R. A. (1995), *Sectarian Influences within Islam in Britain. Community Religions Project Monograph Series*. Leeds: University of Leeds.
— (1997), 'Baba Balaknath: an exploration of religious identity', *Diskus* 4(2). Accessible at URL www.basr.ac.uk/diskus/diskus1–6/GEAVES.txt Accessed on 3 August 2013.
— (1998), 'The worship of Baba Balaknath', *International Journal of Punjabi Studies* 5(1), January–July.
Gilliat-Ray, S. (2005), '(Not) accessing Deobandi Dar ul-Ulooms in Britain', *Fieldwork in Religion* 1(1), April: 7–33.
Hammersley, M. and Atkinson, P. (1983), *Ethnography in Practice*. London: Tavistock.
Hoffman, J. E. (1980), 'Problems of access in the study of social elites and boards of directors', in W. B. Shaffir et al. (eds), *Fieldwork Experience: Qualitative Approaches to Social Research*. New York: St Martins Press.
Jackson, R. (1995), 'Religious education's representation of "Religions" and "Cultures"', *British Journal of Educational Studies* XXXXIII(3): 272–89.
— (1997), *Religious Education: An Interpretive Approach*. London: Hodder & Stoughton.
Jules-Rosette, B. (1978), 'The veil of objectivity: prophesy, divination and social enquiry', *American Anthropologist* 80(3): 549–70.
Knott, K. (1992), 'The role of religious studies in understanding the ethnic experience', *Community Religions Project Research Paper*. Leeds: University of Leeds.
Malinowski, B. (1922), *Argonauts of the Western Pacific*. London: Routledge and Kegan Paul.
McCarthy, K. (2003), 'Roundtable: site visits in the study of religion: practice, problems, prospects', *American Academy of Religion Annual Meeting*, Atlanta.

Nesbitt, E. (1991), 'My dad's a Hindu, my mum's side are Sikhs', *Issues in Religious Identity*. Charlbury: National Foundation for Arts Education.

— (2004), *Intercultural Education: Ethnographic and Religious Approaches*. Brighton: Sussex Academic Press.

Oberoi, H. (1994), *The Construction of Religious Boundaries – Culture, Identity and Diversity in the Sikh Tradition*. Chicago: University of Chicago Press.

Otto, R. (1958), *The Idea of the Holy*. New York: Oxford University Press.

Pals, D. (1999), 'Reductionism and belief: an appraisal of recent attacks on the doctrine of irreducible religion', in R. T. McCutcheon (ed.), *The Insider/Outsider Problem in the Study of Religion*. London: Cassell.

Pawlowsky, P. (1994), *The Basics of Christianity*. London: S.C.M.

Said, E. (1981), *Covering Islam*. London: Routledge and Kegan Paul.

Schutz, A. (1964), 'The stranger: an essay in social psychology', in A. Schutz (ed.), *Collected Papers*, vol. II. The Hague: MartinusNijhoff.

Steier, F. (ed.) (1991), *Research and Reflexivity*. London: Sage Productions.

Thomas, T. (1988), *The British: Their Religious Beliefs and Practices 1800–1986*. London: Routledge and Kegan Paul.

Warren, C. A. B. (1974), *Identity and Community in the Gay World*. New York: Wiley.

Werbner, P. (1998), 'Langar: pilgrimage, sacred exchange and perpetual sacrifice in a Sufi saint's lodge', in *Embodying Charisma: Modernity, Locality and the Performance of Emotion in Sufi Cults*. London: Routledge and Kegan Paul.

Wolcott, H. (1999), *Ethnography: A Way of Seeing*. California: Altamira Press.

10 Religion and gender

Ahmad, F. (2003), '"Still in progress?" – methodological dilemmas, tensions and contradictions in theorizing South Asian Muslim women', in N. Purwar and P. Raghuram (eds), *South Asian Women in the Diaspora*. Oxford: Berg.

Coakley, S. (1988), '"Femininity" and the Holy Spirit', in M. Furlong (ed.), *Mirror to the Church: Reflections on Sexism*. London: S.P.C.K.

Daly, M. (1973), *Beyond God the Father*. Boston: Beacon Press.

Davaney, S. G. (1987), 'The limits of the appeal to women's experience', in M. R. Miles, C. W. Atkinson and C. H. Buchanan (eds), *Shaping New Visions: Gender and Values in American Culture* (*Studies in Religion*, no. 5), UMI Research Project, pp. 31–49.

Dowell, S. and Hurcombe, L. (1981), *Dispossesed Daughters of Eve: Faith and Feminism*. London: S.P.C.K.

Eller, C. (1993), *Living in the Lap of the Goddess*. New York: Crossroad.

Franzmann, M. (2000), *Women and Religion*. Oxford: Oxford University Press.

Furlong, M. (ed.) (1988), *Mirror to the Church: Reflections on Sexism*. London: S.P.C.K.

Furlong, M. (1991), *A Dangerous Delight: Women and Power in the Church*. London: S.P.C.K.

Hampson, D. (1987), 'Is there a place for feminists in a Christian Church?', *New Blackfriars*, January, pp. 1–16.

Johnson, S. and Deforest, J. (1993), *Out of this World: A Fictionalized True-Life Adventure*. New York: Wildfire Books.

Khan, S. (1998), 'Muslim women; negotiations in the third space', *Signs: Journal of Women and Culture in Society* 23(2): 463–94.

Lazreg, M. (1988), 'Feminism and difference: the perils of writing as a woman on women in Algeria', *Feminist Studies*, 14 Spring, pp. 81–107.

Mernissi, F. (1991), *Women and Islam*. Oxford: Blackwell.

Ruether, R. R. (1996), *Women Healing Earth: Third World Women on Ecology, Feminism and Religion*. London: Orbis Books.

Starhawk (1987), 'The women dance naked in jail', in L. Hurcombe (ed.), *Sex and God: Some Varieties of Women's Religious Experience*. London: Routledge and Kegan Paul.

Stowasser, B. (1994), *Women in the Qur'an, Traditions and Interpretation*. Oxford: Oxford University Press.

11 The question of truth

Barth, K. (1956), *Church Dogmatics*. Edinburgh: T & T Clark.

Berger, P. (1980), *The Heretical Imperative*. London: Doubleday.

Boff, L. (2000), *Ethos Mundial: um consensomínimo entre oshumanos*. Brasilia: Letraviva.

— (2001), *Espiritualidade: Un Caminho de Transformaçao*. Rio de Janeiro: Sextante.

Brunner, E. (1980), *The Christian Doctrine of God: Dogmatics* (Dogmatics Series). Westminster: John Knox Press.

Cantwell-Smith, W. (1962), *The Meaning and End of Religion*. New York: Macmillan.

— (1967), *Questions of Religious Truth*. London: Victor Gollancz.

— (1993), *What is Scripture: A Comparative Approach*. Minneapolis: Fortress Press.

Carmen, J. (1980), 'Religion as a problem for Christian theology', in D. Dawe and J. Carmen (eds), *Christian Faith in a Religiously Plural World*. New York: Orbis Books.

Clarke, P. and Byrne, P. (1993), *Religion Defined and Explained*. London: Macmillan.

Cobb, J. (1990), 'Beyond pluralism', in G. D'Costa (ed.), *Christian Uniqueness Reconsidered*. New York: Orbis Books.

Cupitt, D. (1997), *After God: The Future of Religion*. London: Weidenfeld and Nicolson.

Dawe, D. (1980), 'Christian faith in a religiously plural world', in D. Dawe and J. Carmen (eds), *Christian Faith in a Religiously Plural World*. New York: Orbis Books.

Dinoia, J. (1992), *The Diversity of Religions*. Washington: Catholic University of America Press.

Driver, T. (1987), 'The case for pluralism', in J. Hick and P. Knitter (eds), *The Myth of Christian Uniqueness*. London: S.C.M.

Farmer, H. H. (1939), 'The one foundation', in *The Christian World Pulpit* 135.

Geaves, R. (2003), 'Peripatetic mystics: the Renunciate Order of Terapanthi Jains', in C. Partridge and T. Gabriel (eds), *Mysticisms East and West: Studies in Mystical Experience*. Carlisle: Paternoster.

Heim, S. M. (1998), 'Accounts of our hope: an overview of themes in the presentations', in S. M. Heim (ed.), *Grounds for Understanding*. Grand Rapids: Eerdmans.

Hick, J. (1973), *God and the Universe of Faiths,* 1st edn. London: Macmillan.

— (1987), 'The non-absoluteness of Christianity', in J. Hick and P. Knitter (eds), *The Myth of Christian Uniqueness*. London: S.C.M.

— (1990), *The Philosophy of Religion,* 4th edn. New Jersey: Prentice-Hall.

Hughes, D. A. (1996), *Has God Many Names?* Leicester: Apollos.

Katz, S. (1978), 'Language, epistemology, and mysticism', in S. Katz (ed.), *Mysticism and Philosophical Analysis*. London: Sheldon Press.

Kepel, G. (1994), *The Revenge of God*. Cambridge: Polity Press.

Knitter, P. (1987), 'Preface', in J. Hick and P. Knitter (eds), *The Myth of Christian Uniqueness*. London: S.C.M.

Nielsen, N. (1993), *Fundamentalism, Myths and World Religions*. New York: State University of New York Press.

Nietzsche, F. (1911), 'On truth and falsity in their ultramoral sense', in O. Levy (ed.), *Collected Works*, vol. II. London: T. N. Foulis.

— (1968), *Will to Power*, trans. Walter Kauffman and R. J. Hollingdale. New York: Vintage.

Norris, C. (1994), *Truth and the Ethics of Criticism*. Manchester: Manchester University Press.

Parrinder, G. (1976), *Mysticism in the World's Religions*. London: Sheldon Press.

Partridge, C. (1998), *H. H. Farmer's Theological Interpretation of Religion: Towards a Personalist Theology of Religion*. Lampeter: E. Mellen Press.

Race, A. (1983), *Christians and Religious Pluralism*. London: S.C.M. Press.

Rorty, R. (1991), *Objectivity, Relativism and Truth*. Cambridge: Cambridge University Press.

Schuon, F. (1975), *The Transcendent Unity of Religions*. New York: Harper & Row.

Smart, N. (1978), 'Understanding religious experience', in S. Katz (ed.), *Mysticism and Philosophical Analysis*. London: Sheldon Press.

Smith, Z. (2002), *The Autograph Man*. Harmondsworth: Penguin, p. 119.

Stace, W. (1960), *Mysticism and Philosophy*. London: Macmillan.

Stewart, C. and Shaw, R. (1994), 'Introduction: problematizing syncretism', in C. Stewart and R. Shaw (eds), *Syncretism/Anti-Syncretism: The Politics of Religious Synthesis*. London: Routledge and Kegan Paul.

Surin, K. (1998), 'A politics of speech: religious pluralism in the age of the McDonald's hamburger', in M. Heim (ed.), *Grounds for Understanding: Ecumenical Resources for Responses to Religious Pluralism*. London: Eerdmans.

Tillich, P. (1966), 'The significance of the history of religions for systematic theology', in J. C. Braur (ed.), *The Future of Religions*. New York: Harper & Row.

Toulmin, S. (1990), *Cosmopolis: The Hidden Agenda of Modernity*. New York: Macmillan, The Free Press.

Vroom, H. (1989), *Religions and the Truth*. Grand Rapids: Eerdmans.

Ward, G. (1997), 'Introduction, or a guide to theological thinking in cyberspace', in G. Ward (ed.), *The Postmodern God*. Oxford: Blackwell.

12 The internet as a resource in the study of religion

(1978), *Holy Bible: New International Version*. London: Hodder and Stoughton.

Anon (2006), The Net Confessional. www.lorax.org/~cwarren/confessional/index.html. Accessed on 13 November 2007.

Berners-Lee, T. (1999), *Weaving the Web*. London: Orion.

Butler, T. (1999), 'Weaving the Web'. Bishop of Southwark's address to the Weavers' Company, 22 February. Diocese of Southwark Press Release. URL: http://southwark.anglican.org/news/pr075a.htm. Accessed on 2 December 2006.

Church of Fools (2006), URL: www.churchoffools.com. Accessed on 2 December 2006.

Cooke, A. (2001), *A Guide to Finding Quality Information on the Internet: Selection and Evaluation Strategies*. London: Library Association.

Cox, H. (1965), *The Secular City: Secularization and Urbanization in Theological Perspective*. New York: Macmillan.

Fox, G. (2004), Coming clean: the best and worst of DailyConfession.com. URL: www.lorax.org/~cwarren/confessional/. Accessed on 13 November 2006.

Lutz, A. and Borgman, D. (2002), 'Teenage spirituality and the internet', *Cultic Studies Review: An Internet Journal of Research, News and Opinion* 1(2).

McGraw-Hill (2005), *Student Success*. http://novella.mhhe.com/sites/0079876543/student_view0/research_center-999/research_papers30/conducting_web-based_research.html. Accessed on 24 August 2006.

Penslar, R. L. (ed.) (1995), *Research Ethics: Cases and Materials*. Bloomington: Indiana University Press.

Robinson, B. (2006), 'Ontario consultants on religious tolerance'. URL: www.religioustolerance.org. Accessed on 2 December 2006.

Index

A'isha 297–8
advaita vedanta 15, 28, 135, 229
Adventism 33, 76
Africa 55, 64, 129, 147, 160, 184, 187, 190, 193, 289
agnosticism 3, 15, 43, 62, 64, 158, 171, 179, 243, 335
Ahmad, Fauzia 293
Alister Hardy Research Centre 57, 106
Alston, W. P. 35
America 3, 45, 55, 61, 112, 116, 128, 143, 146, 147, 186, 189, 204, 208, 246, 247, 289, 294, 299, 308, 310, 311, 329, 333
Angad, Guru 237
animatism 147
animism 19, 147, 153
Anselm of Canterbury 10, 45, 49
anthropology 2, 8, 19, 39, 41, 49, 51, 54–6, 62, 64, 89, 127, 141, 142, 146, 147, 148–50, 152–3, 183, 184, 190, 195, 198, 204–6, 216, 244, 251, 253, 259, 268, 273, 332, 335
Antonnen, Veiko 202
Anwar, Muhammad 247
Appadurai, Arjun 204–5
Aquinas, Thomas 45, 282, 343
Arberry, A. J. 53, 193
archaeology 1, 43, 47–9, 65, 72, 74, 128–30, 144, 146, 154, 156, 195
Ashoka 46–7, 129
atheism 15, 46, 60, 62, 64, 99, 112, 154, 158, 207, 243, 246, 254, 317, 335
Atkinson, P. 250
Augustine of Hippo 71, 282, 343
authenticity 4, 13, 51, 57, 184, 198, 211–40, 248, 285, 290, 292, 296, 299, 312, 317, 318, 319, 321, 332
Ayer, A. J. 41
Ayodhya 219

Bahá'í 112–13, 115, 187–8, 257
Bailey, Carol 270
Bailey, Greg 225
Bainbridge, W. S. 34, 52–3, 152
Balaknath, Baba 238, 247–9, 253, 256, 263
Balch, Robert W. 81–2, 92
Ballard, Roger 200
Barrett, David 115
Barth, Karl 305, 313, 314
Becker, Howard 32, 33, 152
Beckford, James 52, 85
Beckham, David 26–7
Belke, Thomas J. 110
Bellah, Robert 63, 245
Bentham, Jeremy 105, 110
Berger, Peter 19, 58, 63, 64, 78, 106, 245, 305, 324
Berkeley, George 161
Berners-Lee, Tim 340–1
Bhabha, Homi 204
Bhagavad Gita 22, 49, 72–3, 154, 163, 164, 173, 238, 310
bhakti 72, 136
Biblical Studies 1–2, 16, 48, 137, 202, 276, 278–81, 347
bin Laden, Osama 239, 347
Blackmore, Susan 59
Blavatsky, Helena Petrovna 87, 144
Bloom, William 232
bodhisattva 16, 23, 42, 162, 310
Boff, Leonardo 60, 319
Bowie, Fiona 55
Brahma Kumaris 189
brainwashing 53, 85, 233
Brierley, Peter 99, 102–4
Brodeur, Patrice 251
Bromley, David 345
Brown, Karen McCarthy 80
Bruce, Steve 33, 99, 103, 105, 184
Buber, Martin 176

Buddha, the 12, 17, 23, 42, 87, 128,
129, 174, 175, 189, 191, 195, 197, 223–5,
229, 255
Buddhism 2, 8, 14, 15, 17, 18, 23, 26, 28,
30, 31, 34, 42, 47, 54, 84, 87–8, 91, 93,
105, 110, 114–15, 124, 128–30, 134, 136,
139, 143–6, 153–6, 158, 162, 164, 168,
169, 172–5, 180, 187, 189, 195–8, 200,
214, 218, 222, 223–4, 229, 242, 247, 248,
253, 255–6, 257, 310, 311, 323, 340, 343,
347, 352, 354
Burnouf, Eugene 144
Butler, Tom 353

Caddy, Peter and Eileen 233
Cantwell Smith, Wilfred 202, 306, 312,
316, 317, 318, 332, 336
Cao Dai 187
capitalism 52, 61, 150, 201, 205, 268
Caplan, Lionel 329
Carey, William 132
Carlson, Jeffery 250
Carmen, John 316
Carus, Paul 143
caste 74, 132, 154, 166, 174, 198, 199, 225,
227, 235, 236, 259, 264, 268, 291
census of 1851 93–6, 103, 106
census of 2001 91, 96–8, 100, 105, 117,
125, 345
census of 2011 125
Cesaire, Aime 185
Chakrabarty, Dipesh 202
charisma 151, 194, 195, 219, 221, 232,
265, 330, 331
charismatic religion 51, 92, 106
chat rooms 350–3, 356, 358
China 109, 128, 129, 139, 184, 186, 190,
191, 196, 197, 207, 242, 307
Ch'ondogyo 110
Christadelphians 11
Christmas 70, 79, 100–2, 181, 266
Christianity 1–3, 8, 11–12, 14–16, 19, 24,
28, 32–3, 36, 41–2, 43–5, 47, 49–51, 53,
68, 69–70, 71–2, 82–3, 84, 90, 92, 93–4,
99–107, 110, 116, 121, 123, 128, 131,
132–3, 136, 137–8, 139–40, 154, 156,
158, 164–5, 166–7, 169, 173–4, 176, 178,
183, 185, 188, 190, 192, 202, 207, 212,
218, 220–1, 224, 243, 250, 253, 256–8,
266, 273, 276–83, 285–7, 296, 304–6,
308–18, 321–2, 324, 325, 328, 329, 332,
347, 352, 353, 355–8

Christy, Henry 146
Church of Fools 355–7
Church of Jesus Christ of Latter-day
Saints 11, 71, 72, 112, 113, 114, 116, 117
Clark, Francis 36
Clarke, J. J. 191–2, 207
Clarke, James Freeman 92–3
Clarke, Peter 318
Clement of Alexandria 282
Coakley, Sarah 285
Cobb, John 318
Codrington, R. H. 163
cognitive science 58, 63
Cohen, Percy 35
colonialism 1, 4, 45, 56, 129, 130,
133, 145, 183–209, 213, 268, 289, 311,
315, 322
communism 29, 36, 109, 110, 140, 183
comparative religion 2, 16–17, 60, 133, 144,
147, 159, 189–90, 202, 313, 321
Comte, Auguste 137
Confucianism 110, 183, 187, 192, 196,
197, 307
Congar, Yves 285
conversion 12, 47, 52, 57, 70, 81, 82, 86,
134, 179, 187, 188, 223–4, 270, 281, 352
Cox, Harvey 106, 116, 352
Cox, James L. 178–80
creeds 15, 24, 27, 34, 42, 44, 72, 158, 174
Csoma de Koros, Sandor 144
cult 13, 32–4, 50, 52, 72, 85, 115, 123, 152,
154, 170, 193, 198, 247–8, 282, 330, 343
cultural studies 2, 39, 43, 63, 183, 184,
209, 273
Cupitt, Don 336
Cusack, Carol 353
customs 54, 62, 79, 132, 147, 152, 181,
195, 255–7, 258, 276

D'Aquili, Eugene 60
Dalai Lama 16, 145
dalits 74
Daly, Mary 285
Darwin, Charles 137, 192
Daveney, Sheila Greeve 290–1
David-Néel, Alexandra 145
Dawe, Donald 313–14
Dawkins, Richard 69
Dawson, Andrew 76–7
de la Saussaye, P. D. Chantepie 159
Dead Sea Scrolls 47, 48
Deoband 264–5

Derrida, Jacques 61, 178, 201
Descartes, René 161, 176
Desideri, Ippolito 144
deviance 52, 92
dhikr 227, 243, 248
dialectic 109, 139, 140
Dinoia, J. 314–16
Discordianism 109, 353
diversity 53, 55, 91, 184, 198, 202, 211–40, 241, 242, 243, 245, 246–50, 256, 282, 287, 306, 317, 319, 324, 329, 336
Dowell, Susan 277–9, 285
Dowling, Levi 310
Durkheim, Emile 52, 53, 62–3, 141, 142, 148–9, 184, 304, 335, 351

East India Company 130, 133–4, 144
education 2–3, 11–13, 18, 29, 40–1, 65, 92, 103, 130, 153, 202, 203, 233, 244–5, 250, 277, 340, 348, 354
Eliade, Mircea 26, 161, 162, 165, 169, 175, 181, 220, 240, 335
Eller, Cynthia 287–8, 290
email 98, 264, 341, 346, 348–9, 350, 358, 359
Embree, A 246
Emden, Jacob 309
Emerson, Ralph Waldo 133
emic/etic issues 64, 70–4, 172, 180, 182, 260, 275, 277, 287, 294, 299, 335
empathy 64, 69, 128, 133, 152–4, 168, 170, 172–3, 176, 179, 181, 245, 257, 264, 299
empiricism 21, 40, 52, 53, 58, 69, 89, 121, 134, 137–40, 152, 165, 232, 326
Engels, Friedrich 140
Enlightenment 47, 49, 61, 105, 137–8, 142, 192, 207, 232, 304
environmentalism 18, 201, 286
epochē 64, 159, 179
essentialism 201, 202–3, 246, 276, 293, 294, 322
ethics 17, 21, 25, 30, 35, 42, 45, 53, 75, 80, 81, 101, 105, 118, 120, 121, 134, 174, 184, 192, 197, 215, 257, 274, 305, 312, 315, 320, 321, 348–9, 350, 351
ethnicity 183–4, 188, 189, 204, 205, 237, 247–8, 257, 259, 272, 292, 332, 336
ethnography 2, 51, 54–6, 62, 67, 82, 89, 152, 153, 156, 205, 243, 245, 250–3, 258, 260, 272–3
eucharist 21, 51, 75, 82, 145, 164–5, 166, 175, 256, 356, 358

evangelization 90, 188
Evans-Wentz, W. Y. 145
exclusivism 45, 133, 202, 306–8, 312–16, 318, 323, 336
ex-members 85–6, 123, 267

Family Federation for World Peace and Unification, *see* Unification Church
Family International, The 108
Farmer, H. H. 304, 306, 323–4
Farquhar, John Nicol 133
Fausboll, Viggo 143
feminism 4, 275–8, 285–94, 298, 299, 301
Festinger, Leon 81–2
festivals 9, 10, 84, 87, 91, 94, 101–2, 135, 166, 167, 179, 180, 181, 196, 224, 235, 247, 261, 268
fetish 164
Feuerbach, Ludwig 140–1, 202, 246
fideism 69–70
fieldwork 146, 241–74, 351
Findhorn 231, 233
Finnström, Sverker 205
Fitzgerald, Timothy 188
Flew, Anthony 41, 46, 160
Flood, Gavin 64, 175–7
Flueckiger, Joyce 252
focus groups 123–4
football 25–7, 29, 37
Foucault, Michel 61, 201
Francis, E. K. 247
Franzman, Majella 284, 299–301
Frazer, J. G. 8, 56, 147–8, 149, 154
Freud, Sigmund 51, 56–7, 138–41, 142, 156, 304
Fruzzetti, L. 247
Fukuyama, Francis 207
functionalism 19, 24–7, 148
fundamentalism 9, 10, 51, 184, 209, 237, 298, 306, 328–32
Furlong, Monica 278, 282–3, 285, 286

Gandhi 186
gatekeepers 74, 79, 83, 263–4, 267–71
Geertz, Armin 240
Gellner E. 193–4
gender issues 4, 74, 87, 106, 166, 184, 201, 256, 260–2, 275–301
ghosts 23, 162, 357
Gilliat-Ray, Sophie 270
globalization 45, 55, 184, 201–2, 204, 207, 232, 336, 339

glossolaliation 22
Gnosticism 281–2, 309
Gobind Singh, Guru 49, 214, 234–7, 291
Goddess 286–9, 301
Golden Temple 265–6, 267
Gordon, David 79
Graf, Karl H. 138
Guru Granth Sahib 214, 234, 237, 238, 256, 257, 260–1, 265, 291

Hadden, J. K. 329–30, 345
hadith 228, 265, 293, 296–8, 309
Hammersley 250–1
Hammond, Philip 116
Hampson, Daphne 276, 286–7
Harris, Harriet 330
Hasan, Mushirul 203
Healthy Happy Holy (3HO) 188
Heaven's Gate 82, 92
Heber, Reginald 136
Hegel, G. W. F. 20, 138–41, 162
Heim, Mark 315–16
Heisenberg principle 77, 170
Hick, John 46, 202, 304, 311–12, 316, 317, 318, 320–1, 324, 326–7, 335, 337
Hinduism 2, 8, 9–10, 14, 15, 18, 21, 22, 24, 28, 47, 49, 78, 93, 101, 130–7, 139, 154, 155, 164, 166, 167, 169, 174, 180, 184, 188, 189, 190, 191–2, 195, 198–200, 203, 209, 213, 218, 219–20, 225–9, 233, 237–8, 246–8, 252–4, 257, 259, 260, 288, 291, 310, 315, 318, 328, 332, 335, 339–40, 343, 354–5
Hirst, P. H. 40–2
history 2, 9, 11, 14, 16, 42, 43, 45, 46–7, 51, 59, 62, 72–4, 83, 89, 127–30, 132, 138–40, 142–3, 145, 146, 153, 156, 159, 166, 175, 181, 184, 201, 202–3, 205, 209, 216, 218, 220, 225, 244, 260, 281–5, 297, 311, 324, 328, 331, 333, 336
Hitler, Adolf 27, 110
Hodgson, Brian H. 144
Hoffman, J. E. 263
Hoffman, Shirl J. 25
Hubbard, L. Ron 32, 114, 188
Huff, Darrell 111
Hughes, Dewi 318, 334, 335
Hull, John 202
human potential movement 18, 231
humanism 27, 36, 63, 333

Humphreys, Christmas 145
Hunter, Preston D. 93
Hurcombe, Linda 277–9, 285
Husserl, Edmond 159–60
Huxley, Aldous 60, 319

IbnSina 45
Ice Cream Church 109
idealism 109, 138, 192, 335, 336
ideology 13, 29, 30, 32, 36, 105, 109–11, 186, 198, 204, 277, 329–30, 334
immigration 11, 95, 105, 352
inclusivism 45, 191, 306–7, 312–16, 318, 323, 325
India 3, 9, 11, 20, 47, 72–3, 128–35, 164, 173, 186–7, 189, 190, 191–3, 198–200, 203, 206, 209, 219–20, 223, 225–7, 229, 233, 234–7, 246, 247, 248, 256, 259, 264, 270, 272, 292, 307, 309, 310, 316, 328, 340, 345, 354
insider/outsider issues 1, 4, 8, 12, 15–16, 43, 62–4, 67–88, 132, 153, 168, 174, 176, 191, 220, 236, 239, 241, 251, 254, 257–8, 260, 262, 263–4, 269, 271, 275, 276, 287, 300, 304, 306, 312, 315, 325, 328, 331, 332, 335
inspiration 110, 186, 212–13, 229, 304, 306, 317, 354
institutionalization 33, 92, 151, 212, 218, 219, 230, 287, 300
interfaith dialogue 4, 45, 143, 312, 337
International Society for Krishna Consciousness (ISKCON) 72–3, 91, 177, 189, 337
internet 9, 119, 157, 170, 311, 339–60
interviewing 59, 80, 99, 117–18, 120–4, 153, 171, 248, 259, 265, 266, 272
Islam 2, 9–10, 15, 48, 62, 92–3, 97, 112, 114, 134, 136, 157–8, 173, 174, 183, 186–90, 193–5, 202, 203, 206–9, 212–13, 215–17, 218, 220, 222, 225–9, 233, 239, 246, 248–9, 259–60, 262, 264–5, 270, 290–9, 307, 308, 309–10, 322, 324, 332, 347

Jackson, Robert 202, 245, 246, 248, 250
Jainism 15, 18, 19, 134, 162, 188, 214, 222, 233, 246, 257, 291, 307–8
James, E. O. 189
James, William 8, 56–8, 156
Jedi 98–9, 353

Jehovah's Witnesses 9–10, 11, 32–3, 51,
    52, 54, 71, 72, 79, 91, 97, 112–16, 152,
    153, 169–71, 253, 345, 347
Jesus Christ 14–15, 25, 27, 43, 49–51, 68,
    71, 86, 133, 137–8, 139, 142, 166, 173,
    189, 220, 229, 279, 280, 282, 308–11,
    313, 315, 337, 357
jihad 9, 10, 157, 268, 298
Johnson, Sonia 288
Jones, William 129–32, 136–7
Joseph, R. 60
Juche 109–11
Judaism 14, 15, 17, 19, 20, 22, 24,
    27, 47, 48, 50, 62, 82, 93, 95, 97,
    129, 133, 138, 142, 163, 166, 173, 174,
    176, 186, 189, 212, 213, 215, 218, 220,
    257, 278–9, 282, 288, 307, 309, 314,
    322, 328
Jung, Carl 56–7, 62, 156

Kabir 225–6, 228, 231
Kant, Immanuel 161, 349
karma 42, 135, 164, 227
Katz, Steven 60, 318–20, 323
Kepel, Gilles 331
Khadijah 295, 297
Khalistan 235–6
Khalsa 49, 173, 203, 205, 209, 212, 235–9,
    248, 265, 291
King, Richard 191
Knitter, Paul 312
Knott, Kim 184–5, 247
Kuenen, Abraham 143
Kvaerne, Per 196

Lang, Andrew 147
language 21–2, 34, 46, 54, 58, 62, 67, 69,
    127, 130, 134, 136, 143, 152, 176, 179,
    191–3, 216, 227, 230, 236, 259–60, 264,
    266, 270, 276, 285–6, 294, 300, 319,
    321, 325, 327–8, 353, 357
Lassen, Christian 144
Lazreg, Marnia 294
Leppokari, Maria 239
Locke, John 161
Lofland, John 52, 82
Lopez, Donald 145
Luckmann, Thomas 106
Luther, Martin 28–9
Lyon, David 61
Lyotard, Jean-François 61, 178, 334

McCarthy, Karen 259
McLeod, W. H. 235–6
MacIntyre, Alisdair 69, 70
Mackie, J. L. 46
magic 130, 139, 145, 148, 149, 152, 153,
    165, 192, 195, 197, 216
Malinowski, Bronislaw 152–3, 253–4
Mandelbaum, D. G. 200
Marshall, John 47, 129
Marshman, Joshua 132
Mary, mother of Jesus 33, 166, 248,
    278–9, 280, 295, 309
Marx, Karl 61, 63, 105, 140–1, 304
Marxism 27, 109, 181, 201
media 1, 9–10, 43, 62, 63, 65, 82, 86, 112,
    157, 169, 171, 204–5, 248, 292, 293, 329,
    343, 357
meditation 21, 25, 60, 87, 88, 135, 173,
    213, 224, 226, 310, 320, 323, 354
membership 11, 71, 99, 101–9, 111, 113,
    116, 119, 230, 248, 330
Mernissi, Fatima 297–8
Methodism 32, 33, 95, 357
methodology 1–4, 13, 39–65, 80, 82, 83,
    97, 123, 128, 138, 154, 156, 158–9, 169,
    171, 179, 184, 201, 202, 233, 245–6, 271,
    272, 274, 276, 299–301, 321, 335, 349
migration 55, 184, 185, 189, 204, 206, 208,
    232, 242, 248, 294, 332
Mill, John Stuart 105, 110
missionary activity 45, 55, 81, 87,
    128–9, 132–3, 136–7, 144, 154, 163, 179,
    184, 188–9, 190, 270, 291, 307, 311,
    313–14, 315
Mithraism 188
monasticism 16, 17, 84, 88, 174, 180, 224,
    282, 285, 290, 296
Monier-Williams, Monier 133–6
monotheism 19, 131, 133, 142, 147, 154,
    190, 192, 212–13, 314
Moody, Raymond A. 59
Moon, Sun Myung 18, 68, 81, 188, 253
Moonies, see Unification Church
Morgan, Peggy 65
Mormons, see Church of Jesus Christ of
    Latter-day Saints
Muhammad 12, 13, 24, 48, 93, 142, 174,
    188, 194, 213, 215–18, 225, 247, 276,
    294, 295, 297–8, 308–10
multiculturalism 2–3, 45, 87, 91, 187, 242,
    244, 245, 250, 294, 311

mysticism 53, 58, 60, 131, 145, 152,
    191, 192–3, 200, 217, 218, 222, 227–32,
    237, 243, 250, 285, 306, 308, 312,
    318–23, 326
myth 13, 27, 30, 34, 57, 83, 95, 110, 131,
    136–7, 138, 142, 147–8, 152, 156, 166,
    173, 180, 204, 207, 219–21, 235, 240,
    278, 334

Nanak, Guru 12, 226–8, 234, 236, 237, 238,
    260, 291–2
Nandy, Ashis 185–6
near-death experiences 59, 107
Nesbitt, Eleanor 245, 248, 260, 271, 272
neuro-theology 58, 59–60
New Age Movement 18, 53, 54, 55, 75,
    105, 154, 231, 233, 308, 310, 333, 336
new religious movements 33, 36, 42, 45,
    52, 54, 63, 65, 72–3, 86, 89, 92, 98–9,
    105, 123, 151–2, 154, 158, 171, 187, 205,
    211, 212, 221, 230–3, 242, 243, 251, 257,
    290, 298, 318, 337, 347, 353
Newberg, Andrew 59–60
Nielsen, Neils 331
Nietzsche, Friedrich 61, 333
nihilation 307–8
Nirankaris 188
Norris, Christopher 333–4

O'Dea, Thomas 219
Oberoi, Harjot 237–8, 246
occultism 18
Olcott, Henry Steel 87–8, 144
Open Episcopal Church 358
Orientalism 56, 186, 190, 191, 192,
    195, 207
Orthodoxy 15, 44, 77, 84, 178, 224,
    258, 283
Osiander, Andreas 137–8
Otto, Rudolf 8, 19–24, 58, 63, 161, 162–3,
    165, 169, 221, 245, 317

paganism 188, 287, 290, 297
Palmer, Susan 75
Pals, Daniel 63, 245
parapsychology 59
Parrinder, Geoffrey 60, 189, 190, 319
participant observation 51, 74–6, 153, 168,
    170, 176, 177, 245, 252–3, 266, 272, 351
Partridge, Christopher 106, 324, 329
Paton, William 189, 190

Paul of Tarsus 51, 57, 173, 280, 356
Paulus, H. E. G. 138
Pawlowsky, Peter 258
Penslar, Robin 349
Pentecostalism 22, 72, 116
phenomenology 1, 3, 4, 8, 16, 43, 64, 74,
    83, 128, 152, 154, 157–82, 202, 245,
    246, 299
philosophy 8, 13, 34, 39, 41, 45–6, 50, 58,
    60, 61, 69, 109–10, 131, 134, 135, 137,
    139, 158, 161, 176, 192, 224, 244, 304,
    306, 319, 325–7, 333
pilgrimage 83, 135, 220–1, 226, 228, 234,
    238, 269, 340, 354, 355, 357
pluralism 42, 44, 45, 54, 61, 202, 209,
    305–8, 311–18, 328, 331, 336
pollution 49, 261, 264
polytheism 19, 133, 142, 146–7, 287
postcolonialism 4, 200, 204–9
postmodernism 8, 61–2, 64, 178, 212, 293,
    305, 306, 334, 336
prayer 11, 17, 21, 25, 35, 60, 69, 78, 90,
    148, 159, 162, 173, 218, 220, 221, 227,
    252, 258, 265, 269, 278, 285–6, 320,
    353, 354, 356
Price, Richard 90
primal religion 34, 66, 154, 187, 188
proselytization 52, 68, 188–9, 318
Protestantism 15, 27, 28, 30, 33, 43, 44,
    52, 84, 104, 143, 150, 164, 174, 178,
    183, 192, 202, 215, 216, 224, 310, 313,
    316–17, 318, 329, 335, 336
psychoanalysis 27, 140
psychology 2, 8, 39, 41, 51, 56–9, 62, 141,
    156, 244
Puwar, Nirmal 55

Quakers 11, 19, 33, 34, 95, 177–8,
    179, 181
questionnaires 96, 97, 99, 117–21, 231,
    272, 349, 353
Qur'an 15, 44, 112, 174, 194, 213, 215–17,
    220, 228, 260, 268, 276, 293, 294–9,
    308, 309

Race, Alan 308, 311, 313–18, 323
Raelians 75
Rahner, Karl 46
Rampa, T. Lobsang 146
Rastafari 75
Ravidasis 188

rebirth 162, 174, 197–8, 200, 310
reflexive research 82–3
Reimarus, H. S. 138
reincarnation 59, 154, 273
religious studies 3, 8, 11, 13, 14, 18, 20,
    30, 32, 39–65, 146, 189, 244–6, 258,
    305, 344–5
revelation 44, 47, 50, 61, 151, 207, 212–18,
    220, 221, 222, 227–9, 242, 243, 276,
    279, 293–5, 297, 304–7, 309, 313–15, 317,
    323–4, 331
Rhys Davids, T. W. 136, 144
rites of passage 9, 25, 26, 32, 54, 79, 107,
    152, 154, 247
ritual 10, 20, 21, 25–7, 30, 34–6, 49,
    54, 56, 60, 63, 67, 79, 80, 88, 89,
    140, 147, 148, 152, 154, 162, 174,
    178, 180, 190, 193, 197, 198, 218,
    219–22, 225–8, 230, 235, 237, 240,
    246, 253, 256, 261, 262, 264, 273,
    279, 286, 290, 300, 316, 317, 324, 354
Robinson, Bruce 114, 346
Robinson, John A. T. 103
Roman Catholicism 13–14, 22, 33, 43, 44,
    46, 70, 71, 79, 95, 102, 104, 106, 110,
    147, 173, 174, 178, 215, 218, 258, 263,
    316–17, 358, 359
Rorty, Richard 334
routinization 151
Roy, Asim 195
Ruether, Rosemary Radford
    276, 289–90
Rumi, Jalalu'ddin 227–8, 231, 308

Sahaja Yoga 189
Sahajdharis 237
Said, Edward 186, 200, 247
sampling 40, 96, 117–18, 120–4, 349
samsara 162, 197, 198, 213, 227
Santeria 189
sants 225–8, 234, 237
Satanism 112, 337
Schleiermacher, Friedrich 20, 316
Schmidt, Wilhelm 147
Schuon, Fritjof 216, 316, 319
Schupe, A. D. 329–30
Scientology 18, 32, 33, 75, 112–13, 124,
    170–1, 188, 242, 337
sect 13, 26, 32–3, 50, 52–3, 129,
    151–2, 188, 195, 198, 215, 219, 227,
    242, 330, 336

secularization 11, 13, 53–4, 70, 105–7,
    150–1, 183–4, 207, 209, 321, 324,
    329–30
Semler, J. S. 138
Shaku, Soen 143
shamanism 18, 164, 229
Shaw, Rosalind 332
Shi'a 222, 268
Shinto 307
Sikhism 17, 49, 74, 164, 173, 174, 187–8,
    189, 191, 204, 205, 209, 214, 226,
    234–40, 246, 247–8, 255, 257, 260–2,
    265–6, 273, 291–2, 307
Skype 359
Smart, Barry 61
Smart, Ninian 1, 3, 27, 30, 34–5, 36, 60, 64,
    161, 171–5, 179, 181, 182, 190, 202, 220,
    229, 245, 271, 316, 319, 322
Smith, William Robertson 141–3, 148
sociology 2, 8, 24, 32, 39, 41, 43, 45, 50,
    51–4, 61, 62, 89, 99, 102, 105, 146, 148,
    150, 152, 156, 184, 219, 244, 245, 251,
    273, 294, 324, 329, 335, 351
Söderblom, Nathan 20, 161
Soka Gakkai 84, 114, 116
Spencer, Herbert 137
Spiro, Melford 155, 197–8, 200
Spivak, Gayatri 186, 200, 201
sport 25–7, 36
Srinivas, M. N. 198
Starhawk 288
Stark, Rodney 34, 50, 52–3, 106
statistics 4, 43, 77, 89–125, 169, 170,
    272, 345
Stevenson, Ian 59
Stewart, Charles 332
Stoller, Paul 64
Stowasser, Barbara 295–7, 298
Strauss, D. F. 138
Sufism 193–5, 212, 217, 218, 221, 225,
    227–8, 233–4, 239, 243, 248, 268, 308
Sundkler, Bengt 55
Sunnis 222, 268
supernatural, the 17–19, 23–4, 27, 28, 30,
    35, 36, 42, 53, 58, 64, 105, 109–10, 137,
    143, 148–9, 151, 162–4, 168, 169, 171,
    173, 175, 177, 221, 229, 232, 287, 288,
    310, 335
superstition 2, 87–8, 132, 133, 145, 148,
    164, 172, 180, 191, 192, 193
Surin, Kenneth 202

surveys 94, 96–7, 99–100, 102, 103, 105, 117–22, 123, 272, 349, 359
Sutcliffe, Steven 55, 64, 71, 231–2, 233
Suzuki, D. T. 143
Swearer, Donald 195
syncretism 110, 191, 198, 282, 332–3

taboo 56, 57, 140, 148, 164–5, 262, 291
Talmud 174
Tarachand, S. 199
Taoism 162, 187, 196, 197
Taylor, David 81–2, 92
technology 43, 54, 61, 62, 105, 130, 143, 201, 204, 215, 329, 339–40, 348, 349, 352, 357, 359
textual criticism 2, 43, 89, 134, 154, 202, 209, 216–17
theism 18, 154
theology 1, 2, 3, 8, 14–16, 25, 27, 39, 41–6, 49, 64, 71, 83, 89, 90, 123, 131, 137, 138, 154, 158, 171, 185, 191, 202, 218, 244, 254, 276, 277, 282, 285–6, 287, 304–6, 308, 309, 311–14, 316, 318, 323, 329, 335
Theosophy 87, 144, 310
Thomas, Richard 100–1
Thoreau, Henry 133
Tibet 16, 60, 129, 144–6, 195, 223, 310
Tillich, Paul 26, 27–30, 316, 336
Torah 13, 14, 24, 28, 49, 138, 150, 163, 173, 174, 215
totemism 56, 146, 149, 164
Toulmin, Stephen 333
Toynbee, Arnold 316, 334
transactional analysis 28
Transcendental Meditation 18, 76, 101
transhumanism 112
Troeltsch, Ernst 152
Tylor, E. B. 8, 19, 23, 24, 28, 30, 146–7, 148, 149, 154
typologies 31–4, 151, 180, 206, 329

Udasis 237
ulema 193–4, 217
Unification Church 18, 52, 252

Unitarianism 11, 34, 43, 90, 97–8, 111, 118
Upanishads 135, 154, 192

van der Leeuw, Gerardus 161, 162, 163–5, 169, 171
Vedas 131, 135, 136, 154, 213, 237
vodou 72, 80
Vroom, Hendrik 321, 322–3, 325–8

Wach, Joachim 161
Waddell, L. A. 16, 145
Wahhabis 225
Wallis, Roy 32
Ward, Graham 334
Ward, William 132–3
Waterhouse, Helen 84
Weber, Max 32, 52, 61, 105, 150–2, 221
Weibe, Donald 63
Weightman, Simon 200
Wellhausen, Julius 138
Werbner, Pnina 190–1, 195, 203, 268
Whaling, Frank 35
Whiting, Karen 288
Wicca 112, 290
Wikipedia 344
Wilson, Bryan 105, 106, 152
Wilson, Horace Hayman 129, 134
Wittgenstein, Ludwig 34, 69, 327
Wolcott, Harry 250–1, 272
World Council of Churches 33, 72
World's Parliament of Religions 143
World Religions 10, 16, 64, 89, 92, 97, 129, 134, 144, 153, 159, 185, 187–95, 202–3, 208, 232, 239, 290, 301, 308, 317–18, 320–1, 336, 345
worship 7, 8, 16, 17, 19, 25, 36, 53, 57, 68, 75, 84, 90, 94, 96, 101, 119, 131, 141, 145, 159, 162, 169, 173, 193, 195, 224–5, 227, 238, 253, 255–6, 258, 263, 264, 269, 286, 288–9, 291, 324, 352, 354–6
Wyatt, Roy 51

Yinger, J. M. 24–5, 26, 27, 152

Zen 128, 143, 323
Zoroastrianism 20, 134, 187, 188, 296